American Icarus

ALSO FROM LANTERN BOOKS

Pythia Peay
America on the Couch
Psychological Perspectives on American Politics and Culture
616 pp, 978-1-59056-488-2, paperback

American Icarus

A Memoir of Father and Country

PYTHIA PEAY

For we are strangers before thee, and sojourners, as were all our fathers. —I Chronicles 25:19

Lantern Books ● New York
A Division of Booklight Inc.

2015
Lantern Books
128 Second Place
Brooklyn, NY 11231
www.lanternbooks.com

Copyright © 2015 Pythia Peay

Printed in the United States of America.

Library of Congress Cataloging-in-Publication Data

Peay, Pythia.
American Icarus : a memoir of father and country / Pythia Peay.
pages cm
Includes bibliographical references.
ISBN 978-1-59056-441-7 (pbk. : alk. paper)—ISBN 978-1-59056-442-4 (ebook)
1. Peay, Pythia—Family. 2. Carroll, Joe, –1995. 3. Fathers and daughters—United
States—Biography. 4. Authors, American—21 century—Family relationships. I.
Title.
CT275.P517A3 2014
306.874'2—dc23
2014033070

For Joe,

And for Kabir, Amir, and Abe

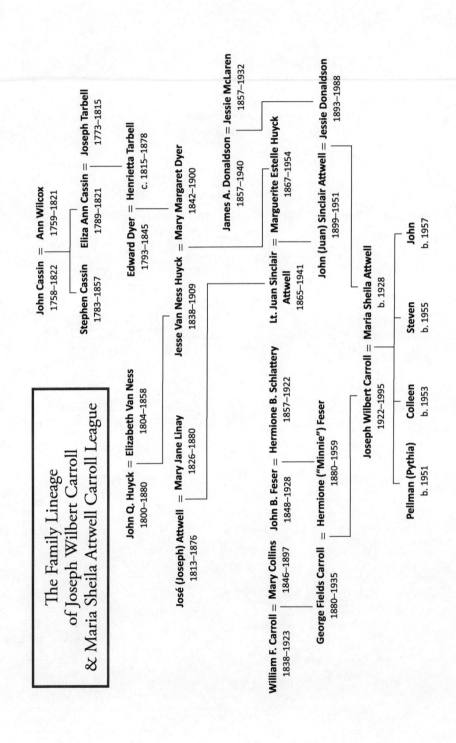

The Family Lineage
of Joseph Wilbert Carroll
& Maria Sheila Attwell Carroll League

John Cassin = Ann Wilcox
1758–1822   1759–1821

Stephen Cassin   Eliza Ann Cassin = Joseph Tarbell
1783–1857   1789–1821   1773–1815

Edward Dyer = Henrietta Tarbell
1793–1845   c. 1815–1878

Jesse Van Ness Huyck = Mary Margaret Dyer
1838–1909   1842–1900

James A. Donaldson = Jessie McLaren
1857–1940   1857–1932

John Q. Huyck = Elizabeth Van Ness
1800–1880   1804–1858

Lt. Juan Sinclair = Marguerite Estelle Huyck
Attwell   1867–1954
1865–1941

John (Juan) Sinclair Attwell = Jessie Donaldson
1899–1951   1893–1988

José (Joseph) Attwell = Mary Jane Linay
1813–1876   1826–1880

John B. Feser = Hermione B. Schlattery
1848–1928   1857–1922

William F. Carroll = Mary Collins
1838–1923   1846–1897

George Fields Carroll = Hermione ("Minnie") Feser
1880–1935   1880–1959

Joseph Wilbert Carroll = Maria Sheila Attwell
1922–1995   b. 1928

Pellman (Pythia)   Colleen   Steven   John
b. 1951   b. 1953   b. 1955   b. 1957

Contents

I

Plaything of Clouds
and of Winds

Nowhere to rest find
The insecure feet
And he is plaything
Of clouds and of winds.
—**Johann Wolfgang von Goethe**, *"Limits of Humanity"*

JOE CARROLL STOOD six foot one inch tall, with blue eyes that could impale a person at a glance and a washboard stomach as hard as a balled fist. Zeus-like, he reigned over my childhood, or so it seemed to me, with thunderbolts and lightning. Master of the stare down, he could fix you motionless without a word leaving his thick Irish lips. Once, when I was about fifteen or sixteen, my brother Steven refused my father's order to get on the tractor and mow the alfalfa field, mouthing off with a smart-ass "Fuck you." No one ever crossed my father, much less swore at him, and he backhanded my little brother across his face hard, breaking his nose. Scared but scalded with anger over this injustice, I dared to confront my father when he came back inside the house. Through the corner of my eye, I could see my brother out by the barn. He was climbing into the tractor's seat, his nose still bleeding. Red drops stained his white T-shirt.

"That's so unfair! You're cruel!" I shouted at Joe's retreating back. "He should go to the doctor's. I bet you're scared of what Dr. Bob will say!" My face was flushed and my body shook. We were standing in the mudroom just off the kitchen, next to the round, white refrigerator with a full keg of Budweiser inside. The one with a spigot Dad had rigged up on the outside for easy pouring. My father was still in his

1

prime: I could see and smell the sweat pouring off him, staining his khaki work shirt. I could feel the physical fury as it ripped through his muscular body. Outside, a humid summer silence hung over the yard like an oppressive blanket. The rest of the family seemed to have melted into the sun. Would he hit me next, I wondered? A girl? His firstborn? His just-a-little-bit favorite child? The one who could sweet-talk him into a better mood?

Stiffening and straightening his back, Joe turned on his heel to face me. His eyes narrowed into steel slits. His face was screwed tight with rage. Lowering himself to look at me, he held my glance with the force of his physical will. Raw fear coursed through my body, spiking my heart rate into a frenzied gallop. The words shot out of his mouth like bullets: "Who. Do. You. Think. You. *Are?*"

My courage failed and I ran to my room. Turning up the volume on my pink transistor radio and burying my head in my floppy stuffed lion, I burned with shame and humiliation over how utterly puny I was against him. All I could think was how cold-hearted and physically terrifying this man who happened to be my father was. And yet, amid the tears and terror, I felt a reluctant awe. Like Gary Cooper in *High Noon* or Clint Eastwood in *The Good, the Bad and the Ugly*, my dad was cowboy cool and handsomely mean. As far as I knew, no one in our family ever mouthed off to him and got away with it.

My father wasn't born a tyrant. In his youth, he was beautiful, with a round and vulnerable face framed by neatly combed wavy brown hair. He had a deep dimple in his chin, full lips, and wide eyes as bright as a pair of newborn stars. In one photo from the family album, he is a cocky, dapper lad leaning his elbow on a tree trunk beside his brothers and uncle. In another, he is a commanding young aviator, standing on the runway with his flying buddies as they prepare to board a Douglas DC-4. In yet others, he is a fresh-faced young husband cutting into his wedding cake with his curly-haired bride standing next to him. Or a new father with his arms wrapped protectively around a chubby baby: me. Like a 1950s *Life* magazine ad, Joe Carroll's sparkling intensity leaps from these pictures, radiating the hunger for life, raw optimism, and against-all-the-odds courage of an America that had emerged from the Depression to win World War II. The very air around him seems to vibrate with the bravado of a country about to enter the jet age, of which he would be a part as a flight engineer for TWA.

These two Joes—the nasty bully and the starry-eyed dreamer—were my father. Growing up, the difficulty was knowing just which Joe would rise with the sun that day. Survival depended on an accurate reading of his mood. Born with the same pale, unsettling eyes of my father, I silently observed the atmosphere about him. Just as Joe was a skilled aeronautical navigator who could instinctively measure such invisibilities as the altitude between earth and sky, so I became as adept at divining his emotional weather as a sailor or a pilot reads the skies for coming storms. His eyes, I learned early on, were the lens that revealed the conditions of his psyche. Sometimes they were clear and kind; at other times they had that murky, on-the-edge-of-madness quality that made my stomach flip in fear. Clues to his mood could also be found in his daily routine. When Joe sat in his brown upholstered chair by the bottom of the stairs that led to our second-story bedrooms, quietly reading *Time* magazine and soberly sipping his cup of Sanka, life was peaceful and good. But when he was slumped over asleep in the same chair, one hand down the inside of his unbelted pants, a Pall Mall smoldering in the wooden ashtray shaped like a ship's wheel with a coffee cup half-full of Smirnoff next to it, things did not bode well. Joe's humming beneath his breath was never a good sign; it signaled the onset of a thunder burst. But whistling (at which my father was superbly gifted) was different. "Moon River," "Danny Boy," "Night and Day"—when he warbled these tunes, all was well in the Carroll household.

What made Joe's moods hardest to figure out was that they did not emerge full-blown at the onset of our family life. No, they unspooled over the years like a mountain climber's rope staked to rock that unwinds slowly—until, loosened, it snakes wildly out of control, dropping the person over the edge. Aimed straight at constructing a new life out of a childhood misshapen by the shock of loss and strange fortune, my father was at his strongest and most confident in the earliest years of our family. And so it was that my first memory of him as a little girl is that of tender love, and exuberance for life in all its warm-earth, sun-drenched beauty.

A parent's face, with its lines, lights, colors, and constantly changing expressions, is a compelling force to a child. I could not possibly remember this, and yet I do: my father's face bent over me as an infant, animated with wonder, holding me in his arms sweetly and with affection. In images etched into my brain, I see him intently concentrated on fixing his tractor, or smiling in amusement at his young family and our games on the dusty patch of lawn that was our front yard.

This precious stability began to erode as I approached adolescence, giving way to the lurch of good days and bad days. The very best days were the ones when Joe was getting ready to leave on a trip or immediately after his return. Then, there was a reassuring measure of order. There would be no scenes. The bottles of beer and vodka vanished, and the house basked under the clean, clear skies of sobriety. Preparing to leave, Joe whistled, shaved, and packed. "Sheila!" he would call out to my mother, looking for the clean socks and pressed handkerchiefs he needed for his suitcase. Long into adulthood, I remembered the lime aroma of Cannon aftershave and the crisp, chemical smell of his newly dry-cleaned TWA uniform.

As Joe's departure neared, the house filled with exhilaration at the approaching liberation. For several days after he was gone, we would be like sailors on leave. Freed from the Joe Carroll rules that bound us, we kids ran around the farm with dirt-smeared faces, made a mess in our rooms, ate hamburgers and French fries from Jack in the Box, slurped Dairy Queen smoothies, and opened the house wide to our friends. We forgot our manners at dinner, left the hated liver and peas uneaten on our plates, and joked and laughed among ourselves without fearing we would be shut up and shouted down.

My mother was also different while my father was away. Although she could get overwhelmed with farm chores and taking care of four children on her own, she also smiled more, painted, crooned Broadway songs as she hung up the laundry in the backyard, invited her girlfriends over to sit by the pool, and giggled and exhaled along with the rest of us. We knew it wouldn't last: my father's rule would be reinstated on his return. But at least for a day or two, we knew we'd be safe, as Joe would be too exhausted to do more than sleep and eat.

And then he'd drink. The hard days were a mirror opposite of Joe's best days and usually occurred at the midpoint between trips. His attention reengaged with the family and the two-hundred-acre farm where we lived, my father's mood would darken precipitously into drunken sullenness. With the emotional barometer falling fast, Joe would mumble like a crazy man beneath his breath, remain silent if spoken to, or shut himself in his bedroom. When the storm finally broke, his temper fell like stinging rain and cruel words poured from his mouth like hailstones, lashing my mother and siblings and even the animals around him into fearful submissiveness.

"Goddammit, ya stupe-head!" Joe would bark at one of us for failing to do an assigned chore correctly. If it was winter, this might be chopping a hole in the ice for the cows. If it was summer, it might mean gathering hickory and oak twigs for the evening barbeque of perfectly smoked hamburgers. Or maybe we didn't run fast enough with his matches, Johnson's baby oil, fly swatter, magazine, or whatever his need was at the moment. During these drinking bouts, Joe exaggeratedly turned words on their sides and elongated vowels so that they came out sounding like a Midwestern Swedish hash: "*Yaaaa stooop-hed.*"

It was the dinner table, however, that set the stage for the most melodramatic of our family dramas. Drunk, pissed off, and out of his mind, Joe became a virtuoso tyrant over grilled steak, garlic bread, and baked potatoes with butter, chopped chives, and sour cream. Called down at six o'clock, we'd each take our seat at the redwood picnic table in the farm kitchen. My brother John and I sat on the bench to the left, my sister Colleen and brother Steve to the right. After serving the food, my mother took her place at the far end of the table. Always last to arrive—and no one could lift a fork until he sat down—my father sat in the maple wood captain's chair at the head of the table.

On a bad drinking day, it didn't take him long to get started. First came the Catholic grace over six bowed heads. "Thank you, Father, for that which we are about to receive," we would pray in unison, paying homage to the big daddy in the sky as well as at the table. And then it would begin.

"Stupid, lazy hostesses," he might say, referring to the crew on his last flight, his eyes darting around the table. "Old, fat cows," he would mumble, glancing in my mother's direction, hoping to draw someone into a showdown at the Carroll corral. Then, "Sheila! Lazy pig. Where's the goddamn garlic bread!" he would bark, sending my mother flying from the room in a gush of tears. Mostly, I sat hunched and mute before this gale force of paternal fury. Other times I took the bait, hurrying to the defense of my mother or the brother or sister who had refused his I-dare-you-to-disobey-me order to eat every last morsel of food on the plate.

As I grew, and the fifties were overturned by the convulsive social change of the sixties, my father used the table as a bully pulpit to hold forth on current affairs. Whether it was about blacks marching for civil rights, feminists burning their bras, poor people on welfare, long-haired hippies, or antiwar protesters marching on Washington against the Vietnam War, Joe loved nothing better than a red-faced shouting match. Something about the successive waves of liberation movements brought out the dictator in him. "Goddamn hippie commies," he'd yell. "They should be shipped out of the country."

I fell for it every time. "Daaaddy," I would wail. "How can you *say* that?" And then we'd go off, trading shots with each other. But it was worse not to engage, to answer his insults with silence; just as the worst fate in life, to my father, was to be like everyone else. Even sober, my father loved nothing better than a hot and testy argument, regarding our family debates as the training ground for adulthood. We were taught to stand up for our beliefs by standing up to him—but only, as we each found out eventually, when he gave us permission.

The trickiest times of all, however, were when the good days collided with the bad, and my father became a dangerous brew of high spirits and brooding melancholy. When these high and low pressure systems came together my father was at his most charismatic: a pure force of human nature that combined everything terrible and wonderful at once. At moments like these, his starlit eyes flashed a rare brilliance that irradiated everyone around him with waves of energy.

Not because he had anything really great or important to show us, but because he had a "Rube Goldberg project" in the works. This was his code name for the launch of a new home venture. One Sunday after Mass, when I was about eleven, Joe theatrically unveiled his latest purchase: a new kind of electric sandwich maker. It had long handles and a round press that neatly chopped off the edges of the bread, creating a perfectly spherical hot sandwich. With great flourish and fanfare, holding the press over the gas flame like a conductor waving his baton, Dad cooked up his version of the Reuben sandwich. As a rule, I hated the bitter taste of sauerkraut, but something about Joe's juicy good humor made me love his corned beef and rye concoction, dripping with grainy mustard and melted Swiss cheese. My sister detested the hypocrisy of these Sunday morning brunches and wondered skeptically why Joe was suddenly trying to play the "good" father. But I loved them, carried aloft by my father's beguiling brand of wizardry that could turn a mere sandwich into food that I thought was fit for immortals.

Then there was the time Joe rigged up new drainpipes that he'd designed to make the rainwater flow more easily from the roof. His decision to do this in the middle of a spring thunderstorm was what we'd later call "vintage Joe Carroll." After some hours noisily clambering around on the roof, Dad called us all outside. The four of us lined up in the rain. Dripping wet, chilled, we dutifully admired Joe's handiwork as the water sloshed through the pipes and onto the soggy ground. "I can't hear you!" Joe shouted over the thunder and lightning, cupping his hand to his ear. "Hip hip hoorah!" we screamed. "Hip hip hoorah!"

A more massive project was one that lasted several hot summer days in between trips. After much bargaining with the shiny-green-suited pool salesman my father called an oily con man—the first time I'd ever heard that phrase—Joe decided to have a swimming pool built. Once it was finished, it fell to the kids to fill it up from one of the muddy farm ponds. Like a chain gang of four, we struggled and strained, snaking long, black, heavy hoses from the pond that lay a couple of acres downhill, up to the pool by the house. When my dad flipped the switch on the pump by the pond, and the dirty brown water started flowing into the pool, a collective shout echoed over the distance between us. Whatever it was, big or small, it was always an ordeal. And my father was always square in the middle of it.

No, there was nothing remotely mild or pallid about Joe. He met life full on, with everything he had. He could grind a field mouse beneath his heel, flail the horses with his long whip, and pick up a cat by its tail and hurl it across a field, causing me to squeal in fright and disgust. Or he could tenderly help my sister care for a litter of abandoned kittens, whistle an Irish ballad, or tell me a bedtime story with such pathos my eyes would fill with tears. He could, in equal measure, be boyish and happy or bullying and morose, generous and good-hearted or bitter and stingy, charming and loving or vindictive and hateful. He was a mess of contradictions and impossible to figure out. He did not like black people, or so he said. But when he discovered that the only black teenage boy in the small town where we lived refused to attend school for fear of being beaten up, my father saw to it that he was enrolled immediately. "Your father isn't prejudiced," my mother used to say. "He just hates everyone."

As hard as I tried when I was growing up, there was no getting around the fact that Joe Carroll was different. Unlike those other fathers who worked regular nine-to-five jobs and had American wives, my father flew airplanes to distant cities and foreign countries and married a charming, flirtatious Argentine woman with curly black hair and dimples to match his own. His twin loves, flying and farming, kept him working constantly, shuttling between earth and sky. He never sat still, unless he was drunk or exhausted, and he never ate dessert. He never belonged to a club, had friends, or enjoyed a regular social life like my girlfriends' fathers. I had to wait until I was ten years old and on a summer vacation with a girlfriend's parents to the Lake of the Ozarks—Missouri's largest resort—to discover that parents got together with other parents and did ordinary things like play cards or go water-skiing.

For all these reasons, no one who met Joe Carroll ever forgot him. Even decades into his decline from a high-spirited youth to a swollen, disease-ravaged old man, he could still elicit exclamations of "Oh, *Joe* . . . Joe *Carroll!*" He was our very own legend, a bewitching romantic who clung stubbornly to his dreams. He created Wild West adventures out of the most ordinary aspects of daily life; suffered wretchedly from a ferocious addiction to beer, vodka, and cigarettes; and was both brightly manic and horribly, darkly depressed.

As the years passed, the original masterpiece that was his face became encrusted with the thick pigment of paranoia and despair. Furrows, jowls, and the blotched red stains and veins of alcoholism obliterated his once-boyish looks. The more he drank, the more I struggled to comprehend this increasingly difficult man whom fate had chosen as my father. As a teenager, wild and a little unhinged from the uncertainty of it all, I would yell, cajole, and act out to get Dad's attention, doing everything possible I could think of to save him. I wanted to rescue my father from the drinking devils that were obliterating his body, sanity, and even, so it seemed to me, the very essence of him as a person.

Brimming with good intentions and puritanical zeal, I ferreted out hidden bottles of liquor and poured them down the drain. I checked out books on alcoholism from the local library and threw them on my father's head as he was napping. I argued, cried, and pretended to have a nervous breakdown. I made ridiculous threats to run off and become a mini-skirted go-go dancer with thigh-high patent leather boots in a California strip club. But beneath all of my kooky drama was a girl who ached inside and was trying to stop the ground crumbling beneath her feet. It just didn't seem possible to me: that the person who professed to love and care for me and my siblings and mother had become fixated on his own destruction. I simply could not take into my heart the notion that someone who had been so full of life could so recklessly court death.

When none of my schemes worked, and my own sanity seemed at risk, I knew it was time for me to get a life of my own. So I left. I did it angrily and impetuously—willfully intent, if not on rescuing my father, then on saving the world instead. Swept up in the swelling countercultural movement that so unnerved and brought out the worst in my father, I glimpsed an opening into a new destiny. Driven from Missouri to California by the wide and beckoning world that lay tantalizingly beyond my bedroom window, and by a desire to be as unlike Joe Carroll as I could possibly be, I became a hippy, moved into a commune, and found a spiritual teacher and God.

I couldn't see it at the time, but I know now that, like my father, I wanted to transcend the chaos of confusion that marked my childhood in exactly the same way he had sought to escape the tragedies of his own youth through flying and alcohol. Just like him, I aimed to break free of the pain-laden ties that pinned my soul to earth. Whatever was out there had to be better than what lay inside my home.

*

All parents are gods. All parents permanently sear themselves into their children's psyches. They loom large because they are the personal carriers of that pair of universal forces known as "Mother" and "Father," upon which a child's very survival depends. For most of recorded history, it has been the father, more than the mother, who has shaped the institutions of the world we live in. There is God the Father, the founding fathers of a nation, and the father as head of the family. And it is the father who, until recently, influenced the child's relationship to the world through his work and engagement in life. According to psychoanalytic theories in the earlier half of the twentieth century, explains Jungian analyst Andrew Samuels in *The Political Psyche*, the father's task was to sternly but gently turn the baby toward "his" world. Samuels quotes the English psychiatrist D. W. Winnicott, writing in 1944 that "the children get a new world opened up to them when father gradually discloses the nature of the work to which he goes in the morning and from which he returns at night, or when he shows the gun that he takes with him into battle."

For a woman born in the early fifties, as I was, when men worked outside the home and women kept house inside, these theories still held sway. The world, for the most part, came to daughters through their fathers. In my case, this was especially true: the passport to my childhood past is stamped with Joe Carroll's sky-borne travels. The image I had of the world growing up was shaped in the image of my aviator father's: foreign, enthralling, a bit dangerous, and far removed from life's daily banalities.

In one memory that wells up from my Missouri girlhood, I recall an annual summer ritual. Lying on the lawn that sloped down to the blacktop county road that divided our farmhouse from the weathered barn, the sweet-smelling grass warm on my back, I'd spend hours gazing into the blue sky. Letting go of my body, I'd drift off into the clouds, swept up in a delicious, dizzying vertigo. It wasn't long before a whirring drone would interrupt my daydream. This sound, forever associated in my mind with languid summer days, was prelude to the silver cylinder that would soon enter my field of vision.

Entranced, I would contemplate the jet as it sailed across the face of the sky, trailing a long white tail behind it like a flying dragon. Squinting and peering, I would try to make out the letters to see if the plane belonged to TWA. Though I could never make out the logo, I liked to pretend that my father was up there anyway, seated at the control panel of the cockpit. In my mind's eye, I could see the hostesses walking around in their sherbet-colored uniforms, brightly serving passengers trays of hot food, aisle by aisle. I could see one of the flight attendants as she knocked politely on the cabin door and handed my father his company cup of Sanka. A cup of Joe for Joe at the instrument panel. In this fantasy, my father would glance down and see me looking up at him from below and wave. Then the plane would disappear into the distance, and my summer daydream would dissipate. In the silence, I would ponder the mysterious whereabouts of my flying father until the boom of the plane breaking the sound barrier would pierce the summer spell, bringing my floating thoughts down from the clouds and the planes above.

My father would return home from his trips with souvenirs infused with the talismanic power of distant places: tiny bottles of cheap French perfume, airplane snacks of salted peanuts, luxurious-smelling hotel shampoos and soaps, brass-colored TWA wing pins, garish plastic drink stirrers, or exotic gifts like the Moroccan pouf hassock or the embroidered Chinese blue silk robe, which still hangs in my closet. He'd enchant us with anecdotes about his fellow pilots,

Bangkok cabdrivers, and tales of glimpses of Earth, the moon, and the stars from the cockpit.

Another memory, as charged with my father's aura now as then, surfaces. The entire family is in our parents' bedroom as my father opens his suitcase and unpacks his bag. He is standing by the bedroom window. Light is pouring in, shaded emerald by the branches of the large oak tree in the front yard. Unlike later in life, we are all glad to have Joe home. Like lightning bugs, we four children buzz around him, glowing. My father takes off his uniform jacket and hands it to me. Spellbound, I hold it to my face and inhale its scent of dry cleaning chemicals, airport lounges, cigarette smoke, and hotel rooms. I am breathing in the places he's been, the sights he's seen, the air he has soared through in the wide-bodied Lockheed Constellation whose air temperature, mechanical maintenance, and engines are in his care.

And so it was that my father literally meant the world to me. For many years, until just before I left home, my father and I shared a special rite of departure. On the day he was to leave, I would wake early in the morning. I would lie in bed and listen as he moved about the house while everyone slept, making coffee, shaving, dressing, whistling softly, and packing. Something about the orderliness of his dawn ritual soothed me; it was something to count on. When I heard the front door shut behind him, I went to the window of my upstairs bedroom and waited. It was a moment between worlds, filled with the humming expectancy of a new dawn, a new day, and the promise of a new sky adventure for my father. I felt no fear for my father's safety. Instead, I sat dreamily at the windowsill, basking in the exaltation of an "anything is possible" moment. Still partly wrapped in sleep, I watched as my father loaded his bag into the back of his pickup and heard the start of the engine crack the stillness. With a splutter and roar of the truck, Joe backed out of his parking spot by the horses' fenced-in pasture then looped around the circular driveway. Just as he passed in front of my window before heading down the hill on his way to the airport, Dad slowed briefly. He looked up at my window and we smiled to each other, then waved good-bye. In that gesture of leave-taking, my father transmitted something nameless yet quintessentially American: a love of doing the daring thing. A passion for going beyond the narrow circle of one's daily life. A yearning after distant horizons.

This silent farewell became the signature gesture of our relationship over the rest of my life. After I left home at seventeen, years rolled by during which we saw each other only in passing. Because our visits took place between trips, Joe often refused to stay anywhere except the hotel closest to the airport wherever I was living, as if the sky had become his permanent abode. During the seventies, when I was finally living in the spiritual commune I had dreamed of, Joe felt awkward and uncomfortable visiting me in my furniture-free meditation/ living room. So, taking my growing family along with me, I became accustomed to visiting him at hotels. In the safely impersonal ambiance of coffee shops and restaurants we caught up over lunches and long dinners. As each of my three sons was born, Joe was introduced to them in lobbies where potted plants stood on soft carpets and Muzak played in the background. In between visits, we kept in touch through infrequent phone conversations.

Eventually, as my own life took off, I let go of the notion of saving my father, gradually releasing him to the forces of fate. Taking refuge in meditation and the notion of spiritual transcendence, I focused only on saving my own soul. This pursuit, I know, delayed my entry into full-scale adulthood and engagement with life. But it was better than escaping into drugs or letting myself splinter into pieces. What the spiritual life provided for me, as it does for many, was a safe place. The sober refuge of meditation and community enabled me to rise above the psychic turbulence of my inner world until I was strong enough to descend and face myself and the story of my childhood.

The process of coming to terms with the legacy of my father didn't begin until I was in my late thirties. Shaken by the unraveling of my marriage, I began to delve into the psychological structure of my self. Where I'd once been contemptuous of anything to do with psychotherapy, I now became absorbed by learning about the dynamics of the unconscious. Entering Jungian analysis, I began reflecting on my dreams and fantasies. Picking through the heap of repressed and discarded childhood memories, I searched for the thread that would lead me to meaning. More than anything, I wanted to make sense of my family past and how it had shaped me. I needed to know what to keep and what to reject, what was mine and what belonged to my parents. None of the things I did to right my wildly tilting interior universe, however, had any effect on my father. It never made him sober or happy or healed his childhood scars. As he grew older, he became increasingly erratic and reclusive. That was always a tragedy. But it was one I learned to live with and accept.

Slowly, as my life began to cohere around its own center, the hurt and raw emotions around my father began to subside, like silt that settles to the bottom of a lake. I began to find pleasure in the simplest exchanges, such as Joe's birthday and the Christmas card he sent with his shaky signature; or the rare moments along the way when, sensing need in my voice, he'd reach out to me and support me as a father. Anger turned to sadness that led in turn to an armistice of acceptance. Finally, the day came when I was called to help him die—this sky god who had filled my childhood from behind clouds, wind, and sunlight. And who was now falling and tumbling to the ground.

The call came in midsummer, 1994. "I never thought I'd make it this far," said Joe. It was a humble admission of a truth that, until now, he'd never spoken aloud. I was slow to answer, heavy with heartache. "I know," I said. And indeed, in that moment it dawned on me that I had always known that for most of his life my father had carried on a romance with death.

We were talking on the phone—me from my home outside Washington, D.C., and my father from Corpus Christi, Texas. It was to this sunny Gulf city named after the body of Christ that Joe and his Mexican-born second wife, Hilda, had impulsively moved from Guadalajara several years earlier. Loading up his yellow Mercedes-Benz station wagon with their belongings, Joe had driven back across the border just far enough to be closer to an American hospital. As it turned out, my father's instincts had served him well. Almost as soon as he moved into his new house—the first middle-class, suburban house he'd ever owned—Joe was diagnosed with prostate cancer. After a successful round of chemotherapy, his cancer had gone into remission.

But Joe being Joe, never quite knowing whether he wanted to live or die, hadn't returned for a checkup.

Frightened by tales of his worsening health, my sister had flown out to see him, put him in the car, and driven him to the doctor's office. As he shivered on the examination table in his paper gown, Joe was gently informed by his physician that his prostate cancer had returned. But this time, it had metastasized to the point that it wasn't going away. My father should do without chemotherapy, said the doctor. Sometimes it was best to let things take their course.

"It's my fault, Pell. Why did I do it?" Joe anguished aloud now, calling me by my childhood nickname. "If I'd gone back to the doctor we'd have caught it in time. But I did it to myself. No one else to blame. No going back now," he said, his voice trailing off, small and frightened. I stumbled for the right words to reassure him. My heart thumped in loud panic against my rib cage. A frightened animal seemed to have taken up residence inside my body.

"Well, we'll do the best we can. Maybe it's not as bad as the doctor thinks," I said, lamely. And falsely. But what do you say to a man who's been trying to destroy himself all his life, and then finally succeeds? In a flash, all the bitterness of my youth resurrected itself, fresh as ever. As Joe had lived, I thought, encased in thick gloom, so he'd die, alone with himself and passed out drunk.

But given that nothing about Joe's life had proceeded according to convention, I shouldn't have been surprised when his death took an unexpected turn, and a strange beauty gave us an opportunity to draw close again. Relationships, as my analyst Tom once remarked pensively, never really end. They live on inside of us.

Even though years had passed, I learned as I tended my father on his deathbed that kinship ties are not subject to time or space. Or even, it seems, such gaping traumas as abuse and alcoholism. At the end of Joe's life, despite the vast emotional and geographical distances that had separated us, the bond between my father and myself still existed, as if preserved intact by the guardianship and grace of a family angel who'd stood watch from the moment I was born. What's more, I gained entrance to a place every child yearns to explore: the inner world of my father. Hovering on the threshold of death, the seal of his past broken by the force of desire to relive the life he was about to depart, memories and confessions poured out in rare, heart-to-heart talks. In those hours, something happened I never thought would—I saw Joe's soul struggle to come alive.

After my father's death, life, as it is wont to do, flowed on. Yet like invisible travelers tugging at my sleeve, the forgotten figures from his past that had surfaced as he lay dying continued to press for my attention. Haunted by Joe's presence in my dreams and by the words of another analyst who'd once remarked that my father had cast a long shadow over my life, something seemed undone. Had I ever, I wondered, really known my father? Seeking to solve the riddle of his life— and mine—I began to look at Joe's life from a wider angle, to sense the larger forces surrounding his lone and lonely figure. I wanted to try to understand the man who was the ground I came from. I wanted to do this because he was so much more than my father. He was that precious shard of the human condition given to me to learn and grow from.

Joe Carroll was, after all, a man of his time, shaped by previous eras as much as his era had shaped my own. Like one of those Chinese nesting boxes, his psyche had been formed by the psyches of each of his parents—and so on back through generations. In other words, I began to realize, volumes of human experience were at work behind the disappointment and hurt I'd suffered as my eccentric, reclusive father's daughter. Whether or not we like it or have even noticed it, as Jungian analyst Marie-Louise von Franz puts it in *Archetypal Dimensions of the Psyche*, we are up to our ears "not only in our biographical past but also our collective historical past." It seemed that I was as much a daughter of my father's and ancestors' eras as I was of Joe Carroll.

And so I began to chip away at the buried psyche of this historical parent of mine. As I did so I gradually realized that my father was someone for whom otherwise typical events like marriage, family, and work became exaggerated expressions of the subterranean beliefs and ideals that shaped the country he was born in. As if the hand of fate had reached down into the soft clay of his life, my father and all he believed in and strived for was sculpted by the American myths:

that curious confluence of Puritan redemption, Manifest Destiny, and American exceptionalism; Greco-Roman ideas of democracy and personal excellence; Calvinist hard work, Enlightenment individualism, and the pursuit of reason. It was the well-worn narrative of heroic extremism, of triumphs won and tragedies survived; of a uniquely American parable of the immigrant-born, self-made individual who tirelessly works himself out of poverty to achieve things never imagined possible. It is, says Jungian scholar James Hillman with colorful wit, "the story of the wild child born in a shoe box who becomes head of GM"—an American creation story ritually reenacted every election, as candidates strive to prove their patriotic bona fides by virtue of the hardships they've endured to achieve their dream. Indeed, America, says Hillman, is much more than a geographical place. It's an idea—a mythic landscape populated by such American superheroes as Superman, the Marlboro Man, George Washington, and Jesus.

These American ideas and ideas *of* America came down to Joe from his father and grandfathers, and his mother and grandmothers. Raised in a large, poor Pennsylvania railroad family during the Depression, he overcame poverty and a Dickensian twist of bad fortune to ride the crest of the postwar wave with skill and know-how. Like others in the Greatest Generation, my father dreamed big dreams, buoyed onward by the American quest to build a bigger and better life than the one he'd been born into. Posted to Brazil as World War II drew to a close, he witnessed firsthand a planet opening up to itself through air travel. When countries began creating their own national airlines, he joined the pioneer ranks of those on the frontier of commercial aviation, flying new routes carved into the air by the Army Air Corps, Pan Am, El Al, Alitalia, Flota Aerea Mercante Argentina (FAMA), and TWA that carried him around the globe. As a girl, I simply took my father's life for granted. Yet, for a young man who'd never ventured too far from home, I see now that these encounters with some of the world's oldest and most sophisticated cultures must have been a lot for his blue-collar, Pennsylvanian soul to absorb.

But though Joe's experiences changed him and made him more worldly, one of my father's more endearing qualities was the way he always remained himself: just your average Altoona-born, Midwestern farmer who planted wheat and alfalfa and raised horses and cattle and pigs and sheep and who happened also to fly around the world. A regular Joe Six-Pack whether in Paris, New Delhi, San Francisco, or Tel Aviv. In the earlier years, I remember him returning home from a trip with bemused bewilderment about the world that he was newly exploring, never quite believing he was living the life he'd achieved. Though he became increasingly jaded and sick, angry and overweight, and depressed, manic, and exhausted, a kernel of his original wonder and adventure always remained.

This spirit, so American, reemerged anew as he drew near death. "You know," he said, shaking his head, "I remember as a boy taking my first train trip with my Uncle Fritz to Washington, D.C., and how, standing at one of the monuments, he told me this was the farthest I would ever travel in my life. And can you imagine where I've been and what I've seen? Boy, kiddo, was he wrong! I wonder what Uncle Fritz would have said about my life, the life he never saw me live."

I'll never forget something else my father once told me, words that I remember as images. It was after he'd returned home and endured yet another torturous stretch of sleepless nights. On his around-the-world routes, he said, sipping from his ubiquitous cup of Sanka and inhaling deeply on a Pall Mall, he flew in the wake of the sun along the curvature of the Earth. On these sky roads, Joe flew in a perennially bright day with no darkness to cue his body when to rest or sleep.

When I think of my father following the sun, it seems to me that he was also the child of the older hero myths, particularly the Greek tale of Icarus, of whom it was told that he flew too close to the sun on wings of wax and plunged to his death into the sea. For although America and the industrial and technological revolution had given my father wings to ascend the ladder of professional and material success, no one ever taught Joe Carroll what to do if he fell. Rising high in the first half of his life, he descended in the second into the depths of alcoholism and madness. Retreating further into isolation, he refused to grasp any human hands extended to him in help. Nor were the rest of us taught how to deal with the family tragedy that unfolded in slow and silent motion. For who cared, really, about the fate of such a regular Joe? Who heard the splash his soul made, as, over the years, it sank ever deeper into despair?

Only as my father lay dying did he try to arrest his descent, and to right his life of extremes. But his attempt at a deathbed reckoning did not come easy. All the ideas that had supported him over the course of his life were of scant use before the immense forces confronting him. Though gripped by a last-minute determination to rectify the things that he'd made so terribly wrong, his emotional resources were scarce. His inner life was threadbare. Little existed to support him spiritually or psychologically. Surrender, dependence, and acceptance were alien to him. "I wish that I'd spent more time learning some of the things you have," he said to me in the middle of one long, wakeful night. Joe's vulnerability, so unexpected, made me cry. Frightened for my father, humbled by death's approach, it grieved me to see how he shrank in terror from the next leg of his life's adventure.

Alcohol, coffee, cigarettes; a grueling work schedule; a relentless, unceasing, inner emotional storm; a demon of restlessness always at his back; his first marriage ended and his children scattered—all these things took their toll on my father. When he died at age seventy-two, the tragic transformation from young god to a ruined wreck was complete. His body swollen, his feet elephantine and huge, his skin stretched tight as a drum, his face reddened and his nose bulbous and misshapen by too much cheap vodka, all that remained of Joe was his sense of humor and his ever-youthful hope for what lay around the next corner. Still, I like to think that as my father left this life for the next it counted for something that he took the courage he'd once possessed in abundance and began tentatively to explore the boundaries of his soul.

Joe Carroll lived at a time when there was little social support and scarcely any acceptance for undergoing the inward journey of spirituality and psychotherapy. Often, I feel sorry that I kept my own interior exploration and analysis a secret from him. No doubt, if I'd taken that risk, I would have been met with humorous scoffing and joking. I can hear his voice now: "Hoo*eee*, Pell, those shrinks are going to make you crazy!" Still, sometimes I wished I'd had more courage to bypass his cynicism and speak to the part of him that might have been quietly listening to what I had to say.

But, in a way, perhaps I can make the journey for him. By putting myself in his shoes as a boy and a young man, I might learn more about my father. In beginning this quest, I turn my spotlight and shine it down the tunnel of Joe's, and my own, past. I examine the pieces of his broken life, searching for clues as to why my father was the way he was, why Americans are the way we are. Why I am the way I am. I don't hope for big answers; just a few insights that could help me, and perhaps some others, make their way into the future. From old photos, fleeting memories, conversations with relatives, genealogical research, recollections and impressions from my father as he was dying, and interviews with psychologists and historians, I carefully reconstruct Joe's life, putting together the pieces with narrative glue the way an archaeologist reassembles a shattered vessel.

Joe's passing began a journey that led him far from this world. I, who could not follow, undertook a years-long odyssey into the mystery of the life and death of the American man who was my father. And to begin, I return to the place he was born: the town of Altoona, Pennsylvania.

II
The Sons of Altoona

Think of anything, of cowboys, of movies, of detective stories, of anybody who goes anywhere or stays at home and is an American and you will realize that it is something strictly American to conceive a space that is filled with moving, a space of time that is filled always filled with moving.—**Gertrude Stein**, The Gradual Making of the Making of the Americans

Y ELLO, PELL! I'M THINKING of moving to Austin. Heard it's a wonderful city, real pretty. Real estate prices aren't bad. I've been on the phone with an agent, and boy, he says he's got a deal for me. Says you can buy prefab log houses that are real neat."

My father and I were on the phone again. I could hear Hilda in the background, rustling pots and pans in the kitchen. Joe was in the grip of a new project and he wanted the whole family in on it. Any concerns I'd had about my father in the wake of his diagnosis of terminal cancer were now banished by the bright flare of his sudden enthusiasm. Even as his life was ending he was busy doing what he did best: planning a new expedition.

"Come on, now. Let's take a family trip for my birthday to check it out," he wheedled. "You and Neen, Steve and John. I'll get the airline passes, pay for the hotel. Whaddya say? Just the four of you, though. Do we have a deal?"

"Okay, Dad, I'll think about it," I replied. But inside, I was furious with him and his madness. "Bidey bo!" said Joe, signing off with his usual farewell, as innocent as a child.

"What's he thinking?" I vented to my brother later that day. "He's going to move in his condition? Build a log cabin? He's *so* in denial."

Looking back, I see that my lapse into pop psychology was itself a form of denial. Instead of confronting the sobering fact of his approaching death, I could go on as I always had, regressing into old habits, fuming and fussing with my siblings about my father's screwball behavior.

But a dream I had later that night changed my mind. Strolling along a river in an old village, I was fixed motionless by the sight of a man standing upright in a wooden flatboat. Paralyzed, I stared in fright. Dressed in medieval clothes, the time-weathered, olive-skinned boatman looked as if he'd stepped straight out of a fairy tale from another century. His fierce black eyes were riveted on my face. Holding my gaze, he deliberately poled his boat toward a massive stone bridge. As he drew nearer the arch in the center of the bridge, the enigmatic boatman, his eyes still fixed on mine, pulsed wordlessly, as if transmitting an urgent message. Then he was gone, vanishing beneath the archway. Jolting awake from the dream, I lay in bed, turning the images over in my mind. Had I encountered the mythic Charon—the ferryman who helps souls cross over to the other side?

This dream helped me to see through my father's defenses. And my own. It began to sink in that Joe's life was ticking away its last minutes. Any interest I'd had in trying to argue with him or change him evaporated. My father was dealing with his illness and dying the only way he knew how: plan a trip, arrange for airline passes, check the stand-by list for seat availability, make shuttle reservations, and call the hotel. It was what the Carroll family did. Confronted with my father's imminent departure from life itself, we would stay in character and reenact the family ritual one last time. What really mattered now, I realized in light of my dream, were the simplest things: to be a daughter, to walk with Joe a little way longer until our fated path came to an end—even if it meant going to Austin to look at a prefab log house that he would never live in. Gentled by this shift in perception, I agreed, along with my siblings, to my father's splendid deception.

And so it happened that on a bright fall day on October 23, 1994, the four of us, with my father and my stepmother Hilda, arrived in Austin. My father had made reservations at a beautiful hotel, with fountains splashing in the high-ceilinged courtyard. There were spas, luxuriously

22

upholstered couches, tall flowering plants, cocktail bars, and hovering waiters. It was the perfect place to act as if my father, after trying to kill himself all his life, was now going to live forever. Later that night, giddy at this rare reunion with his four children, my father took us out for dinner. Walking inside the restaurant, we were stopped cold by the neon-lit sign that hung over the mahogany U-shaped counter. "Joe's Bar," it read, in flashing scarlet letters.

Struck by the symbolism of the sign, the six of us paused as one. Then the old Carroll streak of mean wit took possession of the good will I'd been feeling. Breaking into laughter with my siblings, I insisted on taking a picture of Joe and Hilda beneath the sign. "Come on, Dad," I joked. "A shot for posterity!" I still have the photo; even now it reproaches me. My father stands beneath the garish neon words as if condemned by a fate he cannot shake. He is wearing his trademark blue Mexican Guayabera shirt, which he loved for all the handy pockets and the fact that he could wear it untucked over his pants. A crumpled brown and baggy cardigan is stretched over his shirt. Beneath the sweater his shoulders are helplessly slumped; his face is lined, gray, and haggard, with a look as sad and as close to the grave as any human being I'd ever seen. Standing next to him, Hilda smiles shyly into the camera, her eyes the color of bittersweet chocolate.

The next morning we awoke to a vintage, golden southwestern day. It was my father's seventy-second birthday, and his old companion the sun had come out to salute him. Joe's good mood had returned. Soon, we'd be off chasing his next rainbow. After eating breakfast together, the six of us gathered outside the hotel to embark on the planned city and house-hunting tour. Joe and Hilda had driven down in his beloved yellow Mercedes station wagon—the one he'd shipped from Germany, the one that continually broke down, and the one he loved to fix—and the four of us piled in. Steve took the wheel while my father rode shotgun in the passenger seat. John, Colleen, and Hilda sat in the back. With no room left over, I crawled into the far rear with a pillow.

Joe had always been the family navigator. Now he rustled the map and ran his fingers over the colored lines. As my father gave Steve directions, I commented on how I'd always been "directionally impaired," easily getting lost, unable even to read a map. Dad chuckled and recalled his talent as a young airman, able to navigate a plane from the air without instruments, going by the landmarks below and his gut sense of direction and altitude. "I guess you didn't inherit that talent from me," he joked. No, I said, I guessed I hadn't.

It was true. Often, I was the butt of family jokes for my meandering driving style. Even on roads I knew well, I could easily get lost. When I was under stress, right and left, east and west, north and south went out the window. Later, I read with interest how psychological states of panic, confusion, and disorientation can arise from issues around early childhood separation. Could it be that my talented navigator-father's erratic coming and going damaged my own inner sense of direction? And did the gift of stable and consistent love in childhood have something to do with firmness of purpose and an ability to get where one wanted to go later in life?

That day, none of those questions was on my mind. Instead, I relaxed into a pleasant regression, comforted to be driven by others. For all my father's bluster leading up to our family outing, the day unfurled with languorous ease. All talk about meeting with real estate agents and touring log houses melted in the warm Texas sun. "I just want to get a feel for the area," Joe said now. Wandering around the city, we explored different neighborhoods, imagining where my father and Hilda might feel most comfortable taking up their new lives. My sister, the musician, talked about Austin's vibrant arts and music scene. We spoke of future family reunions we knew would never take place.

Later that night, we celebrated my father's birthday at a charming restaurant on a terrace overlooking Lake Travis. Seated at the head of the table, Joe surveyed the misty, hilly vista spread below us. He turned back to the table with a sigh and gazed silently around the table at the five of us, his eyes lingering on each of our faces. It was a moment shaded with melancholy, wordless and awkward, but heavy with feeling. It lasted only a few seconds, until the waiter approached. Garrulously ordering a drink, Joe turned his attention to the menu. We were treating him, for a change. But suddenly my father wasn't hungry. Just thirsty for alcohol.

When it was time for dessert, Joe refused to eat the piece of cake we'd ordered for him. "Nope, not hungry," he said, waving at the waiter to take his plate away. We sang happy birthday anyway, then made him blow out his candle and make a wish. Together, we raised our glasses to the old man. After a round of absurdly brave toasts—"Here's to a great year!" "Thanks for being such a wonderful father!"—we gave him our gift: a key chain from Tiffany with a globe on it. I'd picked it out myself, thinking it would be a gesture of homage for his wayfaring career. Joe had always received gifts awkwardly. Opening the package and holding up the key chain, he looked more distressed than pleased. "Nice, nice, verrry beeeyooootiful," he said, and hastily replaced the key chain in its bright blue box. Despite the shots of vodka he put away that night, he remained sober and subdued for the rest of the evening.

The next morning, my brother John, publisher of a Texas business magazine, left to return to work. The rest of us climbed into the station wagon for the drive back to Corpus Christi. Midway, we stopped for lunch in Fredericksburg, a tiny resort town devoted to its German immigrant past. The wide main street was lined with churches, antique shops, and beer gardens: my father's idea of heaven on Earth. Sitting on a flowering terrace, Joe downed frosty steins of dark lagers and hungrily sampled plates of sauerkraut and sausages, smacking his lips in Dionysian satisfaction. As the sun beat down on our backs, my father reminisced about the past. His eyes grew dreamy as he looked off into the distance. "Reminds me of Mother's sauerkraut," he said. "Boy, did my old dad like her cooking."

When I pulled into Joe's driveway later that evening, I felt tired but filled with something nameless and long-missing: a familial substance, perhaps, some trace of my original self. The next morning, before the shuttle arrived to take us to the airport, I sat with my stepmother over a cup of coffee. "Thank you for coming," she said. "Your father just wanted to be with the four of you one last time." I tried to take this in, then asked, still disbelieving, "Did he say that?" Hilda pursed her lips and nodded her head in silent affirmation. An hour later, Steve, Colleen, and I left for the airport, each of us headed for our respective homes in different cities. It had been a good visit, and, I thought, perhaps my last. But as I hugged my father good-bye, we danced lightly around any talk of dying. Or love.

As the plane lifted off the ground, I watched as the city by the Gulf began to fade from sight. Gaining altitude, I stared out the window into the endless sky. My thoughts drifted with the clouds to Joe's mention of his parents. Especially his father, that lost grandfather of whom I knew little more than that he'd been snatched from life too young and that he'd been Irish. Why, I wondered, had my father taken us in our youth to some of the greatest cities of the world yet never to the hometown of his boyhood? Why had I seen Florence, Paris, and even Bombay—yet never Altoona, Pennsylvania?

RETURN

For all our freedom of travel growing up, our family never had any nostalgic homecomings to the Appalachian mountain city where my father was raised. There were never any raucous family reunions with grandparents, aunts, uncles, and cousins, or tables overflowing with special family dishes and drink. The town where Joe Carroll was born was as faraway and foreign to me as a city on the opposite side of the planet. Not only was Altoona just a place on the map, my father never said much about his boyhood there. Unlike my mother, who spoke wistfully of her Argentine family, Joe never seemed to be bothered by homesickness. As my brother John liked to joke, it was as if my father, when he left home, had joined the witness protection program.

Once, long after I'd grown and gone, I asked Joe if he would go with me to visit his older sister, who'd never left Altoona. I'd just moved with my own family to Washington, D.C., and Altoona was only a three-hour drive away. In spidery handwriting, my elderly Aunt Helen had written to say that she still lived in the house that she and my father had been born in. She had invited us to see her.

"Our home is big, as you must have guessed knowing that Mother and Dad reared nine children here," wrote my elderly aunt. "I don't hear anything from Joe and will look forward to catching up on him." Nearly thirty years had passed since my father and his sister had last seen each other at my grandmother's funeral. But my father had shaken his head: no, absolutely not. Avoiding my gaze and looking down at the ground, he'd put his characteristic stop to any further conversation on the matter.

"End of discussion," he'd said, a bit sadly. Turning on his heel and squaring his beige cardigan-clad shoulders, he'd taken Hilda by the arm and walked off with a forlorn air, whistling. He could visit me, tour the monuments of the nation's capital, but he could not return to his childhood home. Though not far geographically, the emotional distance would be too great, and too treacherous, to travel.

By the time I finally make the pilgrimage to Altoona, both my Aunt Helen and my father have been dead for over a decade. I struggle with guilt, realizing that I've inherited the Carroll family's pattern of distance from other members. What is the force, I wonder, that propelled us away from each other, atoms rushing outward from the center of our family gravity? As my car ascends the spiraling highway etched into mountainous ridges, an eerie feeling descends. Past and present converge in an altered timescape. I feel as if I'm traveling a labyrinth into the heart of my father's long-ago childhood.

Out my window, ribbons of thick green trees and granite embankments studded with giant boulders enchant my eyes with hints of hidden mysteries. In the distance, rounded hills roll into the horizon like the huddled backs of sleeping animals. Wisps of fog curl among the high bluffs. Tales of the bearded mountain man Rip Van Winkle, kidnapped by dwarves for twenty years, spring to mind. The sky threatens rain, thunder rumbles, and a memory returns from childhood: my father's bedtime-story voice explaining that thunder is the sound of those dwarves rolling ninepins in the sky.

A four-wheeler roars past me, and, snapping back to the present, I round a curve and begin the descent into Altoona. My chest tightens and tears prick my eyes. I had been prepared for a gray, soulless city, abandoned by the railroad industry that created it. Instead, Altoona has the careworn air of a place that, although its best days lie behind it, retains the pulse of tradition. Its cast-off pathos catches at my heart. I am moved by its place in the country's story; touched by the way it has gone on, despite its abandonment more than half a century ago.

Traditional clapboard white houses, old Federal style brick buildings, suburban homes, modern department stores, and domed and steepled churches are nestled in the crook of the mountain arms that encircle and protect the city.

I am reminded of the dream I had immediately after my father died. A herd of giant elephants covered in emerald blankets—the color of my father's body bag, the color of these hills—stand vigil beside a road. Did my father's spirit return here after his death, this place where he first entered existence, his soul's dust to earth's dust? I don't know. But Joe's presence is strong.

Cupped in a valley between two ranges of the Allegheny Mountains in southwestern Pennsylvania, Altoona bears the imprint of what historian Richard Slotkin has called America's "oldest and most characteristic myth"—the frontier. For the most part, we are used to thinking of the frontier as the territory that extends westward from the Missouri River to the Pacific Ocean. But the "oldest West," writes Frederick Jackson Turner in *The Frontier in American History*, lay along the Atlantic Coast. Onto these rocky shores rolled successive waves of Irish, German, French, Welsh, Italian, and English immigrants, possessed of a restlessness and a rootlessness that would fatefully shape the national temperament. "American social development has been continually beginning over again on the frontier," writes Turner. "This perennial rebirth, this fluidity of American life, this expansion westward with its new opportunities . . . furnish the forces dominating American character."

The frontier as a symbol of freedom's limitless possibilities is embedded in the American psyche. It shimmers on the horizon of all our dreams as undiscovered, unpopulated, and untamed wilderness: endless acres of thick forests and lush meadows, saffron-brushed deserts and steep mountain buttes, dangerous rapids and winding rivers, bottomless oceans and starry skies. The frontier exists in our imaginations as the thing that is untouched, the ground untrod by human feet, that virgin place upon which we would make a mark of our own. And so it seems to me ironic that the myth itself arose out of the subjugation of the very thing it celebrates. Alexis de Tocqueville, that astute French observer, wrote in *Democracy in America* that our young nation was fixed upon its "march across these wilds, draining swamps, turning the course of rivers, peopling solitudes, and subduing nature."

Altoona was an early outpost in this American march across the wilds, initially founded on the triumph of man over nature. The city saw itself as heroic conqueror, not of other nations, but of forests and mountain peaks. "They came to join the great adventure," trumpeted a 1924 Altoona Chamber of Commerce publication celebrating the town's seventy-fifth anniversary. It was written just two years after my father's birth. "They were Forty-Niners as truly as were the gold sekers [*sic*] who went to California. . . . Their adventure was to conquer a great mountain range and subdue it to the will of rail transportation."

The "great mountain range" that the Altoona immigrants conquered had long been inhabited as hunting and camping grounds, first by the Shawnee and Delaware, and then by the Iroquois—the six nation confederacy of the Oneida, Cayuga, Seneca, Mohawk, Onondaga, and Tuscarora peoples. Part of the Appalachian Mountain system, the Alleghenies before the first settlers arrived was a dense primeval forest of chestnut, oak, pine, hemlock, hickory, and walnut trees.

As I imagine Altoona then, nature was an exuberant expression of flourishing wildlife. To be outside was to be surrounded by the sound of birds cawing, branches snapping, grasses rustling, ice cracking, rain pelting, rivers surging, and winds whistling. A teeming civilization of animals—bear, elk, deer, and even an occasional buffalo—populated the ancient woods. Trout, salmon, bass, and beavers swam in the clear waters of the Juniata River, near whose headwaters Altoona was located. Indian trails running from east to west traversed these ranges; one of the highest peaks overlooking Altoona, Wopsononock Mountain, was sacred to the native populations.

For centuries, the Indian nations lived on their land without altering the course of a river or the face of a mountain. The "Pennsylvania Forty-Niners," on the other hand, set out to remake the American wilderness in the image of European civilization. The first pioneers, British settlers, began arriving in the region as early as 1775. Indians fought back, then scattered, and giant trees hundreds of years old fell to earth as the colonists cleared forests and built forts for protection. Farms emerged, etched clear-cut from the wilderness.

Where the Iroquois saw mountains that housed the Great Spirit, the European settlers saw minerals and resources to be stripped and extracted for trade in the new world: iron, coal, clay, ore, sand, timber, limestone, and even lead, which would be cast into bullets for George Washington's army. After the American Revolution, canny Philadelphia merchants, competing with those of Baltimore and New York for the rapidly expanding markets of the western United States, saw the need for more efficient routes to trade products made from these raw materials, and to cultivate new markets for the new east coast commodity: steel. By the mid-1820s, a transportation revolution, spurred by the race to the Ohio Valley and sparked by the bare beginnings of the new "Rail Road," which was seen as the answer for trade with the west, was underway.

But if Pennsylvania really wanted to be a significant player in the development of American expansion westward, it would have to surmount its formidable geographical limitations. The journey from Philadelphia to Pittsburgh, Pennsylvania's gateway to the West, faced a blockade of dense, steep mountains and enfolded valleys— the Allegheny Ridge—that rose then unfurled like an emerald carpet toward the Rocky Mountains. Determined to ascend and move beyond this giant of an obstacle, the particular genius that is the hallmark of the American psyche—the engineering smarts, the "Yes, I can do anything!" spirit of sheer, raw gumption—blazed into action, firing innovation. The first step in this commercial transportation endeavor was the creation of the Mainline of Public Works and the Allegheny Portage Railroad, a 350-mile long patchwork of canals, inclines, and rail lines carved across the mountains and overlaid atop old Indian trails.

In an age when a person can wake up on the East Coast and be on the West Coast in time for lunch, it's difficult to conceive of traveling by such a crude, unwieldy transportation system. At various points along this expensive, twelve-million-dollar route, passengers alternated between pack boats ferrying train cars along waterways or, conversely, canal boats lifted out of the water, broken down into three pieces, and transported over inclines in primitive railcars before being returned once again to the canals. At other stages during the ten-hour passage, passenger and freight cars were hauled over steep grades and mountaintops by means of stationary hoisting engines, pulled along by ropes thick enough, in the words of one awed observer, to "fish for Leviathans and Sea Monsters."

For many passengers, the experience of crossing the Allegheny Peaks brought a rare encounter with the heights. In articles and letters from that time, passengers expressed their awe in mythic terms. One described his journey as "Jacob's ladder to be carrying us to the very heavens." As they neared the mountains, wrote another traveler, "their lofty precipices were dimly visible and terrifically grand. It was a moment of intense interest . . . the ascent by night formidable." The project, said another, was "more honorable than the temples and pyramids of Egypt, or the triumphal arches and columns of Rome." Indeed, "these Pennsylvanians," noted a writer for the *Daily Cleveland Herald*, "think the region of Time is over; they are building for eternity."

But as rail technology advanced and commerce flourished among Pennsylvania's competitors, even this ingenious transportation mix proved too lengthy and laborious. Immensely frustrated by its failure to move west more quickly with its business interests, Philadelphia mounted a big push to conquer its transportation problem. On April 13, 1846, the Pennsylvania Railroad was chartered, its mission to get up and over the mountain range impeding progress. In a dramatic and unusual departure from other railroads owned by the railroad barons, such as Cornelius Vanderbilt's New York Central, J. P. Morgan's New York, New Haven, and Hartford Railroad, or Jay Gould's Erie Railroad, the Pennsylvania Railroad, as organized by the state of Pennsylvania, was a shareholder corporation. Under PRR management, new routes, hewed by the brute force of manual laborers, were constructed, and by 1849 steel tracks ran straight from Philadelphia to the base of the eastern slope of the Alleghenies.

There, the Pennsylvania Railroad faced nature at its most implacable: a chasm that dipped steeply, then rose sharply between two mountain ranges. This impasse seemed to defy existing constructing technology and even the ability of locomotives to make such a climb. Determined as ever to push on through the Alleghenies to the west, the PRR set up a base camp to launch a massive construction project. A special mountain division made up of hundreds of Irish laborers was imported from Cork, Mayo, and Antrim counties. Under the guiding vision of J. Edgar Thomson, the chief engineer for the Pennsylvania Railroad, Horseshoe Curve, a masterful piece of engineering, began construction. Rather than aim straight across the plunging ravines, this U-shaped track looped around the inset valley, then doubled back. Perched on a mountain pass that rose 122 feet, laborers used picks and shovels to form a ledge on which they could place the tracks. Easing the steep grade between the two ridges, Horseshoe Curve, remarkably still in use today carrying millions of tons of cargo west and east, allowed the heavy locomotives to gather the power they needed to make the climb to the next peak. It instantly became an engineering marvel admired around the world.

As Horseshoe Curve was being constructed, a tunnel was also being bored straight through the summit of Allegheny Mountain. From this crest, it was an easy downhill descent to Pittsburgh, portal to the rest of the country. By 1858, completion of these monumental construction tasks—Horseshoe Curve and the Gallitzin Tunnels—had reduced travel time between Philadelphia and Pittsburgh from four days to eight hours. The human sacrifice was great. Many were killed or maimed by the backbreaking labor. "Under scorching summer suns and in the drear of mountain winters they worked," says the 1924 Altoona Chamber of Commerce booklet describing this feat. "They dug great cuts in the mountainside; blasted and dug through forests; wrestled with giant rocks; coped with slides and washes of earth."

It was at this juncture of mountain and man-made railroad that Altoona was founded, emerging out of the base-camp community of engineers, laborers, and massing of materials that constructed Horseshoe Curve and the Gallitzin Tunnels. What had been a mere farming and iron-making village grew into a crude center of operations for the Pennsylvania Railroad. From their first attempts to climb the curve, individual locomotives couldn't haul trains or freight cars without booster locomotives. Likewise, trains coming from the west needed booster engines to assist their descent. Because climbing the steep hills of the curve was extraordinarily hard on the steam engines that hauled those early locomotives, repairs were continually needed. Eventually, shops were built to construct and repair the locomotives, and passenger and freight cars. Incorporated as a borough in 1854, the mountain-train town took its name from the Danish railroad city of Altona. The extra "o" established the town's separate identity from its Danish sister. Some say the town's name came from the Indian word *allatona* meaning "high land of great worth."

It was in the shelter of this land of great worth that my paternal great-grandfather found refuge from the famine and wars laying waste to his native Ireland. Born in County Cork in March 1842, William F. Carroll immigrated to this country in 1862. He arrived on American soil during the Civil War, well ahead of the first generation of Ellis Island immigrants. Lacking any family stories, letters, or records documenting my great-grandfather's trajectory from Ireland to Altoona, I turn to Peter Vogt, the director of *Altoona at Work*, a documentary on the Pennsylvania Railroad that plays at the Altoona Railroad Museum. In one of the curious twists of fate that mark my research, I discover that this award-winning filmmaker is a near neighbor of mine in Washington, D.C., his yard studded with railroad artifacts and antiques.

Vogt is a well of information about the history of Altoona and its entwined relationship with the Pennsylvania Railroad. Very likely, he tells me, my great-grandfather had been hired by an immigrant labor manager, a fellow countryman who acted as a broker staffing the American railroads, mines, and factories. Once in Altoona, my great-grandfather Carroll, who could not read or write, took a job with the Pennsylvania Railroad as a blacksmith. His skill, though valuable, Vogt tells me, would have placed him on the lowest rung of the railroad hierarchy. Placed far below the precision work of the machinists, and that of the linemen who drove the trains, Carroll's was hazardous, brute labor. Daily, my great-grandfather toiled with hammers and gigantic pieces of hot steel, manually forming metal into drive rods and wheels, and repairing and constructing enormous boilers and the great locomotives. These were the men, says Vogt, who worked the huge power hammers, manhandling the stuff that had to go under the "pounders." The work environment, he says, "was gigantic, dramatic, and dangerous. The whole place shook and everything was hot." In Vogt's film, a retired "Pennsy" blacksmith recalls the molten steel poured out of cauldrons into giant and small molds to cast parts, and how the whole place reverberated with huge blasts of smoke and fire. "In its heat, scale, and intensity [it] was like being in Vulcan's workshop—a workshop of the gods," says Vogt. "But it was all just part of what it takes to make a railroad and run it."

Except to stress the dropped *O* in our last name—"We were O'Carroll's," Dad liked to say—my father shared no tales about my Irish forefather. Yet all his life, Joe's blood ran green. This inheritance was evident in my father's black-dog moods, his hot temper, maudlin poetry recitations, the prodigious amounts of beer he guzzled, and the Irish lullabies and ballads he sang and whistled.

Probably no memory of my father haunts me more than these songs. Against his roughneck ways, Joe's warbling was unexpected, and it could always break the listening heart. My sister, the musician, recalls that Joe's whistling had an unusual vibrato. Even now, imagining myself back home again, I can see my father, his lips pursed and his head thrown back like a bird. I can hear the bittersweet strains pouring from his lips. I may not have been told much about my Irish great-grandfather. But through my father's notes, volumes of wordless feelings, a hundred years silent, came coursing through.

In the lullaby "Toorah Loora Loora," my father crooned to me about my uprooted Irish ancestor's longing for the family he had left behind. In "Danny Boy," which Joe whistled as he sat in his chair, staring off into some imagined past, could be heard my great-grandfather's lament for his abandoned motherland. In "When Irish Eyes Are Smiling," which my dad whistled as he mended the barbed wire fences on our Missouri farm, were echoed my great-grandfather's brogue as his big hands shaped the molten pivots with the heavy iron tongs. Amid the clamor of these railroad workers, did my great-grandfather, I wonder, sometimes hear the echo of his own father's humming and whistling, long, long ago in the fields of Ireland? Did my Irish ancestry come down to me as strains of sadness and longing? And when did the brogue William Carroll brought with him fade from the family tongue?

In 1872, my great-grandfather married Mary Collins, an Irish girl from Johnstown, Pennsylvania, immortalized in her 1897 obituary as a "lady of refined Christian character." Five children were born to the Carrolls, the oldest being a son named George, who would become my father's father. In 1880, my maternal great-grandfather, John B. Feser, immigrated to Altoona from Germany. He, too, put his capable hands to work for the railroad, as a cabinetmaker. Feser married one E. Hermione; they had six children, the oldest of which was a girl named after her mother. These two eldest children of my great-grandparents—my grandmother Elisa Hermione Feser and my grandfather George Fields Carroll—met, courted, married, and began a major family enterprise of their own. Joseph Wilbert Carroll, as my father was christened, was born October 24, 1922, the eighth child and sixth son of the large Irish-German Carroll clan.

At the time of my father's birth, Altoona's original mandate to conquer nature was well in the past. The city was at the apex of its glory, proud to be the crown jewel of the mighty Pennsylvania Railroad, a near-mythic entity that gave the city its reason for being, marking it with an indelible character. In seventy-five years, Altoona had gone from a farm field to a population of 100,000. The town teemed with the productivity of an enterprising America. Old photos show new streets bustling with hurrying pedestrians, horse-drawn delivery wagons, and garish early Fords. Though my father's family was too poor to shop for store-bought clothes, Gables, with over forty departments, displayed its tempting merchandise in windows of French plate glass.

There was fun, too, from dancing at the Penn Alto Hotel to ice-skating, roller coasters, casinos, and canoeing at the Lakemont Amusement Park. Clubs and organizations, mostly for men, organized Altoona's community of engineers, brakemen, and carpenters: the American Legion, the Brotherhood of the Railroad Trainmen, Elks, Eagles, Masons, Shriners, the Patriotic Order Sons of America, and more. Before heading home at the end of one of the three shifts, or "tricks," that marked the twenty-four-hour work day, train crews and shop men could stop at one of the town's many bars. There, in men-only gatherings, the workers could let down in relaxed camaraderie, where they would enjoy boilmakers: a tall, cold beer with a shot of whiskey. A slew of accents characterized these bar-stool conversations, mirroring the mix of ethnicities populating Altoona. Neighborhoods were parceled into Jew Hill, Dutch Hill, and Little Italy.

This cultural diversity shaped the city's remarkable religious pluralism. In 1924, sixty-nine churches of various Christian denominations lined a street named "the Isle of Worship." There was also a Jewish temple, a Masonic temple, and even a domed Roman Catholic cathedral, Blessed Sacrament, which sat like a bishop proudly overlooking his see from a hilltop perch. Atop Gospel Hill, the highest point in town, evangelists gathered their followers and delivered fiery "sermons on the mount."

But the largest temple of worship of all was the enormous Pennsylvania Railroad complex, with its shops and endless systems of tracks binding the city in the sacred rituals of blue-collar labor. Work was this temple's form of worship: extreme manual effort, exacting discipline, patient reliability, and refined skills all performed in service to a massive industrial undertaking on a scale unlike anywhere else in the world at the time. The cacophonous music and ceaseless sound of whistles and the rush and clackety-clack of the great steam locomotives arriving and departing filled the air with the resonant psalms of heavy industry. Smoke, ashes, and cinders mantled the valley in a film of gray and black. Inside the shops, gleaming steam locomotives, as colossal and immutable as sphinxes, rested on giant platforms for repair. Row after row of engines, wheels, and equipment lined the walls like holy relics in a shrine.

The Altoona railroad repair and production complex, with its labs, offices, warehouses, and shops, was the largest in the world. Everything about the railroad shops, in fact, was writ extra-large, a citywide production of stupendous size and proportion. The enormous blacksmith shops on Twelfth Street housed the biggest steam hammer in the world. Down the block, the legendary 250-ton steam locomotives were "bathed" in the world's largest lye vat, "steel babies" lifted into their tub by a 150-ton crane. Altoona had the largest car wheel foundry and the largest roundhouse in the world. Hundreds of skills to match countless tools were utilized to overhaul thousands of freight and passenger cars. At its peak, the Altoona Works employed over 17,000 people; the 122 buildings that made up the complex covered 218 acres outside and 37 acres of indoor workshop space. Altoona was also home to the world's first and greatest Mechanics library, with over 65,000 volumes of knowledge on the arts of engineering—an industrial Library of Alexandria. Known as the "Standard Railroad of the World" because of its research and testing facilities, the Pennsylvania Railroad garnered a reputation throughout Europe and beyond. It attracted the best in scientific talent, writes Dan Cupper in *Crossroads of Commerce*, producing leaders in civil, mechanical, chemical, and electrical engineering. Crucial in both war and peacetime, the Railroad exceeded every other in the number of travelers it carried and the tonnage it moved. Its track-mileage exceeded 25,000 miles, or enough to circle the Earth.

The Pennsylvania Railroad was also for many years the largest corporation in the world. For over a century, shareholders never failed to receive a yearly dividend. Like the computer and information industries of today, notes Cupper, the Pennsylvania Railroad dominated culture and commerce. So pervasive was the PRR's influence, he tells me, that an anecdote of the time held that whenever a person found themselves in Pennsy territory, they had to specify exactly which "President" they were speaking about. Stated in terms of today's transportation economy, writes Cupper, the power of the Pennsylvania Railroad would be "as if American and United airlines merged with aircraft builder Boeing and then, after constructing the runways, airports, and air-traffic-control systems needed for their routes, took over parts of the Air Force, NASA, and Federal Express." The Pennsylvania Historical Society records that even by World War II the PRR and Altoona Works remained so critical to the national economy that the rail shops and Horseshoe Curve "ranked high on the list of sites to be bombed or sabotaged by Nazi Germany." The mythic reach of the PRR even cast its spell over Cupper's own life. Forsaking his career in journalism to follow the call of the train, he became a conductor on the Norfolk Southern, responsible for the care of passengers and cargo.

Eventually, in a familiar pattern that repeats itself throughout the American story, the Railroad, like Icarus, suffered a fall from its pinnacle. During the 1870s and 1880s the railroads turned into arrogant, monopolistic bullies, angering the public and tarnishing their public image, a stigma that would carry over into the next century. Even as other railroads switched to the more efficient diesel and electric-powered engines, the Pennsylvania Railroad remained entrenched in the past, devising grandiose plans to build better steam engines. In their view, Cupper explains, "that's the way it had always been, and always would be."

By 1952, when the Pennsylvania Railroad finally made the switch to diesel power, it was too late; the once-mighty corporation had been eclipsed by faster technologies produced by General Electric and manufactured more cheaply. At the same time, General Motors began promoting automobile and truck transportation for the newly built Interstate Highway System. Finally came the rise of air cargo and passenger transportation.

So began the slow decline of the railroad, that once omnipotent transportation giant that had driven America's westward expansion, establishing towns and the nation's first parks along its rails. When a frontier disappears in America, as historian David Courtwright notes in *Sky as Frontier*, "a distinctive social world disappears with it, evolving into a more conventional order or moving elsewhere." And so it was with Altoona. Specialized skills, arcane tools, and long-established rhythms of life fell into disuse. The once-sprawling Altoona Works vanished, save for a few buildings, living on only in the memories of rail enthusiasts and in museum exhibits and paid for by highway taxes to encourage tourism. A city, used up and discarded by the quicksilver American dream, struggled to survive into a new era. Ironically, as America wrestles with an environmental crisis today, rail transportation is once again emerging from its long slumber. Trains now offer a clean alternative to the high fuel costs and air pollution of jet travel, and relieve highway congestion caused by trucks.

✳

When I finally arrive in Altoona on a late summer's day in early September, I can smell the pine needles in the wind that rushes down from the mountains. I walk through the quiet streets and reflect on the city of the once-great Pennsylvania Railroad. Today, after what Vogt describes as a period of almost "schizophrenic struggle" over its identity and future, the old railroad complex has been replaced by manufacturing and merchandising centers. Golf courses that cater to retiring baby boomers dot the open green spaces that surround downtown. Through gradual re-organizations, the PRR split into two railroads: Amtrak took over its passenger service; Conrail, and then Norfolk Southern, took on its function as a freight rail carrier. While both Amtrak and the Norfolk Southern Railroad continue on their timetabled rounds, a disconsolate air haunts the city, as if it suffers still the loss of its once-mythic center. For what is a city made of, if not the lives of individuals who share a common fate?

Though I missed meeting my Aunt Helen, her daughter Carol has volunteered to show me the Carroll house where my father was born. I meet Carol—one of many Carroll cousins I've never met before—in the parking lot of the Altoona Railroaders Museum. From there, I follow her car as it snakes up the steep hillside, past the department stores and the golden-crowned cathedral that broods over the city beneath it.

The Carroll house, located where the uppermost edge of Altoona meets the foothills of the lush and misty Appalachians, stands just as it was when it was built in 1909. I get out of the car and crane my neck and look up at the windows. I am silenced by this encounter, washed with feeling. The house is large but understated. Narrow at the front and long at the back, the white clapboard, four-story residence is neatly divided in two: a square, bottom half is topped by an ornately gabled top, with five large windows, two above and three below. A wide front porch with railings and an overhanging roof open to the street. A small trap door beneath the porch conceals a basement bin, where coal was once delivered to fuel the furnace. Built into the side of a hill, the house doesn't possess much of a front yard; steep steps lead down to the street. Behind the house a small patch of yard slopes up into the ridges arching high above it.

It is still owned by the family, but the current occupant, the boyfriend of a second cousin, has declined to let us inside. Still, it's important for me to see the house, not only because my father was born inside these walls, but because it is the site of a family tragedy.

It is among these ridges some seventy years ago that seven tall and skinny Carroll boys with marble-blue eyes ran wild, hunting deer and rabbit. "Ridge runners," or the "Carroll tribe from the hills," my Aunt Renie tells me they were called. This brings to mind Uncle Paul, as he sat beside my father on his deathbed, musing about the Carroll boys who lived on a hill, happily apart, or so he made it sound, from the rest of the town. Though they were poor kids, they'd had a good childhood, Paul told me. Content to roam outside, they'd played their own made-up games and devised mischievous pranks.

I face the house and think of all the unrecorded memories that live within those walls. Carol tells me that our German great-grandpap Feser, as he was called by the family, would visit each Sunday, tying his horse up at the porch railing. I imagine my father and his brothers and sisters running through the house in excitement, spilling outside in a rolling tumble to the dirt-paved street. I can see my grandparents, George and Minnie, still dressed from the Sunday church services, coming outside to greet the German patriarch. There had been no visits from my Irish great-grandfather, or at least during my father's childhood, as William Carroll had died in 1923, one year before his sixth grandson's birth.

I never really knew my father's parents, never even saw my grandfather, and only met my grandmother once, as an infant. Joe, my mother tells me, "was close-mouthed" about his family. So distant are my grandparents from me that my generational link to them as their granddaughter feels wholly unreal. No letters or journals exist, and, as was often the case with many immigrant laborers who were poor record keepers, there are no official documents in my possession to ground them in time and history.

So it is with excitement that in my initial research I come across a 1920 census record of a white male, George Carroll, age forty-two, born in Altoona, 1878. It is the first written record of my grandfather's life I have come across. The sight of my grandfather's handwriting gives me a jolt. As if a broken circuit has been rewired, I feel plugged into my American past. It is strange that, although I know so little about my paternal grandfather, he will end up shaping my life in such a profound and permanent way. In the few photos I have of him, George Carroll's long, angular face presents itself to me across the decades. His gaze is serious; he appears gaunt and inwardly preoccupied. In his expression I see reflected the hollow look of displacement carried down that long chain of Irish immigrants driven to this country by the horrors of the famine and death stalking Ireland during the nineteenth century. The melancholy of these Irish exiles, many of whom identified themselves with the Children of Israel, was passed down from my great-grandfather William Carroll to George, who in turn handed it to Joe.

Tracing my emotional lineage, I calculate the cost inherited from my ancestors. Was my great-grandfather's experience as an exile from Ireland, I wonder, the headwaters of the Carroll family's complexes around alcoholism and depression? Did William Carroll bring with him from Ireland a psyche seared by the loss of his homeland, his loved ones, and even pieces of his own self and soul? Historical research by Ronald Takaki in *A Different Mirror* informs me that, just before embarking, my great-grandfather would have participated in an "American wake"—a bizarre ritual in which he would have been mourned as good as dead, since those he'd left behind would never see or speak with him again. In his passage across the Atlantic on one of the "famine ships" transporting Irish laborers to America, William would have slept in an airless dungeon on a narrow shelf, along with hundreds of other people. Once landed, he would have endured the blunt force of entering and adapting to a very new and different reality from anything he'd ever known.

My great-grandfather would not have known what psychologists now recognize: that a loss of culture is in its own way a trauma to the human psyche. Family systems theorists speculate that it can take up to three generations to work through the effects of an immigration, says psychotherapist Harriet Lerner. Those driven by the traumas of war, poverty, and disease into political exile face an especially difficult time integrating their lives into their new homeland.

What is more, some psychologists also say—and contrary to what most Americans would like to believe—time does not always heal the generations-old traumas suffered by our forebears. Instead, that which is unfinished and unhealed gets passed down a family line, as if an invisible field of unquiet ghosts hovers behind the living. Turning to the work of German psychologist Bert Hellinger, I read about the "interruptions" that can occur to block the natural flow of love through a family line. Families, he says, have their own "conscience" and fate. In *Acknowledging What Is*, Hellinger maintains that historical family traumas are a source of physical and psychological illness. This is not because the family members are bad or evil, he stresses, but "because fate takes a certain turn that touches and affects all those concerned. It begins with the parents, who have parents of their own and come from families with fates of their own. All that has an effect in each new family. The ties ensure that the fate is carried by all. When something bad happens in a family, the need for compensation may extend over generations."

I pause over this last sentence, letting the words sink in. It is with George Carroll that something bad did happen. Picking up his photo once again, I peer into my grandfather's face, examining his expression for clues, anything that will help me to understand where something inside my father went wrong. I see George's physical exhaustion, the anxiety. There is shame in the slump of his shoulders, despair in the heavy droop of his face—traits that today might be diagnosed as depression. But I see nobility, too. The dignity of the laborer who creates out of the muscle of his body. Still, as if I'm gazing at a stranger from five centuries ago, I find it incomprehensible that I am descended from this man—that his genes partly pattern the shape and characteristics of my own body, as well as that of my three sons.

In him is that place of interruption that ruptures the flow of love in my family. As Hellinger recommends in his book, I try to "bring him back into the picture" of my present life, because, as Hellinger says, "when the dead have their place, they are peaceful and are experienced as a positive energy." I want to do this, to acknowledge my tie to my long dead grandfather, for the sake of my father's restless spirit, for myself, for my sons, and for the generations of my American family yet to be born.

In one faded picture, George Carroll stands beside an old jalopy with large, bug-eye headlights. He has on worn denim overalls with long sleeves and baggy pants. Behind him stretches a rolling pasture of stubble, as if a crop has just been harvested. A narrow-brimmed hat is jammed on his head, and his large hands dangle out of his too-short sleeves, bony wrists showing. The hands are not clenched but look open and relaxed. I see, too, that his big knuckles and long fingers are like my father's. I notice the large veins; looking down, I see the same veins rivering my own hands and that have often been remarked upon by friends and family.

Struck by this strange similarity, I feel, for the briefest of moments, sad that I never had the chance to hold my grandfather's hands, to touch the body I came from, to hear an Irish song or story from his lips. But perhaps these wishes are merely fantasies. The gaze beneath George Carroll's hat is unsmiling. He looks dour and worried. These are the Depression years, and George bears the heaviness of those hard times on his thin frame. Gene, my father's younger brother, leans into the picture with his hand on one of the tall tractor tires— his eagerness to be in the picture and close to his father touching in its vulnerability. In another sepia-toned photo, my grandfather, still wearing the same down-at-the-mouth expression, is seated before the rough-hewn, weathered wall of a barn. Three small children with lush blond curls—Helen, Dot, and Jim—sit on his lap. All four gaze away from the camera into the distance, as if someone is calling to them. My grandmother, as I imagine this scene.

Because she lived longer, I know a little more about my grandmother. In an accompanying photo, she is a young, attractive woman dressed in a plain cotton jumper. The same three children now sit on her lap, as if she has changed places with my grandfather. All three kids stare into the camera; my grandmother's gaze is intently focused on her children. Her thick, wavy brown hair is swept up in a bun; curls trail around her face. Like my grandfather, she, too, has a careworn expression, as if weighed down by life's endless tasks. Already, she has four children. Five more boys—Dick, Bob, Paul, Joe, and Eugene—will come along. All nine children were born at home, as my father once told me.

Minnie, as my grandmother was called, was a strongly built woman who stood five feet ten inches tall. As I learn from my father as he is dying, Minnie had suffered a childhood bout of polio that left one leg lame and shorter than the other. Undeterred by this disability, she stood on her feet all day, chasing kids, cooking, and cleaning. In an age when physical needs trumped all others, there was no time to spare for nurturing the emotional well-being of children. And so it was that my father would sometimes remark, as I was growing up, that neither he nor his younger brother, Gene, had been wanted. Somehow, his mother had made this much clear to him, never considering the way her words would ripple across the generations, increasing in emotional velocity until it broke on the shores of my psyche. Or perhaps, I think, my grandmother feigned indifference because the real truth was she cared more than she let on, or might have fallen apart if she'd given too much love.

"Oh, no, Ma didn't want us," my father would say, looking away, the hurt palpable beneath his studied nonchalance. "There were just too many kids." Joe understood, the way anyone would, the burden on his mother of raising so many children, especially a crippled woman who hobbled about her chores. Still, as a little boy, Joe developed a habit of sleep-walking. Once, he said, his parents woke up and found him gone. In the dead of night, along dirt roads bordering the forest, he'd walked for over a mile, until he'd arrived at the front stoop of a neighbor's house, where he was eventually discovered. Something in Joe's tone of voice as he recounted this story always left me unsettled. Had the daemon of travel that would determine his fate, I wonder, already taken possession of him? Or was he seeking out another family to fill the empty places pot-holing his psyche?

Jungian analyst Lionel Corbett suggests a link between my father's sleepwalking and being an unwanted child. Corbett is trying to help me locate the fissures in my father's developing emotional infrastructure. Joe's paranoia and social anxiety as an adult lead Corbett to suspect the possibility of some kind of early abuse. Or, at the least, that a sense of danger pervaded Joe's primary relationships. Joe's symptoms and his studiously offhanded remarks indicate to Corbett that my father had grown up in a household where his caretakers felt to him unreliable and untrustworthy. Even after leaving home, Corbett says, my father would have carried this early atmosphere with him, imprinting his surroundings with the traumatic echo of his past.

My father's shaky tie to his mother ensured that their relationship would be a complicated one. Despite Mother Carroll's ambivalent feelings toward the next-to-youngest of her brood, the little boy Joe loved his mom back twice as strong, layering a fine golden gloss over her flaws. I know this because, as a young girl, my grandmother was the starring heroine of my bedtime stories. In these real-life fairy tales, Mother Carroll appeared as the overworked but kind mother who stood on her feet all day baking delicious meals and washing laundry by hand as she took care of seven strong-willed boys and two equally stubborn daughters.

My very favorite tale, the one I asked my father to tell me again and again, was about the time the Carroll boys got up at night, crept outside, and dug an underground pit in the hills behind the house. Into this hole in the ground they stashed food stolen from the household pantry—homemade pies, bread, churned butter, cheese, and jams my grandmother had labored to make during the day. Each night after bedtime, the seven would sneak outside for nocturnal parties in the wooded hills. Overprotected child that I was, this sounded divine to me, mischievous in a Huck Finn/Tom Sawyer sort of way. Always a good girl, I secretly longed to be as free as a boy, to do something as sneaky and fun as my father had done when he was young. Sometimes, under the cover of night, my father said, he and his brothers would steal chickens from a neighbor's henhouse. I can still remember my mouth watering as my father described the way they'd pluck a bird, salt it, roll it in mud, then roast it over a fire. I remember his descriptions of warm, vine-ripened tomatoes and fresh sweet corn, filched from surrounding farms. When my grandmother, alarmed by the gradual disappearance of food from her pantry, discovered her sons' midnight robbery, she lined them up in a row and dressed them down.

"Oh, Mother was mad," my father would say, widening his blue eyes and smiling impishly as if he was still the naughty boy. After scolding her sons, Mother Carroll administered each one a dose of castor oil. At this part in the story my father would make a face, recalling the bitter taste. Then, Mother Carroll made them get shovels and fill in their underground pit. A special bedtime ritual always closed out this story: my father would pick my sister and me up, one at a time, in his strong, sunburned arms. Swinging us in the air, he would yell, "One . . . two . . . three . . . wheeee!" dropping us on the bed as we laughed ourselves silly. After that, we'd kneel beside our beds, make the sign of the cross, and, led by my suddenly penitent father, recite our evening prayers.

Years later, I hear a darker version of the bedtime story from my cousin Patrick, son of Joe's older brother Bob. In this "little horror story," as my cousin describes it, his father and no doubt my own along with some friends locked another kid in a crypt or small space—most likely the dug-out pit of my father's bedtime stories—and left him there overnight. When the Carroll boys released their captive the next day, the boy's hair had turned completely white. It was, says Patrick, an event that haunted his father all of his life—as perhaps it had Joe, too.

Another oft-told story that stuck with my father was about the time he got a job to save money for a motorcycle. Mother Carroll warned him, however, that if he bought it, she'd stop speaking to him. But my father hankered after this motorcycle and purchased it anyway. I remember the day he bought his motorcycle as if I'd been there myself: standing on the porch with my grandmother as she watches her son proudly wheel up the hill in front of their house, yet experiencing my father's mix of anxiety, guilt, and daring as if his feelings were mine.

Just as she had promised, Mother Carroll kept her vow. For days, she refused to speak to Joe, or even acknowledge him. Eventually, my father said, he couldn't stand being shut out from the circle of her affection and he sold his motorcycle. "I didn't believe Mother would do it, but she did. I just couldn't take it anymore. I just couldn't take the guilt every time I got on the bike and rode down the driveway," Joe would say, shaking his head in puzzlement.

A good part of my father's shame as he told us this story must have stemmed from what he didn't tell us: that his father had died, and that he didn't want to be the cause of any more suffering to his mother. His sensitivity to my grandmother's moods, his dependence on her, fits with the way Joe appears in the few photos I have of him as a youth. I cherish these photos, for in them my father's gaze is undefended, fresh, and vulnerable; his hair curls and curves off his head in charming tufts. He looks the way a man does before the shield of emotional passivity— the contemporary man's modern-day armor—has been raised against vulnerability. Still, the motorcycle was the first indication of my father's lifelong addiction to fleeing the unpleasant sting of pain, his first attempt to make use of a mechanical object as a vehicle to separate himself from his past. His first step on the American hero's quest to find his frontier.

SON OF ALTOONA

As I look back over the early years of Joe's life, I wonder about his psychological inheritance, not just from his parents and grandparents, but also as the son of an American railroad city. How culture shapes the inner world of the individual was a question that preoccupied one of psychology's early pioneers, Erik Erikson. In his studies of various Native American cultures, Erikson came to see how the values, beliefs, and perspectives of culture are transmitted via child-raising techniques that help individuals adapt to their surrounding social community. These techniques inevitably mold a child's emotional character as well.

Erikson's insights lead me to wonder how my father's personal psychology was shaped by being born to a hardscrabble, blue-collar railroading family during the height of the industrial age and the depths of the Great Depression. Joe Carroll's childhood, I realize, was different in the extreme from my own; no continuity of tradition binds us across the generations. The grandson of a blacksmith and the son of a machinist who spent his days servicing the steel bowels of mammoth train engines, Joe Carroll was born into a family that worshiped in the church of American industry. In the laborer's suppers his mother prepared, in the withdrawn, strained silences of his father, Joe's life was steeped in a world of the relentless feeding of engines: trains, tractors, motorcycles, and automobiles. Daily life ran on the fixed rhythms of the train-track schedule. The sharp whistle of the trains punctuated the days and nights of Altoona much like the cathedral bells marked the hours in the medieval cities of Europe. Technological ingenuity and industrial progress through the domination of nature, I come to see, was the core myth of Altoona and the railroad it serviced.

Marked from birth by Altoona's myth of industrial progress, Joe was endowed with a fascination for the magic and power of machines, and possessed by a workaholic intensity that heedlessly disregarded the toll on his body. Able to soar above troublesome emotions, his soul forever yearning after the toot of the train, Joe was bred with an inborn drive to master nature, including his own human instincts. Old photos show him bent over the open hood of a car or truck, his head and shoulders bowing over some faulty valve or piston. It's an image that says a lot, as I well remember Joe describing an engine with more curiosity and affection than he ever expressed about his four kids. Non-mechanical person that I am, though, even I can understand technology's lure: how concrete, and fixable it is; how clean of the irrational and the human.

But as much as the myth of Icarus sounds a warning about flying high, so too does it sound a cautionary note about engineering. Daedalus, father of Icarus and the inventor of his crude wax-and-feather wings, is known as the mythic father of technology. His name, writes Thomas Cahill in *Sailing the Wine-Dark Sea*, means "cunning fabricator," a man able to "work on unknown arts, to alter nature." The first in a long line of inventors who rather than take life as it was sought to improve on it, Daedalus can be seen imprinted on Benjamin Franklin's experiment to harness electricity while flying a kite, Thomas Edison's invention of the telephone, the U.S. Interstate Highway System, the Wright brothers' plane, the NASA shuttle, and Steve Jobs' Apple computer. So bound has technology become to America's identity that it's as if, after his son's tragic fall, Daedalus took wing and landed on American soil.

Even the railroad, as some observers noted at the time, seemed to spring out of the essence of America. The new form of transportation "appears to be the characteristic personification of the American," wrote the French Guillaume Poussin following his visit to America in 1851. And in fact the gifts of the Iron Horse—"fire-spars flashing from his gleaming eye," as Dickens put it—to the young country were many. The railroad unified disparate regions spread across immense distances into a nation and opened new webs of communication and connection. It strengthened a budding democratic system of social equality, created standard time zones, and helped launch the engineering profession, fast food, corporations, speculation, debt, credit, and big financiers.

Yet in a recurring theme around technological progress that continues to play out over the centuries, the railroad destroyed as much as it built, and generated as much anxiety as excitement. Newspaper editors and thinkers, writes Craig Miner in *A Most Magnificent Machine*, wrote regularly of the "bewildering" effects of the railroad. Many worried about the displaced Native American tribes and the erosion of a more rural, simpler "Old America." Other observers linked the railroad with the rise of too much "effervescence" in American society. They fretted over its "nervousness and irritability," and the way railroad culture instilled haste and restlessness in the country's citizens. For in a paradoxical twist, as much as the railroad brought the country together, it also fueled America's hunger for expansion, driving families and communities further apart.

Thinking along these lines brings to mind my conversation with psychoanalyst James Hillman. He analyzes America as a country that hates limits. Psychiatrically, he says, this is a manic condition, a state in which "a person has unbounded energy and a flight of ideas; everything is speeded up. If you try to put limits on someone with mania—if you interrupt them, confine them or try to stop them from what they're doing—they can fly into a manic rage. The mania in this country is without borders."

In her study of the way a manic condition affects an individual, Jungian analyst Verena Kast writes that such a person "suffers from a compulsive urge to be active and from a heightened drive that can hardly be slowed." Filled with boundless strength, Kast writes in *Joy, Inspiration, and Hope*, manic persons behave as if they are immune to ordinary needs like sleep or downtime. Exempt from fatigue, they are constantly busy and on the move, exhausting everyone around them. Common among geniuses, writers, artists, and inventors of all kinds—not to mention many business movers and shakers—mania is often envied for its frenzied states of inspired creativity. But in yet another variation on the Icarus myth, mania can turn just as suddenly into its opposite, depression. This emotional disorder is labeled bipolar disorder: the sudden downturn of giddy elation into listless heaviness and immobilizing melancholy.

Mania's drive, Kast explains, corresponds in its essence to a "deep contemporary longing to be carried up into the heights." Thus the cure for the state of mania, she says, quoting the Swiss existential analyst Ludwig Binswanger, lies in learning to strike a balance between the vertical and the horizontal. In other words, because the experience of falling or crashing is a sign of having gone too high too fast, it's wise to avoid becoming high-flown, soaring to such altitudes that what's below disappears from view.

But what happens when there is no ground to anchor the manic ride of the highflier, the dreamer, the frontier-chaser? In their immense zeal to create a new civilization out of the old, my father's forebears began the process of destroying the very foundation that supported them, the earth they stood on. As much as my father liked to think of himself as a practical man with his feet planted firmly on the earth, groundlessness, the severance from nature's rhythms, was as much a part of his inheritance as his Irish temper and his German blue eyes.

Once, in an example of my father's whacked-out mood swings, I recall being awakened around two or three in the morning by the whine of farm machinery. Peering out my bedroom window into the darkness, I could see the headlights of my father's John Deere tractor, shining like the two eyes of a wild animal. It was just after the summer harvest. My father had returned from a trip, had tried to sleep but couldn't, and so had gone to work plowing under the stripped stalks of wheat into neat rows of mounded, fresh dirt. Back and forth, back and forth he went, beneath the spectral moonlight. He was all alone in the night, with nothing but the stars above and, perhaps, the faint memory of his own exhausted father standing beside a primitive American vehicle in fields of stubble.

I cannot say for sure whether my father, or his father or grandfather before him, suffered from manic depression. I do know that for my father, sleep and relaxation never came easy. Alcohol was one of the only ways he knew how to bring himself down from the stimulation of overwork. Even his past had been split from him in the mad rush to achieve his new life.

But sitting at my cousin Carol's round kitchen table that September afternoon, sorting through the pictures we have each brought out to share, I make a startling discovery. My father—who lived like a man in a witness protection program, who severed his ties with his birthplace, who left his mother, sisters, brothers, cousins, and foster parents behind, in Wordsworth's words in "Tintern Abbey," "more like a man/ Flying from something that he dreads, than one/Who sought the thing he loved"—possessed more photos of his Altoona family history than anyone else in the Carroll family. Even as Joe spent his life fleeing his past, he kept with him these images of his childhood.

It is another curious fact about my upbringing that the first time I had seen these photos was when my father was dying. In the weeks before his death, we sat together, side by side, musing over the pictures of his long-dead relatives. Sent on a mission to find them for his hospice workers, I'd come across them in a corner of his paper-jammed cupboards. "Who are these men?" I asked him one afternoon, holding up a sepia-toned, cardboard-backed daguerreotype. Turning the photo over, I see that it's dated 1895, and marked on the back "property of Mrs. G. F. Carroll." My grandmother.

A "seat gang" of ten men from the second floor of the Trimming Shop at the Altoona Car Shop on Chestnut and Third Street, as my grandmother has labeled the photo, pose for the camera. Their long work aprons are stained and dirty; their shirtsleeves are rolled up. These are the men, I learn from Peter Vogt, who cut and sewed the leather for the seats that lined the luxurious passenger cars of the old steam locomotives. They are cabinetmakers who crafted the decorative molding and woodwork trim, tradesmen who carved master molds called pattern makers for steel train parts. They are large, with raw-boned strength; their forearms and hands are muscular and capable. Their faces are broad and furrowed, scrubbed clean and pleasant. Some are half smiling in amusement; others look tired and ground down. Most have long handlebar mustaches bristling over their long cheeks. The one sitting off to the far left with an optimistic look on his face, says my father, is my German great-grandfather, John B. Feser.

As we sat that day gazing into the faces of these workers, Joe and I fell silent. I found myself wondering about these men who were the undergirding of my life and who also laid the first transportation grid of the country I live in today: my two great-grandfathers, my grandfather, my father and his brothers. These sons of Altoona. Profound respect for the discipline, humility, and honest devotion these ancestors gave to the labor of their lives surges through me. I note the way I draw on these qualities in my own profession as a writer, and thank them silently in my heart for this inheritance—not of money, but of character, patience, manual endurance, and physical strength. These "Pennsylvania Forty-Niners" who "found a wilderness and builded [sic] an industrial empire" and who conquered the "triumphant conversion of steam to a useful agent" were indeed, as celebrated by the Altoona Chamber of Commerce, master builders.

But as much as we inherited the bolder, brighter virtues of courage and perseverance from our laborer forebears, so we also bear in our American psyches and on our shoulders their physical weariness. We are a depressed nation, I believe, because we have not stopped yet to rest. Exhausting one industry, we immediately begin another. We are chronically tired because we cannot halt our manic building and development, cannot stay in place and take care of what is already there. This obsession may have been magnificent at one time, but it is outworn and has exacted a steep emotional toll. It has gone on too long. From the distance of a century, I ask my ancestors, now in their eternal sleep, to dream American dreams that are more rhythmic and sustainable in nature, and to rest in the soft hills of Altoona, land of good worth, where they lie buried.

III

The World in
Solemn Stillness Lay

Although we know that after such a loss the acute state of mourning will subside, we also know we shall remain inconsolable and will never find a substitute. . . . And actually this is how it should be. It is the only way of perpetuating that love which we do not want to relinquish.—**Sigmund Freud**, from a letter to Ludwig Binswanger on the loss of his son (quoted in *Loss, Sadness and Depression* by John Bowlby)

JUST DRIVE ME OUT of town and shoot me with a gun."

Joe was on the phone again. He was in another one of his wild, high-rolling moods. "Just throw me in a ditch and leave me there. Let the birds take care of my old carcass. It's what you'd do to a sick animal, put it out of its misery. Did it on the farm all the time. Boy, am I gonna stink when I'm dead. Hooeee!" Pausing as if to drive his craziness home like a spike to my sanity, he hollered out an order to my stepmother in his typical Joe-jumbled mix of Spanish and French, "Hilda, bushky! Uno mas cerveza, s'il vous plaît!"

On the other end of the line, I cupped my forehead in the palm of hand. It had been several weeks since our family trip to Austin. My father's goofy gallows remarks, I suspected, camouflaged his growing panic over the ledge cancer had led him to. Beneath his words I could hear the familiar dialect of guilt and worthlessness. Feelings that had pushed him to this precipitous place in his life as much as his illness had.

"Dad—Daddy! How can you say that?" I protested into the phone. But I was scared. Dying is not something they teach you, the way you learn how to drive a car. Nor does anyone educate you in the loss of a contentious, kooky parent like Joe Carroll. Only hours before, I'd been unnerved by a sibling who'd told me that Joe had been inquiring about how to mail order large amounts of pharmaceutical medications in the event he couldn't take the pain of his spreading cancer. He may have seemed like he was joking. But a thin steel wire threaded his words with calculated intention.

"Geez, Dad. You know people can't just dump dead bodies by the side of the road. Besides, it's illegal," I said, trying to reason with him. "Oh, hell's bells, Pell. Sure they can," Joe shot back. "I don't want you to spend a dime on my casket. The funeral industry's nothing but a scam. I'm telling you, just shoot me, throw me out of the car, and roll me in a ditch. Capiche? Bidey bo, gotta go now." Hanging up the phone, I stared hard out the window, seeking answers in the sky to the riddle of my father. Even in death, Joe stubbornly spurned a permanent resting place. It seemed he would be defiantly rootless to the end of his life. If he had to die, then by God it was going to be on his terms.

Caring for Joe since his diagnosis of terminal prostate cancer was proving cumbersome. Hilda could look after him inside the house, cooking and cleaning. But her limited English, coupled with her inexperience of and contempt for American culture, made it impossible for her to contend with doctors, Medicare, and health insurance. Nor, having failed her test three times, could she even drive a car. My father himself now rarely drove farther than the grocery and liquor stores a few miles from his house on Corpus Christi's commercial strip. But the pain medications he was taking, along with his daily doses of Budweiser and Smirnoff, turned even these small jaunts into perilous excursions.

Just recently, he'd backed out of his garage, forgetting to use the automatic opener. Gunning his station wagon, he'd smashed the rear fender, leaving a gaping, splintered hole in the garage door. After that, he'd parked the offending Mercedes and, laughing at the gods, had gone out and bought himself the latest model Lincoln Continental. Sleek, black, and flashy, it stood in his garage in arrogant contempt of the hole in the door that he refused to fix. No, Joe was not about to die easy. He was, to quote his favorite Dylan Thomas poem, not going gentle into that good night.

And then, a miracle—one of those that sometimes breaks our

way—happened. Frustrated by his unyielding obstinacy, my father's new oncologist had assigned him to hospice care. Not because he'd be dead anytime soon. Not even his new oncologist had mentioned that word yet. No, it was because Joe had announced to his startled physician that, should it become necessary, he'd be making no more trips to the hospital. "Can't smoke, can't drink, won't go," he'd told her. His decision had left her with no other choice.

First to visit him were two warm-hearted Latina social workers. Sitting by Joe's bedside, a tiny gold cross glinting around her neck, Maria Hernandez had taken his large hand in hers. "Joe," she'd said, her brown eyes piercing his fogged blue ones, "you're going to die. It's time to face your death. We're here to help." These words averted my father's dying story from its brutal arc, bending it gently toward grace. The right words, in the right way, and by the kindest of healers, had finally been said.

"Yup. Told me straight up," my father told me over the phone in a sobered tone. "Now that I can say it I can face it. Don't know why anyone wouldn't tell me before. Told me I had to get to work preparing for it." Again, as when he'd told me he had cancer, I was the one who couldn't speak, couldn't even offer any words of comfort, because of the emotion choking my throat.

Over the following weeks, my father began to tackle the project of dying with the same enthusiasm he'd brought to all his life adventures. Joe was still Joe, of course. But the sawtooth edges of his personality had softened considerably. For sure, they'd been rubbed down by his prostate operation, as well as the estrogen and morphine he was taking to treat his cancer. But the ongoing visits from Maria and Gloria, his other hospice social worker, also had an effect. Their medicine was simple: it consisted of listening. Sitting beside my failing father as they shared coffee, they'd simply asked him to tell them his life story. Setting down the timeline of events that had befallen him, they explained, was part of the work he had to do to face the end of his life.

In increasingly frequent phone calls, Joe expressed his astonishment over the novelty of this exercise. He was as fascinated now with exploring the geography of his memories as he'd once been thrilled by the first taste of warm croissants with melting butter in the street cafés of Paris. No one had ever really listened to Joe in this particular way before. A stranger to therapy, he'd never benefited from Freud's radical discovery that listening can heal. Certainly, the thoughtful, almost philosophical attention Joe was receiving from Maria and Gloria was creating a kind of détente in on our own long-troubled relationship. "Yello, Pell, why don't you come out for a visit?" my father asked in a rosy-toned voice one day. "We can order takeout from Red Lobster. Yum! Fried shrimp. Bidey bo, gotta go. Call me back."

Entranced by this sweeter, gentler father, I did just that. I arrived at his home a week later and found the drapes of Joe's suburban home closed against the bright Texas sunlight. Tobacco fumes from his and my stepmother's chain-smoking choked the rooms. Even the air-conditioning vents seemed to breathe Marlboros and Benson & Hedges. I longed to escape through the green-and-gold lacquered front door, to breathe air unpolluted by the acrid stink of cigarettes and stale coffee. Some things, I thought, would always stay the same, would always be hard to accept.

However, after a sandwich at the kitchen table that overlooked the sparkling Gulf inlet where Joe's small boat bobbed in the waves, I began to revive. My father was tired, but eager to talk. He beckoned me into the living room and sank into his roomy, vinyl La-Z-Boy with a belch and a big sigh. "Pell, can't find those old photos, know they're around somewhere. I've been trying to find them for the hospice gals. Look in the filing cabinets in my bedroom, would you? That's a girl."

He was referring to the built-in cupboards along the wall. I spied the photos immediately: a haphazard stack of old and fading images stuffed in a shoebox. I returned to the living room and found my father nearly asleep. His head lolled to the side, his eyes fluttered open and shut, and his hands were relaxed open on his knees. I sat down across from him. "Dad, would you like to take a nap?" I inquired softly, tapping him lightly on his knee. He started awake. "Heavens, no! Bring out those photos. Let's see what's in there. You show them to me."

One by one, I showed them to him: the old, the dead, the long-forgotten. Holding up the photo of the strong-jawed woman in the ankle-length black dress with its white apron, my father's eyes sparked in recognition. "That's Grosmutter, my German grandmother," he mumbled. "Oh, she was tough. But she helped Mum out." I came across the photos of the Pennsylvania Railroad seat gang, the old Altoona house, his maternal aunt Ann, his long-lost brother Bob, and photos of relatives whose names and faces he could no longer recollect. Soon, as if summoned by the smoky cigarette haze, a crowd of colorful invisibles began to move restlessly about my father's living room, clamoring to be heard by us, their descendants. In the deepening pull of memory, my father began to shift in his chair. I brought out the photo of my grandfather, standing lean and tired beside his tractor.

"Ah, my old dad," my own said to me. Leaning back in his recliner, his eyes closed as if the effort to remember was too much. His body still, Joe began to mumble about his parents. The large-screen television was blessedly mute; the hum of the air conditioner filled the darkened living room with white noise. I leaned in closely to catch his words. I wanted to hear this, wanted to know if he would say more about the tragedy that altered the course of his life. Yet his attention wasn't directed to me, but somewhere back in time, far from the Texas living room where we were sitting. "My dad," said Joe, his voice sweetened by the honey of nostalgia, "he worked so hard. I hardly ever saw him. So many kids to feed."

After a reflective silence, Joe picked up the trail of his thoughts again. "But every day after school, I would run down the road to meet him on his way home from work. And every day," my father continued, opening his eyes directly into mine, "Dad would give me some little scrap from his lunch pail he'd saved just for me. Then we would walk back home together, just the two of us." I marvel at this bite of food from my grandfather, and how it lived on in my father's memory as a morsel to be passed on to me; so small a gesture, yet made immortal by love.

Christmas

"What happened to your father," my mother tells me, "was more like a movie than real life." To me, it seems like a Dickens novel. It is the tangled place in the skein of my family history; the Gordian knot of the Carroll clan. Pieced together from fragments told to me growing up, by other family members, and by things my father said as he was dying, the story goes like this: When my father was twelve years old, my grandfather had a stroke. With one side of his body paralyzed, George Carroll was forced to leave his job as a mechanic with the Pennsylvania Railroad. Bedridden and wheelchair bound, he spent his days secluded in a curtained bedroom on the second story of the Altoona house. Sometimes, Joe told me that quiet Texas afternoon, his mother would ask him to take a tray of food up to his father.

"I couldn't, I just couldn't do it. I was too scared to see him. He looked terrible, and I stayed away from *that* room," said my father with a shiver—even as he himself sat bloated and disfigured from cancer, heart disease, emphysema, and alcoholism. "He had changed so much. He didn't look like my father. I didn't recognize him." Strange sentiments for me to hear from my father, as I felt the same about him.

On Christmas Day 1935, when my father was thirteen, my grandfather seemed to take a turn for the better. Though advised by his doctor to avoid any overexcitement, George Carroll felt well enough to come downstairs to share the afternoon holiday meal. The rest is as familiar to me as the Nativity story itself. Each scene, repeated to me over the years, is engraved in my memory—a series of bleak Christmas cards reminding me of the Norman Rockwell family my father never had. In this tableau, my father sat next to my grandfather. It was a day to feel good, to eat, and to take pleasure in sitting around the table together. Young and high-spirited, Joe joked around, patting his father on the back, urging him to take second and third helpings of the Christmas meal. It was the height of the Depression, and such meals were rare.

Suddenly, with no warning, my grandfather's skin went clammy. His face turned white, he drew a harsh, rattled breath, then froze. At exactly 1:20 P.M. his head dropped forward on the table, and stayed there, still. At first, there was only silence, the invisible sound of life rent by death. Then the impact hit and there was shock, disorientation, and pandemonium. Brothers, sisters, cousins, aunts, and uncles scrambled to their feet, knocking over chairs and abandoning plates of still-warm stuffing and pie. They tried to revive Father Carroll; the brothers carried the limp body of their crippled dad to bed, while the sisters covered him with blankets. Mother Carroll touched her husband's cheek with her hand. There were tears on stunned faces, and the doctor was summoned to the house. But it was too late.

That night, George Fields Carroll's body was laid out in the parlor. No one but my sister and me remembers this part of the story: how Joe's older sisters took their brother by the hand and brought him before the corpse. In the gloom, as my father used to tell us, they blamed him for causing the death of the family patriarch, for thumping his invalid father on the back and encouraging him to eat more food. Young Joe was defenseless, taking upon himself shame in the way children often do at times of tragedy. "They were mad at me about Dad's death," was all my father would say in later years about his estrangement from his sisters. My mother remembers that it was Joe's mother, not his sisters, who Joe felt had blamed him. Decades later, as I tell my analyst Tom the story, he shakes his head in sympathy. "It is the picture of the helpless child."

On the morning following Father Carroll's death, a Catholic priest from St. Theresa's, my grandfather's parish, paid a visit to Mother Carroll. The pall of sadness and confusion hung over the house. My father hovered on the stairs in the background, an anxious boy listening in to a conversation that would change the course of his life. Outside, the landscape shimmered in the winter cold, a glazed frieze of snow and ice.

"Mrs. Carroll," the priest said, "I've come to see about arrangements for your husband's burial." In order for her husband to receive a proper interment, the priest explained, "the Church requires a particular kind of casket," one that cost a certain amount of money. But this was the middle of the Depression. There was no money.

Newly widowed, my grandmother was forced to weigh the pros and cons of a demand from the priest of a religion to which she didn't even belong. When his parents had first married, my father tells me in our talk that afternoon, his mother had been German Lutheran. Mother Carroll had never converted to her husband's church. According to the patriarchal customs of that time, it was the father's religion that determined the family faith. Thus, all nine Carroll children had been baptized Catholics. But my grandparents, influenced by the religious diversity flourishing in Altoona, had been flexible about their respective faiths. And so on Sunday mornings the Carroll brood would wander off for services with either parent.

Only once did tension mar this progressive arrangement, provoking the only argument my father said he ever witnessed between his parents. "Never saw them fight," Joe said on that hot Texas afternoon in 1994. "I couldn't believe it when they did, because they'd never argued before." Because of her bad leg, Joe said, his mother sometimes had trouble walking long distances. One Sunday, a man from her congregation showed up to drive her to church. On seeing this, George became upset, and Joe heard them "exchange words." Jealous and unsettled, Father Carroll forbade his wife to be taken to church by this "other man." But Mother Carroll stood her ground and went on attending Lutheran services with the help of her new friend.

As my grandmother sat with the priest that dismal day, she was being asked to take what little savings she had and spend it on the correct casket to ensure her husband's survival in the next world. But there were worries enough in the everyday world in which she was going to have to live for a good time to come. The Depression coupled with my grandfather's illness had already convulsed the family. Along the way, the older children had all dropped out of school to care for the younger ones as they came along, and to work, join the army, and marry. That still left Joe, thirteen, and Gene, eleven, to be looked after.

In the end, my grandmother gave in to the demands of the priest. Whether Mother Carroll felt it was owed to her husband, or whether she was intimidated, I'll never know. Perhaps she was tired and had simply lost the heart to resist. The funeral costs, my father would say later with great bitterness, left them destitute—unable, he claimed, even to stay together as a family. All the rest of his life, until days before he died, my father nursed a corrosive resentment toward God and the Catholic Church. Yet when it came to raising his four children, Joe followed in his own father's footsteps, marrying a woman outside the Church but baptizing each of us Catholics.

After his father's funeral, young Joe, as he used to proudly relate this part of his biography, got busy. He was, after all, a bred-in-the-bone, haul-yourself-up-by-the-bootstraps American. Euphoric with entrepreneurial ideas, he went door-to-door in his neighborhood, hiring himself out to do yard work or repairs to bring in money for the family. This couldn't have been easy. The Depression years in Altoona were stone-hard. Even the Pennsylvania Railroad, says Jeannine Treese, executive director of the Blair County Historical Society, felt the brutal slump; nobody was buying railroad cars, there were fewer passengers, and the numbers of trips were down. Employees were kept working only one or two days per month, simply so they could receive a paycheck. That way, if they'd fallen behind on their property taxes, laborers could show their stub to the tax office as proof of employment—allowing them to pay later when the economy improved. Like other locals, the Carrolls walked along the railroad tracks, picking up pieces of coal that fell from the trains so they could heat their home. Hungry hobos came daily to the back door, and my grandmother would hand out whatever leftovers she had—even as Joe himself stood in breadlines for food.

I feel pride now at Joe's resilience. Could I have responded in the same way, I wonder, if the same tragedy had repeated itself in my childhood? Surely, my father showed remarkable character in his responses. Surely, too, as psychologists would agree, the defenses he erected against the onrush of grief he felt helped him adapt until he would be strong enough to bear his feelings without being destroyed by them. Except that time never came. And so this adolescent trauma marks yet another place in my family line where grief became a debt deferred from father to child.

In one of his early essays, "Mourning and Melancholia," Freud describes the internal "work of mourning" that seems so mysterious because "we cannot see what it is that is absorbing" the bereaved so entirely. The result of this inward process, Freud concluded, was ultimately purposeful. It served love, he wrote, by perpetuating the bond of intimacy with the person who had died. The late English psychiatrist John Bowlby devoted an entire volume, *Loss: Sadness and*

Depression, to the psychological aftermath of death. His case histories of toddlers, teens, sons, daughters, fiancées, mothers, and husbands in the grip of sorrow are testimony to the profound depth of human connection. Although the response to loss varies widely, Bowlby differentiates between "healthy mourning" and "disordered" forms of grief. In the family where bonds of affection and dependency are regarded as childish and weak, or where emotional displays like crying, being angry, or being clingy are condemned, for instance, conditions are ripe for what Bowlby terms "thwarted grief."

Children exposed to this kind of family environment in the midst of tragedy, Bowlby argues, "grow up to be tough and hard," overly competent and self-reliant, and difficult to live with. "Immune to mourning they may be; but at what a price!" he exclaims. Some, he notes, may even react to grief and loss with euphoria, or unnaturally high moods of elated energy and happiness that can lead to manic states. In this mood, a person feels that the loved one is not needed at all, that one can do very well alone. Inevitably, this mood collapses into its opposite: despair. In later years, these people are at greater risk of depression, alcoholism, and suicide. Isolated, these "psychiatric casualties" can even cause the breakdown of others around them. It is a diagnosis that sounds uncannily close to my father.

From Bowlby and Freud I turn to Sylvia Perera, a contemporary Jungian analyst. I share with her the tale of my grandfather's death. Perera points out that had my father been helped to work through all the emotions around the sudden loss of his father, he might have avoided the unconscious bonding with death he carried with him through life. "We can only speculate what such an event may have stirred in him," Perera continues. But Joe "may have carried a chaos of emotions— love, grief, anger, and guilt—all of which can accompany the death of a parent at any age. When the grieving process can't be resolved, this can leave deep emotional wounds and defenses against them. His sense of terrible guilt and responsibility might have been a way to manage these strong emotions. In addition, [he] was an adolescent, beginning to feel his independence and rebellion against parental control. Who helped him to sort and regulate the intensities of all those emotions?"

she asks, knowing of course that the answer was "no one." If only his mother or someone else had extended warmth and empathy to the young Joe as he dealt with his guilt and grief, says Perera, it would have helped him to cultivate a more grounded and "realistic sense of identity. It might have helped lay his guilt to rest through understanding in a stable, supportive relationship."

The existential psychiatrist Irvin Yalom also comments on the motif of guilt in my father's story. "Guilt is ubiquitous in survivors," he comments. Indeed, in his research, Yalom tells me, he has noted the curious fact that "people almost search for a way to accumulate guilt" around the death of a loved one. "It's as if the person believes that if they caused the death in some way, then they are responsible for it. The next level is that if they had done something differently, then the death wouldn't have happened." But this line of reasoning, says Yalom, belies "an unconscious way of trying to deny the inevitability of death." If in fact it is in the nature of our loved one to die, he explains, "then it is in our nature, too—and this is going to happen to us." A tragic death such as my father faced in adolescence, Yalom continues, is "burned into memory."

My grandfather's sudden departure, I begin to realize, is the point in my father's narrative where, forever after, Joe becomes a kingdom divided: one part earth, one part sky; one part scared and needy boy, and one part hero. I can feel the spirit of Icarus begin to take possession of him, sense the currents of air swirling around his feet and rustling the feathers of his wings, feel the pull of the warm and inviting heat of the sun as he gently lifts off the ground. I hear dimly, in the background, the voice of a worried father—his own father—warning his son to be cautious, to choose the middle course.

Yet the middle way was never Joe's, and soon he was quickly scrambling up the ladder of life. Enamored from a young age with horses, he began working in the stables of a wealthy couple, Dr. Pellman Glover and his wife, Dorothy. As my father began to win over their affections, the doctor and his wife, aware of my grandmother's perilous financial situation, offered to take my father in.

Impressed by his talent for hard work and his charm and ebullience, Dr. and Mrs. Glover agreed to support and educate young Joe—almost, but not quite, as if he was their own son. Gene, the youngest, also benefited from the Glovers' largesse, and it was arranged for him to be sent away to the Milton Hershey School, a wealthy boarding school for male orphans. At the same time, in a Dickensian twist of fate, the Glovers hired my grandmother to move in with them as well. Not as a guest, not even as my father's mother, but as the housemaid who would clean, cook, and do the laundry—even for her son. In the Carroll family narrative, my father's adoption by what was called an "upper-class" family and his mother's role as their home help became the centerpiece of our family pathology. It was seen as a weirdly mixed blessing, gossiped about by successive generations of Carrolls.

"I have always thought," writes my aunt Eileen, Gene's wife, "that part of your dad's problems stemmed from the fact that he was taken out of the family and sent down the street to live with the doctor and his wife, while his mother was the servant in the house. Can you imagine sitting at the table with your own mother taking orders and serving you your food, yet never [being] allowed to sit at the same table? He was raised entirely differently than the rest of the family and I think he looked down on them."

My mother knew very well how it affected my father. "I always thought that was the worst thing that could have happened to your dad," she tells me. "I never understood why the Glovers did that. The reason they asked your father to come and live with them was because he was so hardworking and smart. So they brought him into their household, and the idea was to give him a wonderful education. Then they brought in his own mother as hired help. It totally mixed him up so that he didn't know where he belonged. Was he a Glover or a Carroll? Was he the boss's son or was he the maid's son?"

This skewed family constellation was often given as the reason for my father's sexist, hostile attitudes toward women. "The reason your father grew up expecting women to serve him," claims my mother, "is because his own mother was his servant, while he was the pampered foster son." Backing up her point, my mother recalls standing in the kitchen making mashed potatoes. My father walked in and began to criticize her: "Now you've got to beat them real hard, that's what Dr. Glover always said to—" Joe was stopped mid-sentence by the expression on my mother's face. "I knew he was going to say 'Ma,'" said my mother. "I just looked him in the eye and said, 'What do you think I am to you?'"

"That's what Dr. Glover always told Ma," my father replied, finishing his sentence.

My mother, who had a bold streak of feminism, was having none of this. "Well," she responded, with a Latin shake to her black curls for extra emphasis, "you are *not* Dr. Glover." Then she hesitated in her story, reluctant to say anything critical about his mother. "Mother Carroll was always very sweet to me." My mother's tone softened. "She was to be admired. She did the best she could. And the Glovers thought they had done something noble."

That was certainly the vantage point of Uncle Paul, who, my cousin Sharon tells me, maintained that the Glovers' generosity is what allowed Gene and my father to lift themselves up, get an education, and pursue exciting careers in aviation. Still, there were many times growing up when I wished that I'd had a father more like Sharon's father. Uncle Paul may have run a simple drapery business, but he was teddy-bear sweet and comfortably safe. More importantly, my uncle had licked his drinking problem; and what's more, he'd done it for his daughter— something my father had failed to do for any of his four children. Yet there was no changing the hand fortune had dealt my father, or, in turn, me. Life had served the players in this family drama a hard call; they'd answered it, as my mother said, in the very best way they could.

I try to imagine what it must have been like for my father that day as he packed his few things and walked half a block downhill to the Glovers. I feel for this scared, yet hopeful, skinny boy as he leaves his known world behind. His new caretakers may have lived in the same town, even the same neighborhood, but their social standing marked them in a world apart. The Glovers, my cousin Carol explains, "were way above us. We were just poor people and they had that beautiful house and our grandmother worked there for years. They traveled in a very classy circle with a lot of doctors, and their friends were influential and into riding at the Hunt Club."

When I remark to Carol that I thought America wasn't supposed to be divided into classes, she looks startled. I want to remind her of John Adams and Benjamin Franklin's plain beginnings, and Thomas Paine, a school dropout who rose to be one of America's most brilliant heralds for freedom and equality. I want to tell her about those democratic ideals George Washington and Thomas Jefferson stood for that distinguished us from the rigid aristocracies of old Europe. I want to quote Abigail Adams, as David McCullough does in *John Adams*, who once proudly admonished an English social climber about the "mechanics and mere husbandmen" who'd conquered the British nobility. But I remain silent.

As different as the Glover house was from the Carrolls', so, too, were Dr. and Mrs. Glover from Minnie and George Carroll. Minnie was a stout, capable woman who walked with a limp; Dorothy Glover was tall, slender, and reserved. Smoothly styled beauty-shop waves of hair framed her angular face. In the photo I have of her, she wears pearls and a tailored dress with a pair of feminine, black leather lace-up high heels. Her eyes are cool, but kind.

In the same photo, Dr. Pellman Glover sports a bow tie and a suit; a flower is neatly pinned in his lapel. His hair is neatly parted and pomaded, his shoes a glossy expensive leather. An ophthalmologist, greatly respected around town, he has a serious expression and wears an air of self-conscious authority. Behind his reserve, his eyes glint with impervious smoothness. Dr. and Mrs. Glover sit together before their massively ornate fireplace with Jiggs, a grotesquely fat bulldog that is the sole object of their affection, and who, it was told, used to slobber all over their furniture.

For that is the other difference between the Glovers and the Carrolls. When my father moves in, he becomes the adopted son of a childless couple. In my mind's eye, I see my thirteen-year-old father as his refined foster mother takes him by the arm and guides him into the hushed, book-lined living room with the stone fireplace, black leather couch, and heavy oil paintings. Later that day, he is shown to his bedroom on the main floor. When his mother arrives with her things, she is taken to her quarters above the garage.

That evening, in the formal dining room, my grandmother serves supper. Set apart by the white apron pinned to her housedress, Mother Carroll does not join the family at the table. She eats later, by herself, after the table has been cleared and the dishes washed. Down the road, Joe's older sister Helen, now married with children of her own, has moved into the Carroll house. Why, I wonder looking back, couldn't my grandmother have remained in the family house with them? Why did she leave her house to live as a maid and serve her son in another man's house? Did she, too, feel guilt over her husband's death? Was she punishing herself by casting herself out of the family as a mother-in-exile?

The years after Joe and his mother moved in with the Glovers flew by quickly, a grace note of peace and stability. Everything that had gone before slipped unnoticed into a stream of underground memories. My father began living, to quote Freud, psychologically beyond his means. Each day, he got up and went to school. Each day, his mother cooked, cleaned, and served the Glovers and their foster son at the formal dining room table. A weathered report card of my father's from Keith Junior High School 1938/39 shows a perfect record of attendance and good grades; it also records his mother's signature. Another photo reveals my father as a lanky basketball player on the high school team. Which half of my father's family, I wonder, cheered his team to victory?

As the country began to ease out of the Depression, my father began to slip away from his own hardscrabble past and lead the life of a country gentleman's son. He dressed in T-shirts that showed off his muscles, wore cool white leather shoes with pointed brown tips, and drove a shiny convertible his foster father bought for him. In jodhpurs and turtleneck he sat astride thoroughbred horses on English saddles at the Altoona Hunt Club, soaring over jumps or riding to hounds with the local gentry. On weekends, he visited the Glovers' country home in Hartleton, where he played darts and croquet in an English-style garden. There, he forged a friendship with Ollie Boop, a Pennsylvania farmer who instructed my father in the ancient arts of agriculture: how to plow a field, sow crops, watch the weather, and bring in the harvest. A simple man my mother described as "common as an old shoe," Ollie Boop made a lasting impression on my father, who even talked about him on his deathbed.

Parallel to my father's rise was my grandmother's slow slide downward. Over the years, she grew increasingly strange and a little mad, withdrawing into a private world of her own. She began relating to others, including her own children, as a servant. Even after retiring from the Glovers and moving in with my uncle George's family, Mother Carroll continued exactly as she always had. Working late into the night in order to have a fabulous meal ready to put on the table the next day, she would serve her son's family promptly at dinnertime, her trademark apron around her waist.

Yet never, recalled my cousin Paula, would our grandmother sit at the table with the rest of the family. "You never saw her eat anything. I don't know whether she considered it unladylike, or whether she was losing her mind." Somewhere along the way, Grandma Carroll began hoarding food, stuffing bread and meat in her apron pocket and beneath her nightgowns in her dresser drawer, or under her bed, where it molded and rotted.

And somewhere along the way, my father slipped right out of her memory, displaced by her youngest son, who became the sole focus of her affection. "Gene was her baby," said Paula. "He could do no wrong. If he was eating, you couldn't even vacuum the rug. You had to stop." When Grandma Carroll broke her silence, it was only to talk about Gene. "Do you know my Gene?" she would say. "Do you have a Gene? I have a Gene." When I ask Paula if Grandma Carroll ever mentioned my father, she paused. "No. I never heard her speak of anyone else."

Despite the different conditions fate had assigned to them, the Carroll boys grew up to be alike in many ways. None of them seemed burdened by the mask of melancholy worn so heavily by my grandfather. Instead, "the brothers," as they were called, were gregarious and charming. Tall, broad-shouldered, lean, they all had the same wolf–pale blue eyes, full lips, and smooth, caramel skin. Each of the seven brothers had a deep cleft in his chin, marking them as teasers—ones who loved to dance, smoke, and drive fast.

So handsome that they "left her in awe," recalls my cousin Carol, the Carroll boys had "personality plus." In one photo on the front lawn of the old Altoona house, Dick, Jim, and Paul smile into the camera, leaning into each other with laughter rippling across their faces and danger running through their bodies. Strong-willed and self-centered, the brothers developed a reputation for black humor, wit for relief, and a mischievous mean streak. They also, each one of them and even, it was said, the two sisters, were drinkers. "They were all good guys. They just had a problem with drinking. If you knew one who didn't drink," said my cousin Paula, "he was odd." Reunions were an occasion for these drinking devils to come out and wreak their mischief. "When the brothers would come home to visit," says Carol, "all they did was drink. I would get nervous because I was just a little girl."

After the war, the brothers scattered across the country, claimed by marriage, the military, and careers. Family reunions grew more infrequent. In one of the last family photos from that earlier era, my grandmother stands, a heavyset, timeworn woman in a navy and white polka-dot dress. She is surrounded by five of her seven sons. My father squats on his heels on the edge of the group; his young, tanned face is furrowed with anxiety. In his expression, I can see the first traces of withdrawal. The pain of his childhood is beginning to trace its mark on him and the carefree, happy Joe is slowly receding.

As the forties faded into the fifties, my father and his brothers and sisters continued their slow drift apart. Children were born, and the distance between the Carrolls and the cataclysm of their grandfather's stroke grew wider. In 1959, Mother Carroll died, and the family came together from around the country one last time to grieve and to drink in raucous Irish abandon. Eight years old, I stayed behind on the farm along with my siblings. At the funeral, Dorothy Glover told my father that now "he belonged to her." What Joe thought of this remark he kept to himself, for, as my mother recalls, he withdrew from her, refusing to even speak to her during the gathering. It would be the last time Joe would go home. But each year during the Christmas holidays in the decades that followed, in Carroll families around the country, the brothers turned as one to alcohol to blunt the shock of a memory that refused to die.

My younger cousin Sharon—one of only three cousins I grew up knowing—remembers Christmases with her father, my uncle Paul, as less than happy occasions. "Daddy never celebrated much," she tells me. "Sometimes he used to hang a fifty-dollar or a twenty-dollar bill on the tree." Once, she said, the nuns from her Catholic school came to visit because Paul had given the Church a donation. "He was so drunk," she said, "he went outside and put a fifth of whiskey in the trunk of their car. This was my school principal and Sunday school teacher! When I asked him what he thought they were going to do with it, he said, 'Drink it.' And he was probably right."

"Christmas was hell," recalls my cousin David of his childhood with his father, my uncle Dick. "It just exacerbated his alcoholism. It was a time of intense conflict between all the Christmas carols, wonder, glory, happiness, love—and then the sheer horror of it all with the drinking and the poverty." Dick, along with Bob and George, is one of the Carroll uncles I'd never met. He was only sixteen when Father Carroll died at the Christmas table, David tells me. Having dropped out of school along with the rest of his older siblings, his father had felt the loss very keenly. "He had such a sense of responsibility for his mother, and for his younger brother Eugene," recalls David.

So exiled did the Carrolls become from each other that it's only as I research this book that I stumble across my older cousin David. My newfound relative, I discover, is a noted naturalist, artist, and author, as well as the recipient of a MacArthur Fellowship for his lifelong work in the marshes of New Hampshire. But being born a Carroll has had its effects on my brilliant cousin's life, too, I learn. The first eight years of his life, he tells me, were unhappily spent in Altoona, in the shadow of the big house "high up on the hill." His family recollections are so eclipsed by the Carroll memory blackout, that, until I tell him, he doesn't even know our grandparents' first names. What remnants exist for him of that time, he writes in *Self Reflection with Turtles*, are "of harpy aunts and furtive alcoholic Carroll brothers."

David tells me that he couldn't revisit Altoona as I did because he wouldn't "come out alive." Just as my spiritual quest broke me out of my troubled home, so, too, did nature liberate David. The discovery of a "new, natural world" that was completely separate from the railroad yards, churches, and stuffy parlors of his past, he says, was "a satori experience that changed my life for its entire duration. I'd found a world that was not a human construct, but was another whole way of being and seeing. That was a huge metamorphosis for me." His entrance into this new world, says David, wasn't just escapism. "It was a pass key out of a world I knew I had to leave."

During my conversation with David, I feel immense relief combined with a kind of sweetness of kinship that comes, strange as it may sound, from being born out of the same flawed family soul. I am not alone; I am not crazy; he knows what I'm talking about. Here is someone else who also had an alcoholic Carroll father, someone else who in his deepest emotional self knows something of the same family complex I wrestled with, and someone else whose calling in life had been shaped by similar chaotic forces. From the time he was five, David tells me, he began reading his father's cheekbones from behind "to tell whether he'd been drinking or not, because I had to know how things were going to go." As he grew older, he would sometimes have to struggle with his father to prevent him from getting in the car, or, should that fail, retrieve him from the local bars.

How I knew that feeling, and how I knew it especially at Christmas! For most of my childhood years, the hours leading up to Christmas Eve and morning were heavy with tension. The story of how my grandfather died on Christmas Day and how the Glovers took in Joe had, from the beginning, become firmly embedded in the family imagination. Like a medieval passion play, it was re-enacted each year. On December 25, the baby Jesus was born; my grandfather had died tragically, and so, I sometimes felt, had my father. Contributing to the surreal mix of human and divine drama, Christmas was also my mother's birthday. Her first name, Maria, was after Mary the mother of Jesus. Even feeding the cows and horses on Christmas morning became part of this Midwestern manger tableau. For a small-town farm girl with an overactive imagination, it was a lot to absorb.

As Christmas Eve approached, with excitement rising and the smells of cooking wafting through the house, my father would begin to drink. Huddled in the big farm kitchen, I'd confer with my mother. Through the windows, bare oak tree branches waved against a gunmetal sky, and the horses in their pasture ran and kicked up their heels in the frosty air. Inside, my mother's Christmas greenery and country-primitive ornaments animated the kitchen. It was cozy, scary, sad, and bad all at once. Yet again, the story of how my grandfather died on Christmas Day would be taken out and recited, our family's version of "The Night Before Christmas."

"He's like this because your father's father died on Christmas Day, dear," my mother would say distractedly, peeling the potatoes at the sink, or standing at the ironing board as she pressed our clothes for Mass. "He blamed himself. He was taken in and raised as the rich son of the Glovers. His mother cooked and waited on him. And then he crashed the convertible they gave him and never paid them back. And they put him through college, which is why he was able to leave his past behind and work for TWA. Imagine the guilt! All that guilt. I think that's why he never stayed in touch with the Glovers after he left home. Too guilty."

As the oldest, it sometimes fell to me to keep my father sober enough to get through Christmas, especially the late-night drive to attend Midnight Mass. Despite all the talk of developing tendencies of denial, children of alcoholics hone extremely fine detective skills: their survival depends on it. Over the years, I learned that, for brief intervals beginning on Christmas Eve, Joe would start disappearing into his bedroom. I can still hear the sound of that door closing, and the gripped-in-the-gut mood of anxiety that would descend over the house. It didn't take long to figure out that he'd gone to steal sips from the bottle of Smirnoff he kept hidden in his top bureau drawer, along with his stack of monogrammed white handkerchiefs and the *Playboy*s stashed beneath his boxers.

Though my mother did everything to stop him, her hysterical screaming and heavy-handed verbal attacks only escalated their conflict into yelling matches. "Jo*seph*!" I can still hear her exclaiming in exasperation. "Shei*lah*!" he would respond, in his slurred, slow speech. "Oh, go to hell," my mother would murmur darkly. "Goddammit to hell," my father would snarl in return.

One Christmas Eve, as I sat strategizing with my mother on how to handle my father on one of Christianity's holiest nights, she turned to me. "Why don't you go and talk to him?" she said. "You have a way of handling him so that he doesn't lose his temper." Keeping the peace became part of my birthday gift to her, and so, in and out of the bedroom I would go, keeping a valiant vigil over my father's sobriety. I became quite talented at this domestic maneuver, calculating the minutes after he had closed the door behind him. My interruptions had to be perfectly timed: long enough to allow him to take a sip or two; yet not so long that he would get drunk.

"Daddy, can you come out and watch TV with us? *Frosty the Snowman* is on," I would yell outside his door. Or, "Daddy, I need to come in and talk to you about a Christmas secret." Or, "Dad, Mom wants to know if you want cranberries with Christmas dinner." Or, "Dad what time should we feed the cows tomorrow morning? Before church or after church?" I developed a talent for soothing and being smooth, for calming my father with a minimum of fuss or drama. I counted myself a success if Joe was able to ferry us all in our boat-size Chrysler station wagon along the country roads to Midnight Mass, relatively sober. As we sat in the pews along with the other families, I would thank Jesus, Mary, and the Mass for working their healing magic on him.

After Mass, if our plan had worked, we could drive home beneath the stars in peace without wrecking ourselves on the side of the road. And if my father hadn't nodded off during the service, we would stop for a late-night snack at the Blue Springs Truck Stop. Over frosted cinnamon buns and hot chocolate with marshmallows, I could begin to relax. My father was clear and sober; my job was done. With any luck,

Joe might even stay sober until Christmas morning when we opened gifts, and later, for turkey dinner and my mother's birthday celebration. There might even be some warm moments around the television as we watched Bing Crosby and Rosemary Clooney in *White Christmas*. Or, if a Perry Como Christmas special was on, we all might laugh, as we sometimes did, when my mother swooned over the suave singer in one of his pastel cardigan sweaters, accusing her of having a crush on him. Or so I always hoped.

STORIES OF SUFFERING

Each of us, says psychotherapist Miriam Greenspan, is handed a story of suffering at birth. The story we inherit from our parents, she tells me, comes down to us as a double narrative. There are the facts—the deaths and births, political upheavals, obstacles overcome, and tragedies suffered—that are passed down orally. And then there are the psychic emotions, the nonverbal energies, that color the telling of the story. Children are especially porous to this latter, unspoken background of their parents' lives.

The story of suffering I inherited from my father was a tale of guilt—guilt I assumed unknowingly, as if I and not my father had sat beside my grandfather on that ill-fated Christmas Day. Guilt I assumed for love of my humble, hardworking grandmother, my father's maternal maidservant. Guilt that seeped through all my father's bedtime stories of her, stories that melted my heart for both mother and son caught in their trap. Guilt, I realize now, that led me to identify with my grandmother. Outside my conscious awareness, I developed a deep bond of loyalty to her, eschewing wealth in favor of humbler activities, such as scrubbing, cooking, and caretaking, refusing nannies and housekeepers in favor of doing it all myself. In a dream I have, I run up the stairs of the old Carroll house to my grandmother's bedroom. There I find an image of her body tacked up on the wall, her legs and arms splayed like a human map. Tiny threads tacked around her trace different areas on her body. "So this is where it all begins!" I exclaim in the dream. My Grandmother Carroll complex.

The tendency to stay stuck in family traumas, observes psychoanalyst Michael Eigen in *Coming Through the Whirlwind*, was first noted by Freud. Something in his clients, Freud noted, refused change, even after a breakthrough. He puzzled over his patients' tendencies to get caught in the undertow of the past, resisting growth and remaining mired in repetitive patterns. One reason we repeat our early traumas, Freud theorized, is because we are driven to master them. We also perpetuate behaviors of the past, he felt, for reasons of love and loyalty.

The study of how the past influences the present has been a lifelong professional interest of Dr. Jerrold Post. In his current role as the director of George Washington University's political psychology program, Post teaches his students about the importance of knowing one's personal "psychobiography," or how we're psychologically shaped by the significant others in our lives, as well as the events of our era.

Sitting across from Post in his office, I relay the Christmas Day episode in my father's boyhood. Leaning back in his therapist's chair, Post listens carefully, closing his eyes as if dropping off to sleep. His eyes open wide when I finish.

"It's a very puzzling inheritance," he comments. "The younger brother [Gene] was in the home, but they [the Glovers] didn't adopt him; they sent him away. Then they plucked your father out of all the family. How would that make your father feel toward his adopted parents who put him in that position?" Post shakes his head somberly. "And what was his mother feeling? How did she feel seeing this other warm woman almost steal her son away from her?" Although Post's comments are in the form of questions, they jar loose new perceptions of this decades-old event. My own naiveté surprises me. How had I never considered these angles on Joe's story before?

Because of what happened to my father, muses Post, "who he was as a man and the relationship of men to women would have become a major issue in his life. Losing his father, and then being chosen by a man who was cold and dull, who at the same time brought in his mother to care for him—it sounds like it set up confusion around a woman's role," he says. "He was socialized to be waited on and fawned over as a boy. It's a very peculiar model of relationship between a son and his mother." As I listen to Post, it occurs to me that my father doesn't seem like the lucky "chosen" one anymore. Certainly, says Post, this early trauma set the stage for my father to have a lost and lonely life; a person who would have trouble maintaining relationships with his family and friends.

"Here was a man," continues Post, "who was full of himself and who sought to live his dream. But part of that restless drive stemmed from a profound dissatisfaction with himself, too. He couldn't embrace his life fully, loving his wife or his daughter. Part of your father's drive was to fill up the emptiness inside of himself."

I next take Joe's story to New York psychotherapist Charles Strozier. A student and colleague of Heinz Kohut, the founder of self psychology, Strozier has written that exploration of the past can help to repair unsettling feelings of fragmentation. Through remembering and restoring broken narratives, a person is enabled to feel more whole and "historically continuous" along an axis of time. Like a psychological detective, Strozier begins searching for clues to the mystery of what happened Christmas Day, 1935. The trauma that occurred, he believes, inflicted on Joe a "narcissistic wound," a kind of emotional sore spot around which he constructed his personal identity. The notion that he caused his own father's death, in other words, became a narrative that organized his life story. Narcissism and its attendant themes, I soon discover, will become a major theme in my father's psychology, as well as the country that shaped him.

"Joe's slapping his father's back obviously didn't cause his father to die, and it's surprising that his family would then treat him as if that's the case," muses Strozier. "So I would wonder about the dynamics in the family that would have allowed an event like that to be turned into a story where your father was held to account for having caused the death of his father. It doesn't make sense." He asks me an unexpected question: "When your father got angry, did he get rageful?"

When I answer in the affirmative, it is as if Strozier has found his clue. Rage, he tells me, is the hallmark of "narcissistic self-disorders." It is sparked by extreme vulnerability to criticism. It typically occurs in the person who lacks a stable sense of identity and selfhood.

Most people, for instance, says Strozier, can handle the usual jabs and hurts of everyday life without feeling destroyed by them. But to a person with a shaky sense of self, he continues, even the mildest insult can be experienced as "total and all-embracing." Emotions scatter into wild confusion, and the person crumbles to pieces. They may feel a terrifying sense of fragmentation, loss of control, and, worse, annihilation. What emerges as a byproduct of this frightening process, observes Strozier, is narcissistic rage, or, as he explains, "undirected aggression, a fury which has no real object, but will seek out objects in its world, will strike out at those nearest and dearest, will do crazy things, and can engage in verbal abuse or, in extreme cases, criminal violence." Though the results of such rage can be tragic, it has a purpose: it holds the person together, preventing them from falling apart.

This was most likely the case, continues Strozier, with regard to my father's psychological development. The telling detail, he explains, is that the other relatives I spoke to in my family don't recall Joe's recollection that he was the one who caused his father's death. The more likely sequence, says Strozier, is that Joe, after patting his father on the back, and then seeing him die not long after, would certainly have worried that he had killed him. These feelings of guilt may have been further fueled, Strozier adds, by someone who might have made an offhand remark in passing, suggesting the same thing. Because young Joe was "psychologically different," he continues, with a fragile sense of self, this would have been taken in by him and magnified as not only the family's, but also the world's, condemnation.

And so, even though almost nothing existed to support the shame Joe took upon himself, declares Strozier, "in your father's psyche that judgment assumed exaggerated proportions and turned into the monumental myth of his childhood." Living by this negative myth set off a cascade of self-destructive patterns over the rest of my father's lifetime: a vulnerability to insult and injury that triggered in him fragmentation, collapse, and the erosion of any firm inner ground; rage and fury, followed by a desperate attempt to right himself. And, last, bitter regret over the people helplessly caught in the storm of his emotions—me, my sister and two brothers, and my mother.

This harmful pattern also fed my father's alcoholism. Grandiosity, often a symptom of narcissism, explains Strozier, feeds mania, which in turn fuels drinking. "This puffiness, the beating of the chest, pretending to be more, is seen so much in alcoholism," he says. "People who are grandiose protest too much. You know it, as you can feel their attempt to bolster themselves in an exaggerated way. But in that very exaggeration they make themselves vulnerable. When something happens that touches the original narcissistic injury, they become vulnerable, once again, to total collapse and fragmentation."

Turning Strozier's insights over in my mind, a memory surfaces of my father. In it, I am a young mother, happily married with children and living in Santa Fe, when my father and stepmother arrive for a visit. On the verge of retiring, Joe had been looking for ways to make some extra money. He'd brought with him packages of brightly colored, clown-like paper maché figures. Surely I could interest some of the shopkeepers of Santa Fe in these cute imports, he said. Never a very good businesswoman, I made a few half-hearted attempts at sales calls on my father's behalf. One shopkeeper had laughed in derision, saying that the town was filled with these kinds of cheap tchotchkes.

"How'd it go, Pell?" Joe asked me when I got home. "C'mon, did you make some really big sales?" Dollar signs were glinting in his eyes, and he was in one of his up-swinging moods. Without thinking, I repeated the shopkeeper's remark. I was immediately sorry. In an instant, my father's whole body changed. His shoulders slumped and his body slackened as he slid forward in his seat and turned away from me, his face closed tight. I tried to rekindle his enthusiasm.

"That was just one store," I said, pleading with him. "We can try again." But it was too late. Joe began shaking his head. "Nope, nope. That's it. End of discussion." Heaving himself off the couch, he disappeared into his bedroom. I knew exactly what he was going to do. When he left my house, he left behind the Mexican dolls, along with a number of empty vodka bottles. For years, until they finally disintegrated, I brought the colorful figures out each Christmas. If my father happened to be visiting, he never mentioned them.

We speak of narcissism these days with a kind of flippancy, as the marker of a shallow or selfish person. Yet we overlook the story of suffering underlying this affliction, seeing only the external bluster and bombast of the person who suffers this disorder. We ignore the way the wounds of narcissism can turn a family into a perpetual passion play, a Greek drama of hurt, rage, revenge, and bitter reproach. Just like the Carroll family, and, I suspect, many other families as well.

✳

Stretched out in his La-Z-Boy, my father had grown tired of looking at photos of his past and was ready for a beer break. "Bushky! Uno mas cerveza, s'il vous plaît," he called out to Hilda for perhaps the fourth time that day. "Que est un numero uno?" he added, turning to me with an "Aren't I something?" twinkle in his eye. "You are, Joe," said Hilda tiredly but politely, handing him a cold Budweiser.

In this small rite of exchange between my father and stepmother I glimpse the deeper psychological forces at work in his life: the woman he has finally found who will serve him, as his mother once did, unreservedly. Someone, too, who would never criticize him, and who would reflect back to him his status as the great Number One. "America," droned a commentator on television that day, "is the most powerful country on the Earth. Surely we can find a way to fix our health care system."

"Humph," my father grunted. "Can't these people take care of themselves?" As he dropped off for his afternoon nap, I sat for a while in silence. The ghosts quieted as if they, too, had returned once more to their eternal rest. Gathering up the photos, I began putting them back in their box. One slipped out of my fingers onto the carpet.

Leaning down to pick it up, I saw that it was a picture of my mother when she was a young, newly married woman.

IV

Love and War in South America

What we call the self—one's inclusive sense (or symbolization) of one's own being—is enormously sensitive to the flow of history.— **Robert Jay Lifton**, *The Protean Self*

IN THE DAYS AND weeks before my father died, it became hard for him to speak. Sentences were trails of halting words strewn with grunts. This was frustrating, both to him and to everyone around him. After a lifetime of silence, Joe's feelings, midwifed by his hospice aides, had found their voice. Now pressure was building from within to say the things that needed to be said before he vanished from this world. But it was growing late. The spread of cancer combined with emphysema had reached his throat and would soon throttle his vocal cords. Propped up in his super king size bed, the television blaring, my father battled to express the thoughts haunting his eyes.

It was midmorning on the third day of my visit. What I had thought would be a brief stay now stretched indefinitely. I had just applied a fresh morphine patch when my father began to grow agitated. He was trying to tell me something. I sat beside him on the edge of the bed. His hands flailed in the air, his face grimaced with effort, and his body tensed and heaved as he strained to speak. I reached for a pad of paper and put it in his hands, but he was too shaky to write. Side by side we sat, each of us crushed by the weight of the unsaid.

What might he be trying to communicate? Maybe, I thought, more memories of his childhood had surfaced. Or perhaps he wanted to tell me something about his will, that mysterious testament of which, so far, very little had been spoken. In the lengthening silence, I began to entertain thoughts of the impossible: that this crusty, closed-mouthed, tight-hearted man of a generation altogether different from mine was trying to say how sorry he was for the messes he'd made with his drinking. And that, before he died, he wanted to utter the words that none of us had ever heard: that he loved his kids, and he was proud of them.

My father's mumbling broke into my thoughts. I lowered my left ear close to his mouth. In my wildest fantasies, I couldn't have imagined what he grunted: "Your mother . . . such a bastard to . . . to . . . sorry, sorry, sorry, sorry . . . flowers . . . flow—" He stopped, his exhaustion so great; tears trickled down the furrows of his jowly cheeks. But I understood. "You want us to send flowers to Mom. You feel sorry for what happened?" Joe nodded, lay back on the bed, puffed out a sigh, and closed his eyes.

"But Dad *hated* Mom! They *hated* each other," my brother says when I drop this explosive piece of news. I hang up the phone and turn over my sibling's words, trying to make sense of my father's confession. My parents' twenty-five-year marriage had imploded, a victim of the storm of emotions between them over the last half of their marriage. Their divorce had been fought out in court over three years, and it had been vicious.

Yet even in exploring this, the most conflicted relationship of his life, my father's hospice workers had been able to drain poison from a heart infected with bitterness. In addition to recalling the narrative of his past, they'd told Joe, the work of dying also involved reconciling with those he'd loved, and hurt. And there was no one Joe had hurt more than my mother.

The opposite of love, wise people have suggested, is not hate but indifference, which cools the coals of a burning heart. By that measure, my parents' marriage was made for the pens of poets and playwrights. Indeed, it had always been more of a romance than a relationship, a turbulent affair, equal parts love and hate. History and passionate symmetries of the spirit had brought them together; canyon-size cultural and temperamental differences had split them apart. Propelled by the rush of war to distant lands, Joe had fallen in love with a woman as different from him as a character out of a fairy tale is to a person in the real world. As in any good fairy tale, a series of fateful events led to my parents' meeting.

ROMANCE ON THE RÍO DE LA PLATA

Maria Sheila Attwell was born on a bright Buenos Aires Christmas morning in 1928. The doctor who delivered her was in a hurry to get home for his holiday dinner. In his haste, he neglected to wash her properly. It was an oversight, according to family lore, that caused my mother to break out with a terrible case of eczema. So each day for the first year of Maria's life, my mother's Spanish nurse bathed her in olive oil, from her round head to her little toes. Because of this, "bonnie wee Sheila Mary," as she was lovingly called, grew up to have skin that tanned a golden amber.

With her thick eyelashes, sapphire eyes, coal-black curly hair, and curvy figure, Sheila Mary, so everyone said, looked just like Elizabeth Taylor. "Bouncy," recalls my mother's old school friend Pixie. "No. Let me rephrase that. Your mother was bubbly." My mother's infectious humor, my aunt Fiona confided in me, could sometimes prove embarrassing. Carried away on waves of mirth, Sheila had the humiliating habit of occasionally peeing her pants.

Yet afflictions often have their usefulness, as would prove the case in my parents' first encounter. Joe and Sheila's fates crossed in January 1948 while each was on holiday in the Paraná delta. About three hours north of Buenos Aires and named for the wild jaguars that once roamed there, this lush ecological wonder of riverine habitats, forested wetlands, marsh deer, and islands is geographically well suited for the paths of strangers to cross. The rivers of three countries—Paraguay, Argentina, and Uruguay—meet and spill into the Río de la Plata, an estuary that flows between Argentina and Uruguay into the Atlantic Ocean. Though remote, it was, and still is today, a popular vacation resort. Funky cabins on stilts and lavish vacation homes dot the islands inlaid among the waterways. Getting there is not easy. The first leg of the journey is by

the journey is by train to the port town of Tigre, followed by a floating
river bus that ferries passengers and supplies across the rivers.

In a photo of my mother with the words "the day I met Dad"
inscribed on the back, her wavy hair blows provocatively in the wind
and an elusive smile tugs at her lips. It must have been hot and sultry
that January day in the tropics; in another photo she is dressed in short
shorts with a blouse tied at her slender midriff. Seated in the glare of
the sun, Sheila and her best friend Millie have their heads thrown back
to the sky. Their long, bare legs are stretched out before them, and their
faces dare the camera. They look as coquettish as two 1940s pinup girls.

Sometime that same day, Millie and Sheila went down to the pier to
watch the boats sail by. Millie's attention became riveted by two young
men in a passing rowboat. "Look at that guy with the dark curls!" Millie
exclaimed. My mother, however, had her eyes set on the other man.
"But look at that blond," she countered. Barely nineteen years old,
Millie and Sheila became shy and girlish and were overcome by a fit of
nervous giggles. Suffering her usual stigma when she laughed too hard,
my mother had no choice but to jump in the river to save herself from
embarrassment.

Sheila was a strong swimmer and in no danger of drowning. Still,
she put on a show of helplessness, flirtatiously flailing her arms. With
her grin, those eyes, and a wet shirt she must have made quite an
impression. My father was instantly hooked. He and his friend Dixon
rowed over and fished my mother out of the river, hauling her into
their boat. It was the catch of Joe's lifetime. As they began chatting, my
mother learned that my father was a flight engineer with Argentina's
first intercontinental airline, FAMA. He was visiting the delta, he told
her, while on a layover between trips, along with his friend, a fellow
crew member. As it so happened, the house the two young airmen had
rented was only two doors down from where my mother was staying
with Millie's family.

After an idyllic afternoon sailing the river, Joe asked Sheila to go
out with him upon her return to Buenos Aires. But my mother's hosts,
the Claxon family, were staying on holiday for another week. Joe was
scheduled to leave the day after that for New York; he wouldn't be

back for a while. Thinking she would never see the handsome airman again, my mother thought, "Well, that's it with this American." But Joe had been struck hard by the pretty girl he'd fished from South American waters. He wrote to her from New York, saying that he couldn't forget "one Sheila Mary with the black hair and blue eyes." When he returned on his next flight, they began dating. Over the following year, a courtship blossomed that would merge their separate lives into a single current flowing into the future.

✳

At the time that my father's life intersected with my mother's among the marshes of the Paraná delta, he'd been flying professionally for over a year. How Joe Carroll came to be a flight engineer manning the instrument panel of an Argentine FAMA DC-4 in the aftermath of World War II is a tale of odd crooks and bends along history's byways.

With the draft age set at twenty-one, Joe had taken some jobs after he'd graduated from high school around Altoona, working as a freelance mechanic in grease-stained garages on his beloved cars, trucks, and motorcycles. He'd also spent time at his local airport hangar, tinkering with transportation's latest wonder, airplane engines. But as the country mobilized for war after Pearl Harbor, Joe, with his twentieth birthday approaching, grew nervous. The draft age was now lowered to eighteen and Joe began looking for a way to avoid service.

Dr. Glover, who didn't want the foster son he'd trained to hunt foxes being sent off to die on a battlefield, came up with an alternative plan. When he'd taken Joe in, he'd promised to give him three things: food, clothing, and a good education. Now, even with Joe's older brothers in the army and young men everywhere joining up, Dr. Glover urged my father to go to college. As it happened, the War Department had just announced a plan whereby those who wished to complete their education before being called to serve could do so by enlisting in the Enlisted Reserve Corps, or ERC. As a little ditty went at the time, "You'll get two years of college, boys, two years and maybe four, all you've got to do is join the Enlisted Reserve Corps." Drawn to the steel guts of engines and the field of transportation like his father and his grandfather before him, Joe accepted Dr. Glover's financial support and Mrs. Glover's expectations of success. In what would be a permanent leave-taking, he departed the steep hills of Altoona to enroll in Parks Air College of Engineering and Aviation in St. Louis, Missouri.

It's an odd fact about my father that, many years after the war's end, he openly told my brothers that he'd enrolled at Parks Air College in order to avoid the draft. This was at a time when he spent every mealtime drunkenly railing against those "goddamn peacenik longhair" Vietnam draft dodgers. Eventually, of course, my father had been forced to enlist, so why bring it up at all? Or why not say that the college he attended was part of the war effort? Why confuse things and slant his personal war story in a way that diminished his stature as strong man of the Carroll family?

Like his father and his grandfather before him, my father had been trained to conceal rather than reveal. And, like many children of that generation, my siblings and I were left to speculate on the motives behind Joe's actions and words. Trying to figure out our father, in fact, was something that, over the years, the four of us engaged in with endless speculation. One reason Joe might have stalled enlisting, my brother John thinks, was because, with four of the Carroll brothers already on the battlefields, he might not have wanted to risk causing Mother Carroll more worry. Dad may also, my brother believes, have simply felt scared.

Admitting to any of this, of course, would have made my father look like less of a man in his sons' eyes. To say he'd tried to skip out on the war was more in keeping with the image he promoted of himself as a tough son of a bitch who didn't give a damn than a sensitive youth protective of his mother. Or, worse, a young man frightened by war. Still, by making this offhanded remark, my father revealed that beneath the rough-guy exterior a second Joe existed. This was the wordless Joe who whistled, read poetry, listened to music, and had delicate feelings, but who, encased like a mummy in modern manhood, hadn't been raised to discuss them.

The fact that I cannot find a single piece of paper or military memento among my father's records documenting his stint in the service further deepens the enigma around his wartime experience. When I find out that a fire has burned over 80 percent of all military records from 1973 on back, and that Joe's military locker was destroyed by a flood in a storage facility in Israel, I begin to feel a kind of despair. Joe's only remaining record of his military service, my mother tells me, had been his dog tags. For years, he'd kept them in the top drawer of his dresser—only to lose them when Joe and she left the farm. All I have to go on is the collection of cryptic half sentences about what he did during World War II, spoken in the familiar fugue of shame, puffed-up pride, and goofy words that came down to my family and me from my father. Got sent to Natal, Brazil. Flew cargo planes. Repaired planes and took plane parts back to Africa. It was a staging ground for the invasion of Japan. Had a Brazilian girlfriend, boy was she sweet. Loved Rio, man it was "beeooouutiful." There was brief mention of dangerous missions aboard patrol bombers, or PBYs. And a speck of an island in the middle of the Atlantic Ocean where planes refueled on the way to West Africa.

Sometimes, I recall, my siblings and I would tease my father about what a "hardship" his military service must have been. "Oh, Brazil," we'd chortle with the sarcasm of youth, rolling our eyes in mockery. "Must have been tough." Facing his four accusers, his prowess as a man on the line, Joe would raise his head, wave his Pall Mall in one hand, his can of Budweiser in the other, and yell defensively, "It was dangerous! Planes crashed in the jungle!" Or, "We were preparing to invade Japan. We thought we were going to die!"

At first, I'm tempted to skip over this interlude in Joe's life. I want to leave it at that. After all, he was no great war hero. How hard, really, could flying in the tropical climes of Brazil have been? But I begin to have a nagging sense of this period before Joe met Sheila as yet another piece of his psychological puzzle. His encounter with that Portuguese-speaking country, it seems certain, sparked a lifelong fascination for flying, foreign countries, adventure, and Latin women. It spoke to something in him. But what?

What I discover—not just about my father, but about Brazil and the story of aviation—is unexpected. As a regular Joe caught up in the colossal forces of history, my father's war experience was, surprisingly, more eventful than he'd ever let on. During my research, hidden pieces of his character come to light that change my perceptions about him. In telling his story, I aim to focus his narrative through the lens of the "different light" that author Susan Griffin describes in *A Chorus of Stones*—that light in which "one can begin to perceive the edges of one shared movement in what we have called the private and the public worlds, one motion shaping and shaped by all that exists."

BIRTH OF AN AIRMAN

Stringbean thin, high on hopes and dreams, Joe entered the lecture halls and airplane hangars of Parks Air College in June 1942. It was not only a pivotal year in the war, but a hinge point in the history of American aviation.

During the first two decades of the twentieth century, Americans had grown obsessed with flight. Inevitably, as historian David Courtwright notes, flying was cast in the mold of the American myth of the frontier. It became the high frontier, the air frontier, the new industrial frontier, and so on. Untrammeled by regulation, the heavens appeared as free for the taking as the grasslands of the West had been to the earliest pioneers. The parallels, in fact, were unmistakable, and soon the once peaceful heavens had turned into a Wild West of the air. Planes and pilots tossed and rolled among the clouds like tumbleweeds in the desert. Taking to the skies the way they once took to the open range on horses, mail pilots outraced their counterparts on the ground and became the new American cowboys. A vintage photo of airmail pilot "Wild Bill" Hopson featured on the cover of Courtwright's book *Sky as Frontier* shows a young tough dressed for open cockpit in a heavy zip-up suit with fur collar, boots, and helmet. His legs are planted defiantly apart, his goggles are pushed back on his head, and a cigarette dangles from his fingertips. His face is the familiar mask of impudent, can't-tie-me-down bravado that marked these "early birds" of aviation, as they were called.

No paved runways, control towers, air traffic controllers, or radar tethered these bold sky-chasers to the ground. Flying by the seat of their pants and the sense in their guts, the earliest pilots were guided by the sight and smell of bonfires, train tracks, and flashing beacons, and even then only rarely. Fog or storms could cause them to become disoriented and stray from their course, turning them in an instant into dead birds plummeting to the hard earth. Death and disfigurement by plane crash were routine. So dangerous was the job of airmail pilot, writes Courtwright, it was considered "the next thing to suicide."

Unflappable in the face of the threat flying posed to human life, Americans embraced their newest incarnation of the pioneer with relish. The more danger involved, the more they gasped, gawked, and swooned. Exhibition fliers became the glamorous sports heroes of their day. Aerial showmen called barnstormers—so-called because they got their start performing above the farms of rural America—startled audiences by walking out on wings, parachuting to the ground, and performing spins, dives, loop-the-loops, barrel rolls, and other aerial tricks. Stunt pilots in rickety biplanes, some with bucking broncos tattooed on their tails, performed in air circuses that could draw crowds of seventy-five thousand and more.

After World War I, army pilots who'd endured the tortures of open-cockpit, high-altitude flying joined the circuit. Reenacting aerial dogfights in planes emblazoned with deaths' heads, the planes began competing at faster speeds and higher altitudes. After the show, these gypsy pilots offered rides to crowds who jostled to pay fifty cents or a dollar for a spin in the air. But though critics and newspaper editorialists voiced their concern, barnstormers and mail pilots continued toppling from the heights to their deaths. Like the Roman mobs who thronged the Coliseum, gawkers and young boys were drawn to the spectacle of death, recounts Courtwright, hoping to see an airman plummet and break his neck.

This obsession with smashing the barrier between human and sky was, states Courtwright, overwhelmingly a masculine undertaking. Sure, there were women aviators, he writes. But flying in the early days was "a young man's game." Like the ranchers, miners, and lumberjacks of the late 1800s, America's first aviators were individualistic, free-spirited, itinerant risk takers in search of peril and hazard. The airman's culture was made up of hard-drinking, chain-smoking, card-playing, womanizing carousers who loved playing "to the boys."

An icon in this first shock wave of American aviators, and one of Joe Carroll's personal heroes, was Charles Lindbergh. All these years later, I can still remember the faraway look of reverence that would fall over my father's face as he contemplated his sky hero. And no wonder. A farm boy who delighted in nature like my father, Charles Lindbergh would become the apostle of commercial aviation, advancing a new era of flying.

Lindbergh scaled the heights of frontier aviation, driven by the same holy fervor for danger and chance-taking as those who'd gone before him. The prospect of dying, he claimed, focused his mind. It was the price he paid for the perspective gained as he scaled the heights of heaven. Lindbergh could in fact write like an angel about flight's transcendent effects. "Trees become bushes; barns, toys; cows turn into rabbits as we climb. I lose all connection with the past. . . . I live only in the moment in this strange, unmortal space, crowded with beauty, pierced with danger," he remembered in his compelling *Spirit of St. Louis.*

Lindbergh's talent as a writer set him apart from the virile brotherhood of fliers. But he was different in other ways. He didn't drink or smoke. He had a strong respect for safety and good judgment. More a planner than a gambler, Lindbergh relied on analysis and sound judgment as much as cocky fearlessness. Unlike barnstormers who flew on a pint of gas, skipping motors, and shaky struts, writes Courtwright, Lindbergh used "proper equipment, proper technique, and flew with a proper pilot." He was also keenly observant and had an innate gift for navigation. Like my father, who also possessed instinctive navigational skills, Lindbergh could "read the contour of the hillside" and the "tricks of wind and storm and mountains" as if translating esoteric geographical texts.

It was Lindbergh's obsessive habit of making safety checklists on his equipment, claims his daughter Reeve Lindbergh in *Under a Wing,* that helped him successfully navigate his legendary solo flight across the Atlantic. To the thrill-seeking public, Lindbergh's cautionary preparations mattered little; in their eyes, everything about his historic passage was emblematic of the against-all-the-odds American hero. As the pilgrims had set sail across the Atlantic, as the pioneers had braved the plains of the West, and as the Portage Railroad had crested the Allegheny Peaks, so was Lindbergh the lone pilot heading into a groundless horizon of "blinding white mist." Hidden away in his tiny cockpit, Lindbergh wrote later in his memoir, he felt submerged "in the magnitude of this weird, unhuman space, venturing where man has never been." Am I, he wondered, a living "earth-bound body, or is this a dream of death I'm passing through . . . a spirit in a spirit world?"

After Lindbergh came down to earth from his trailblazing flight, the American public went crazy with delight, crowning him their cowboy hero of the heavens. He became celebrated as "Daredevil Lindbergh," "Slim," and the "Lone Eagle." For a moment, wrote a bedazzled F. Scott Fitzgerald in *Echoes of the Jazz Age*, people set down their glasses in country clubs and speakeasies "and thought of their old, best dreams. Maybe there was a way out by flying, maybe our restless blood could find frontiers in the illimitable air."

Lindbergh became an American legend at only twenty-five. Self-determination coupled with a disciplined but daring nature had helped this tall, lean youth to navigate his plane through ocean fog, dazzling sunlight, and sleepless nights of endless space. Now his steady temperament would help him withstand the intoxicating heights of fame, avoiding a crash. Spurning movie and endorsement offers, young Lindbergh, writes Courtwright, turned his celebrity to the promotion of aviation. Flying, he felt, could help break down prejudices and differences between nations. But first, he felt strongly, there had to be greater respect for safety within aviation. On a countrywide tour, he encouraged cities to build safe landing fields and improve their airports. Taking a job with Transcontinental Air Transport—the predecessor to TWA—Lindbergh helped plan new routes, weather-reporting stations, radio ranges, and beacons.

Lindbergh's efforts were the culmination of a growing recognition of the extreme danger of flying's first days. Too many crashes and too many young men cursed to their deaths by the Icarus myth began at last to anchor aviation within the limits of earthly reality. As the twenties drew to a close, the federal government moved to regulate the burgeoning commercial aviation business, leading in 1936 to the formation of the Civil Aeronautics Authority. For some old-time fliers, the new regulations felt as confining as the barbed-wire fences that ended the free-ranging lifestyle of the early settlers of the West. In the words of one gypsy pilot who flew deliveries of "medicine" during Prohibition, relates Courtwright, it was like exchanging the sky for the "humdrum ground." Lindbergh's appealing combination of American can-do-ism, romanticism, and grounded sense of practicality, however, would help aviation bridge its early buccaneer style with the age of professionalism and safety.

After his plane went into a tailspin, causing him to lose his left eye and nearly killing his two passengers, a St. Louis businessman named Oliver Parks arrived at his own personal epiphany. A former Chevy salesman with a zeal for taking to the air, whose pilot's certificate bore the signature of Orville Wright, Parks realized that ten hours of rushed instruction were not enough to train a pilot in the perilous art of flying. In 1927, the year of Lindbergh's solo flight, he opened the doors to his flight school, Parks Air College.

Drawing on his skills as an auto salesman, and building on the spirit of reorganization sweeping aviation, Parks attracted legends like Amelia Earhart, Howard Hughes, and even Charles Lindbergh to his college classrooms. In-depth courses were offered in all aspects of aviation, including aerodynamics, aeronautical engineering, air transport, managing airline passenger flights, and flying instruction. Parks's vision was in keeping with the times: revealingly, perhaps, passenger service would begin to take off, as it were, during the Depression. Mail planes transformed themselves into fledgling commercial airlines. Feather-fragile wooden planes gave way to lozenge-shaped, all-metal aircraft with thunderous propellers. On the cutting edge of this transformation, Parks quickly became one of the leading air colleges in the world, touted as the "Harvard of the Air."

By the early 1940s, though aviation was safer than it had ever been, it was still the province of young men out to assert their bona fides as swashbucklers and sky gypsies. Recalling his own aviation school days of that era, pilot Ernest K. Gann described his exultation in the airplane as a "joyous instrument" that could be "rolled, slipped, spun and dived," in endless delight. Likewise, my father and some of the other young pilots, as he once told my brother, used to take the school's planes out for joy rides. At the cemetery near Parks, they'd practice dizzying spins over the graves. Joe's story comes as no surprise to Randy McGuire, assistant archivist at Parks College. Despite Parks' strict rules of conduct, he says, "there were a lot of crazy shenanigans" during the college's early days. Any student caught doing something like that today would be kicked out. But, McGuire says, "these early airmen were a breed apart; they were all daredevils in those days. They were amazed by the aircraft they were flying, and the things they could do in them." Neither is McGuire surprised to hear about how quiet my father had been about his old school days. "So many of these guys were loners. You had to pry things out of them. I hear it over and over again," from their sons and daughters, he tells me. Somehow, I'm not surprised to discover that even my father's school records from Parks were burned in a fire.

The danger the young airmen flirted with as they grazed death with their graveyard spins, McGuire feels, was preparation for the maelstrom of war that would soon engulf them. In 1939, President Roosevelt, alarmed by Germany's Luftwaffe, had called for an expansion of American air power and aircraft production. In response, Henry "Hap" Arnold, chief of the Air Corps, began to mobilize a massive training program across all levels of aviation, from pilots to maintenance technicians, ground instructors, gunners, bombardiers, parachute riggers, metal workers, and mechanics.

An airman who'd been taught flying by the Wright brothers, Arnold had the idea to enlist the help of civilian air schools. To that end, he summoned to Washington the presidents of three of the nation's top civilian flying schools, including Oliver Parks of Parks Air College. Out of this conference, according to *The Army Air Forces in World War II:*

Men and Planes, emerged the first plans for what was to become the standard practice for flight training during the duration of the war.

In 1941, Roosevelt raised annual production of fighter planes to 50,000; also that same year, the Air Corps was reestablished as the Army Air Force. By the time the Japanese attacked, the AAF had entered its Second Aviation Objective, with an annual production goal of 30,000 pilots and 110,000 technicians. In 1942, three wartime training programs were authorized that would step up pilot production and technical training in phases, culminating in 93,000 pilots and 600,000 technicians annually. Looking back after the war, General Arnold noted that although the outbreak of war found the AAF in "low gear," they soon had a more powerful force that "was growing every hour."

Thus, while Joe had gone to college to avoid the draft, or so he had said, he now found himself among thousands of airmen being trained as part of the war effort at aviation schools around the country. He enrolled in aircraft maintenance engineering courses, studying precision measuring instruments, radio and civil air regulations, hydraulic systems, fundamentals in propellers, and navigation and meteorology, which put him on track to become a flight engineer. According to his airmen's certification records that I am finally able to track down, and which include some of my father's own handwritten notes, Joe had also been certified as a ground instructor. Shortages of instructors were a major problem, and so, just midway through his two-year program, Joe was enlisted into the War Workers Training Program, teaching about aircraft engines at a local vocational school in the evenings.

Joseph Wilbert Carroll graduated from Parks in June 1944 as a ground instructor and an airplane and engine mechanic. In his graduation photo, my father stands in the back row of his class. Dressed in a light summer suit, he looks both bashful and pleased. Next, he moved on to Sikeston, Missouri. Located midway between St. Louis and Memphis, Sikeston was the site of Harvey Parks Airport, a flight training school for airmen entering the Army Air Corps. Soon after, on July 26, 1944, at Jefferson Barracks south of St. Louis, my father was inducted into the Army. From what I can piece together from family memories and singed Army record fragments, my father moved next to Burbank, Los Angeles, where he began employment with Western Airlines.

Along with America's swelling fleet of commercial airlines, such as TWA, Eastern, United, Pan Am, and American, Western had come under contract with the War Department and was both an army airbase and commercial airline. By 1942, after the bombing of Pearl Harbor and with German U-boats threatening supply ships' Atlantic passage to Europe, the need for a speedier worldwide system of air transport to the far-flung theaters in Africa, China, India, the Philippines, and Australia had become urgent.

In June 1942, the Air Transport Command (ATC), a division of the Army Air Corps, was formed out of the Ferrying Command that had delivered planes for Great Britain. To help transport the thousands of tons of cargo that had begun building up at ports, planes were painted and refitted as supply carriers, reservist pilots were called to active duty, and hundreds of civilian pilots were made "service pilots." Airline executives were commissioned for key command posts, while veteran pilots became pioneers of developing distant military air routes over land with rudimentary landing conditions—all with a keen and competitive business eye to developing future airline routes after the war's end. Though not as romantic as the bomb squadrons and fighter planes, the ATC added a new dimension to warfare, creating a global air transportation system that had never existed before. "The emergencies of the war," wrote Oliver La Farge in *The Eagle in the Egg*, "led us to the threshold of the Air Age."

In true Carroll style, a high-spirited Joe inaugurated his new job with Western Airlines by setting out on a footloose adventure. Rather than drive or fly across the country, he returned to Pennsylvania and then rode the rails with one of his brothers, east coast to west. It was a final tribute to his youth, a farewell to the staccato blast of the train whistle, and a gesture of homage to his buried father and grandfather. I can't recall which brother accompanied him, but I do remember the bedtime stories Joe told us about that wild ride.

Schooled by the railroad patriarchs of his family, Joe had grown up riding the rails. As he spoke of grabbing on to boxcars, I shivered with fear. My father's blue eyes flashed as he told stories of unkempt hobos and nighttime campfires in deserted lots. A strange light seemed to glow beneath the surface of his skin, as if a being from another planet had taken up residence inside my father. Something in his voice kindled the spark of the wanderer in my child's heart and, all in a flash, I'd be riding the rails myself, the thickly starred sky shining through the slats of the boxcar roof, strange towns and cities hurtling by. My eyelids drooping, I half expected that while I was sleeping my father would slip out the door and ride the rails once again through the dark of night to a place where I could never follow.

Joe's new-earned skills were quickly put to use at Western Airlines. He checked the arrival and departure of planes, overhauled crash-damaged engines, and taxied planes down the runway. He quickly rose up the ladder, becoming crew chief and even dating the daughter of one of his bosses. When he changed his mind and broke up with her, his spurned lover took her broken heart to her father, who then fired Joe. I don't know if this had a role in what happened next. But on May 31, 1945, Joe turned up at Fort MacArthur Air Force base in San Pedro, California. Here his records show him as an enlisted man "recalled to AD," or active duty, from the ERC. The war's end was just two months away. But no one knew that at the time.

Unfazed by the run-in with his former boss, Joe arrived at the base filled with the brashness and bravura of a freshly minted navigator with engineering and flying skills. The confidence that lures a man to a life of flight, writes Gann, is "almost indestructible. He believes, he *must* believe absolutely, in his personal fortune and destiny." True to the hypermasculinity bred in the bone of the airmen of his time, Joe found a way to needle the guys in charge. When a high-ranking officer landed at the base, my father was assigned the task of servicing the plane for its departure. Worried about his aircraft's safety, the officer thought one of the tires needed replacing before it took off. My father disagreed.

"This tire doesn't need to be changed," Joe insisted, giving it an arrogant kick. "It's got at least three or four hundred more landings in it." But the officer would not be persuaded. Standing on the tarmac, the officer and the young mechanic got into a heated argument. Unintimidated, my father held his ground, refusing to change the tire in question. In the end, it was the officer who backed down from the standoff. But not without the last word. "I'm going to fix you," he threatened my father, his voice tight with anger. "I'm going to send you to Brazil." And then he stalked off to board his plane.

The officer made good on his threat, and, after being sent to Camp Luna in Las Vegas, New Mexico (an ATC staging base and training camp), Joe qualified to be sent overseas. It was as if, in kicking the tire on the officer's plane, Joe had let the air out on his own overblown pride. Being assigned to Brazil just as the war in Europe was winding down, I think at first, hardly seemed like a way to get back at someone. But as I follow the trail of my father's story to South America, I discover that this country's role during World War II formed a little-known backstory to the bigger tale, replete with its own danger and intrigue. Indeed, it's a rare book on the war, writes historian Frank D. McCann in *Brazil and World War II*, "that mentions the Brazilian bases, the strategically important Natal–Dakar air route, the naval campaign in the South Atlantic, or the Brazilians in Italy."

ZÉ CARIOCA, OR JOE BRAZIL

The Brazilian–American military alliance began in late 1938. The possibility of Axis military bases being set up in the Western hemisphere had become a matter of concern to the American government. After France fell to the Nazis in 1940, worries increased that, should Britain fall next, the Germans and Italians might move to occupy Latin America as a stepping stone from which to invade the United States. Of greatest importance was Brazil, with its undefended northeastern coastline leading up to the Panama Canal and the southern tip of Florida.

A covert relationship between the two countries—out of sight of the Germans, McCann tells me, as well as the journalists chasing the troops in Europe and the Mediterranean—began to develop. In hopes of securing the string of rudimentary airbases that stretched from the northern Amazon basin to Rio de Janeiro, the United States began shipping military and industrial equipment to Brazil. In

November 1940, the negotiations began to pay off. Through back-channel maneuvers involving a secret contract signed between Panair do Brasil, a subsidiary of Pan American World Airways, and the War Department, an agreement was negotiated that allowed the U.S. Army and Navy to begin developing and fortifying Brazilian airbases.

Rapid developments in the war proved the strategic value of this course of action. When General Rommel's tanks began surging across the deserts of North Africa in 1941, the British became desperate for reinforcements, supplies, and planes. Brazil's northeastern "bulge" jutting out into the South Atlantic, write historians Conn and Fairchild in *The Framework of Hemispheric Defense*, quickly became very strategically important. The closest point in the Western hemisphere to Africa's Gold Coast, the region offered an ideal jumping-off point for the limited-range planes of that time. Brazil's year-round favorable weather and gentle trade winds were a further boon. Soon the coastal cities of Recife, Belem, Rio, and especially Natal became key staging bases for the Allied transport system supplying the British in Africa.

In the years leading up to Pearl Harbor, Brazil, despite its secret alliance and support for American military bases on its territory, had officially maintained a position of neutrality. A skillful "poker player," as McMann describes him, President Vargas enjoyed a fruitful trading partnership with both Germany and America. Then there was the longstanding tension between Argentina and Brazil. If the U.S. wanted Brazil's support, it would have to side with them against their longtime foe, a choice the United States was reluctant to make. The Germans had also become, according to ATC pilot Ernest Gann, an increasingly popular force throughout South America, particularly in Brazil, Colombia, and Bolivia. They dominated the airlines, sending Luftwaffe pilots to learn long-range and jungle flying, and to open routes into the interior.

But when the United States entered the war, President Vargas came under increasing pressure from the Allies to form an open alliance. The defenselessness of the airfields in northeast Brazil seemed to invite a German air advance from across the South Atlantic. What's more, Japan's attack had cut the transpacific air routes and the North Atlantic route was impassable during the winter. This made the South Atlantic route, as Conn and Fairchild write, "the sole remaining airway from the United States to the fighting forces in the Old World." After some resistance, Vargas took the initial step of severing diplomatic relations with Germany. Meanwhile, support among the Brazilian people swelled for the Allies, especially after Hitler, believing that Brazil's cooperation with the United States indicated it was in a state of war, retaliated with submarine attacks off the critical northeastern coastline. Still, Vargas continued his waiting game, even while participating in diplomatic negotiations with the War Department for increased arms shipments. Though General Marshall did not want to move forces to the Brazilian bulge without Brazil's consent, fear grew, write Conn and Fairchild, that the Brazilians might stall the further build-up of American troops and unrestricted flight operations so vital to the European and Mediterranean theaters of battle.

"I cannot tell you how important I think this Natal danger is," wrote Secretary of War Stimson in a personal appeal to President Roosevelt early in 1942 on the urgency of satisfying Brazil's demands. "With the redoubled necessity of planes for Burma and China; with the French fleet moving in the Mediterranean; with subs in the Caribbean; we can't allow Brazil, who is not at war, to hold up our life line across Africa."

By June 1942, a joint Brazil–United States Defense Commission had finally been formalized and by August 1942, a spate of attacks on its ships by German U-boats accomplished what diplomatic relations had failed to do, and Brazil openly declared war on the Axis powers. With their relationship now in the open, the U.S. Army Air Force moved quickly to locate the South Atlantic Wing of the Air Transport Command at the Natal airbase of Parnamirim. Soon Natal became the fulcrum of the most important air route between the hemispheres. Conn and Fairfield called it the "air funnel to the battlefields of the world." Others called it the "trampoline to victory." To those pilots and crews making the run it was known as "Fireball run," or "the Fireball Express."

The route began at Morrison Field in Miami and extended through the Caribbean and Brazil as far south as Natal. At Natal, it turned eastward across the Atlantic narrows to the African coast and then reached across central Africa to Khartoum, where it divided. The main line, as documented in Air Force history records, extended "north to Cairo to eastward through Habbaniya and Basra to Karachi, then across India and Burma into China, with a branch line up to Tehran in Iran. An alternate route led eastward from Khartoum, passed through Aden and skirted the Arabian coast into Karachi, where it joined with the route out of Cairo." To protect them from the enemy, many of the foreign bases and their exact location were kept secret.

Excepting Natal. As the headquarters of the South Atlantic Wing, Natal grew into the largest American air- and navy base outside U.S. territory. At times, more than five thousand American troops were stationed in this Brazilian Casablanca. With a steady stream of incoming and outgoing troops, and planes landing and taking off every three minutes, *Life* magazine headlined it "the wartime crossroads of the world." The War Department designated it "one of the four most strategic points in the world," along with Suez, Gibraltar, and the Bosphorus.

Animated with that terrible enchantment so peculiar to war, Natal flamed briefly as a star in the galaxy of legendary wartime cities. To consolidate the relationship between Brazil and the United States, President Roosevelt came ashore in 1943 to meet with President Vargas; together they toured the air force, navy, and army bases. Jack Benny, Humphrey Bogart, Clark Gable, Duke Ellington, and Bette Davis stopped over on their way to Africa to perform for the troops, casting an aura of glamour over this teeming paradise located just steps away from an impossibly blue ocean. Legendary fliers like Antoine de Saint-Exupéry and Charles Lindbergh passed through, as did dignitaries such as Eleanor Roosevelt, Ernie Pyle, and Madame Chiang Kai-shek. Axis spies and Brazilian fascists shadowed the streets and ports. Nightclubs advertising free admission "for all" welcomed young boys and men from the farms and small towns of America.

For most privates, the encounter with the sensuous country of palm trees; garish parrots; tarantulas; fresh, sweet pineapples; and white sand was unlike anything they'd seen back home. Certainly, my father had not. Yet in a flip of stereotypes, it wasn't the Brazilians who loosened up the Americans, but the reverse. As the retired Brazilian Air Force Colonel Fernando da Costa and his wife recalled to the *New York Times* in 1994, the American boys had much to teach the Catholic town bound by old-world customs. There was the boogie-woogie, Rayban sunglasses, kissing girls in public, drinking out of bottles, canned beer, dancing the jitterbug, calling everyone "my friend," and wearing shorts and sport clothes instead of suits and ties.

Despite its position as a key wartime city, Natal never became a battlefield or an enemy possession. The role of troops stationed there was threefold: to protect, to maintain, and to transport. What threat there was lurked at the edges of the city, in the deceptively pretty waters where enemy submarines crawled, intent on bringing down transport ships and planes. Twin-engine bombers flew search-and-rescue and anti-submarine runs, patrolled the Atlantic coastline against invasion, and skirted gunfire from the German subs. But the primary military activity revolved around the Air Transport Command, that less-than-glamorous arm of the Army Air Force made up of aircraft and civilian personnel from both the Army Air Corps and the commercial airlines. Like my father.

These weren't the swaggering flying aces and bomber pilots of movie lore who waged epic air battles over Britain, Germany, Africa, and Japan. They were the scrappy pilots and sharp-eyed navigators who never knew when or how much they'd get paid, and who jokingly described their planes as little more than a trucking business or a flying boxcar. Yet they brought to their tasks the same guts and brio that marked their generation of pioneer airmen. Many had started flying during the heady, pre-commercial days of barnstorming. Men like Air Force Colonel Joe Mackey, charged with launching the South Atlantic route, who had camped out at airfields as a boy, snatched handkerchiefs off markers with the tip of his plane as a stunt pilot, and had written "Okay, Paris," in the sky in a French air show. Or like Lee Hipson, an ATC pilot whose gold teeth were souvenirs from one of the many crashes he survived during his early days as a parachutist and flying instructor.

These crazy-for-flying airmen turned their talents to good use in the war. Without the supply operation they ran in the workhorse Consolidated C-47s and C-54s, and giant cargo ships like the C-87, the Allied forces could not have won. Artillery, ammunition, toilet paper, metal wastebaskets, engine parts, fuses, bombs, surgical instruments, Chinese money, mail, medicine, wounded soldiers, military personnel, gasoline, German prisoners, steel girders, and all the "depressing junk of war," as Gann put it, weighed the planes down, making it difficult at times to maintain safe altitudes. Undeterred by exhaustion, cramped cockpits, or dangerous flying conditions, plucky pilots and navigators fueled with youth and patriotism climbed into their planes eager to begin the 28,000-mile relay run from Miami to India and back again, often in as few as eight or ten days. They may not have engaged in air battles. But they did face death-by-crash over forests, deserts, mountains, and oceans, as well as sniper fire from enemy bombers and subs.

By 1944, the reputation of the ATC and its intrepid crews had begun to spread. Reporters and photographers vied to hitch rides on flights girdling the globe on the modern-day version of the Pony Express, where the crews changed but the planes kept going. Photographs and tales of their adventurous exploits were splashed across the pages of American magazines like *Life* and the *Saturday Evening Post*. "The Fireball is the longest, fastest, air-freight line in the world. It is a sort of emergency ambulance for tired and battle-scarred planes," wrote the *Post*'s war correspondent David Wittels of his airborne odyssey over four continents and great oceans. "It has been operating only a few months and has been a military secret most of that time. Now it can be revealed that the Fireball is the backstage reason for much of the recent success of our Air Force in the China–Burma–India area."

These writerly accounts of ATC exploits reveal wartime America's glimmering fascination for the world that was opening up to it through the experiences of our boys posted abroad. "Below us were the incredibly winding rivers of India, the fields like crazy quilts instead of the geometric patterns at home, the walled castles and the drab little villages, the milky, opalescent green of partly flooded rice paddies," penned the inspired Wittels. "The C-87 'Fire Ball Express' glistens under an African moon as mechanics refuel and check motors at Khartoum in Anglo-Egyptian Sudan," reads a *Life* magazine photo caption from June 5, 1944. This emerging, exotic world would beckon the young ATC airman who was my father into his own lifelong career in commercial aviation. As with others, it would also presage a lifetime pattern of restless country hopping. For all the crews involved in these "tremendous undertakings," writes Gann, contrast was so routine that "they thought nothing of waving farewell to pink-faced Scots in the night and, after a dreamlike period of suspension during which nothing was to be seen, swooping down in the dawn over Mohammedans bent toward Mecca."

Probably the most legendary feat of the ATC was the passage across the Himalayan Hump. In 1942, the Japanese invaded Burma and cut the Chinese off from the world. It became necessary to airlift thousands of tons of fuel and food to the forces of General Chennault. Passing over the jagged mountain peaks of India and Tibet, the ice and snow and the dizzying, disorientating altitude led to a high accident rate. Hungry and frozen, these men, as the wartime saying went, "lived like dogs and flew like gods."

As far as I know, Joe didn't make it as far as India or the Himalayas. From what I can piece together from what he told us, Joe's leg of the Fireball run was probably up and down the coast of Brazil, across the Atlantic narrows to Africa, then back again to Brazil. These missions did indeed, as Joe claimed, have their dangers. Even at the time my father flew, after the fall of Germany, enemy subs lurked offshore. Then there were the patched-together planes of wartime guided by rudimentary systems of navigation.

In recounting ATC flights he flew over Brazil, Ernest Gann describes flying with no oxygen over mountain peaks whose heights were unrecorded; large areas marked on maps UNEXPLORED; rainforest canopies so dense and green he feared crashing into them more than the ocean; and cumulonimbus clouds off the Gold Coast so gigantic and threatening he named them the "grandfathers" of thunderstorms.

Stationed in Latin America for twelve years, senior curator at The Museum of Flight in Seattle and Latin American–aviation historian

Dan Hagadorn says his most memorable flights were over the Amazon basin. In a tone of near-reverence, Hagadorn reminisced about the pattern lightning and storms that "extended in every direction as far as the eye could see." Even today, he confides, Brazil, with its weather, mountains, and vast stretches of open, uninhabited, primeval landscapes, is "one of the most difficult areas in the world to fly over—and in the forties, with its vintage World War II airplanes, it was even worse. If you went down, you were gone."

The transatlantic hop from Brazil to Africa—and especially its refueling stop—was nearly as legendary as the Himalayan Hump and as dangerous as the Brazilian rainforests. This was the route mentioned by my father, and I read about it with interest. Ascension Island was a pinpoint of red volcanic rock in the South Atlantic that fell midway between Natal and Accra in Africa. A British possession, Ascension had been transformed by American engineers into a landing strip named Wideawake Field, after the raucous birds that made their home on the island.

Pilots certainly had to be wide awake to find Ascension, as it was afloat in what a *Life* magazine photographer called "the landless void of sky and water," rimmed by empty stretches of shark-infested seas. In the event that the navigator with his octant and protractor—a role my father claimed to have played—missed the island, pilots made up a ditty that went like this: "If you miss Ascension / Your wife gets a pension." The late CEO of the Motion Picture Association of America Jack Valenti, who was a fighter pilot, described in his biography *This Time, This Place* the elation he felt when at last the island emerged through the mist of rain, clouds, and surging seas: "Suddenly we saw it, a patch of land thrown up by the Atlantic. Hello, hello, you lovely little lost bitch of an island."

By the end of the war, the Air Transport Command girdled the globe, and had become the largest airline in existence. Routes had been established to never-before-seen, unmapped regions. Runways had been gashed into jungles and etched into the icescapes of Newfoundland, bringing civilization to deep wilderness. As the ATC pilots and their crews grew intimate with the weather and topography of North

America, Europe, Africa, India, and South America, they absorbed, writes Gann, "an entirely new world which previously no man knew very much about." Voyages that had previously required days or weeks now took hours. For these aerial voyagers, writes Gann, "our sea was of all three dimensions; we sailed it sitting down, without either the benefits or confinements of tradition, and we were obliged to develop our own sense of what was right and what was wrong."

My research so far had yielded a vivid picture of the ATC flights my father flew during the war. But what exactly was Joe doing in Brazil in the last months of the war? By then, the skies over Africa and Europe had quieted. Hitler had been vanquished. Yet in that ominous summer of '45, few thought the war had ended. It was, as Michael D. Gordin writes in *Five Days in August*, a "frantic and confused time that no one yet realized was the final summer of the Second World War." One last enemy, Japan, remained. "Keep in mind," adds Dan Hagadorn of that time, "that the atomic weapons were so top secret that even many of the Army and Navy senior planners didn't know of the bombs' existence. They really thought we were going to have to invade the home islands of Japan. As a consequence many things were in motion worldwide in the military to prepare for that event."

Fighting on fronts around the globe, American military forces were widely scattered. As the Allied forces mobilized for the invasion, a top-secret redeployment plan in the works for well over a year was set in motion by the American high command. On May 20, 1945, eleven days before my father showed up at Fort MacArthur Air Force Base, the WHITE PROJECT got underway. Tasked to the Air Transport Command, the project involved the return of army transport and combat planes stateside. Parallel to that was the GREEN PROJECT, a program for flying troops and military personnel from the European and Mediterranean theaters to the United States for rest-leave before war against Japan. In addition to the aircraft crews making the trip from abroad, an additional 33,000 men were brought in to help fly home some 50,000 troops per month. Somewhere in that massive mobilization was Army Air Corps Private Joseph W. Carroll.

Favorable headwinds out of Casablanca made the Brazilian airway the quickest route back to Miami. Just as Natal had served as an air funnel for fanning troops and aircraft to the world's battlegrounds, now it acted in reverse. ATC troops were responsible for clearing incoming planes by briefing the crews, checking aircraft for safety and weight and balance requirements, and dispatching the flights. War-worn planes—many of them previously serviced by gunners and clerks in the guise of mechanics—had to be readied for upcoming battle. Smuggled pets, weapons, and overweight baggage were found and removed. In all, some 2,282 aircraft that summer, among them heavy bombers, Flying Fortresses, and twin-engine airplanes, made the westward crossing through Natal.

According to *The Army Air Forces in World War II: Traffic Homeward Bound*, the airlift home "was a tremendous demonstration of the massive airlift of manpower . . . the most striking of those marking the end of war. Nothing like it had happened before." Indeed, it must have been a spectacle, a site worthy of Homer: this sun-blessed vision of a paradise, transformed into a massive military hub, rife with fear. And confusion.

At its peak in July 1945, some 30,000 troops passed through Natal. Doctors, nurses, and cooks serving hot meals twenty-four hours a day attended the steady stream of incoming and outgoing troops, foreign nationals, civilians, and medical evacuees. Security was tight and counterintelligence personnel checked planes for sabotage. A gloomy mood of low morale beset the base when ATC troops clashed with Air Force bombers whose units had been forced to disband upon arrival in Natal. Beribboned fighter pilots who'd been engaged in gunner-to-gunner battles in the skies were now told their combat skills were useless. Reassigned as mere clerks, guards, or even truck drivers, they grew mutinous.

Forced to work alongside each other, the Army Air Force combat pilots lorded it over their fellow noncombat officers and crews. In mess halls and barracks, they rained down epithets like "Alien to Combat," or

"Army of Terrified Civilians." At Parnamirim Field, an Officers' Club dance was aborted when arrogant top guns danced to a song whose theme was "To Hell with the ATC." The friction and frustration wore on my father, as, he later confided in my mother, he, too, felt worn down by the scorching equatorial sun and the scorn of the "wearer of battle stars" belittling him. It was, he told her, "a hellhole of heat and humidity."

But in a telling piece of aviation history, the Air Transport Command crews became fired by a nonmilitary mission of their own. It had nothing to do with war, and everything to do with American enterprise. These airmen, amazingly, had their sights fixed on the future—and that future was air passenger travel. Thus Air Transport Command officers, most of whom were on leave from civilian airlines, did everything in their power to convert homeward bound soldiers into passengers who, when the war was over, would be sure to buy tickets on America's airlines. Today may have been war, these hopeful entrepreneurs reasoned, but tomorrow everyone would return to the friendly skies of passenger flight.

So it was that tired and dusty privates battered by war were given forms to record their impressions of their flight home and were politely asked to make suggestions or list complaints about the comfort of their return flight. Some wished that they'd been issued summer uniforms for travel through the tropics; others would have appreciated maps of the countries over which they'd be flying. But most were appreciative of the advantages of air travel. "I have enjoyed my trip . . . and would like everyone in the ETO to get the chance to fly home," wrote one infantryman. "The air crews are very courteous regardless of rank, and being a private myself, I know," wrote another.

In an effort to earn the future business of these soldiers and make their journey home as cheerful and pleasant as possible, hot meals were served. Because these were the days before cabins were pressurized, blankets were handed out to keep the soldiers warm at high altitudes. My father was assigned his own special task in this promotional game: an interior makeover of the cabin that would be used by an important Air Force general on his return to the States. This time, Joe didn't blow his assignment. Instead, he enlisted the help of his Brazilian girlfriend who, in all the chaos, he'd met and fallen in love with. Together, my father and his girlfriend cleaned, decorated, and even hung her homemade curtains in the general's cabin.

But there was even more to my father's wartime story than decorating a general's cabin, flying cargo and airplane parts across the narrows of the South Atlantic, or readying battleworn planes for the invasion of Japan. During one of his long afternoons of dying and remembering, Joe spoke to my sister and me of flying secret missions from Los Angeles to Rio de Janeiro, by way of the Andes Mountains. With our eyes as wide with wonder as when we'd been little girls at bedtime, Joe told us how the crew had piloted their plane through steep mountain passes, in the dark of night and with no lights, so the enemy wouldn't detect them. He'd flown some of the earliest flights through the Andes, he'd said; there had been no instruments and at times they'd been so turned upside down they'd hung from the ceiling. It was, my father mused, the first time he'd realized his extraordinary gift for navigation. Even during such heart-stopping, disorienting moments, he could always tell at what altitude the plane was flying.

This tale of intrigue proves mystifying. Nowhere do I find mention of an ATC route that led through the Andes and across to Brazil. Possibly Joe made these flights while stationed at the Western Airways army base in Los Angeles. As one Air Force historian tells me, it was a time when "anything was possible." Nor would there have been any reason, he says, for my father to have made up this story. Secret supply missions were known to have taken place, but no records of the crew would have been kept, and the records of the mission itself would also have been sealed. Very likely, he adds, my father would have been ordered to be at the airport at a specific time. He would have been given his destination and route and told that if he told anybody about it, he'd be killed. Whatever was in the cargo hold would probably have been kept secret from him. Another Air Force historian wonders aloud at the unusual discrepancy in my father's record between his induction into the army in 1944 and his reenlistment to active duty at San Pedro in California in 1945. He questions whether my father had really worked for Western Airlines. In a turn of conversation that takes me off guard, he theorizes that my father might very well have been a part of some secret intelligence operation.

Feeling like a secret agent myself, I continue to track down proof of this Los Angeles–Andes–Rio air route. Ernest Gann flew much of the same turf as Joe claimed to have flown, and in Gann's aviation memoir I come across an account that matches my father's. Assigned by the State Department to fly a Lockheed Lodestar to an airbase in Rio de Janeiro on the eve of World War II, Gann and his pilot flew— unequipped with oxygen, accurate maps, or emergency equipment— down the west coast of South America, then veered eastward at Lima, Peru, across the Andes. Once through the Andes, it was westward across Bolivia, and then on to Rio de Janeiro on the southeastern coast of Brazil.

Flying at heights barely lower than the Tibetan plateau, Gann recalled "staggering" through mountain passes at eighteen thousand five hundred feet. Groggy and delusional from lack of oxygen, he was surrounded by "tiny blue stars spinning . . . and sliding together as they might in a kaleidoscope." Reading Gann's account, I experience a sense of gratification. Because alcoholism has a way of filtering everything through fumes and veils of distortion, any verification of truth is a precious restoration of trust. And I find it here.

Whatever my father was up to during the war came to an abrupt halt on August 6. Then, everyone involved in the massive preparation underway at Natal was stunned by news of the nuclear bomb that had been dropped over Hiroshima. As Japan's surrender became imminent, the massive troop redeployment began to fall off. By the end of September, the transatlantic airlift had slowed to a stop and was terminated. From what I can reconstruct, my father returned to the States for further overseas training at Camp Luna in New Mexico and Nashville, Tennessee, then returned to Brazil for another year, running air and sea rescue missions and performing aircraft repair and maintenance.

Here again, the question of whether my father was involved in secret intelligence operations comes up, as it will at future stages in his career. One historian asserts that without question my father was involved in undercover work, as it was very rare at the time for soldiers after the war to live in another country. "These guys were like baby Jason Bournes," he tells me, referring to the secretive and lethal agent of Robert Ludlum's trilogy. "They didn't want to involve their families, especially girls." A Freedom of Information request to the FBI turns up nothing (the FBI had jurisdiction over South America during the war; the CIA took over in 1947). An FBI historian, however, tells me that record keeping then was poor, and comments that it was still "a likelihood" that my father had been involved in some sort of intelligence. Joe's previous experience in the service, he says, would have stirred agents' interest in him. After the war, as another Air Force historian asserts, Central and South America were thought to be a hotbed of spies for Nazi Germany, "watching everything."

As with so much else surrounding my father's past, I will probably never know the answers to these riddles. On January 9, 1947, Sergeant Joseph W. Carroll was honorably discharged at Morrison Field in Florida. In the military photo I have of him, captioned "Daddy" in my childish handwriting, my handsome, proud father smiles broadly from beneath his ATC Flight Instructor's cap. Somewhere in all the commotion of war, Joe had continued to move up the ladder of both aviation and the military—from private to sergeant; and from an airplane engine and machine technician to navigator, instructor, and a seat in the cockpit as a member of the flight crew.

But South America had left its mark on my father, and he was in no rush to settle down back home. After returning to the States long enough to become certified as a flight engineer, Joe took advantage of the three-year contracts offered to American aviators by foreign countries building national airlines of their own. Like other "airmen of fortune" at the time, he moved to Buenos Aires and took a job with the fledgling Argentine airline, FAMA.

THE AGE OF NUMBING

Having known so little about my father's military experience, I found myself unexpectedly drawn through my research into the blast and might of war. As I studied the pages of history that Joe lived, dry text turned into sounds, sights, and smells. In an instant, I found myself on the tarmac of a military base by the rainforest-rimmed beaches of Brazil, amid throngs of American soldiers. The roar of planes filled my ears and the heat of the sun beat down on my shoulders. In a dream, I soared in a plane through silent spaces of endless water and sky, fearful that I wouldn't make it to land. Staid Air Force documents transformed themselves into a thrilling detective mystery. I, a lifelong pacifist, surprised myself by how easily I became enchanted by conflict's allure. I discovered, as James Hillman writes in *A Terrible Love of War*, that war is a mythical happening, catapulting individuals out of ordinary reality into heightened states. For this reason, writes Hillman, no other account save myth can convey war's pairing of inhuman tragedy and the divine intoxication of battle—the product, I imagine, of war's proximity to that swirling vortex of history that sweeps everything into itself.

After all I've discovered, I now marvel at all my father *didn't* say. He was more the hero, to me at least, than he'd ever allowed. Unless I'd made the effort in writing this book to dig deeper into his story, I'd never have discovered that, despite his obfuscation and short-hand bulletins, Joe Carroll had risen to the cause of his time and done what was asked of him. Surely, he must have felt the rush of history through his veins as he ferried supplies over impenetrable forests and submarine-infested oceans. Surely, blood-deep fear must have accompanied him as he flew secret missions across the Andes Mountains— silent, by the thread of instinct, suspended in the black of night. Even so, the short list of facts Joe shared in the years after the war with his wife and children conveyed hardly anything at all of the emotional magnitude of that time. The code of his profession didn't help. Airmen, I learn from Gann, were set apart by their "almost psychopathic modesty." Nor did the code of the military help. "If your father didn't distinguish himself by getting injured or killed in the line of duty, he vanished into obscurity," an Air Force historian tells me. "It's up to relatives like you to bring someone like him to light again."

My father's experience was not so different from others his age. As it has been said many times, the Greatest Generation served their country well. But their tight-lipped style of communication and repression of emotion did not serve them well in turn. Larry Decker, a California psychologist who works with veterans, says that World War II vets "just didn't talk about" their experiences. The storied silences of that generation, however, could not inoculate them against war's psychological aftereffects. These were the men and women who, in stoic fashion, endured economic hardship during their childhood, fought in World War II in their early adulthood, and then returned to marry, work, and raise their children.

They accomplished all this while pretending as if they had not grown lean and worried during the Depression. Or had lived through the most horrific mass killing the modern world had ever seen, or had their souls blinded by the glare of the first atomic bomb. Forced by circumstance to rebuild their lives from the ground up while ignoring what was going on inside, many of them fell, too, like my father, into bottomless pools of alcohol and depression. For though he was a gifted navigator who could pilot a plane through steep mountain passes, or bring it in for a landing without radar through rain, sleet, and snow, no one ever taught Joe Carroll how to ferry his soul back into his body to face the humdrum of daily life, and the inevitable gray weather of boredom and disappointment.

Many a time when we were growing up, my father's dark moods hung over the house like those old-fashioned black crepe streamers that mourners used to drape around their homes after a death in the family. None of us had words to explain Dad's sudden dives downward and inward, just a sixth sense of something menacing in the background. Easily spooked, I feared ghosts flitting in the darkness and robbers under my bed. My sister dreamed of snakes writhing on the wall and lions roaring in our parents' bedroom. Bravely, my brother sang songs in his bed, while my youngest brother developed an inconvenient habit of running away.

"Children often pick up those things that are 'unlived' in the life of the parent," Jungian analyst Jerry Ruhl tells me. Many of his clients, says Ruhl, are children of parents who suffered through a historical tragedy, such as the Holocaust or World War II. Often, he says, "they come into therapy with unexplained feelings of deep depression and guilt that don't seem to be related to their current life circumstances. This dynamic is probably what's behind the biblical admonition that the sins of the father are carried unto the fourth generation." Certainly, one of the legacies I inherited from my father, I confide in Jungian analyst Lionel Corbett, was the feeling that his suffering was mine to bear, and my responsibility to redeem. "He unknowingly put his suffering into you," Corbett replied. "All parents do that, in some form. Whatever we can't solve we hand on to our children. So there was a displaced experience, where he put his pain into you and you had to deal with it."

I was not alone in the Carroll family in my experience. Of Joe's older brothers who served in the army, it was my uncle Bob who suffered the worst of war's miseries. On captain's orders, he'd had to execute a deserter fleeing from his own unit. It was also Bob who, upon surprising a dozen German officers in a basement, had heroically raised his Tommy gun and shouted "Hände über Kopf!" ("Hands on head!")

After the war, he would credit that Thompson submachine gun for not being killed. Bob was dead, however, by the age of fifty-six from alcohol and cigarettes. My cousin Patrick tells me that Bob was "a quiet man" who became a skilled carpenter, installed garage doors, and loved to read Shakespeare. Susan Blackston, Bob's daughter from his second marriage, recalls that her father was very proud of having served in the 101st Airborne Division (506th Parachute Infantry) and of his wartime bravery in three major battles, D-Day, Operation Market Garden, and the Battle of the Bulge.

But there were lasting wounds: the large scar on his knee, which earned him a Purple Heart; the haunting memories of the trenches; the horrible cold; and the paratroopers he'd witnessed being shot in trees, unable to get away because their parachutes were tangled. There was also the guilt that tortured him over the wife and two daughters he'd abandoned after the war, when he'd fled across country to California, then married again; the severed ties with his Altoona family; and the sobriety he was unable to maintain. It wasn't until I was a young adult that news of this lost uncle surfaced; it came in a letter from his widow, who'd written to tell us he'd died. Susan told me that my uncle used to sob when he was drunk, wretched over having had to kill a man from his own unit. "It seemed to me he had a look of horror behind his eyes," she wrote, "as though it was permanently etched there."

"I don't think he ever had a moment's peace," recalls Susan. "He dreamed of the horrors of war when he slept and when awake he was in a constant struggle with alcoholism—either fighting against the intense cravings, or succumbing to them. And yet, in spite of it all, I never doubted his love for us; unspoken, but true."

Claire Saxon, whose own father died in a crash shortly before she was born, while he was flying the "Hump" on a mission over Burma for the ATC, is president of the Air Transport Command Association. Dedicated to preserving the memories of these remaining veterans, she puts me in touch with several World War II ATC pilots. In self-deprecating emails laced with humor, they share tales of their missions in remote regions of the world, including references to the bottle of "mouthwash" in the package from home, or a flight so harrowing not "a sober breath" was drawn. Given the razor's edge they flew between life and death, who could blame them? At the end of the day, recalls Saxon, it was common for pilots to celebrate at the club with drinking games to crown the "best of the best" as they outlasted their buddies after a rough mission, long days of the pressures of war, or simply a boring workday. Many in the military, she says, had a bottle of "the stuff" tucked away in a foot locker or desk drawer, just in case they couldn't get to the club in time.

Post-traumatic stress disorder, or PTSD, was a diagnosis that arose after Vietnam and was unknown to the veterans of World War II. Even if the term had been in use, they would have scoffed at it. Vietnam vets who breached the soldier's code of silence, Decker tells me, were judged by their elders as "crybabies, drug abusers, and losers." Nonetheless, he says, World War II vets suffered just as high an incidence of alcoholism, suicide, and unemployment as those who fought in Vietnam. A study of U.S. male veterans of *all* wars between 1917 and 1994 in the *Journal of Epidemiology and Community Health* found that those who had served in the military committed suicide at a rate

2.13 times that of other men. They were also 58 percent more likely to kill themselves by gunshot.

A 2013 George Washington University study found that suicides among current U.S. troops overall average nearly one a day, the highest rate since the wars in Iraq and Afghanistan began a decade ago. Vets now account for 20 percent of *all* U.S. suicides; the youngest vets and those returning from Iraq and Afghanistan have suicide rates four times higher than other vets.

James Hillman makes the interesting point that PTSD suffered by veterans occurs within a wider syndrome: the numbing of the American homeland and its addiction to security. PTSD, Hillman writes with compelling force, "breaks out in peacetime because peace as defined does not allow upsetting remembrances of war's continuing presence. War is never over, even when the fat lady sings on victory day." As in the case of my uncle Bob, peace for veterans is not an absence of war, Hillman continues, but "its living ghost in the bedroom, at the lunch counter, on the highway." Society rejects the disturbed emotions of its vets just as it rejects the wider epidemic of depression. This rejection makes us ill-equipped, writes Hillman, to help vets tortured by the absurdities and horrors witnessed during war.

In his use of the word "numbing," Hillman has drawn from the work of America's noted psychologist of war, Robert Jay Lifton. When he was a young man working with survivors of Hiroshima, Lifton was among the first to recognize the psychological changes nuclear warfare had triggered in the human psyche. His view of the atomic bomb as an extreme example of violence without feeling led him to coin the term "psychic numbing." He has described this phenomenon in *Hiroshima in America* as a "diminished capacity or inclination to feel," as well as a "paralysis of mind," a "psychic closing off," and an "insensitivity to death."

For the Japanese who survived the nuclear holocaust, Lifton found, psychic numbing could be a useful defense mechanism: in the interest of long-term survival, it prevented victims from being overwhelmed by the terrifying images confronting them. For Americans who had created the weapon, psychic numbing acted as a barrier against the horror and fear evoked over the attack. But as a people, Lifton writes, we developed a *habit* of numbing toward Hiroshima. Over time, numbing became a way of being, slowing our gut responses to other large-scale human disasters.

Psychic numbing has also functioned as a protection against the guilt that contaminates the American psyche where Hiroshima and Nagasaki are concerned. The bomb, Lifton tells me, is America's "raw nerve." Where Hiroshima and Nagasaki are concerned, he says, "we have this agitated, anxious feeling, and so we don't like to look at it. Above all, we've spent the better half of a century avoiding coming to terms with its human effects." America is no worse than other nations who were at work developing the bomb at the same time, he adds. "But it happens that we were the ones to make the bomb first, and to use it, and this has had its impact on us." Thus the raw nerve exists, he concludes, "because we have a need to fend off any kind of guilt or self-condemnation."

"Futurelessness" is another postwar phrase coined by Lifton. With the release of the first atomic bomb, something happened that had never happened before: human beings now had the power to wipe themselves out. Totally. The biological continuity of the human race had become imperiled. The imagery of massive death and extinction began to lurk behind the backdrop of everyday life. The destructive image of the bomb, wrote Lifton in *The Broken Connection*, now entered into "every relationship involving parents, children, grandparents, and imagined great-grandparents and great-grandchildren." Every personal tragedy became colored by an end-of-the-world anxiousness. A chill settled over America. Irony, absurdity, nihilism, and apocalyptic fantasies of annihilation spread like an emotional ice age.

Psychologically, writes Lifton, this gave rise to a phenomenon unique to our era that he terms "doubling," in which individuals go through life with both a "measured self" and an "apocalyptic self." The former is the everyday self that finds meaning in love and work. The latter is preoccupied with nuclear annihilation and death in general and contaminates ordinary life. When combined with America's young and relatively shaky sense of identity, futurelessness created a potent mix. From it, notes Lifton in *The Broken Connection*, can be traced the origins of the live-for-the-moment abandon of the beat and hippy generations and that of survival communes and religious fundamentalism obsessed with Armageddon. Indeed, the specter of futurelessness haunts the United States with increasing ferocity, says Lifton, as "it's always the possessors of nuclear weapons who feel most vulnerable to them."

As a child of the Cold War, I remember well how my own "apocalyptic self" cut into normal life. Night after night for a period of time, I dreamed of fighter planes flying over our farmhouse, dropping bombs over innocent family picnics. No amount of soothing from my mother could ease my fears. No prayers could make the planes stop their nightmare flyovers through my dream world. Such interventions were of scant help when I was practicing desk-dives during bomb drills at elementary school in the event of nuclear attack—as if my wooden desk could save me from death by radiation. My sister recalls wanting to move to Florida, only to be told by my father that she'd be in greater danger because she'd be closer to Communist Cuba.

It could also be the case that my fear and sensitivity as a girl to bomb-dropping planes was because my father flew for a living. War and peace, bombs and planes, fathers and fighter pilots—all became fused in my imagination. Nuclear threats threatened my nuclear family. After all, no bombs could be dropped were it not for the planes that delivered them. The Boeing B-29 Superfortress that delivered the two bombs over the skies of Japan, writes aviation historian T. A. Heppenheimer in *A Brief History of Flight*, was one of the largest aircraft of World War II, as well as one of its "largest and costliest gambles." Rushed into combat to replace the Boeing B-17, it had a longer range, flew higher and faster, and could carry a bigger payload. With an immense wingspan of 141 feet, a slim length of ninety-nine feet, and four-engine propellers, the B-29 was a fierce and elegant military aircraft symbolic of America's emerging superpower status. Customized for the Hiroshima mission, it was outfitted by Boeing with the most advanced propulsion and avionics systems and radar equipment of its time. It was the first bomber to house its crew in pressurized cabins. Gun turrets had been removed to hold either the "Fat Man" or "Little Boy" versions of the atomic bomb.

The pilot chosen to command the B-29's historic mission had to be so emotionally constituted as to be undeterred by any revulsion over the execution of his mission. That commanding Air Force officer was Colonel Paul W. Tibbets, who sweetly christened the B-29 the *Enola Gay*, after his mother. A barnstormer from the old days, Tibbets sat in a secure perch aboard the massive B-29, and the altitude of 31,000 feet from which he dropped Little Boy insulated him from the hell unleashed below. Speed, too, must have helped. To avoid the blast, Tibbets, as planned and rehearsed in advance, made a quick 155-degree turn just in time to avoid the "giant purple mushroom," as he later described it, that boiled upward to a height of 45,000 feet "like something terribly alive."

Beneath that plume an estimated 70,000 Japanese civilians were incinerated, 100,000 injured, and a city leveled to smoke and rubble. "Fellows, you have just dropped the first atom bomb in history," Tibbets is reported to have said to his horrified twelve-man crew who, aside from one other officer, had not been told the truth of their mission. Years later, as Lifton writes in *Hiroshima in America*, he asked Tibbets to comment on how it felt to be the first man to drop the atomic bomb. "I felt nothing about it," he replied. "This wasn't anything personal as far as I'm concerned, so I had no personal part in it. . . . It wasn't my decision to make morally. . . . I can assure you that I sleep just as peacefully at night as anybody can sleep."

Remorse may not have troubled Tibbets's sleep; it was left to other veterans to suffer in their dreams what he could not. The issue that preoccupies me is not so much whether dropping the bomb was the strategically correct decision for ending the war: it is that we've refused to let into our consciousness the colossal scale of human loss and its implications for the very future of the human race itself. How is it that in this country—save for the Holocaust—all horror has been stripped from our official telling of World War II, and only victory remains? How is it that the *Enola Gay* is housed in a pared-down exhibit at the Steven F. Udvar-Hazy Center, far from the Smithsonian National Air and Space Museum in the center of the capital, with no mention of the Japanese who died and suffered as a consequence of its bombing mission? How is it that World War II is commemorated as a triumphant circle of wreathed pillars on the Mall, with little to mark the suffering borne by our veterans? And how is it that my father's experience of World War II came down to me in such spare, terse sentences?

Charles Strozier has some thoughts. The glamorization and mythmaking around World War II that has recently taken hold of the American imagination, he says, didn't flourish until the aftermath of the Vietnam War—one of America's most deeply felt failures. Few during World War II itself, he says, thought that it was such a "great and wonderful war." Most of the American public embraced the conflict and recognized that it was one worth fighting. But it was also experienced, he says, as "a searing event, an awful nightmare of destruction and disaster."

When I ask what happened to distort America's memory this way, Strozier turns by way of explanation to the psychology of my father. Joe's exaggerated guilt over the death of his father and the injury to his self-esteem he suffered, Strozier reminds me, resulted from the fragile inner structure on which his identity rested. The same repetitive pattern of narcissism and grandiosity at work in my father, says Strozier, can be seen in the way America reacts to any failure or perceived insult to its superpower status. The narcissistic wound Joe suffered over the death of his father, for instance, is similar to the wound America suffered around Vietnam. Failing to reach the sun—or win the war, or build the mightiest army, or maintain the richest economy—America collapses inward, a young Icarus falling in despair.

This pattern was repeated again after the terrorist attacks of September 11, 2001. "The sense of invulnerability we had built up again was literally shattered by this event," says Strozier. Witnessing the destruction of "these majestic towers that stood for all our power," he explains, was collectively experienced as a narcissistic wound. The rage response that followed—the wars in Afghanistan and Iraq, the worldwide "crusade" against terrorism, the uncritical embarking on a foreign mission without reflection or understanding of history—was, he says, "predictable." As was the public response of patriotism that was an attempt to conceal the vulnerability that had been laid bare for the world to see. The psychological danger for Americans is that the more despised we are, Strozier warns, the more wars we want to fight, and the more we find ourselves trapped in a world of uncertainty.

*

My father was not alive to see passenger jets being turned into deadly weapons, and I'm glad he was spared the sight. But it occurs to me that among the fragments of my father's war memories, I never once heard him speak about Hiroshima or Nagasaki. Nor, as an affectionate aficionado of aircraft, did he mention to me the formidable B-29. Sometimes I ask myself why, during my father's flashbacks as he was dying, I didn't press for more details. A taboo seemed to block my questions: shyness in the face of his approaching departure, not wanting to disturb or upset. Or maybe it was my own emotional resistance at work; the habit of psychic numbing infused into our father–daughter relationship. Hearing my father speak so intimately felt awkward. I just wasn't used to it; his words sounded foreign to my ears.

But emotional memory has an animal intelligence of its own. Having hibernated like a bear, it wakes one day and lumbers into the light. On the day that he described his secret missions to Rio, my father ended with a brief but telling statement. "Hoo, boy, was I scared!" He shook his head. "Never knew if we'd make it or not." It was the first time I'd heard him admit fright in such a real and sober way. After falling quiet for a few moments, my father began to speak again. Now his words came with more difficulty. "Did I tell you about my Brazilian girlfriend?" he asked, his sick voice quavering. He tried but failed to remember her name, this young girl who was by now either dead or an old woman with her own memories. But it was clear she'd lodged permanently in his heart. "Oh, she was so pretty," he added, as if not quite believing such a romance had really occurred, in a far-off time, and in a far-off land like Brazil. She'd had her eye, this Brazilian girl, on marrying my father. "She wrote letters to my mother!" Joe said in wonderment. "Old Mum. She didn't know what to think."

As Joe grew wordless again, I considered whether it was illness that was making it hard for him to speak or an uprush of feelings that had closed his throat. In fact, I discover later from my mother that my father's relationship with his Brazilian girlfriend had ended sadly. On leave after the war, Joe had proudly showed his foster father a picture of his new girl. Her skin must have been dusky and her face exotic, as Dr. Glover reacted strongly. "Don't you ever bring anything like that into this house," Joe's foster father had said. And so my father hadn't.

My investigation so far makes me realize that by the time Joe met up with my mother that sunlit day on the Argentine delta, he already carried a lot inside him. Just twenty-six years old, the eyes of his heart had witnessed many things—things he had no skills to understand, much less speak about. He'd seen his father die in front of his eyes and had borne the burden of that death on his adolescent shoulders. He'd become a man early on, sundering his sweet boyhood attachments, only to be taken in by foster parents who treated him like a prince and his mother as a maid. He'd cast his lot with a profession launched by drifters, dreamers, and star-chasers. He'd been catapulted into war in a country worlds away from the one he'd been raised in. He'd dared his life over mountains, oceans, and forests, and then been shunned and scoffed at by the "real" heroes. Because of luck, fate, and a bomb, he'd been given a second chance at life. He'd fallen in love with a woman who had loved him back, and then had allowed that relationship to be robbed by the cold man who had stood in as his father.

On the outside, Joe Carroll had emerged from these ordeals victorious, a flying ace who aced life's tests and had wings pinned on his chest to prove it. On the inside, however, he was a dangerous brew—a poisonous mix of shame, fear, optimism, pride, energy, rage, and a bottomless need for love and excitement.

My mother perceived none of this. She saw only a part, rather than the whole of him: a charismatic airman who would airlift her out of her life and into the American dream. On his side, my father was just as blind, seeing in my mother the animated warmth and carefree joy missing from his childhood. My mother and father were not wrong to look past each other's more wounded sides. They were young and doing what we all do—following life's river, foolishly, courageously plunging into its strong currents.

Would any of us marry anyone, I wonder, if we saw what history had done to them, and how life had mangled the good soul and the beautiful imagination?

V

The Girl from Argentina

Thus not only does democracy make every man forget his ancestors, but it hides his descendants and separates his contemporaries from him; it throws him back forever upon himself alone and threatens in the end to confine him entirely within the solitude of his heart.—
Alexis de Tocqueville, *Democracy in America*

T HE DAY AFTER MY father confessed his regret over my mother, the house fell quiet. It was early afternoon; our hospice team, who'd been proud of Joe's breakthrough, had just left. Tired out from all the exertion, my father was napping. Hilda had gone to the grocery store with Jenny from next door. It was time to call Sheila.

Trailing a long phone cord, I stepped outside the sliding glass doors in the kitchen. The sun threw fingers of light on the wooden deck. My father's boat bobbed forlornly in the choppy waves. Quickly, so as not to give in to my desire to throw myself into bed and fall into the deep sleep my body craved, I dialed Sheila's townhouse in a suburb of Kansas City. Talking to my mother about my father's cancer and slow decline had not been easy. As the event horizon of Joe's death had drawn nearer, our conversations had grown dense with underground emotion. When I conveyed Joe's deathbed apology about being "such a bastard" to her, my mother grew quiet.

"I want you to know," said Sheila in stilted tones, "that I always loved your father." As a young girl growing up in Argentina, my mother had suffered from a lisp. The proper teachers at her private girls' school, however, had drilled it out of her with diction lessons. Whenever she felt anxious, my mother had a habit of falling back into the stylized accent of her girlhood. The crisp enunciation of this learned speech pattern had the effect of chilling any emotion. Each sentence became a protective border against unruly feelings that threatened the well-ordered existence she'd come to inhabit in her older age.

I sighed. Despite her formal tone, I knew my mother meant what she had said. Behind her verbal shield, Sheila was a woman of turbulent inner feeling. The shock of Joe's apology must have been great. "I want you to know that I've been thinking about your father, and I've discussed it with Pixie and Fiona," she continued stiffly, referring to her childhood friend and my aunt, "and, and . . . I want you to know I forgive him." Then, "Should I come out? Would you like me to be there? I could stay in a hotel. Would you like me to be at the funeral?"

This was unexpected. Sheila felt excluded, I realized, from this most major of family dramas—the death of the Carroll patriarch. As an ex-wife myself, I could understand. Even though she and my father had been divorced for almost twenty years, and even though his drinking had nearly destroyed her, my mother wanted to share in this turning point. There was, after all, the life they had shared, and the old dreams that cast shadows over the evening of her life. Sheila's immigration to America and her marriage to Joe had been the signature myth of her life.

I wanted my mother to be there; it felt right. But it also potentially undermined the delicate structure underpinning our days as we tended my father's dying. Hilda, my stepmother, was a keyed up bundle of contradictory behaviors and emotional extremes. On one hand, she grieved exorbitantly, moaning and crying over my father's approaching death. On the other, she spent endless hours on the phone to her family in Mexico, planning her life after Joe's death. In her betwixt-and-between state, Hilda would have split apart under the stress of my mother's presence. But maybe the truth was that it was I who could not have dealt with my mother. Even under ordinary circumstances, the repression Sheila maintained against her dammed-up emotions was always threatening to break, flooding me with her anxious, nervous fussing and crush of tears.

"No, Mom," I responded, saying nothing of my internal dialogue. "I don't think it will work. But I'll let you know as soon as anything happens." I could hear the weight of disappointment in her voice. I felt guilty excluding my mother, like a selfish daughter assuming executive powers that were not mine to exercise. Who was I to stop her from saying good-bye to my father?

My mother never brought it up again. Generosity of character had always been one of Sheila's better traits, and she never held my decision against me. But exile was not new to her. Maria Sheila Attwell had come to this country as a girl of twenty. Taking her American husband's hand, she'd turned her face north without a backward glance at her Argentine homeland. Or so she had said; so she had believed. As a new immigrant, she'd become skilled in the art of marking life's milestones time zones apart from the large, multi-generational family of her childhood. Throughout the first decades of my mother's American life, news of weddings, christenings, funerals, miscarriages, divorces, and political upheavals arrived on thin, onion-skin paper long after the event. A rare phone call and telegram marked urgent news of births and deaths. As difficult as it was for my mother to live through my father's death via telephone calls, she knew well how to manage her grief in the space apart from the rest of us.

Yet it should also be said that, immigrant that she was, my mother was every bit as American as my father. On that sunny day in the Argentine delta, my mother recognized something in the young aviator that called to her. From the moment Joe extended his hand to Sheila, lifting her into his boat, they became fellow citizens in a shared mythology.

"America," says Jungian analyst Benjamin Sells, "is a myth that is worldwide. There are no borders. The person sitting in China wanting to emigrate here is already American, drawn by the beacon of liberty that America sends out around the world." But it is not just any person, says another psychologist, who can make the daring leap from culture to culture. In the majority of people who come to America, explains Mihaly Csikszentmihalyi, a "tremendous process of natural selection" is at work. Because to move here means a break from one's family and native country, those who end up in this country are more individualistic to begin with. "If you take any Central European or Vietnamese village, for example," says Csikszentmihalyi, "the person who will end up in America will be the one who is able to break away with less pain from his roots."

The spirited courage, independence, and damned-if-I-won't-do-it-my-way individualism in my mother—those triple trademark American qualities that made it possible for her to forge a new life in a new country—had long been in the making. Or so I discover in the yellowing pages of family trees, letters, photographs, and recollections from relatives both long dead and still living that come down to me from the maternal side of my family. In contrast with my father's broken lineage, a trove of information exists to help guide me in my search. As I pick my way back in time along this trail, excitement begins to quicken within me, as if a kind of sleeping ancestral body is stirring to life. Why had I never seen the extraordinary things concealed in my mother's heritage? Why had I allowed the wealth of family papers to remain out of sight in boxes and drawers? I am discovering what Studs Terkel wrote of America: that we have amnesia.

Somehow I am not surprised when, as the century-and-a-half fog that has shrouded my mother's line begins to disperse, a pattern emerges of yet another legacy marked by travel, transportation, and the yearning for horizons. For, sure enough, my maternal DNA, I soon learn, was infused with the roaming spirit and migratory wanderings of seafarers and long-distance voyagers. Tracking the landings and departures that mark my mother's ancestral lineage, I come across a discovery that upends everything I've thought about myself as the daughter of an Argentine immigrant. It is through my South American–born mother that I am descended from early settlers to this country, dating all the way back to the seventeenth century. What is more, long-dead American ancestors of mine once lived and now lie buried in Washington, D.C., the city where I have lived for almost three decades. In discovering this, I feel like a character in those stories of the lost treasure that is sought far and wide and then found close to home. For the precious chain of continuity between past and present that I've been seeking through this book lies in my very own backyard.

FROM AMERICA TO ARGENTINA

The ancestral stepping-stones that led from America to Argentina and then back to America again begins with the story of my maternal great-grandfather. James Donaldson was born in Glasgow, Scotland in 1857. A proud, hot-tempered man with a long-handled mustache and bushy red hair, Donaldson sailed the world as a marine engineer with the British Merchant Navy. His Scottish roots were deep and long and, like those of his wife, daughter of the wine merchant McLaren, went back generations. A standout in this field of Scots ancestors is the Reverend Alexander Stewart, who bore the title Nether Lochaber. A noted minister who once gave a sermon before Queen Victoria, the Rev. Stewart, I learn, was a Celtic scholar, *seanachie* (storyteller), and naturalist. A statue of the revered Stewart still stands on the western Highlands where he once preached and walked the hills. I ponder Nether Lochaber's photo and feel affection for this spiritual ancestor: This is a relative after my own soul, and, instinctively, I embrace him across time.

The Donaldson family of two sons and three girls—among them my grandmother, Jessie—were practical, churchgoing people. Their small, coal-heated cottage in Dundee doubled as the parsonage for the church next door. They made their own jams and medicinal remedies, cooked on a wood stove, and boiled their clothes clean in cauldrons of steaming water. My aunt Fiona remembers them in her memoir as hearty hymn singers with a gregarious social life and a passion for dancing Highland reels. My slender grandmother, it was said, liked to hike up her skirts and dance the sword dance on the dining room table. Art, books, poetry, and intellect were also important. The two older sons were sent to the University of Glasgow; it was expected that the girls would soon follow. The Donaldsons' lives were broadened as well by the travels of their merchant seaman father who—just like my own experience with an air-faring father—brought home tales and mementoes of foreign cultures from New York to India and who even took my grandmother Jessie and my great-uncle Jimmie with him on a trip to China.

In the early twentieth century, financial hardship struck the Donaldson clan. Plans for my grandmother and great-aunts to attend university were quietly shelved. My grandmother, still young, was apprenticed to a milliner's shop to help support the family. To all who knew her, my grandmother Jessie, much like her forebear Nether Lochaber, was possessed of a poetic and refined temperament. She must have endured shame at being sent out to do humble needlework, as she kept this episode from her past a secret well into adulthood.

These bleak circumstances, coupled with his outward-going nature, spurred James Donaldson to look abroad for work. As it happened, Argentina, rich in exportable resources such as beef, wool, and wheat, was being trumpeted worldwide as the country of the future. Inspired by its economic promise, my Scottish great-grandfather decided to cast his lot with the millions of French, British, Germans, Russians, Spanish, and Italians streaming through the Port of Buenos Aires. In 1912, he bid farewell to his homeland and sailed to Argentina to set up his own engineering company. After a separation of three years, and with his business successfully launched, Donaldson sent for his wife and three daughters, Cissie, Jessie, and Gertie. His two sons, Jimmie and Archie, were fighting in the trenches of World War I and would come later. At the time my great-grandparents made this leap into a new life in a new country they were fifty-five and fifty-eight years old.

Perhaps the security of modern times has softened me, or maybe my own razor's edges have dulled with time. But I find myself astonished on two counts: my great-grandparents' age, and the fact that James Donaldson sent for his wife and daughters in the thick of war. In 1915, as in World War II, the South Atlantic was a dangerous place crawling with German subs. In the event of shipwreck, the three daughters, all in their early twenties, each had a gold sovereign sewn into a little bag pinned to their underwear.

Was this magic coin meant to block a bullet, I wonder wryly, or to trade with natives should they wash up on an abandoned island? At any rate, thus protected, my great-grandmother and her daughters set sail as part of a convoy. And, in fact, the Donaldson women's thirty-day passage aboard the merchant vessel the *Esequibo* met with hazard. When forced to run a German blockade off the coast of Argentina, the ship in front and the ship behind were both torpedoed and sank.

Undeterred, the *Esequibo* sailed on toward its destination. Before docking, the Donaldson daughters were instructed by their mother that if they had any grievances about their new country they could complain all they liked to her. But they were forbidden to say a word to their father. Any show of fear or pining for the relatives and friends they'd left behind was banished to the ancestral basement, to be unpacked by a granddaughter—me—a century later.

Once arrived, the Donaldsons settled in Olivos, a leafy suburb of Buenos Aires. They christened their new home Glen Shee, or Glen of the Fairies, after one of their favorite places in Scotland. Emblazoning the family crest of a roaring lion on the garden gate, the family filled their house with the copper, silver, furniture, and oriental carpets they'd brought with them from Scotland.

Argentina had been settled by conquistadors in the sixteenth century; its official language was Spanish and its predominant faith was Roman Catholic. Just as in North America, new arrivals rarely mixed with the indigenous peoples, whose population dwindled as those of European origin swelled. Accordingly, the Donaldson family became part of the Argentine Anglo-British community. This group of expatriates, my aunt Fiona tells me, was "more English than the English" and about "fifty years behind the times."

The Donaldson sisters' free-spirited Scottish streak did little to ease their entry into the more socially conformist British community. The Scotland they'd been raised in had helped pioneer the European Enlightenment, cultivating a progressive culture that valued humanism and scientific rationalism—and that questioned any authority that could not be justified by reason. More independent-minded than their counterparts, the three Scottish sisters quickly found jobs. They read the latest novels, went rowing on the Río de la Plata, and danced with single male friends.

Influenced by the rise of the suffrage movement roiling Britain, my grandmother Jessie, I'm told, formed strong opinions about jobs and votes for women, and, most especially, birth control. With money earned from her work, Jessie even bought a car, becoming one of the first women in Buenos Aires to own a license.

Yet for all her convictions and avant-garde ways, Jessie could play the coquette. After suffering a bout of typhoid fever that left her temporarily bald, she wore a little cap lined with fake curls. Her doctor, she claimed, grew sweet on her and brought her a bottle of Veuve Clicquot champagne. It was, she said at the time, about all she could drink. As it came to pass, marriage and assimilation to the Argentine-British community would greatly modify the Donaldson sisters' progressive feminist beliefs. Gertie, the youngest, was the first of the sisters to marry. Her husband, José Romero, had come to Argentina from Spain. Next was Cissie, who married Rex Hurst, of English ancestry. It was Rex who introduced my grandmother Jessie to her future husband and my maternal grandfather, Juan Sinclair Attwell.

Juan Sinclair Attwell had been named after his own father, who was also of Scottish origin. But the Attwells had been among the earliest settlers to Argentina, preceding the Donaldsons' arrival by nearly a century. By the second decade of the twentieth century, my great-grandfather Attwell belonged to a family that was well established, and he staunchly identified himself as an Argentine citizen. The name father and son bore, Juan Sinclair, reflected the custom of the time whereby the first name was Spanish and the middle name was English. Here again, on the Attwell side, are clustered yet more seafarers. My great-grandfather Juan Sinclair, my great-great-grandfather José, and my thrice great-grandfather Guillermo were all officers in the Argentine Navy.

It is through the diplomatic travels of my Argentine great-grandfather Juan Sinclair Attwell that my ancestry loops back to America. Throughout the years, I've known him only as the stiff man standing to attention in the formal portrait that has hung on the wall of my home. His image is yet another one of those family ghosts that I've brushed past countless times, armloads of laundry, children, books, or groceries directing my attention to the present. For years, I admit, I've been a little fuzzy about exactly which side of my mother's family this stuffy-looking family patriarch belonged to.

Now I take his portrait down, remove it from its frame, and study the details. In the sepia-toned photo, Lieutenant Attwell is dressed in the full regalia of the Argentine Navy and standing beside a Victorian side table. Beneath his ornately curved and brocaded naval hat, his jut-jawed face, turned in proud profile, is stiff and serious. His thick mustache bristles. Gold chains and buttons decorate his chest, gold-fringed epaulets broaden his shoulders to a severe line, and thin white gloves sheathe his hands. His sword hangs by his side in its silver-tipped scabbard, engraved with the antique phrase that he'd chosen as his mission in life: "To serve the Fatherland and be useful to Society." My forebear is proud of following in the footsteps of his navy father and grandfather before him. And of his new appointment as Argentine naval attaché to Washington, D.C.

Lieutenant Attwell arrived in New York on his twenty-second birthday, October 31, 1887, and proceeded directly to Washington. The young, rural capital was in the midst of a building boom; the muddy canals and swampy lowlands of pre–Civil War days had given way to homes, businesses, and paved streets and sidewalks. The small area that made up the central part of the city surrounding the White House and the Capitol was relatively metropolitan, with broad avenues, cable cars, and a population of 100,000. Tall schooners docked in the city's ports on the Potomac River; the forty-year-long construction of the Washington Monument—the tallest building in the world at the time—had just been completed. Grover Cleveland was president. Diplomatic life flourished, including at the Argentine Office of Legation on Massachusetts Avenue, the famed Embassy Row of later years.

The new foreign post fit my great-grandfather as elegantly as his naval uniform. He mingled easily at diplomatic dinners and balls, relishing his encounters with the capital elite, as they're called today. Representing Argentina at the first Pan-American Conference, J. S. Attwell engaged in discourse with other South American delegates on the contentious issue of the Monroe Doctrine and inter-American trade. He took a tour of several states that included "splendid banquets," presented lectures at Cornell's Cosmopolitan Club, and even met with the presidents of the Southern Railroad and the Pennsylvania Railroad—exactly at the time my other great-grandfather was laboring as a soot-covered blacksmith. As cultural interlocutor, naval attaché Attwell also wrote pamphlets and newspaper articles touting the benefits of Argentina to the Americans. In turn, as my great-grandfather noted in his memoir, he explained America to the Argentines through articles in newspapers such as *La Prensa*.

In 1893, as secretary of a committee seeking to settle a boundary dispute between Argentina and Brazil, Attwell met face-to-face with President Cleveland. But it was the first lady who left a lasting impression. In his memoir, Attwell waxes poetic over Mrs. Cleveland, describing her as "the perfect mistress of the White House," known for her "gentle manners, her culture, and her beauty." Indeed, my great-grandfather was quite a ladies' man and took keen notice of the many young, single, and, as he put it, "good-looking ladies" of the nation's capital. One of those young belles would turn out to be my great-grandmother.

Juan Sinclair Attwell had just begun his second diplomatic tour when he began his courtship of the woman he would marry. At a diplomats' ball, his glance fell on a dark-haired young woman across the room, her face coyly hidden behind a black gauze fan (still framed and hanging on the wall of an Argentine cousin's house). This seductive ploy on the part of Miss Margaret Estelle Huyck initiated a flirtation that culminated in a wedding in 1894. As a local Washington, D.C., paper noted under the headline "The World of Society," the April 11 ceremony was followed by a reception at the home of her parents, Mr. and Mrs. Jesse Van Ness Huyck. According to the announcement in the *New York Times*, the Argentine minister and other members of the delegation were present, as were members of the Huycks' extended Washington family. The newlyweds' honeymoon trip would take them to South America, by way of Paris. The charming bride's friends, it was noted, hoped that Lieutenant Attwell would be kept in the country on his diplomatic mission.

My American great-grandmother Margaret Huyck's photograph has also hung on my wall for many years. Her wide, sable eyes have patiently observed me as I've dashed past her on the business of my twentieth- and twenty-first-century life. I, who by a turn of fate now live in the city of her birth, have come to her story late, at the age of fifty-seven. It wasn't as if I'd never been told that my great-grandmother had been born and raised in the city where I'd come to live. It was one of those bits of knowledge that had dimly existed in the back of my mind, but until now this fact of my family heritage hadn't seemed all that important to me. I'd been distanced from my great-grandmother not so much by time, I began to realize, as by my family's numbed memory, as well as America's deep-set alienation from its own immigrant past. Seeking to recover yet another lost connection, I study the great-grandmother I never met, and yet whose life prefigured mine.

An alabaster-skinned, shy young woman with thick eyebrows arched over serious eyes stares back at me. In their inscrutability, Margaret's eyes are like curtains pulled over a vanished world, forever lost to me. Her chestnut hair, the color of my own, is knotted on top of her head. She wears the long, tightly cinched skirts of the nineteenth century, and a high lace collar chokes her neck. In an earlier family photo, taken before her marriage, Margaret stands in a close-knit circle with her parents, sister, and brother. They are gathered in a photographer's studio, not far from their home on I Street, just minutes from the White House. Tracing my fingers over the lines of an old family tree I retrieve from the back of my aunt's family album, I finally see what I'd never seen before: that my great-grandmother's family—my family!—has resided along the East Coast and throughout the Washington area since colonial times. Among them are a Revolutionary patriot and navy heroes, judges, farmers, lawyers, merchants, slave owners, and a Sergeant-at-Arms—all through my mother, the Argentine immigrant whose bloodline ties me back to Washington and the sunrise of America.

Poring over family papers and trekking through archives, I learn that Margaret Estelle Huyck's father, my great-great grandfather Jesse Van Ness Huyck, was a highly regarded, well-off, and socially connected Washingtonian real estate broker with a seat on the Washington Stock Exchange. His rise to prominence began during the Civil War and over the course of forty years, J. V. N. Huyck, as he was called, became the city's oldest established broker, carrying out some of the city's largest property deals from his office at 1505 Pennsylvania Avenue.

This family patriarch, his small stature offset by his double-breasted suits, monocle, and upper-class air, was descended from two Dutch families, the Van Nesses and the Huycks, who'd immigrated to the New

World in the early seventeenth century. First to arrive was Jan Huyck, who sailed up the Hudson River in 1626 with his brother-in-law Peter Minuit, the first colonial governor of what is now Manhattan, and who put down the roots of a huge family tree that eventually spread throughout upstate New York. Vice Admiral Aert Van Ness, an officer in the Dutch Navy, also sailed to these shores in the early seventeenth century, and also settled in upstate New York. Van Ness's son, the Honorable Peter Van Ness of Kinderhook, became a chief justice, and three of his sons grew up to hold positions of power and influence in the new republic.

It is Peter Van Ness's oldest son, and my sixth second cousin, General John Peter Van Ness, who first linked the Van Ness family's fate to Washington City, as the barely existent capital was then called. John Peter arrived as a congressman from New York in 1801, when Thomas Jefferson was president. After marrying, John Peter eventually took up residence in a magnificent, city-block-wide estate designed especially for him by Benjamin Latrobe, architect of the Capitol. Today, it is the site of the Pan American Union Building—a small irony that has not gone unnoticed by my Argentine family.

Situated just blocks away from the White House, the Van Nesses entertained such American notables as John Quincy Adams and the writer Washington Irving. After completing his term in congress, J. P. Van Ness continued his upward climb, becoming president of one of Washington's first banks and brigadier general of the city's militia. During the War of 1812 he commanded his troops to be ready to fight the British invasion "at the sound of a trumpet"—only to escape to the high shores of the Potomac, where he and his wife and friends watched a glowing horizon lit by the fires of the burning Capitol. Elected mayor twice, General J. P. Van Ness, it was written, "gave a strong start to everything essential to the city's life." As it was also written, he was a slave owner. At his death, the worth of the "human chattels" he'd owned was listed as part of the value of his estate. Upon examining a portrait of Van Ness as an old man wearing a snobbish, snarling expression, I decide that, despite his appointment with history, I do not much care for this aloof Washingtonian ancestor.

The lineage on my great-grandmother Margaret's maternal side proves no less interesting than her father's Dutch progenitors. Two English brothers, Jeremy and Thomas Dyer, initiated this branch of her family tree. Settling in Prince George and Prince Charles's counties just outside modern-day Washington in the early 1700s, the brothers married and started families. A cryptic note on the family tree, "Once Sergeant-at-Arms of the U.S. Senate," is scribbled by the name of Jeremy Dyer's grandson Edward, my third great-grandfather. Curiosity spurs me to pay a visit to the Senate Historical Office on Capitol Hill. When a kindly historian brings out a file bearing Dyer's name, an electric thrill of ancestral connection runs again through my body.

Edward Dyer, I learn, was only the fifth to hold the office of Sergeant-at-Arms. Among his duties, Dyer would have escorted the president during his visits to the Senate, kept custody of the gavel used to begin Senate sessions, and overseen security for the Senate Chamber. According to his obituary, Dyer was "universally esteemed" for his "excellent qualities and manly virtues." In those tumultuous days, when brawls were common and pistols easily drawn, I'm told, the Sergeant-at-Arms would by necessity had to have been capable of commanding authority.

My anticipation over this early American ancestor grows when I'm told that, in some remote file cabinet in the Senate building exists a photo of Dyer's official portrait. When, after months of waiting, I finally slide his picture from the large envelope that arrives in the mail, a slender, dark-suited, white-collared, clean-shaven, pale-skinned, English-looking, thin-lipped, and immensely serious nineteenth-century man materializes before me. Dyer's large, direct eyes lock mine in a steady gaze, and it is clear that here is an American idealist, one of those refined yet fiery patriots, like Thomas Jefferson or Thomas Paine, for whom these United States provided an all-consuming passion. Dyer, in fact, died in office in 1845 during the administration of President John Tyler. His portrait holds a special place in my study, his fine face with all its concealed stories looking over me as I work, imparting a protective atmosphere. Something in him, I feel, works still through my fate, taking the American experiment in directions he may never have imagined during his lifetime.

After his first marriage ended in tragedy—his wife and all seven children died—Edward Dyer married for a second time, to Henrietta Tarbell: Margaret Huyck's grandmother, and my third great-grandmother. If I thought I'd discovered as many patriots and adventurers as were possible in one family tree, however, I am in for more surprises. Not only do I unearth yet a third lineage of maritime tradition through this matriarchal ancestor, I learn that I am descended from seamen who'd served in the United States' first navy. One so distinguished himself during the Revolutionary War that I—who have always abhorred the actions of those early American imperialists who oppressed the Native Americans and enslaved Africans—might even lay claim to membership in the Daughters of the American Revolution.

Take Henrietta's father and my fourth great-grandfather, Commodore Joseph Tarbell, whose Navy commission was signed by President John Adams. Assigned to the defense of Norfolk during the War of 1812, Tarbell was given command of a flotilla on the James River. During a battle with a British squadron, he sank three of their boats, killed ninety, and captured forty-three prisoners, forcing the British to flee. In 1815, Tarbell died suddenly, aged thirty-five, on a chill November evening in Washington City. He left behind a wife, my fourth great-grandmother Eliza, two young daughters (including Henrietta), and the legacy of a navy destroyer that in 1917 was named after him.

Tarbell's commanding superior during the War of 1812 was another navy swashbuckler, and another name on my family tree: Commodore Stephen Cassin, Eliza's brother, my fourth great-uncle, and, according to our family tree, a hero of the Battle of Lake Champlain, which took place during the War of 1812 as the U.S. Navy battled to block the British from invading the northern states from Canada.

On September 11, 1814, as the opposing fleets engaged in combat, Cassin's sloop *Ticonderoga* became separated from its squadron and surrounded by English vessels. Cassin walked the ship's rail as "showers of canister and grape" rained around him, fighting off assaults and calmly staring down the enemy's attempt to board. For his valiant feats that contributed to victory over the British, Cassin was honored

136

with a Congressional Gold Medal, a burial spot at Arlington National Cemetery, and not one but two ships named after him.

Stephen Cassin's guts and genius were inherited from his father, John Cassin, the headwaters of this side of the family tree, and my fifth great-grandfather through his daughter Eliza, Joseph Tarbell's wife and Stephen's sister. John Cassin, too, I learn, has a file, an official portrait, and a backstory so inseparably linked to our country's founding that it's worthy of its own book. In a visit to the hushed library at the Washington headquarters of the Daughters of the American Revolution—with sun shining gold through long windows across old, thick texts from the American Catholic Historical Society—I discover the Irish-descended Cassin stepping from the mists. According to documents on file that certify him as my own authentic American patriot, Cassin joined the Pennsylvania Militia at seventeen, where he served as a private under the command of George Washington at the Battle of Trenton. Yes, *the* Battle of Trenton in which, on Christmas night, Washington and his rag-dressed, barefoot soldiers crossed the ice-choked Delaware River in freezing rain and snow, surprising and capturing the sleeping enemy soldiers.

After the Revolution, Cassin, who was said to have maintained a "warm personal friendship" with George Washington—who even presented Cassin with an oil painting of himself—became a merchant seaman, sailing to France. In 1799, he was tasked to help found the U.S. Navy. He moved to Washington and served as second-in-command at the Washington Navy Yard. He testified before President Jefferson's Congress to fund, restore frigates, and fight pirates in Tripoli. During the War of 1812 he returned to the Delaware River to command the naval forces protecting Philadelphia. Still on active duty in his late fifties, Master Commandant Cassin became commanding officer of the Navy Yard at Norfolk, Virginia, and then Charleston, South Carolina, where he died in 1822.

In existence for nearly two centuries, John Cassin's portrait, a miniature etching by the French artist Charles Balthazar Julien Févret de Saint-Mémin, has been housed at the National Portrait Gallery. On a beautiful Washington spring day, I organize a viewing party made up of myself, one of my sons, and an elderly couple—my newly discovered Cassin cousins descended from Stephen, who live just ten minutes from my house. When the museum attendant opens the oversize folio with her plastic-gloved hand, pulls out a thick ivory parchment sheet lined with miniature portraits of Federal America, and then points to Cassin's profile, our small group stands and stares. One by one, we approach the table, each of us entering into a kind of spellbound communion with our ancestral past, at once old and yet so new.

As if in church, we fall silent, for the fine, near-photographic detail of the etching springs John Cassin to life before us. His thick hair curls down around his ears and over his broad forehead. His face is wide, round, and crosshatched with wrinkles. His nose is pugnacious, his eyes are heavy-lidded, and his neck is thick beneath his heavy woolen navy uniform. He is a burly man, and his chest, decorated with nautical buttons, gold braids, and wide epaulets on his shoulders, is proudly pushed out. Near fifty years old at the time he sat for this portrait, this ancestral elder compels the child in me to reach out. I want to put my hands around his face, turn it toward me, and look directly in his eyes. But fate has only left me his outward-looking gaze. Reorienting myself to the direction Cassin faces, I see the far horizon, feel salt spray on my face, and thrill to a ship's swift motion into the distance.

The lives and characters of the ancestors I've had to work so hard to uncover were much closer in time to my great-grandmother, Margaret Estelle Huyck. What I read as brief entries in history books, or garner from family legends and records, came down to her as living stories that wove her into the fate of the United States, marking her with the call of the sea, the glamour of foreign cultures, and the lure of politics.

Before she married and left for Argentina, Margaret and her sister May had moved in Washington's social circles; the sisters and their mother had spent several years abroad, traveling widely throughout Germany, France, Italy, and Switzerland. In one photograph before her marriage, my great-grandmother is seated against an elaborately carved, high-backed bench, her hair piled high, her hands folded in her lap, and a white fur draped around her shoulders as if for some official occasion. So it was that on that spellbound evening when my great-grandmother Margaret locked eyes with the impeccably dressed Argentine gentleman across the room, it was as if everything in her North American past to that point had prepared her to be whisked away to South America by a pompous diplomat and high-minded naval officer.

After Juan Sinclair Attwell's marriage to Margaret Estelle, the couple took up the lives of foreign diplomats. Their two sons, Sinclair and Norman, were schooled abroad in Switzerland, France, Italy, Washington, D.C.—where the Attwells lived with the Huyck family— and finally in Buenos Aires. Although Juan Sinclair had converted to Catholicism for his new wife, he never went so far as to become an American citizen. His bond to Argentina was too deep. Besides, this great-grandfather of mine didn't really like the United States. "The facts on the ground," Lieutenant Attwell wrote in his memoirs, were "more eloquent than the words of certain American diplomats." He referred to "US hemispheric hegemony" and criticized the country as the "great colossus" that had been "expanding its domains since its independence from Britain." Instead, it was my American great-grandmother who adapted to her new culture, becoming Señora Margarita E. H. de Attwell, as she was listed in a Diplomatic List for the Department of State in 1901.

For all the dash and promise that attended her marriage at the outset, Señora Attwell's life ended sadly. It's hard to say, exactly, when she turned into the heavyset, melancholy, severe woman my mother remembers as a child. After Lieutenant Attwell retired early due to heart problems, the family lived for a while in the wilds of the Argentine Chaco, where Juan Sinclair raised pineapples and planted American cotton, an enterprise that failed. During that time, Margarita busied herself translating a Spanish novel into English. Her book, published in 1900 by Little, Brown and Company, now sits on my writing desk, a talisman of the woman writer in my family tree. After returning to Buenos Aires, my great-grandfather Juan Sinclair turned his attention to the Officers' Naval Club, while my great-grandmother Margarita helped found the American Women's Club of Buenos Aires. Clinging to the American identity that had become more fragile in exile, she searched in vain for a Spanish translator of Mark Twain. She became ever more devoutly Catholic.

In a passport photo of her around this time, Margarita's face has taken on a tired and strained look. Dark circles ring her eyes, her jaw is clamped, her jowls sag, and her mouth is drawn in a tight line. Gone is the pretty young woman who'd charmed the handsome naval attaché from behind a black fan. Perhaps she is returning from a visit home to Washington, where she'd been called back to bury her mother or her father. Perhaps, I think, this American woman doesn't want to go back to the country of her Argentine husband. Or perhaps the troubles caused by her two sons are beginning to weigh on her.

In his early twenties my great-uncle Norman had suddenly gone mad, and had been institutionalized. Sinclair, Margarita's older son and my grandfather, also brought worry and disappointment through his engagement to my Scottish grandmother, Jessie Donaldson. For one thing, Jessie was seven years older than Sinclair. Jessie's humble upbringing, I imagine, may also have been a drawback to her as a future daughter-in-law.

Strongly identified with her elite Washingtonian background even while living abroad, Margarita may have hoped for a more socially advantageous marriage for her son. One of the family stories passed down recounts the time my great-grandmother had been invited to a diplomatic dinner in Buenos Aires held in honor of an important dignitary. Seated next to each other at the formal table, the statesman had turned to my great-grandmother and, with an aloof smile, had remarked: "You and I are the only people here who really know what gracious living is."

But the worst mark of all against my grandmother Jessie was her Scottish Presbyterian faith. Nurtured in the parishes and convents of nineteenth-century Washington, my great-grandmother's Catholicism had grown fanatical in exile. Both of her sons, Norman and Sinclair, had been baptized in the Church; marriage outside the Church was unthinkable. For four long years, Jessie and Sinclair persisted in the face of my great-grandmother's formidable opposition. Finally, when Señor and Señora Attwell were traveling out of the country, my grandparents were married in a small civil ceremony.

Marriage into the family did nothing to ease the strain between my grandmother Jessie and my great-grandmother Margarita, which grew worse over time. When she was a girl at school, my mother recalls, her grandmother Attwell frightened her by sending priests to her school to convert her to Catholicism. Both Juan Sinclair and Margarita were formal with and unaffectionate toward their only two granddaughters, Sheila and Fiona. Neither was the elder Attwells' marriage happy. During one memorable Christmas meal for which the entire family had gathered, my aunt Fiona recalls, Señora Margarita Estelle asked Señor Juan if he'd gone to confession. When he responded that he hadn't, she began to cry, scream, and wail loudly. How could she even eat, she raged at him in front of everyone, when he hadn't received this holiest of rites? Soon everyone at the table was in tears, and the Christmas meal ended in chaos.

As she grew into old age, Margarita, a voracious reader, suffered from cataracts. After an operation to remove them from one eye, she got an infection, which soon spread to her other. The result, which could have been prevented today, was total blindness, and two glass eyes were placed in the empty cavities. Confined to her apartment, Margarita Estelle, a gifted musician from youth, continued to play her piano.

Each afternoon, her husband left her alone and took himself out for tea at the Ideal, one of Buenos Aires's oldest and most elegant hotels. For several hours, Juan Sinclair held court with passersby or family visitors. Still, it was remarked of Lieutenant Attwell that he seemed a lonely man. On April 30, 1941, he passed away. As it was noted in the *Buenos Aires Herald*, "Full naval honors were rendered" at his funeral. His coffin, it was recorded in his obituary, was "draped in the Argentine flag, and bore the dead officer's hat and sword."

Yet one more tragedy lay in wait for my American great-grandmother. In 1951, at the age of eighty-four, living in a nursing home, her elder son Sinclair died suddenly of a stroke. When my aunt Fiona broke the news to her, she replied, blind and dazed, "You mean Sinclair . . . my boy?" Her loss must have been great; Fiona tells me that

Sinclair had faithfully visited his mother every day. Three years later, Margarita Estelle Van Ness Huyck Attwell followed her husband and son into death.

FROM ARGENTINA TO AMERICA

Margarita Estelle and her daughter-in-law Jessie remained at odds throughout their lives. But though they likely never discussed it, immigration was one thing the two had in common. Both came from a tradition of seamen and navy officers. Both set sail for new lands as young women in their twenties. Both of their sea journeys were launched by a man: my great-grandmother to follow her husband, and my grandmother to follow her father. Both left behind homelands steeped in memory and tradition. Generations of family customs and daily rituals were disrupted, to be replaced by border-crossings, lengthy ocean passages, momentous departures from and arrivals at distant ports, and the mixing and mingling of languages and food.

Of the two women's immigration experiences, however, my grandmother Jessie probably had it easier. She'd had a stable, cozy family life in Scotland. Relocating to Buenos Aires, she'd arrived *en famille*. For most of her adult life, she'd been surrounded by an extended clan that preserved many of the old customs of Scotland.

This was in marked contrast with my great-grandmother, who, I discover to my profound sadness, passed down no stories whatsoever of American life to her Argentine granddaughter, my mother. At some point, or at least as far back as my mother can recall, she stopped returning home to the States to visit her family, thus marking another dramatic "cut off" point in my family tree. This in turn shaped my grandfather Sinclair, who'd followed his diplomatic parents around the world, attending school in Washington, D.C., and different countries. As he'd once confided in his oldest daughter, my aunt Fiona, he'd grown up never really feeling at home anywhere. My grandfather would carry this restive dissatisfaction with him into his marriage and home life.

For in spite of the passion that had marked my Argentine grandparents' courtship, the marriage between Jessie Donaldson and Sinclair Attwell foundered. The current of romance running through both their natures had enabled them to endure an extended engagement. But the ardor that had sustained them in opposition to Sinclair's formidable mother failed to translate into the affection of daily life. The tedium of marriage and raising children did not serve them well. Motherhood, too, was not an easy path for Jessie, who was hospitalized no less than six times after my mother's birth, and who frequently had to place her newborn daughter in the care of her mother, father, and sisters. In this way, my mother's psyche is linked with my father's: both suffered maternal deprivation in early infancy.

Sometime during the course of Jessie and Sinclair's marriage, my grandfather began having affairs. He took up with his secretary, with other women in their community of Olivos, and even with one of my mother's schoolteachers. He traveled out of town on frequent "business" trips, most likely accompanied by the "lady friend" of the day, as my mother's friend Pixie recalls. At home, he was a kind, if absent-minded and detached father who spent most of his time tinkering in his garage with inventions. His entrepreneurial enterprises, such as manufacturing radio tubes during World War II, kept him preoccupied; at night he sat outside beneath the stars, dreaming of the day when radio waves would travel to the moon.

Her pride hurt by his affairs, my grandmother began to cultivate herself socially, playing bridge and developing friendships with the "smart, intellectual" set of Olivos, as my aunt remembers. Well and widely read, she collected poetry and even wrote her own memoir. As she grew older, the soubrette in her waxed ever stronger and more outrageous. No one I ever knew could hold a cigarette and cock her head and smile quite like my Granny Jessie.

Growing up, my mother was innocently oblivious to her parents' flawed marriage. Though they were not wealthy, and had few material possessions, her family's life was rich in culture, friends, and relations. Sheila and Fiona were sent to a private girls' school where grades were called "forms." They studied Shakespeare and Keats and learned to speak French—a classical education that surpassed what my father had received at Altoona High School. Luncheons and balls among the British-Argentine community structured her social life. Along with her family, Sheila sang "God Save the King" during Sunday services at the Scottish Presbyterian Church. People around her referred to England as "home"—whether or not they'd been born there, or even visited. In this conservative community, boys were judged to be acceptable or not based on whether they spoke English; dating a "native" was taboo. Still, because of Sinclair's deep Argentine roots through his father, and because of Jessie's broad-minded ways, my mother traveled in both the Argentine and British circles of Buenos Aires.

In 1946, when my mother was eighteen, postwar Buenos Aires churned with people from around the world. Nazis fleeing Germany swarmed the city, as did Allied and U.S. secret intelligence forces. The military strongman General Juan Perón had been elected president. His wife, the infamous Eva, who had a fondness for helping Nazis find refuge, cast a distracting glamour over the country's growing instability. The mood in Buenos Aires at the time, my aunt Fiona recalls, was that "everything was going to hell in a handbasket." After nearly a century of industrial expansion that had put Argentina's living standards on a par with Europe's, severe inflation, social unrest among the *descamisados*, or "shirtless ones," and high unemployment had thrown the country's future into uncertainty.

The roiling political climate of Buenos Aires barely touched the edges of my young mother's life. At the time, she says, she knew only dimly that "things were going on" in the factories and industrial areas on the outskirts of the city. For her the Depression was over, the war had ended, and she and her sister and cousins were young and carefree in a city known as the "Paris of South America." The outdoor cafés, elegant, old-world buildings, and broad boulevards were their playground. On Saturday nights, Sheila, Fiona, and their cousins and friends went to small clubs where they danced the samba, the fox-trot, a little bit of swing, and, of course, the tango. Sunday afternoons brought more dancing at the Belgrano Club.

A telling story about my mother's beauty took place at a charity dance headlined by Louis Armstrong. Heading up a conga line, Sheila snaked and shimmied past the legendary crooner. Something about the smiling, blue-eyed girl with the black curls must have caught his glance. Stepping to the edge of the stage and leaning down, Armstrong crooned into her beaming face, "Where'd you get those dimples, baby!" Her boyfriend, my mother recalls, bragged about the incident for days afterward.

It was during this postwar period that Joe Carroll's fate crossed with my mother's on the Río de la Plata. The cast of friends and family awaiting him could not have been more receptive. My grandmother Jessie may have once been a proud feminist. But where her two daughters were concerned, marriage was uppermost in her mind. My mother's desire to be an opera singer, or possibly a diamond cutter, had been firmly vetoed. Instead, she'd taken a position as a part-time English teacher. My aunt Fiona's scholarship to study abroad in England had also gone by the wayside. As my grandmother claimed, intellect made her a less desirable candidate for marriage.

Even history conspired to showcase my father's best talents. "It was the late forties. We'd just come out of World War II," recalls my mother's girlhood friend Pixie. "While England came out of the war victorious, it was pretty bedraggled. But Americans were the glamour figures of the war." Merely because Joe was an American pilot, said Pixie, my father had charisma and magnetism and a sort of "swaggering maleness" that set him apart from the softer boys she and my mother had grown up with. (See note on p. 426.)

At my parents' first encounter, however, all that my father had undergone and, perhaps, all that was to come, cast an aura about him of postwar intrigue. A veteran of over 107 Atlantic crossings, he possessed the kind of brash confidence that comes from achievement born of danger. My mother certainly saw him that way. As a young man, she told me, "your father was happy and daring. There was something about him. He had a mysterious, brooding air. I know it sounds very *Jane Eyre*, but in my eyes he was exciting and adventurous."

Exciting and adventurous. Like background melody, these two notes sound again and again throughout my family narrative of world-roaming explorers. This recurring theme would strike major chords during my parents' early romance. After their initial meeting on the Argentine delta, they continued to see each other on Joe's layovers between trips. Though my aunt Fiona remembers my young father as a "rather shy and quiet, but very polite young American man," she also recalls that he had a lovely smile and dimples to match Sheila's. Jessie and Sinclair seemed taken with the handsome American courting their daughter well enough; on layovers Joe sometimes slept on their couch in the living room.

Early in 1949, Joe abruptly resigned from the Argentine airline FAMA. His call to adventure this time came in the person of a high-spirited American flyboy named Kenneth Fuller, a buddy who'd worked alongside my father as a captain for FAMA—and who was now aiming his sights on the Middle East. Israel had just been born as a nation. Lacking professional flight personnel and even aircraft, the young country had begun hiring experienced fliers for their new national airline. "A lot of Americans answered Israel's call for help," aviation historian Brett Stoley tells me, "either because their Jewish buddy from the war went, or just for the excitement of it, or to help because it was the right thing to do, regardless of their religion." Joe returned first to Altoona, where he worked on the Glovers' farm, commuting to New York to help get ready for delivery Israel's very first aircraft, two second-hand DC-4s purchased from American Airlines. He continued his long-distance courtship of my mother, and on August 22, 1949, he sent a telegram to Jessie and Sinclair: "Respectfully request permission marry Sheila."

There was never any question in my mother's mind about joining her life to my father's. As she confided to Fiona, she was determined to make a home for my father. "He was the great love of my life and absolutely nothing could have ever stopped me from marrying him," she tells me. I don't doubt her. But was she also influenced in her decision, I wonder, by the powerful immigration patterns in the generations that had preceded her? As my great-grandmother Margarita had found herself responding to the naval background of my great-grandfather, and as the ancestral chords in my grandmother Jessie had resonated with her husband's naval lineage, had Sheila been captivated by my father because his globe-girdling lifestyle meshed so well with her own family history?

Hesitation about my parents' engagement came from an unexpected quarter: Sheila's father. Taking his youngest daughter aside, Sinclair gently told her that he didn't want her to go. Carefully, he voiced his concern about the "differences" between the young couple. He didn't say it, my mother remembers, but the word "class" was in the air. Even though his daughter would be returning to the country of his own mother's birth, Sinclair was reluctant to let her marry a man whose background was so dissimilar.

But maybe my grandfather also understood something of the consequences that came from following a spouse abroad. Desperate to stop Sheila from leaving the country, he offered to find my father work in Buenos Aires. When that failed, he reminded her that in Buenos Aires she was loved and known—but that now she was going out into the unknown, where no one would know her as they had at home.

However, nothing my grandfather said could stop the force of nature that was my parents' romance. Joseph Wilbert Carroll and Maria Sheila Attwell were married on September 6, 1949. Their wedding ceremony did not take place in Buenos Aires, but in Altoona, Pennsylvania. Nor did it occur at the old Carroll home, but at the home of Dr. and Mrs. Pellman Glover. This did not seem to bother my father's mother, who proudly showed Sheila off to her friends, telling them her daughter-in-law-to-be had come "from very far away." According to the account published in the local paper, "Argentina Girl Is Bride at Nuptials of Joseph Carroll," the bride was "lovely in a pale blue suit of Italian Tussor silk and a small, head-fitting, white-feathered hat." The mother of the bride, Granny Jessie, was present, as was the mother of the groom, Grandmother Carroll. Because for unknown reasons Sinclair had been unable to attend, Sheila was given away by Dorothy Glover's elderly father. As the newspaper article noted, a "number of cables from Argentina were received following the ceremony."

My aunt Fiona remembers my mother's wedding as one of the saddest days of her life. Heartbroken because she'd been left behind in Buenos Aires, Fiona sat alone in the dining room, she recalls, and "cried and cried and cried." When Sinclair and Fiona's uncle Jimmie, Jessie's brother who was living with them, came home from work, they opened a bottle of champagne and raised a toast to Sheila and Joe. Then they sat by the fire and laughed and cried some more.

Wrapped in a haze of bliss, my mother was simply too happy to be sad at the absence of her Argentine family, including even my American great-grandmother Margarita, who sat alone in blind darkness. What must she have been thinking, I wonder now, as her granddaughter prepared to close the circle by returning to America? In the newspaper photo taken that day, Joe and Sheila stand facing the camera—arms linked triumphantly, chins up, exultant smiles on their faces. On the morning after their wedding night, my father's older brother Paul came by for a visit. When my mother came downstairs to greet him, her dark hair framed by a lovely white silk dressing gown, he caught his breath. He'd never, he said later, seen anyone look so radiant in all his young life.

After their marriage, the movable adventure of Joe and Sheila's marriage began. Five days at the Glovers' country home, followed by a month in New York, where my father worked to get the DC-4 ready to fly to Israel. Then it was on to Paris, where my mother stayed while my father flew back and forth to Israel and worked on finding housing. "Big hotel. Joe sick. Pensione alone. Museums. Night clubs. Notre Dame, Seine, Eiffel Tower in one walk. Farewell," wrote my mother in her journal as she prepared to leave Paris. Approaching Israel, she jotted down, "Israel. The land as I first saw it from the cockpit. Drive to Tel Aviv and then out to settlement."

While my father was away, Sheila hiked and picnicked with newfound friends among the ruins and olive groves. For a time, my parents left Israel and lived in Rome, as my father flew some of El Al's earliest international routes. There, too, Sheila ventured out to explore with friends. "We came on an old fortress that was built in 1000, and had a moat around it and tall turrets," she wrote to her parents. "If I could only let you get a feel of it all, with deep blue skies, and all the hills covered with peach and apple blossoms. Boy! It was one of my happiest days." In an incident she didn't share with her parents, Sheila and Joe took a trip to the Isle of Capri. There, they swam nude in the blue grotto. "Stress *laughter* and *gaiety*," she writes in her notes of that day. Then it was back to an apartment in Israel, where they celebrated their first wedding anniversary.

Maybe it was the magic that came with being in a place where history was live in the making, but from the beginning, Sheila was entranced with Israel. The ancient history combined with the exhilarating mood animating the new nation jolted her alive. In letters to her parents, Sheila was heady with discovery as she explored the Mediterranean beaches in front of the Bat Yam apartment complex where they were living, and the customs and cuisine of her host country. Living abroad had come easily to her, as if it was second nature. As indeed it was. Compared to later years, when my father became a recluse, the young couple led a gregarious life, going to parties and restaurants. They rode camels in Nazareth and Joe took up English riding again. In one photo from that period, my father sits astride a bay horse in his jodhpurs and boots; in another, my mother poses on a headstone as old as history, her head turned in profile against the blue Israeli sky. The two pictures, she tells me, are her favorite photos of my father and herself.

Those first days of my parents' marriage in Israel would be set apart in their memory from all their other experiences abroad. It was as if they, too, had played a small part in something both historic and healing in war's terrible aftermath. In one memorable incident, my mother remembers the generosity shown them on their first Christmas, when their new Israeli friends sent them flowers and gifts. Photographs of my father reveal him radiating pride and a kind of sheer joy at being alive. In a photo celebrating El Al's inaugural flight to Vienna, he stands at attention on the tarmac, smiling broadly as he and his fellow crew members are greeted with flowers by local officials and photographers. The El Al insignia, wings that enfold the Star of David, glitter on his uniform cap.

In something of a miracle, I find a living witness to that time. Now ninety-one and living in New York, Ozzie Goldman, who worked for El Al during the exact period as my father, exclaims over the phone in an aged voice, "I remember Joe! We were the team selected to pioneer the airline from scratch. Most of us went to Israel for the adventure, but it turned out to be the happiest of experiences. No one expected to get up at 5:00 A.M. daily, sing all the way to work, and suddenly realize that there was something in life much more important than money."

But not all was perfect in Joe and Sheila's Middle Eastern paradise. Sheila's beauty and extroverted charm could, and did, stir trouble. One weekend, they attended the bar mitzvah of a local family's son. Putting on a pale blue dress, Sheila felt pretty, and she was glad to be included in the Jewish coming-of-age ritual. In the midst of the dancing and talking, a man walked in. The music stopped and the crowd grew silent. Then applause broke out, and everyone made way for him. As the music resumed, the mysterious stranger strode through the crowd to my mother. Bowing deeply, the man, who wore a black patch over one eye, asked her to dance. Judging by his reception, my mother knew this man must be someone important, someone she could not refuse. Sheila accepted his offer and the two twirled in silence to a fox-trot; not a word was exchanged. As soon as the dance was finished, a very jealous Joe took Sheila by the arm, said "let's go," and ushered her away. As my mother discovered later, her dance partner was Moshe Dayan, the famed Israeli military commander who had a reputation as a notorious ladies' man.

There were other brushes with Israel's unfolding fate. When the United Nations partitioned Palestine between the Jews and Arabs in 1947, anger spread throughout the Arab world. In Aden, the capital of Yemen, anti-Jewish violence erupted. In a covert rescue mission dubbed Operation Magic Carpet, Israel mobilized British and American transport planes and American and El Al crews to airlift an entire Jewish community from the southwestern tip of the Arabian Peninsula. Once again, Joe found himself part of a wartime air feat dazzling in its risk and daring. Beginning in January 1949, nomadic Yemenite Jews streamed across hundreds of miles of desert into the capital of Aden. Most refugees had never seen an airplane. Fuel was scarce. Planes were shot at. Dust and sand were hard on the engines. Nervous Yemenites, packed onto wooden benches, weighed down planes. Forced to fly on routes that took nine hours with faulty instruments, and deprived of radio, writes aviation historian Marvin Goldman, British officials warned crews that should they be forced to land on Arab soil, they could all be killed. Yet no major mishaps occurred, and by the time the airlift ended in September 1950, nearly 50,000 Yemenite and Habbani Jews had been carried to Israel.

And, yet again, as with Joe's military service in Brazil and his job with an Argentine airline, questions arise among some historians about Joe's "interesting trajectory" in the near aftermath of the war. As a research scholar at the Simon Wiesenthal Museum points out, these suspicions are not that far-fetched. The Nazi war criminal Adolf Eichmann, for instance, was captured in Argentina by men wearing El Al uniforms. At the time, he explains further, various governments commonly used airlines to carry out covert missions, and "the use of airline pilots for intelligence activities did take place, as it was an easy way to get someone in and out of different countries."

In the spring of 1951, my mother became pregnant. Not many children are told their conception story, as I was. I can't recall exactly when I was informed. But somehow I grew up knowing that I'd been conceived while my mother and father were on a picnic in the Valley of Sharon, a place of biblical legend. Still hanging in my closet is the embroidered Israeli blouse my mother wore in the first months of her pregnancy. Now that my parents were expecting their first child, my father felt it was time to return to the States. He applied for airline jobs back home and was quickly hired by TWA, which was headquartered in Kansas City, Missouri.

Shortly before he began his new job, Joe and Sheila lived for a brief period in England. My father was flying the London–New York route for El Al, and my mother began to have a difficult time being apart from him. I'd never thought of Joe Carroll as the kind of man who would write love letters. Perhaps no child thinks that of his or her parents. But while he was on a trip that was longer than expected, Joe's heart flared open, and in a tender mood he penned his pregnant wife these words:

"Dearest baby," he wrote to her on thin paper now faded to gray. "How I have missed you! Time has never passed more slowly in my life. . . . I should be back Thursday morning and trust that you will be in a healthy condition as I intend to have a wonderful party for us—and I want to remain *just* with you for a week. . . . I don't want to leave the house or have you leave even for a few minutes. Honey, I surely hope that you will feel the same as I about our ever being apart for such a long time. . . . Please believe me I don't ever want to be away from you again. With all my love until I get back, when I will show, rather than write, just how I feel. Forever, Joe." In a PS, he added that there was money for her in his dressing gown pocket.

It was in London that my father asked my mother to marry him a second time. Like his father before him, Joe felt it was important that his children be raised in the Catholic tradition. And so, in a small village outside of London, he cajoled a local priest into marrying them—even though, as the priest said jokingly, "it was too late for premarital counseling."

In a photo taken that day, my mother stands beside a jovial, cassocked priest before massive carved church doors. This time, Sheila is dressed in a black suit with a white corsage. A bump shows prominently around her thickening waist. The priest is turned toward her, as if he cannot help but defer to the force of life emanating from her. Her smile is the same bright wattage as the one she wore on her first wedding day. She is on her way to a new country and to motherhood. Behind her, I see the spirits of all her roaming ancestors: whispering, warning, encouraging, and watching.

Joe and Sheila arrive in New York on the Fourth of July, 1951. It is a fitting date for the inauguration of their new American life.

IMMIGRATION: THE WHOLE STORY

"You marry, and you think you are marrying just that woman or that man, but not at all," wrote Jung. "Their whole ancestry down to the ape-man crowds into your marriage and naturally into your psychological relationship." A human life is nothing in itself, he continued, it is part of a family tree. "We know too little about our forebears. . . . We are all tremendously influenced by ancestral facts."

From an American perspective, Jung's emphasis on ancestry can seem old-world and outdated. In America's cultural "creation story," the individual begins where the past ends. According to this myth, a person is not predetermined by what came before, but forges a separate life through a combination of willpower and living in the present moment. Not only are we the land of opportunity, but the land of perpetual rebirth and starting over.

I love the fresh appeal of this myth as much as anyone. I have lived most of my life by it. The thought of being beholden to long-dead relatives with antiquated belief systems feels oppressive. In light of the stultifying effects of aristocracy and family tradition on individual creativity and initiative, I understand why separating from the past was so critical to the founding of our democracy. But when you have a mother who is the only foreign-born person in town, or a grandmother who visits from half a world away, you are that much closer to the intensely emotional experience of immigration.

In the small, white, Midwestern town where I grew up, Sheila stood out, as my ex-husband once poetically described her, like "a rose in the desert." As a girl, I observed my mother as she engaged in the difficult process of working out her identity in her adopted country. This process was made more complex by the projections of those around her. For if my mother had tilted toward being English in Argentina, she would become full-blown Spanish in Oak Grove, Missouri. Although she spoke perfect English, her intonation, perfected in her Argentine girls' private school, marked her as a non-American. As our friends used to say, "Your mother has a funny accent." Besides, there was no getting around the fact that she was from South America. Indeed, there were times, recalls my mother today, when the farmers and townspeople, warm-hearted as they were, looked at her as if "she had castanets in her hands and a red rose in her mouth."

What I remember most about my immigrant mother, however, were those moments when her Argentine past would abruptly intrude into our lives. As if the Carroll Christmases weren't already loaded with enough emotional minefields, it was also the one day of the year my mother phoned home. Even now, I can see the narrow, tall hall table by the front door of the house and my mother's back to me, as she stands there on Christmas Day, raising her hand to the black phone on the wall.

I see her as she dials the local operator on the party line to place the long-distance, very important, very expensive call all the way to Buenos Aires. Before email, Skype, and cell phones, calling overseas was a very big deal. Often it was both her Christmas and birthday present.

"Yes! Operator! Operator!" Sheila would shout into the receiver, her diction biting through the telephone wires. Her shoulders and neck would quiver with tension. "I'd like to make a telephone call to Buenos Aires, Argentina. Yes! Argentina! 21-313-1642. Yes. Operator. Did. You. Get. That? Repeat back, please," she'd demand. A long, tense pause would follow as the party line was cleared and the connection was made. In Olivos, the family had been waiting, gathered around their own black telephone. Then, like rapid machine gunfire, the phrases spat out: "Mummy! Mummy! Bueno, bueno . . . *vieja*. Fiona!" This was followed by a stream of highly charged English and Spanish words, intermixed with a few Scottish "wees."

Ordered into silence, the five of us would sit in the living room, still as stone and frozen to our seats. Reception was bad, and Sheila had to strain to hear. Even my father hung his head and sat motionless, a *Newsweek* magazine flipped open on his lap. The calls never lasted longer than a minute or two—just enough for my mother's family to hear each other's scratchy voices on the crackling line, to wish Feliz Navidad, Merry Christmas, Muy Feliz Cumpleaños, Happy Birthday, and to say "I love you" repeatedly.

These calls always ended badly. After hanging up, with her back still turned to us, Sheila would double over and sob. Gasps and heaves would shake her body. It would seem like hours before she'd turn around again, wiping her eyes with her hands. Once she'd retrieved her composure, my mother might tell us a few stories of her childhood Christmases in Argentina. There, it was always summer during our winter. Where we received ice skates and sleds, gift-wrapped bathing suits had been under her tree as a girl. After sailing on the Río de la Plata, she'd tell us, the big family of aunts, cousins, and uncles would gather for noisy, festive meals. As I chopped holes in the ice-covered pond for the cows and tossed hay for the horses across frosty fields, I would try and fail to imagine a Christmas like my mother's.

Another memory: I am sitting in the kitchen, probably no older than nine or ten. My mother is standing at her ironing board. The aroma of fresh, steamed cotton fills the room as I snack on Betty Crocker brownies, lost in pleasant daydreams. At that moment, the thought occurs to me that I know nothing about my grandfather, except that he is dead.

"When did your father die?" I ask my mother. Startled out of her reverie, Sheila tells me, calmly, that he died while she'd been pregnant with me. I muse over this prenatal event, try to grasp its importance, but cannot. Then, "What was he like?" I persist, curious about this man who'd been so close to my mother and yet was a stranger to me. "Well, he was a very kind man," my mother said. "We used to go for ice cream. He took us to the beach. I loved him very much." Ignoring the sudden flush of red in her cheeks, the quivering lips, I press on. I want stories. My mother tells them, until, raising and lifting the iron with increasing intensity, tears begin streaming down her face. "Why are you crying?" I ask. "Because talking about him makes me miss him," she says. "It was all so long ago and far away."

If I grew up without ever knowing my grandfather Sinclair, I did have vivid impressions of my grandmother Jessie's periodic visits—if only because they were so charged with melodrama. And if my mother was like a rose in the desert of Oak Grove, Granny Jessie on our farm was like a fine lace handkerchief that snagged on the burry weeds growing in the muddy barnyard.

After they married, my father turned against Sheila's parents as a way of severing her relationship to her own past. Joe in fact never once returned with my mother to visit her Argentine family. Given my father's work in the airlines, and his access to discounted tickets, this was remarkable. Nor did he approve of her visits home. Once when my mother wanted to return to Buenos Aires to see her family, Joe made her leave my ten-month-old brother with the next-door neighbor. Possibly this was insurance in case her plane crashed, or in the event she had any ideas of not coming back, for even then my parents' marriage was subject to cycles of uncertainty. Even so, Joe grew so paranoid during Sheila's absence that he called the U.S. Embassy, accusing her of canceling her return flight home, and, I suspect, kidnapping her two young daughters.

Joe had especially disliked Granny Jessie's refined ways. Making no effort to conceal his repugnance, he would childishly ignore her during her visits and go out of his way to play tricks on her. One summer, just before my grandmother's arrival, Joe made my mother shave my two brothers' heads. Called "baldies," the haircuts were meant to prevent ticks from getting tangled in my little brothers' hair. As Jessie gingerly climbed out of the pickup truck upon her arrival, she was shocked to see her two little grandsons running around with shiny skullcaps. "Oh, Sheila! Joe!" I remember Jessie gasping, as she staggered a few steps, swooning at the sight. After a nasty fight between my mother and father at the dinner table one night, she cried out, "Joe, how could you? After we've just said grace!" Many nights, Jessie would go to bed and, stung by Joe's cutting remarks, cry herself to sleep.

Despite my affection for Granny Jessie, it was a relief when the day came for her to return to Buenos Aires. Once her bags were packed, her perfume fortified to a cloying degree, Granny Jessie presented herself to the four of us, lined up at the telephone stand by the front door. One by one, Granny Jessie pressed a sticky lemon "sweetie" into our palms, then kissed us good-bye. Tearfully, she promised to "save her pennies" for her next visit. Before she climbed into the pickup with my father for her drive to the airport, Jessie clung to Sheila and both wept. Because, as my grandmother always made sure to tell us, she might die before we saw her again.

As much as my parents loved, even adored, each other in the beginning, their relationship suffered under the intense pressures of my mother's immigration and isolation from her family. Unlike immigrants who move to large cities where their nostalgia for home is satisfied by the food, rituals, and communities of their birth culture, my mother was a solitary exile in Oak Grove. Complicating things further, her ancestry was a thick tangle of cultural strands: Who was she, really? Drawn together when they first met by a shared American dream, Joe and Sheila's relationship foundered when it hit the ground, their love pulled apart by divergent backgrounds that acted like magnets to separate them.

The differences between them were on sharp display in the dissimilarities between my two sets of grandparents. My Pennsylvania grandmother Carroll lived in a railroad town in the Appalachian foothills. She scrubbed floors and labored over a stove, both for her family and as a live-in maid for her son's foster parents. My poetical Scottish-Argentine grandmother Attwell, on the other hand, had a gardener and a maid who cooked and cleaned. Minnie Carroll was a stalwart, modest woman who bore and raised nine children. Though marriage was central to her idea of a successful woman's life, all her adulthood Jessie Attwell voiced strong opinions on the importance of women's voting rights and access to birth control. Grandma Carroll was a buttoned-up, church-going, apron-clad servant to her family. Granny Attwell was a flirtatious, whimsical, liberal-minded romantic who smoked, styled her short hair in waves, read widely, believed in religious pluralism, quoted the Bengali poet Rabindranath Tagore, wore silk flapper dresses, and had a glamour shot taken of herself wrapped in an ivory satin stole as a gift to her father.

As different as Granny Attwell was from Grandmother Carroll, so were my two grandfathers worlds apart. The men in my father's line came from poverty and were among America's first migrant laborers. They wore overalls and caps pulled down over coarsened, lined faces, and labored on the greasy, dangerous bowels of train engines. The men in my mother's line were dapper, poetry-quoting, worldly, well-traveled men of culture and diplomacy. They paused for teatime in Argentine outdoor cafés, talked politics, presented papers, loved the ladies, and knew how to dance the waltz. If hard labor, tragedy, and physical self-sacrifice marked my father's side of the family, worldliness, intellect, statesmanship, and romantic idealism marked my mother's.

I am equally proud of the two family trees in which my life is rooted. And it is to my parents' credit that, when they fell in love, they looked past the differences in their backgrounds. After all, it is just that kind of meritocracy that America has strived to honor. To escape the limitations of birth, religion, and heritage was one reason why our ancestors crossed the ocean in the first place. Still, the differences between my two sets of grandparents would become the dividing line between my mother and father. The problem was, neither one of them knew it—because neither one lived in a culture that took the past or the effects of immigration into account as forces that shaped the present. Even if my parents did sometimes catch glimmers of the issues that divided them, they hadn't been given the tools to work with them.

One of their sillier ongoing arguments, for instance, revolved around the proper way to hold a knife. My father insisted that the well-mannered *American* diner cut the meat and then placed the knife down while switching the fork over to the right hand. My mother, however, upheld the *European* style of cutting one's meat and then forking the bite into one's mouth with the left hand, without putting down the knife. My siblings and I often used to wonder where my mother's social airs had come from. We knew she'd gone to an exclusive private school, but even that didn't seem to account for her aura of aristocracy.

We never realized that it had come directly down to her, through her father, from her well-connected Washingtonian forebears. But then, neither did she. Once when Granny Jessie was visiting, Sheila recalled, they'd been watching television. When a report came on about a politician in Washington, D.C., my grandmother turned to her and said, "That's where you're from." But, said my mother, "I had no idea what she meant."

My mother often suffered intense frustration over not being seen for her culturally complex background, which included being part American. This surfaced in what seemed at the time a very strange incident around my third year of elementary school. One afternoon, the ladies from a local chapter of Missouri's Daughters of the American Revolution paid a visit to my classroom. My teacher announced that they'd be picking one new member from each class. When I told my mother about this contest, I was surprised to see her bristle. Though membership in this odd-sounding organization meant nothing to me at the time, I could see that it meant a great deal to her. Yet how could I possibly qualify as an American "daughter," I recall wondering, even at that young age, when my mother was from Argentina?

When the women of the local DAR inevitably picked another girl instead of me, my mother took the news hard. "*You* should have been chosen!" she huffed, her chin high. But she could never really explain why I'd lost, or why it was so important to her that I should have been one of those daughters. Some fifty years later, in the midst of researching this book, I share with my mother the Revolutionary War patriot that I'd discovered in her background. "So," she replied, with a deep sigh, "I could have been in the DAR after all. I wonder if knowing that would have made me feel less different in this country."

My mother's immigration story is ironic in that it circles back around to the United States. But in its exaggerated example, it highlights the way immigration cuts off the psychological vein of our ancestry. It amplifies why all of us, at some deep level, identify so strongly with being an outsider—yet another familiar American theme. For don't we all have stored in the attic of our psyches immigration stories, mythologies, and histories that preceded our arrival to this land? Wasn't the American Revolution waged by immigrants, "boat people" with no green cards or visas fleeing oppression? And don't the branches on all our family trees, except those of the Native Americans, ultimately trace back somewhere else? All our relatives were once strangers in a new land—long-dead relatives who were shy and didn't know the customs, who hung in the back of store lines, and were beaten up or even killed if they took a "wrong" step, who dropped their heads in shame because their clothes were funny, or who felt humiliation because they couldn't make their thickly accented words understood.

It is this profoundly personal underside of immigration that rivets my attention. The public debate that focuses so obsessively on borders, fences, quotas, visas, illegal aliens, green cards, and language requirements adroitly deflects attention from the subjective ways immigration shapes us as individuals, and as a country: grief over the faraway shore that was never mourned; feelings of rootlessness and a sense of not belonging; confusion around cultural identity, both as individuals and as a country; and an essential loneliness.

The many disparate nationalities grouped together within our borders have, as well, placed enormous pressure on the American psyche. In order to maintain social cohesion without fragmentation, we've had to hold ourselves together through exaggerated, patriotic affirmations of our collective American identity. The same holds true for individuals struggling to forge a singular identity out of an inner melting pot of ethnicities. Some lop off their origins in favor of being purely American, while others never let America wholly into their hearts. As long as we see immigration through a purely legal lens, as long as we refuse to recognize the trauma caused by our split-off pasts, we will never begin to grasp the ongoing ancestral dramas playing out behind the scenes of our daily lives.

Amir Afkhami is a psychiatrist at George Washington University in Washington, D.C. "The immigration story in America," he tells me, "is an iconoclastic story of people coming to the New World and remaking their lives." In this "schoolhouse, rosy story" we've all been told, he says, "people who are downtrodden work their way out of political and economic oppression. Rising up the ladder of success, they better themselves and their children in the Promised Land."

Rimming this bright dream of immigration to America is the dark edge of loss and disappointment that is too often ignored, continues Afkhami. It is well documented, he notes, that among immigrants to the United States there is "a higher than normal rate of depression and psychiatric illness." For one thing, many immigrants arrive burdened by expectations of success from their home country. When new arrivals aren't able to meet that expectation, they can suffer a lot of psychic distress, such as depression or alcoholism, he says. Then there are the psychological effects caused by a disruption in family and community networks, and the loss of culture. Isolated and estranged, often forced to live in shelters or single-room occupancies, some immigrants endure multiple stresses that can lead to serious breakdowns. Added stressors include conflicts that can arise as traditional family behaviors collide with more liberal American customs.

Given all the psychological and legal obstacles around immigration, one might ask if the immigrant experience is still a worthy American ideal. When I put this question to Blaine Fowers, a psychologist at the University of Miami, he notes that the very thing that appears to divide us—the fractious clash and clang of cultures within our borders—can also work positively to keep democracy alive and vibrant. Engaging in the "rough and tumble" debate between opposing beliefs, Fowers argues, triggers dialogues that generate fresh perspectives. Even the very values that shape us as a nation—among them respect for the individual regardless of race, class, or creed—are the fruit of the immigrant experience. Rather than threatening our identity, immigration from this perspective becomes fundamental to our American identity.

It is in my conversation with noted Jungian analyst Edward Edinger, however, that I catch a glimpse of a transcendent, even spiritual, purpose to America's multicultural heritage. A scholar of America's underlying myths, Edinger explains to me that history has as its goal "unification, and that means political unification and psychological unification." In that regard, he tells me, America represents a kind of "advanced laboratory." We are, he says, "the one nation that on principle has turned itself into a microcosm of the world as a whole. We've got the most open borders of any nation in the world, and on principle we are a nation of immigrants from all over the world," with communities "all over the United States that represent every major ethnic and national entity in the whole world. So when something goes on in another country, there's a demonstration in front of the White House for that particular community."

This makes America, says Edinger, referencing Lincoln, "the last, best hope of the world. We really are, and if we don't make it, the world hasn't got a chance." But if we're able to integrate our cultural diversity into a unity without fragmenting from the pressure, then the world, he says, "has a model that makes it likely that it can make it, too." Edinger points to the nation's motto, *E Pluribus Unum*, or, "From the many, one" as words that exemplify our national struggle for unity. These words, he believes, speak also to the individual's struggle for wholeness. "The peace being sought among the diverse nationalities fighting and destroying each other," he says, mirrors the psychological process that goes on in an individual, when "a fragmented psyche that is made up of unconscious complexes—and that work against the conscious ego—can be progressively brought into a state of unification." In his view, the early colonists' journey toward the Promised Land of the New World represents the collective archetype of the journey toward individual development and wholeness both individuals and nations aspire to achieve.

Edinger's insights make me think that the current of something much larger was moving through my parents' marriage, as well as my own compulsion to retrieve the lost bits and pieces of my family past. Sorting through my own immigrant story, I begin to feel whole, put right, and put together. Ill-fitting puzzle pieces of ethnic identity begin to assume an *American* pattern. For even the notion that I am a creative composite of all the cultures that make up my identity, points out Benjamin Sells, is itself quintessentially American.

And then there are my ancestors who, once lost, are now found. In dream after dream as I work on this section, they come forth to meet me. One night, I dream that I am walking through a rural landscape, when the earth opens to reveal a valley filled with early American settlers. Two women dressed in plain eighteenth-century clothes step out of the crowd; they have been assigned to me, the dream communicates, as guides. In yet another dream, I open the palm of my hand to find an antique silver pocket watch engraved with the initials "E. D.": my English forebear, Edward Dyer, handing me an emblem of the "time" he lived in.

Then there is the dream in which I discover a pair of women's navy bell-bottoms in my closet: a gift of courage in feminine clothing, as I interpret it, from all those dauntless naval officers in my line. Another night, I open the door of a room that has been closed for over a hundred years; in it, my American-Argentine great-grandparents Margarita and Juan Attwell lie in a four-poster bed. Rising up from their long sleep, my great-grandmother places an exquisite diamond necklace around my neck; going into his closet, my great-grandfather brings out a navy medal and puts it in my palm, placing his hand over mine—gifts that convey their gratitude for being found.

In a final, powerful dream I descend far below ground. I enter a cave and sit before an ancient, dark-skinned man dressed in a brilliantly colored robe. Gesturing passionately, he exhorts me to teach my children about their ancestral past. I stare into his weathered face and his wide eyes transform into ancient maps of the world. Waking up, I wonder: Was this an encounter with the archetype of History? Learning my mother's own immigration story has in fact located me along the timeline of world history as it unfolded through the lives of my ancestors.

This foray into my distant past culminates with a pilgrimage to the graves of my Washingtonian great-great-grandparents, Mary Margaret Dyer and Jesse Van Ness Huyck. It has taken months of research to find them, and when the manager of Mount Olivet Cemetery calls to tell me he's finally located my ancestors' plot, I am charged with anticipation. Now that these burial sites marked on my family tree have been proven to exist, I cannot wait one more day to see them. Barely stopping to comb my hair and grab my camera, I race outside to my car. Less than an hour later, I arrive at the cemetery, located in rolling green hills on the outskirts of the city. The manager, who has paged through the place's crumbling records on my behalf, walks outside to greet me. He leads me among the graves and chats pleasantly about the capital's oldest cemetery, where the wealthy, the politically distinguished, the ordinary, and the outcast—who once lay in unmarked graves in the potter's field, he points out—are buried.

And then, on the crest of a small knoll overlooking Washington, there it is: the simple, weathered white cross that marks the burial spot my great-great-grandparents share. It is an unremarkable grave. Nevertheless, the encounter strikes hard, and my chest tightens with feeling. I receive another shock of surprise when, close by, I discover the grave of Mary Margaret's father, my thrice-great grandfather Edward Dyer, Senate Sergeant-at-Arms, whose pocket watch has come down to me in my dreams. His resting spot is distinguished by a worn stone replica of the Washington monument and is over one hundred and fifty years old. Seeing that I am struggling with emotion, the manager politely leaves me alone with my long-departed family. Having never visited the grave of a relative before—not once!—I become momentarily confused. What is the proper protocol? Should I have brought flowers or should I say a prayer?

Then, instinctively, I know what to do. Sinking onto the summer-warmed ground beneath the cloudless sky, I hug my knees and gratefully absorb the peace welling up from below, arising as if in recognition that here, after a century and more, sits a family member come home. As I rest in companionable silence with my forebears, whose stories I am just coming to know, something clicks into place—the sweetness of being loved by the old ones, and the feeling, carried on behalf of a long chain of wandering ancestors and now laid to rest, of a circle closed, and of belonging.

My father, as he was dying, knew nothing of Jung, or of such sweeping concepts as world unification. Until late in life, he had little interest in his own ancestry, much less Sheila's. But in marrying my mother, I see now, Joe had sought to join his personal life with the larger world. He hadn't entirely succeeded in this; it was an ideal that had been much bigger than him. But in his attempt to make peace with my mother in the last days of his life, he was trying to right both an old wrong and an inner imbalance. I like to think that this was an expression of the better American spirit working in him—trying to make whole, equal, and fair all the disparate parts of his life.

Master Commandant John Cassin, Sheila's fourth great-grandfather, served as a private under George Washington at the Battle of Trenton during the Revolutionary War. Later he became second-in command at the Washington Navy Yard; during the War of 1812 he commanded naval forces in the protection of Philadelphia, and was also commanding officer of the Norfolk Navy Yard and the Charleston Navy Yard.

Edward Dyer, Sheila's second great-grandfather, was fifth Senate Sergeant-at-Arms in the administration of President John Tyler. He died in office in 1845.

Mary Margaret Dyer Huyck, Sheila's great-grandmother, was a native of Washington, D.C., the daughter of Edward Dyer and Henrietta Tarbell Dyer Boone, and the wife of Jesse Van Ness Huyck.

Jesse Van Ness Huyck, Sheila's great-grandfather and Mary Margaret Dyer's husband, arrived in Washington, D.C. during the Civil War. He established one of the city's earliest real estate offices around the corner from the White House, and became a prominent businessman with a seat on the Washington Stock Exchange.

Margaret Estelle Huyck, Sheila's grandmother, as a young woman in Washington D.C. The oldest daughter of Mary Margaret Dyer and Jesse Van Ness Huyck, Margaret traveled abroad and enjoyed a socially vibrant life in the city's political and cultural circles. After a courtship, she married Argentine Navy officer Lt. Juan Sinclair Attwell.

Lt. Juan Sinclair Attwell, Sheila's grandfather, was a third-generation Argentine of Scottish descent who, like his father and grandfather before him, served in the Argentine Navy. In 1887 he was appointed Naval attaché to Washington, D.C., where he met Margaret Estelle Huyck at a diplomat's ball, married her, and, after some years abroad, moved to Buenos Aires.

LEFT: **John B. Feser,** middle row, far left. Joe's maternal grandfather was born in Germany and emigrated to Altoona, Pennsylvania in 1880. The photo is dated 1895, "Property of Mrs. George F. Carroll, and is labeled the "Seat Gang, 2nd floor of the 'Trimming Shop' at the Altoona Car Shops."

RIGHT: **"Grosmutter" Feser,** Joe's maternal grandmother, was also born in Germany before emigrating to the U.S. She helped her daughter and Joe's mother, Hermione Carroll, to raise nine children.

ABOVE: **George Fields Carroll,** Joe's father. Like his Irish immigrant father, who had been a blacksmith, George worked for the Pennsylvania Railroad as a mechanic, until he became bedridden from a stroke during the Depression. He died on Christmas Day, 1935.

SECOND LEFT: **The Altoona Carroll house** where Joe and his two sisters and six brothers were born is located at the foothills of the Allegheny Mountains overlooking Altoona. Joe lived there until the age of 14. It remains in the Carroll family, and looks almost the same today as it did nearly a century ago.

THIRD LEFT: **Pennsylvania Railroad.** A vintage photo of the railroad laborers that belonged to Joe's mother, Hermione Carroll.

ABOVE: **George F. Carroll** with three of his children, Helen, Dorothy, and Jim.

RIGHT: **The Carroll brothers in uniform around Mother Carroll**. This photo was put together to celebrate Mother Carroll's sons, who, with one exception, all served during World War II. From the top right to the bottom: George Carroll (in the only non-military photo, George is wearing his Altoona bus driver's cap, as he was too old to be drafted during World War II), Gene, Bob, and, at the bottom, Joe. From the bottom left to the top: Dick, Paul, and Jim.

BELOW: **Joe with four of his brothers**. This undated photo is likely a photo of one of my father's rare visits back home. After his mother died in 1959, when he was 37, he never went home again. Top row, from left to right: George, Paul, and Joe. Bottom row, left to right: Jim and Gene.

TOP RIGHT: **Joe**, seated, and his younger brother Gene as teenagers in Altoona.

ABOVE: **Joe at the Altoona Hunt Club**. Dr. and Mrs. Glover were members, and Joe learned how to jump horses and "ride to the hunt."

TOP LEFT: **Dr. Pellman and Dorothy Glover**, Joe's foster parents. The wealthy couple took my father in after his father died. They are seated before the massive fireplace in their elegant home, along with their beloved bulldog, Jiggs.

ABOVE: **Joe's Altoona High School** graduation photo.

CENTER LEFT: **Fiona and Sheila Attwell** in Buenos Aires. This photo of my mother (on the right) with her older sister Fiona was taken shortly before they each married, and began lives and families of their own.

ABOVE: **Sheila with friends on the Tigre River**. This photo was also inscribed on the back "the day I met dad."

CENTER RIGHT: **Sheila and her girlfriend**, sunning, "the day after I met dad."

TOP ROW LEFT: **John (Juan) Sinclair Attwell**, Sheila's father. A fourth-generation Argentine, Sinclair was the son of American-born Margaret (Marguerita) Huyck Attwell and Lt. Juan Sinclair Attwell.

TOP ROW CENTER: **Jessie Donaldson Attwell**, Sheila's mother. Born in Scotland, Jessie emigrated with her parents and two sisters to Buenos Argentina in 1915, during World War I, where later she met and married John Sinclair Attwell.

TOP ROW RIGHT. **Sheila on "the day I met dad."** These are the words inscribed by my mother on the back of this photo. It was taken during my parents' fateful meeting, while each were vacationing with friends at the Paraná delta.

TOP LEFT: **Joe and Sheila's Altoona wedding**. The afternoon ceremony on September 6, 1948 was held at the home of Dr. and Mrs. Glover.

ABOVE: **Joe and Sheila** cut their wedding cake.

LEFT: **Joe on the Mediterranean shore in Israel**. After their wedding, Joe and Sheila moved to Tel Aviv, Israel, where Joe started a new job flying for Israel's first airline, El Al.

BELOW: **Sheila in Israel**, visiting ruins by the Mediterranean.

TOP LEFT: **Joe and Sheila** with Israel's first airline, El Al. They are standing on the tarmac of Tel Aviv Airport in front of one of El Al's first planes.

MIDDLE LEFT: **Joe sailing on the Tigre River** with his buddies in Argentina.

BOTTOM LEFT: **Joe goofing around with fellow El Al pilot**. There was a spirit of camaraderie among the El Al crews, as they knew they were part of Israel's new beginning as a country.

TOP RIGHT: **Joe in his TWA uniform**, smoking a cigarette. This photo was taken just after Joe and Sheila's move to the farm, and just before he was to depart on one of his early trips for TWA.

MIDDLE RIGHT: **Joe relaxing in Tel Aviv, Israel**.

BOTTOM RIGHT: **Joe drinking beer** in Israel.

TOP LEFT: **Joe by the roadside** in front of a cornfield. This photo was taken on Joe and Sheila's cross-country drive from Altoona to Kansas City, where my father had taken a new job as a flight engineer with TWA.

TOP RIGHT: **Sheila by the roadside** in front of a cornfield. She is pregnant with her first child, Pellman.

LEFT: **Main Street, Oak Grove, Missouri** (undated photo). Our farm was located three miles outside the town.

BOTTOM: **"Shalom Acres"** Carroll farm in the early days.

VI

Israel on the Missouri

This hour I rode the sky like a god, but after it was over, how glad I would be to go back to earth and live among men, to feel the soil under my feet and to be smaller than the mountains and the trees.—**Charles Lindbergh**, *The Wartime Journals of Charles A. Lindbergh*

IT WAS A SLOW day for dying. Joe was stretched out in his La-Z-Boy, stilled into sleep by morphine. Through the drapes, the Texas sun was slanting toward late afternoon. Lulled by the silky silence, I settled into a reverie. The sight of my father's exhausted face, his ill body slumped over, stirs my heart. Joe is a proud man, and he wouldn't want me to feel sorry for him. Still, I can't help growing anxious. How easy it would be, I think, if my father could just slip from life into death. Escaping the heavy confines of earth, as he'd always done, for the lighter spheres. Perhaps that was the better way for an aviator to die. Not dust to dust, but air to air.

But Memory was not finished with Joe. There were yet more paths into the past for him to walk. Even as he slept, the process of reflection that had been midwifed in him by his hospice guides continued to work. His eyelids flickered, and wordless sounds escaped from his mouth. Dreams (of the past?) rippled over his weathered face. Suddenly, Joe's eyes flew open, sharp blue and fastened on my watchful gaze. He had ventured backward, I am about to learn, to the Missouri farm of my childhood.

"Old Mr. Shelby. Old Mr. Shelby. Just a handshake, just a handshake." The memory must have been a powerful one, as my father's head began to nod back and forth. The swollen fingers of his large, pale hands trembled in his lap as if he were reliving that fateful clasp. Mr. Shelby, a local merchant of few words and gray eyes, had sold him his first one hundred acres of Midwestern land.

"I didn't have all the money for the down payment, couldn't even borrow the mortgage from the bank," Joe continued, speaking of a time some forty-five years ago. "So old man Shelby carried it on a handshake. Said he knew I'd pay him, said I had a nice young family, and that I could pay it over time, when I could afford it. Didn't even draw up a contract until later. Your mother and I were new to town, but he liked us. Not like people do business these days."

I absorbed this news with disbelief. Financial deals done in America on a handshake? Pay later, with no written contract, no legal counsel? Not in the country where I lived, where home mortgages were complex financial transactions involving real estate agents, investment managers, and bankers. It was almost as if he were talking about a different century altogether.

But my father was speaking again. I leaned in closely, as if hearing tales of a land long vanished. "Do you believe it? The townspeople were always so good to me. Remember old Tom, who ran the grain elevator? At harvesttime, I used to bring him my wheat to take to market. But if I didn't have the money, he'd let me pay him later, when I could. Same with Frank, who ran the gas station. If the tractors and trucks needed a fill-up, he'd say, 'Don't worry about it, Joe. Just pay me when you can.'"

Joe's weakened voice was beginning to give out. As he started to cough, I encouraged him to rest for a while. But my father was still in the grip of his story. He cleared his throat and began to speak again. His face took on a defenseless look, and his lumpy, hangdog jowls sagged lower. His next words surprised me.

"What did you think of the farm?" he asked tentatively. His shyness took me by surprise. "Are you glad you grew up there? Not too many people had the kind of childhood your mother and I gave you . . . the cows, the horses . . . the wheat and alfalfa fields." Joe's face watched mine intently.

An uncomfortable silence followed my father's words. He'd asked such a simple question, and yet it had provoked in me an uprush of strong feelings. Had I liked growing up on the farm? The real answer was a very conflicted no and yes. The isolation had at times made me feel trapped. The claustrophobic confines of the town where we'd gone to school had pressed in on me. At home, I'd felt enclosed in a hothouse emotional atmosphere freighted with continual family upheavals.

But I'd also loved the land as some might love a grandparent, or even a holy being. Where my parents had failed to sustain me, I'd felt the deep nourishing of nature's rhythms grow me into a human being. I'd also, in middle age, come to appreciate the virtues of an American small town, and the long-lasting friendships I'd formed, as if out of the Missouri earth. And I'd come to value my encounters those long years ago with a dying breed: those slow-spoken American farmers with their generous knowledge of the earth grounded in centuries gone by.

I gauged my response carefully. I felt self-conscious, and careful of causing my father hurt. More than anything, I wanted things to end on a good note. "Sometimes, I wished I'd lived in a big city," I said, aiming for gentle honesty. "But I did love the farm. Thank you, Dad. It was a different and interesting childhood. You gave me things I haven't been able to give my own children." I wished the words hadn't been so hard to say, yet they felt right and true.

Joe grunted in satisfaction. His glance shifted from my face to the unseen dimension enveloping him. Once more, his eyes grew unfocused as he peered again into his past. "Boy, did I love farming," he said. "Loved flying, too, but hoo, boy—farming was . . . was . . . I don't know." His words faltered to a stop, then started up again. "Old Ollie Boop," he said, his voice resuming. "Old Ollie taught me everything."

"Who was Ollie Boop?" I asked, curious about anyone with such a name.

"Old Ollie worked on Dr. Glover's farm, outside Altoona," explained Joe. "He taught me all about farming. About tractors, and planting crops, and farm animals. How to grow a crop, fertilize it, and bring it in. Oh, Ollie was a good family man, a good farmer, he was." Joe paused, his eyes widening, as if startled by a new thought. "Damn, I loved farming, and I loved flying," he repeated. "But which one did I love the best? Was I a farmer, or a flight engineer? I'd like to know that before I die."

Growing up with a father whose life had swung on an erratic hinge between earth and sky, between a receding nineteenth-century world and the modern age, I, too, would have liked to have known the answer to that question.

DOWN TO EARTH

It seems fitting that the land where my father first sought to bring his roaming spirit to ground lay at the heart of the American continent. St. Louis, Missouri, was where Joe had learned to fly. The small town of Oak Grove, twenty-eight miles east of Kansas City along I-70, was where he would put down roots as a farmer and a father.

Flying west from Washington, D.C., on a clear day, a person can look down and mark the change in landscape as the long, thick band of the Alleghenies falls off abruptly. Rolling down from these steep, dense ridges, the land fans outward. Here begins that middle western region of the United States where herds of buffalo once grazed among rippling grasses. Set in the center of this part of America is the state of Missouri. As far back as ten thousand years, the Mississippian Indians, as well as the Osage, Shawnee, Kansas, and Missouri nations, spread out in settlements. In his version of the ballad "Shenandoah," Bob Dylan sang of the "big, wide Missouri." The folk singer Bob Dyer also sang of the "river of the big canoes" and "a muddy river wild and free." Others have called it "Big Muddy" and "Dark River" for its high silt content. To me, it resembles a chocolate ribbon.

In 1682, a French explorer named René-Robert Cavelier, Sieur de La Salle, immediately claimed the Kansas City area for Louis XIV. French and Canadian fur trappers soon followed, trading with the Indians along the river. In 1803, Thomas Jefferson conducted a real estate deal with Napoleon Bonaparte, famously called the Louisiana Purchase, and it included the Missouri region. To know better the new territory for which he'd paid $15 million, Jefferson sent Captain Meriwether Lewis and Second Lieutenant William Clark on an expedition that would eventually reach the Pacific Ocean. In 1804, the explorers camped on the massive limestone bluffs overlooking the Missouri. By the 1840s and 1850s, the river settlement had turned into a frontier town outfitting the steady stream of settlers headed west for gold and land. Indians, buffalo hunters, Mexicans with $100,000 in silver coins, and mule drivers with blacksnake whips, write the authors of *Kansas City*, filled the saloons, steamboat landings, and dusty streets. It was here, at the "wild, western edge of Missouri," that metropolitan Kansas City would one day be developed.

Missouri's stolid nature and its reputation as the fixed point of the country belied the state's role as a kind of turnstile for America. If in our national mythology the road always leads west, then that road passes through the gateway of Missouri. Today, St. Louis's soaring silver arc bears testament to the Santa Fe, Oklahoma, California, and Oregon trails that once originated in eastern Missouri. The author Wallace Stegner described the massive exodus that flowed across the continent in these evocative words:

> Insofar as the West was a civilization at all between the time of Lewis and Clark's explorations and about 1870, it was largely a civilization in motion, driven by dreams. . . . With a continent to take over and Manifest Destiny to goad us, we could not have avoided being footloose. The initial act of emigration from Europe, an act of extreme, deliberate disaffiliation, was the beginning of a national habit. It should not be denied, either, that being footloose has always exhilarated us. It is associated in our minds with escape from history and oppression and law and irksome obligations, with absolute freedom. (From *Where the Bluebird Sings by the Lemonade Springs*)

Some among the adventurers roaming across the Missouri plains put down roots and stayed. These were the homesteaders who cleared the land, raised up barns, brought in livestock, and planted fields of grain. Their efforts transformed a prairie outpost into the bustling "capital of cow towns," as it was called, whose beef would one day be praised around the world. "Here stands a city built o' bread and beef," wrote the poet C. L. Edson.

Most of us are used to thinking of America as having only one kind of frontier, but as the historian David Courtwright has noted, young America was notable for having not one, but two. Type-I frontiers, for instance, were based on farming and were located in fertile regions. As Courtwright explains, "They attracted farm families, had relatively even numbers of men and women . . . many children, and high birthrates." Indian conflicts aside, he writes, these settlements were "permanent and peaceful," where most men were married and vice was limited. Type-II frontiers, on the other hand, continues Courtwright, were of an altogether different character. These were the movable economies based on "ranching, mining, lumbering, or other forms of extraction." High numbers of transient, single male laborers, with a low ratio of women and scarce numbers of children, populated these economies. Socially and demographically, at least, early twentieth-century aviation was a Type-II frontier.

Both types of frontiers would have a role in shaping the destiny of Missouri. As much as the pristine prairies had given rise to agriculture, so, too, would these flat lands eventually attract aviation. Missouri's landlocked position and its relatively level topography practically begged to be used as a launching pad for flight. The big sky and wide-open runways of land beneath it seemed specially designed for landings and takeoffs. In this way, the mythic locus of air travel lay deep in the heart of Missouri before the first airport was ever built. In Norman Rockwell's painting *Kansas City Spirit*, a muscular man with his shirtsleeves rolled up stands among skyscrapers, cattle pens, and sheaves of grain. His gaze, however, is directed to the airplane sailing through the blue skies behind his right shoulder. A person can grow up loving the Missouri land, as I did, and yet still look both east and west, north and south, and dream of far horizons.

For all these reasons, it made sense that Kansas City would become the location for the headquarters of America's iconic airline, TWA. The city's centrality, note authors Karash and Montgomery in *TWA*, had made it a hub for wagon trains, railroads, and trucks passing through. In the 1920s, city officials had lobbied hard to win the coveted position for their metropolis as a halfway point for flights across the country. In August 1927, fresh from his victorious solo voyage across the Atlantic, Charles Lindbergh had dedicated a muddy field on the banks of the Missouri as the site of the future municipal airport. Crowds ten thousand strong came out to cheer America's golden boy of the airy heights. Soon, enormous hangars and overhaul bases rivaling Altoona's giant train workshops began to grow up on the city's outskirts. Three years later, the fledgling airline, Transcontinental & Western Air, or T&WA, launched its first coast-to-coast passenger service—with Kansas City as the overnight stop. As a highly paid consultant, Charles Lindbergh had lent his name to the airline, which also became known as the "Lindbergh Line" and "The Airline Run By Fliers." When it was time for the airline to choose a home base, Lindbergh cast the deciding vote in favor of Kansas City.

SHALOM ACRES

According to his logbook, my father took his final flight for El Al in the last week of July, 1951. Departing from New York, where he was staying with my mother, he flew to Gander, Newfoundland; London; and Keflavik, Iceland, before returning on August 1 to New York. It would be his last working international flight for some years.

After loading their new convertible, Joe and Sheila drove cross-country to Kansas City. Along the way, they stopped by the roadside to snap photos of each other. In one, a very pregnant, smiling Sheila, looking like some modern-day fertility goddess, stands before a cornfield. Row upon row of tall, golden stalks rise behind her. In his photo, my father looks similarly content, basking in the sun and the field's fertile promise. Of all the photos of my father, this is my favorite; something in his relaxed smile reflects the kind of rare peace so difficult for him to attain. As they drove onto the bridge in St. Louis that would take them across the Missouri River, the spirit of the West blew into my mother and she impulsively stood up, flung her arms wide, and shouted, "I'm crossing the wide Missouri!"

Arriving in Kansas City, Joe and Sheila took a room at the Rosemont Hotel. My father began training for his new job as a flight engineer for the red-lettered airline, now called TWA. Sheila, eight months pregnant, rested, awaiting the arrival of their first child. Early on the morning of November 4, during the first snowfall of the year, I entered the world.

Although I took my place in a long line of dream-seekers, I was nonetheless christened with a name that yoked me to my father's fate: Pellman Sharon Carroll. Pellman, of course, was the first name of my father's foster father, Dr. Pellman Glover. It was to prove a name few had heard of and even fewer could pronounce: Pinnamin, Pullman, and schoolteachers who asked me at the start of each year "Are you sure your name isn't Carol Pellman?" were among the teasing and confused reactions. But it wasn't the name that would come to bother me so much as its provenance. Aside from the fact that it was a man's name, being called Pellman felt like a sacrificial fee offered to a stranger to whom my father felt indebted. Obligation, not love, lay behind this bond to the foster parent my father still referred to as "Dr. Glover."

Then there was Sharon, my middle name. This was not the American version of that name. Rather, it was Jewish, pronounced Sha*ron*, after the valley where I'd been conceived. I liked this name a little better than Pellman. At least it contained my parents' romance, as well as religious history and a psalm-like resonance. The gesture, I like to think, linked me to my parents' participation in a new world that was trying to move beyond religious prejudice—a cause that would one day inspire my own life. Still, as the Italian Jungian analyst Luigi Zoja muses, there was "some kind of myth-making process at work between you and your father." My father named me, a girl, after the foster father with whom he had a complex relationship, Zoja notes. Now I, in return, have renamed him Icarus.

The names our parents give us are interesting clues to the pieces of psychological history they pass along to us. A family name links us to a favored relative; names from outside a family tradition may say something about those attributes or cultural links important to them. Even an ordinary name ties us to the conventions of society, overshadowing the infant's potentially unique self. Maybe this is the source of a baby's cries, as, in its first hours, it feels the weight of the human condition already heavy on its tiny shoulders.

Certainly, I was not a peaceful infant. My mother, who was only twenty-two at the time, recalls that I cried inconsolably. Sitting alone with me in the Rosemont Hotel while my father was away being trained for his new job, Sheila was unable to comfort me—or herself. As I bawled without stopping so she, too, wailed beside me. Heartbroken for her father, I imagine, who'd just died, and whose funeral she'd been unable to attend; lonely for the support of her faraway Argentine family; and, though she never said so, for the freewheeling, traveling lifestyle my birth had ended.

Many years later, my analyst would nod her head sadly over this birth story I'd coaxed from my mother. Nona felt for my immigrant mother's isolation in a new country. She also felt for the infantile fears that could not be soothed away in me, and for the fragile first bond between mother and daughter. Sheila herself had been handed off to her Scottish grandmother and other relatives as a newborn; the period of early infancy for each of her four children would never prove easy for her. This was something she had to suffer in silent abandonment, as these were the days before the term "postpartum depression" had come into use.

A short eighteen months after my birth, my Irish-named sister Colleen was born. Blonde, fair, curly-haired Neen, as Dad called her, was given the middle name of Fiona, after my aunt. By then, my parents had rented a small house in Raytown, a suburb of Kansas City. Two years later, after the birth of my brother, Steven Joseph, my parents bought the farm. "Oh, don't get me wrong," my mother tells me today. "Your father loved you girls. But when your brother was born, he had his son." Yet one more son, John Donaldson Carroll, whose names linked him back to my mother's family, would be born in 1957.

My parents moved to the farm in 1955. All across the country, suburbs of tract houses were springing up like mushrooms after the rain. My father's brothers were living and raising their children in them: among them Gene, in Hazlett, New Jersey; and Paul, in Tallahassee, Florida.

But not my parents. Driven by his dream of being both a flier and farmer, Joe turned his sights in the opposite direction, the countryside. My mother, born into a generation where the wife followed the husband, had no choice except to go where my father led her. Yet Sheila also loved the land. As a girl, she'd dreamed of marrying a rancher and living on an *estancia* in the Argentine pampas. When my father drove her to Oak Grove and showed her the farm he'd picked out for his growing family, my mother stood quietly, taking in her surroundings.

All her life, when faced with moving into a new house or apartment, my mother had cultivated the habit of measuring the psychic mood of a place. This sensitivity to the invisible was something she'd picked up from her Scottish mother, who believed in fairies, as well as the Spanish *curandero* (or traditional healer) who'd worked for her neighbor as a gardener, and who had befriended her as a young child. As my mother would tell me later, the *curandero*, seeing some of his gifts in her, had intended to train her in his arts until her marriage to Joe cut off that potential path. Now, Sheila checked her canny instincts once again. Her glance took in the half-century-old two-story house with the black shutters, the wide front porch, the scruffy patches of grass, and the thick giant of an oak tree that stood in the front yard. The house itself was perched on top of a hill; some said it was the highest point in the county. A bright green valley checkered with neatly squared, fenced-in fields spread down and around it in tiers, like a full, quilted skirt. It was early summer; the sky overhead was a clear, pale blue.

"I can live in that old house," Sheila said, as she turned to her husband. Her words may have been tinged with psychic faith. But they also came out of that broad, brave streak that shot through my mother's character. For this was no easy dwelling: it had a pump in the sink, a wood-burning stove in the living room, and an outhouse for a bathroom. A steep spiral staircase, unsuitable for small children, joined the first floor to the second. Outside, the wire-enclosed yard was mostly dirt. The one hundred acres of farmland had been "worked" before, as they said in those days, but now it lay uncultivated. Twenty acres surrounded the house; the remaining eighty lay down a long dirt driveway and across a blacktop road. Three dilapidated, paint-scraped barns came with the property: one beside the house, and two across the road.

My mother's only stipulation was that she would not move to the farm with three children under four until there was a bathroom and running water. This was hardly an obstacle to my father. Delighted to have my mother's support and brimming with enthusiasm to get started on his new project, Joe began negotiations with the owner, old Mr. Shelby. Soon the farm, with its fallow pastures, crumbling barns, and family of trees, belonged to the Carrolls.

Joe and Sheila could not have chosen a more traditional American setting in which to raise their family. But the impressions of their travels were still with them. Searching for a name, they christened their farm "Shalom Acres," from the Jewish word for peace. It was a noble ideal, inspired by their witness to the historic birth of Israel. But giving one hundred acres of Midwestern land in the middle of nowhere a Hebrew name—with no actual Jews within the town limits—was telling. Even from my father's first handshake with Mr. Shelby, he was never really wholly of the farm. At heart, he still belonged more to the world at large than to this plot of earth under the Missouri sun.

At first, recalls Sheila, neither she nor my father gave "a minute's thought to the town, or to what was going on there. We didn't pay any attention to it. It was less like moving to Oak Grove, and more like moving to the countryside." As long as the town had the one thing that really mattered to my mother—a library—she knew she'd be fine. "Once a week I'd go to the grocery store, then to the library to get books, and, last, to Sally Wilson's Florist Shop, where I would spend my last dollar on flowers," she recalls.

Growing up, I always sensed that my family didn't quite fit in. Taking my questions to my father once, he told me that though the idea had been to raise us in Oak Grove, we weren't really supposed to be part of it, but on the outside of things. He'd wanted to raise his kids with the small-town values of decency, honesty, and hard work, Joe had said. But at the same time, he'd wanted us to be well-traveled sophisticates.

After I left home, I took the same question to my mother. What had motivated her and my father, I wondered, to move to a place three miles outside a bare, one-stoplight town with no movie theaters or even a hint of urban culture or architecture? After all, Sheila was from a world city rich with art, music, and a swirl of nationalities. Even Altoona, with its grand hotel, amusement parks, profusion of faiths, and whistle-stop railroad culture, had seemed worldly in comparison. My mother didn't even pause at the question. The farm, she said, had been her "Tara," referring to the Civil War plantation in *Gone with the Wind*.

There can be no getting around the fact that my parents were romantics who took a paintbrush to their world, illustrating it in a slapdash style of bold and contrasting colors. Their habit of infusing everything around them with imagination, even a plain place like Oak Grove, made everyday life, well, much more than ordinary. In this, as with other aspects of their lives, however, my parents were living out another American trope: that of the land as the "land of our dreams." Like those westward-headed pioneers before them, my parents projected their personal reveries and hopes onto the farm as if it could be molded to their desires. "Nature is always somehow human-made, if not directly with our hands, certainly with our minds," James Hillman writes in his book, *Beauty Without Nature*. "Imagination is perpetually creating nature. . . . There is not a thing called nature, there's an idea called nature."

And if America is also an idea, as many have argued, then the land is where those beliefs come to ground. Chief among the great myths projected onto our vast continent is freedom. The cowboy on his horse would fade to nothing without the majesty of the great spaces of the open west. Independence and self-sufficiency are deep-rooted in images of fields of waving grain. Freedom ranges "from the mountains to the prairies," as the anthem goes. It was the search for free land that drove many of the earliest settlers to arrive here in the first place. Either the soil of their homelands had been stripped by centuries of over-farming, or it was held by the grip of the aristocracy.

This was the case with the French immigrant J. Hector St. John de Crèvecoeur, who in the 1760s settled on a 250-acre farm in Orange Country, New York. In *Letters from an American Farmer*, he describes his newfound country as "this great American asylum" where "the poor of Europe have by some means met together." Can a country be called one's homeland, de Crèvecoeur wonders, "that had no bread for him, whose fields procured him no harvest, who met with nothing but the frowns of the rich, the severity of the laws, with jails and punishments, who owned not a single foot of the extensive surface of this planet? No!" Through de Crèvecoeur's eyes, the new land of America conferred upon each owner unparalleled liberty: "Here are no aristocratical families, no courts, no kings, no bishops, no ecclesiastical dominion," he writes. "Some few towns excepted, we are all tillers of the earth. . . . We are all animated with the spirit of an industry which is unfettered and unrestrained, because each person works for himself. . . . We have no princes for whom we toil, starve, and bleed; we are the most perfect society now existing in the world. Here man is free as he ought to be."

The Puritans, on the other hand, saw their new land through a slightly different lens. For them, the rocky shores of Plymouth offered a place to practice their religion free from oppression. Much like my parents, they transferred their vision of America as a "New Jerusalem" to the land itself. America was seen as a kind of paradise on Earth, a place where sinners could be reborn. The essence of colonial Puritan belief, writes historian Sacvan Bercovitch in *The Puritan Origins of the American Self*, lay in the conviction that the New World, like Canaan of old, belonged wholly to God's work of redemption.

Yet another potent idea settling early America was that of the land as a horn of plentiful abundance and material wealth. This was the mindset brought to the green shores of Maryland and Virginia by those Europeans Bercovitch describes in the wonderfully lush phrase as "lover settlers." To these paramours, the land was feminine in its allure, all-giving in its fertility. Through their eyes, writes Bercovitch, quoting from their writings, the land was both "fairest of nymphs," as well as "nourishing mother" and "undefiled virgin." In this paradise, as Bercovitch quotes again, "the deer were tamer and more plentiful than prostitutes in London; the unexplored interior beckoned before the 'ravished' planter like so many 'Beauties of naked Nature.'"

Lovely though these metaphors sounded, there was a menacing undertone that, Bercovitch notes, foretold "the later concept of the rape of the land." In fact, many of the early settlers would be stirred to revulsion by nature—and the native civilizations that lived here—as cruel, heathen, and bestial. "Conflict with the Indians defined one boundary of the American identity: though we were a people of 'the wilderness,' we were *not* savages," writes historian Richard Slotkin in *Gunfighter Nation*. Indeed, part of the problem of America from its inception, James Hillman tells me, "is that the natives, as well as the slaves, represented the repressed body. I suspect that a great deal of the projection upon the natives had to do with the fear of the body and the fear of eros. I don't mean sexuality. I mean their whole way of living."

Violently driving the native peoples from their tribal lands, Americans continued to seed the continent they'd seized with their own idealistic principles. During the eighteenth century, notes historian Gary Wills in *Cincinnatus*, Roman myths were revived to "glorify agriculture." The Founding Fathers were to place great virtue in the rural life, especially as an antidote to political power and the temptations of city life. Thomas Jefferson, John Adams, and George Washington were all deeply devoted to their respective agricultural estates, to which they each retired after their careers. Farming technique was George Washington's "principle intellectual discipline," wrote Wills, and "his favorite topic of conversation. . . . His friends knew that the way to please him was to send him new seeds, or cuttings or animal breeds." At heart, notes historian David McCullough in *John Adams*, both Jefferson and Adams "were countrymen, farmers, with an avid interest in soils, tillage, climate, and 'improvements.'"

As a girl, I had my own fantasies about the farm where we lived. These were not the airy dreams of nature as some lost paradise found. No. Sanity was what I found in the fields and forests where I grew up.

Oh, there were times when I followed in my parents' footsteps, investing the rural world around me with vivid imaginings. And there were pockets of nature that deeply frightened me—mostly where my father cast his shadow. But more than anything, nature was for me a sensible and stabilizing place that offered a refuge from the wild human drama of my family life. When I stepped outside the back door through the mudroom with its beer keg refrigerator, the touch of earth on my bare feet offered immediate reassurance. The smells, sounds, and sights that wrapped me in their embrace evened my seesaw emotions. The steady solar clock of the rising and setting sun, the hills with their unchanging faces that mirrored each day, offered precious regularity against my father's constant coming and going. Earth's gravity kept me in place and never failed to heal.

The farm I grew up on still stands much as it did over fifty years ago when I first lived there. But because so many small American farms have fallen beneath the scythe of big agriculture, I feel a duty to record it as I knew it then. Each field, pasture, barn, pond, shed, herd of animals, and farm artifact comes with its own tales and memories.

Just outside the back kitchen door, to the right, was the cistern. A heavy, rectangular, cement lid covered the underground spring that filled this well. An iron pump stood on top, from which the house's earliest owners once drew water. The water below ground must call out to the water in our bodies, for the cistern was where my mother would often go to cry. Slamming the screen door behind her after a fight with my father, Sheila would perch on the edge of the well and wail. Tears would pour down her cheeks and mucus would run from her nose. Her strong emotions frightened me; hovering behind the door, I felt helpless to help her. In later years, Joe built an oddly shaped plywood structure over the cistern. It had a broad base with a bench, a tallish tower in the middle, and was painted a bright lime green. Though it looked nothing like the real thing, Joe grandly titled it the Taj Mahal, and said it would muffle the loud suction noises that came from the pump. I wonder whether he was hoping it might do the same for my mother's cries of sorrow.

Directly facing the back kitchen door was the storm cellar, where we took cover when tornadoes threatened. Our cellar was a hobbit-size, raised earthen mound covered by a riotous tangle of petunias, pansies, and morning glory cultivated by my mother, and into which a tiny wooden door was set. Narrow stairs inside led down to a small, dirt-floored space with moist stone walls. Tornado season, which began in the spring, was the signal to pack our keepsake bags with those things we couldn't live without in the event our house was leveled. Into my Barbie-embossed mini-case went my Trixie Belden mysteries, my diary and pen, and my pink transistor radio.

There is no equal in beauty to a Missouri sky in spring. As a storm would begin to blow in, the moisture would draw out the perfume from the daffodils and sweet clover and the air would turn wet and fragrant. As enormous white cumulus clouds amassed, the sky would appear to lower itself almost to the ground, lifting the hair on our scalps in fear and excitement. A tornado sky, however, stopped just short of a storm. The winds that had picked up would suddenly cease, the air would still, and the sky would turn an ominous, sickly, yellowish-gray.

When that happened, we instinctively knew that, somewhere, a nasty funnel might be in the making. Grabbing our bags, we'd all wait at the kitchen table for the signal: a police car siren blaring along the county roads. Yet even after the siren had passed by our house, we had to wait for the final indicator: the one that came from Joe. Nervously, we'd watch his face.

"Joe, I think it's time," Sheila would say, thrumming her fingers on the redwood picnic table. "No, not yet," Dad would say, glancing out the window. "Damn sireens, damn Oak Grove poh-lees-men, they never get it right. Don't know why I pay taxes." As far as my father was concerned, every government employee, local on up to federal, was crooked and wanted only one thing: his money. The feelings of mistrust were mutual. Once my mother asked a county official to fix a dangerous pothole on our road. "Good thing your husband's away," he said. "I'll do it for you, ma'am, but not for that old man of yours."

As Joe drew out his waiting game, minutes would tick by, the silence thickening with fear. Then, finally, "All right, let's go!" he'd shout, having drawn things out as long as he could. As we opened the cellar door, the dank smell of earth would rush up to greet us. Descending the crumbling stairs, we'd squeal in fright at the spiders and insects we knew hung about us in the corners. We huddled on folding chairs in the flashlight-flickering shadows, the universe dark and uncertain about us, and talk. What would happen if the tornado wiped everything out and leveled our house? Would the dogs, horses, and cows survive if they got picked up and then put down again? And what about my close girlfriends Cheryl and Connie, who lived on neighboring farms down the road? I worried for them, too.

When Joe had determined that the tornado had either passed us by or been a false alarm, he'd walk up the steps and, with theatrical aplomb, fling open the storm cellar door. Playing the moment to the hilt, he'd pause dramatically. As the five of us held our breath, we'd all wait for Joe to announce whether our world still stood or had been destroyed. Though a tornado once touched down a few miles from our home, wrecking the house and barns of one of the girlfriends I'd feared for, no tornado ever touched Shalom Acres. "All clear!" Joe would shout, and we'd race thankfully back up the stairs and out into the warm sunshine that was sending shafts of promise through the clouds.

To the right of the storm cellar was a clothesline that on a typical sunny day was hung with fresh laundry. At right angles to the line was a row of fragrant pastel peony bushes, like a pink hyphen sketched into the lawn. In later years, the pool and an exotic hibiscus tree that my parents made a big fuss about would be added to this square of green. A gravel driveway divided this portion of feminine-ruled lawn from the weathered barn that stood on the other side.

This area was Joe's command center, and it had a distinctly masculine, workmanlike air. On most days it was cluttered with a metal tangle of farm machinery. Grease and the odor of gasoline clung to everything. I loved the aroma of these machines almost as much as the scent of the daffodils that lined our driveway. Pickup trucks and all kinds of enormous flatbed and storage vans came and went over the years. A short white tower topped by a round gas tank stood on the far side of the barn, which housed the tractor and the stuff that went behind it, including the cultivator, tiller, and various plows. The barn was also where the horse equipment was kept: an ornate pony cart painted red and gold; along with reins, bits, Western and English saddles, whips, horseshoes, and horse blankets. Barrels of chemicals, fertilizers, and lime stood in shady, dusty corners. Mice and thick, long black snakes scurried and slithered out of sight.

Sloping down from the barn to the road below was a terraced hill. This was the alfalfa field, and it was one of my favorite places. Here I watched the seasons change. In winter, the ground lay white and cold with snow. The small pond in the lower right-hand corner would freeze several inches thick with ice. In the spring, after Joe had tilled the field into a brown canvas of mud-rich soil, tiny green shoots would burst through the earth. In the ecstasy of springtime, I raced with my kite along the ridges, blown about by flower-scented winds. In the summer, the field transformed itself into a dense carpet of purple-tipped green stalks and red clover that tasted as sweet as sugar on my tongue.

On a summer's evening, when we kids were little, Joe would sometimes take us down to the pond. He'd sit on the bank and watch us muck around for tadpoles. Once, I fell on my knees on a large crawdad. I thought that I'd fallen on a pile of sharp sticks and stood up, laughing off the blood spurting down my legs. Already, I'd developed the habit of hushing over fear or anxiety. But my father turned pale with fright. He swooped me up in his arms and raced back up the hill to the house. Even now, I can still hear his heart thumping beneath his shirt. He handed me to Sheila, and she undressed me and put me in the bathtub. As the water turned dark with blood around my body, the whole family crowded into the bathroom, marveling at the claw mark on my knee. Later, gauging the size of my wound, a neighboring farmer claimed he'd never known of such a large crawdad in these parts. The scar marks my leg to this day, a permanent tattoo of my Missouri childhood.

Mid-to-late summer was harvesttime, when the gods of nature crossed swords with the force that was my father. Joe followed the weather closely now, as he had to mow the alfalfa field at exact ripeness and before the rains came. In the days afterward, when the alfalfa lay drying, I'd creep out to the field's edge and breathe deeply the narcotic smell of freshly mown hay. When the alfalfa had dried to the right shade of pale green, the farmer with the hay-baling machine arrived. As the tractor wove among the rows with its boxy attachment, Joe would stand at the top of the field and watch, beer can and cigarette in hand. In a fluid motion, stalks were sucked up then spat out as bales that were left to dry to gold. These were the days before such things as rounded bales. If the rains came before we could get the hay in, there would be no feed for the livestock in winter, and Joe would have to buy hay. He worried about this every year, and we worried along with him.

When it came time to load up the hay and store it, my brothers, especially as they grew older, were sure to be called on to help out. But sometimes Joe would order all of us to work. "Pell! Neen! Steve! John!" he'd call out. "March! March! The rain's a-comin'. All hands on board. That's an order!" he'd shout through the house, stomping his work boots and loudly sloshing down cold beer. As much as I loved the farm, I hated doing chores. When it came to lifting bales, I wasn't much help. But I loved to race behind my brothers as they'd lift and throw the heavy bales onto the back of the long flatbed truck.

When they'd finished, the truck with its wobbly stacks of hay would slowly make its way down the driveway, across the road, and through the gate into the barnyard. The truck would then back up to the big barn. Shaped like an archway, the barn had two rounded sides that curved up to a pointed roof. It had two windows above the high door; together, they formed the eyes and mouth of a wide-eyed face. Many times over the years, I watched my father as he methodically, one by one, swing by swing, stacked the bales to the barn's cathedral rafters. The musty air would swirl gold with flecks of fairy-tale straw as the four of us leaped among the towering stacks of hay. Should a mouse be foolish enough to scurry in my father's path, he'd crush it beneath his boot with a loud crunch and a satisfied "gotcha!"

When I was older, and my father worked less and drank more, the barn became a place of retreat. I'd escape to the back, the tall stacks of hay behind me, and stare out the little window at the serene, rolling pastures. There, tucked into my little alcove of hay, I wrote poetry and dreamed up alternative futures for myself. Two recurring, but competing, fantasies ran through my mind as a young girl. In one, I lived in a small town in a large and cozy house with my husband and our happy family of lots of children. In the other, I walked along the shores of a foreign sea, a single woman, intrepid explorer of distant lands. Even then, my father's conflicts were beginning to work themselves out in me.

In the early fall, when the leaves had begun to redden and the persimmons had ripened to dark orange, a large semi would pull into the barnyard. I knew what this portended: slaughter time. It didn't matter whether I was allowed to watch or not—I kept my distance. But there was no escaping the sound of bleating cows slamming their hooves against the metal walls of the truck, a noise that reached all the way up the hill to my bedroom window. In one black-and-white photo, a skinned cow hangs from a hook over the fence. Neatly filleted, its head, hooves, and gut removed, the white carcass swings like an animal ghost. After being sent to the local butcher and neatly packaged into different cuts, the cow would return to our farm, on our dinner table, in the form of liver, pot roast, meatloaf, or thick and juicy barbequed steak and hamburgers.

In winter, the barnyard was where we fed our herd of brown and white Hereford beef cattle, fattening them for the upcoming year. Before he left on a trip, Joe would have stacked at the barn door the exact number of bales the cows would need each day while he was gone. When it was my turn to do this chore, I'd snip the metal wires holding the bales together, scatter hay around the frozen yard, and then open the side gate to let in the jostling herd. I was always careful around them; these were enormous, strong, and quick-moving animals before whom I was a mere girl.

After I completed this task, I'd face into the chilly Midwestern winds and head down to the pond in the lower pasture behind the barn. If there had been an ice storm I'd slip and slide my way along fields that were slick and dangerous. Around me, tree branches glittered against gunmetal skies, calling to mind Thomas Hardy's lines from "The Darkling Thrush": "When Frost was spectre-grey, / And Winter's dregs made desolate / The weakening eye of day." Picking up the axe my father had left at the pond's edge, I'd hammer at the thick ice until water bubbled through.

In the spring and summer, this large pond, surrounded by rolling pastureland, was transformed into an oasis. A graceful old weeping willow, patient listener to the Carrolls, stood on its raised banks. Here we had family picnics, and here Joe taught us how to skip stones across the pond's surface. Just beyond the perimeter, the cows grazed in fields of sweetgrass and wildflowers, cooling themselves in the shade of oak and hickory trees. In the early years, if Joe was home from a trip, he'd send the four of us down to this part of the farm to gather up wood for the evening barbecue. Cows, trees, ponds, alfalfa—all were part of the sustainable life we didn't even know we were living.

Then there was the wheat field—twenty acres of fertile farmland across from the alfalfa field and to the left of the barn. The cycle of seasons played out here, too. In one of my most vivid memories, I'd been invited into town to play with one of my best friends, Virginia. As was the custom when my father was home, I had to ask his permission first. Sheila drove me down to the road that bordered the bottom of the wheat field, where Joe was plowing under the winter stalks to prepare for spring planting. Taking off my shoes and socks, I climbed the fence, then raced across the field toward my father on his tractor. The fresh clumps of overturned earth beneath the soles of my feet were cool and plush. The pungent smell of the soil hit my nostrils as if I were a pig rooting for truffles in loamy mulch. The sun beat down on my head, and a force of happy energy surged through every cell of my body. I was only ten or so, but I recall taking in the whole sweep of the plowed field, with my father on his tractor beneath the blue sky, and knowing in one illuminated second the great secret of nature. My delight must have shown on my face, for when I finally reached my father, shouting out my question over the tractor's roaring engine, he beamed back an immediate "Yes!" I raced back to my mother and all felt right with my world.

As the summer months moved indolently toward fall, the family would gather in the evening on the front porch. We'd look down the hill and watch to see how close the wheat was to ripeness. By mid-to-late July, the field would have turned into a rippling ocean of opulent, yellow waves. The morning of the big harvest day started down by the barn. With the four of us lined up watching, Joe would jump up into the bulky Allis-Chalmers combine. Perched high above us in the clear, plastic-encased cabin, he was like Zeus. Heat and anticipation would radiate off his body in waves.

Engines weren't very reliable back then; in addition, Joe bought a lot of his machinery used. Consequently, many of my farm memories involve endless waiting for engines to start. If the combine cut off, it would, to use my father's made-up word, have to be "yoixed" and coaxed. When that happened, he would order us into silence—"Quiet!"—as if the temperamental engine wouldn't turn over if one of us made a sound. After a few moments of priming the engine by pumping the pedals, Joe would push the ignition button. If we were lucky, the engine would cough hopefully, sputter, cough again, and sputter yet again, before finally roaring into action. As we cheered, Joe would let out a shout and raise his fist in triumph. Then, very gingerly—combines were awkward machines that could easily tip over—he'd begin to maneuver it across the barnyard and into the sloping wheat field.

His khaki work shirt stained with sweat, Joe would ply the rows of wheat he'd patiently tilled, seeded, fertilized, and sprayed with thick, oily weed poison over the preceding year. As the combine inched along, it plucked up the slender stalks with their bursting buds. Freshly shucked grains streamed into the eighteen-foot flatbed truck, with its high sides in place, being driven alongside by a hired farmhand. When we were little, Joe would sometimes give the four of us permission to ride in the back. Dressed only in our underwear bottoms, we'd roll like puppies in the soft mounds of wheat, the velvety softness luxurious against our young skin. It was like swimming in liquid gold. Once, one of the farmhands claimed that you could make gum out of the grain. Scooping up the hard and tiny pellets into our mouths, we'd chew and chew until, just as he'd said, we'd made our own tacky-tasting wheat gum.

Later, at the grain elevator, where the wheat was dumped into pits, elevated to the top, and then dumped into tall storage bins, we'd cap off the day with cream Popsicles that melted down our cheeks and ran sticky on our sun-browned chests. In the background, the low voices of the farmers in their denim overalls would mumble as they waited

186

their turn, talking wheat prices and weather. Finished with our treats, the four of us would run up and down the dark wood halls of the musty old grain elevator that had stood as long as anyone could remember.

If each section of the farm was its own world, the horse pasture was where my father would try to recreate the equestrian experience he'd shared with his foster parents. Grooming the Glovers' horses in their stables when he was a boy had won Joe a place at their dinner table. Now he would turn to horses as a way to keep his own family together.

As my brother John says, the Carrolls like to do things the hard way. It was a habit we'd learn at my father's knee, and it was vividly exemplified in the way Joe went about his horse project. The goal was to have six horses, one for each of us, so we could all ride together. But my father wouldn't just buy us each a horse. No, Joe would breed and train them himself, one at a time. As he broke in each horse, he'd teach one of us how to ride as well. The brood mare Joe chose as matriarch for this experiment was a lovely chestnut with a graceful neck, mahogany eyes, and a black mane. Inaugurating a tradition whereby each horse would be christened by my mother with a Spanish name, our new mare was called Catarina. Not long after Catarina arrived in the horse pasture, my father brought in a stallion for a visit.

Months later, as I was playing outside by the horse pasture, I spied a small dark shape hovering at Catarina's side. I shouted excitedly for my father, who came running. Was it a shadow, we wondered, or a newborn foal? As my mother, sister, brothers, and I stood on the fence and watched in quiet suspense, my father walked out into the field, slowly approaching Catarina. Leaning down, he separated the small dark shape she was protecting. A gangly-legged colt with a golden coat stepped into the sun. Waving us out to the field, but cautioning us to be "quiet as mice," Joe allowed us to creep closer. I still recall the tender protection that emanated from my father in that moment. He was as gentle with the mare and her foal as he was with his own four kids, who were wide-eyed with wonder.

To the firstborn child, me, would go the firstborn horse, decided Joe. Because the foal had first appeared as a dark shape, my mother decreed that his name would be Sombra, Spanish for shadow. Not long after Sombra's arrival, Joe bought another mare. Because she'd be my mother's horse, Joe named her Bonita, as she was pretty like Sheila. After several more visits from the stallion, Chiquita arrived, for Colleen. Then came Mia, for Steve, and Sancho, for John.

Breeding the horses was just the beginning of the Carroll equine chronicles. Over the years, each of the horses would be trained to obey Joe's will. In one photo, my father stands in the pasture, nose to nose with Bonita. Her head is high, but so is my father's. Joe's hands grip the reins tightly beneath her jaw, and horse and man stare into each other's eyes. There is no question who the master is.

When it came time to break in one of the colts, the four of us would be called outside to watch. Huddled together along the fence, our hearts beating fast with a mix of dread and fascination, we'd watch as Joe took his place in the center of the pasture. A lead rope tethered him to the young horse on the other end. He'd slowly take out the long, leather Argentine whip he'd hidden behind his back and begin snapping and cracking it in the air. At my father's command, the horse would gradually walk, trot, then gallop, over and over again. Eventually, after some days of this, the horse would become accustomed enough to my father to allow him ever so slowly to place a bit in its mouth.

This sight must have impressed itself deeply on my mind, as I still recall the moment when the bit went in for the first time, and how the horse jolted backward, shocked by the bite of cold steel. After the bridle came the saddle, without a rider. The last step in this initiation was that day when, after saddling up, Joe would cinch the girth tight, put his foot in the stirrup, swing his leg over the horse, and leap into the saddle. Immediately, the horse would arc its back and begin bucking and kicking in tight circles. Finally, the horse would stop bucking, and the two would go off in a smooth, running gallop.

As scary as breaking in the horses was, being taught to ride them was scarier still. Joe would summon the four of us to the front yard. "Get down here!" he'd shout up the stairs. "Run on out to the barn and get your bridles and saddles. That's an order!" I'd shiver with nerves and excitement over what was to come next. Sombra, a half Shetland, could be mean, and he would nip and kick his heels at me before I'd even slid the bridle over his tossing head. When they were little, my brothers would tear up at my father's command, their lips trembling. They'd run to my mother and beg to be allowed to stay inside. But Joe's sons were an extension of himself. And no son of his would ever be allowed to be a knee-knocking little sissy-boy.

"Come on, get a move on," my father would order as we scrambled around, whining and grumbling. "Don't forget your horse bait!" Soon, riding gear and corncobs in hand, we'd be lined up at the fence. Now that there were six horses, catching one of them was a feat of skill and daring. Opening the gate, Joe would walk out into the field. Extending his hand with a corncob cradled in his palm, he'd begin whistling softly under his breath. At the far end of the pasture that bordered a small grove of trees, the horses would lift their heads and prick their ears forward. Snorting in excitement, they'd paw the ground and lift their tails.

Then, all at once, they'd gallop straight for my father. Joe never flinched. When it came to standing your ground, he looked as if he'd invented the phrase. He knew they'd never run over him. And indeed, the horses never failed to pull up short in a cloud of dust, tossing their manes and jostling around him. For a moment, we'd lose sight of Joe. Tension mounted as we would wait and watch for him to reappear, like Jehovah out of the whirlwind.

Emerging, Joe would shout at me. "Pell! Get over here. Bring your bridle." Dreading my position as the oldest, and my stomach queasy, I'd creep toward my father amid the prancing, rearing horses. As afraid as I was of getting kicked by one of the horses, though, I was even more scared of my father. It never once occurred to me to disobey him. "Don't worry, they won't hurt you," he'd say. "Just don't let them know you're afraid. You're the boss." If only I could handle him the same way. Years later, when my sister was in analysis, she recalled the fear she'd felt as a small girl in the midst of all the flying hooves and tails, trying to catch her own horse. "Who was your father trying to train?" asked her analyst. "The horses or you?"

Despite all the fear and trembling that surrounded the horses, no one ever got hurt or broke a bone. But there were enough near misses to keep us on edge. One time, for example, Joe took my sister and me out for a training exercise. He led us on our horses far out into the fields and found a steep ridge that sloped down and then turned sharply uphill. Our instructions were to carefully guide our horses as they picked their way through stones and weeds while staying in our saddles. After we had jumped our horses across the small gully, we were then to scramble up the hill. On this occasion, Joe went first, and my sister followed.

Suddenly, our family dog, a German shepherd named Grande, appeared out of nowhere and leaped straight up into the air by my sister's side. Chiquita was a big quarter horse, and Colleen, who was only around eight or nine, was tiny on her back. In silent, stunned horror, I watched as Chiquita bolted, sending Colleen over the top of her head. I was perched at the top of the ridge watching, and my stomach heaved with panic that my little sister was going to be killed. Too late to stop her momentum, Chiquita took a flying leap over my sister. Her back hooves came down on the other side of Colleen's limp body, grazing her rib cage. Joe jumped off his horse, scrambled down the hill, and scooped my sister into his arms. After seeing that, aside from a few scratches, she was unharmed, my father began to sob. It was one of the very few times I saw him cry.

As with everything connected to my father, there were moments of sheer terror and pure glory where the horses were concerned. In one photo, I sit on Sombra's back, a little girl of five or six, smiling proudly into the camera. My father is holding the reins as we stand before the wide front porch. It would take years for me to completely overcome my fear. But as I grew into adolescence, I became adept at walking out into the swirling throng of horses all by myself and catching, bridling, and saddling Sombra. A deep bond grew between my horse and me; I loved my spirited Shetland with his golden coat. He was magic in my eyes, a flying carpet and mythic Pegasus all in one. The day came when I roamed over the farm on horseback, galloping across the fields, a free girl beneath the sky.

Probably my most memorable horse ride of all, though, was when I was around twelve or thirteen. It was early evening on a warm July Saturday night. My sister and I were upstairs in our bedroom, listening to the Top 10 countdown on the radio, as we always did in those days. Abruptly, Joe's voice broke into Petula Clark's voice crooning "Downtown."

"Pell, Neen, turn that damn radio off. Let's go for a ride," my father yelled up the stairs. "That's an order!" We grumbled and exchanged skeptical glances but knew it was useless to argue. In the pasture, we saddled up our horses beneath the light of a huge full moon. The earth bloomed dark emerald. Joe led us through the woods and away from the house, the footsteps of the horses falling softly on the thick forest carpet. In the bright glow of the moon, the trees stood like ships' masts at full sail across the ocean of sky. Thickets of fireflies lit up the air around us and combined with the stars overhead to surround us in an enchanted net of twinkling lights. The frogs, cicadas, and owls were animal concert to our human silence as we rode silently through the night.

We emerged from the stand of oaks and maples, and my father led us down a hill toward a pond. Without saying a word, my father made straight for the water. I was directly behind Joe, and when I saw where he was headed, I pulled on my reins. This was something new, and I didn't know what to expect. Would Sombra even know how to swim with me on his back? Would he balk and toss me over his head? And what about the poisonous water moccasins that lurked in the local ponds?

"Come on, Pell! Let's go, Neen!" yelled Joe, as he plunged into the pond's moon-reflecting waters with an exultant whoop. Glancing backward at my sister, I raised my eyebrows, then, giving my horse a kick, I turned and followed my father. Whatever apprehension I'd felt was not shared by my horse. Sombra stepped easily into the pond and kicked off the shore. Buoyant and light beneath me, his thick neck strained forward and his strong legs pumped through the silver water.

My world tilted. Swimming on the back of a horse wasn't anything I'd ever experienced, and I haven't since. I became merely a slip of a human being in a powerful animal universe. Sombra, whom I'd trained to obedience, was now the master graciously bearing me on his back. Reins were useless now; I had to wholly trust my horse to carry me through these waters. Intensely in the moment, all my senses engaged, and gripping my knees tight so as not to fall off, I felt flush with the thrill of it all.

All too soon, it was over. As they arrived on the other side of the pond, each horse scrambled awkwardly up the embankment, the three of us slipping and sliding in our wet saddles. The tall grasses and bulrushes brushed our drenched legs with mud and burs. Sombra and Chiquita violently shook the water off their hides, nearly unseating us, and my sister and I laughed in giddy relief. For days afterward, the two of us basked in the high of our "midnight moonlight ride," as we later called it. Such moments of grace with Joe were rare. They were to be hoarded against that time when the curtain of darkness would descend once again.

Other corners of the farm held their share of stories. The upper edge of the alfalfa field bordered property that belonged to a farmer who looked as if he'd walked straight out of Grant Wood's *American Gothic*. Farmer Hull wore stiff denim overalls and a straw hat. His face was as brown and crevassed as a dirt field, and he lived on the hill behind us in a house that was shaped like a tall and narrow saltbox. Once when my mother had taken us to his house trick-or-treating, he'd slammed the door in our faces with a curt "Got no candy." My mother thought his sour nature was due to his wife, who was said to be a little insane.

Each spring, Farmer Hull would gather winter's dry brush and set giant bonfires, letting them burn untended through the night. After that, he'd emerge onto the field with a nineteenth-century-style manual plow, pulled by two enormous draft horses with pie-size hooves. As I hung on the fence and gaped in awe, he never once looked my way. He didn't like my father much either, who'd complained to him that the bonfires could leap the fence onto our property. When it came time for old Farmer Hull to retire and sell his land, he deliberately ignored my father's offer to buy it, selling his property instead to the owner of our local grocery store. This made my father so mad he forbade my mother ever to shop there again, forcing her to drive to the next town over.

Across the road from Farmer Hull's property was a private family cemetery. This small plot of land, its ivy-covered gravestones carved with the names of people freshly dead and long gone, was another of my favorite places. For a girl who lay awake at night scared of ghosts, something about this little graveyard was oddly comforting. Finding private hiding places of my own would become a kind of compulsion. Only among the tree-shadowed gravestones, which flickered with the wraiths of lives past, could I be sure to be left alone with my thoughts. Here, too, was where I first tasted the power of storytelling. In the summertime, as dusk fell, I'd sometimes gather my siblings and take them up the hill. I'd seat them by the gravestones and put my own twist on the latest Edgar Allen Poe tales of horror I'd been reading, making them (to my great satisfaction) squeal in fright.

I heard stories, too, from our neighbor Lenny Corn, who with his wife Sally lived down the hill from us, at the corner of Old Coburn Road and the county highway. Lenny had a shock of white hair and blue eyes to rival my father's. Years before, one of his legs had been amputated. Since then, Lenny had spent his days sitting in his chair by the window, his wheelchair close by, watching life go by. It was said of Lenny that there wasn't anything that happened in Oak Grove that he didn't know about. My father liked Lenny, and the feeling was mutual. Perhaps my father saw in him something of Ollie Boop, the Pennsylvania farmer from his childhood. Lenny had a quiet calm about him and was known to everyone as a gentle, kind man.

Many a humid night, Joe and Sheila would load us up in the back of the pickup and drive us down the hill to Lenny and Sally's. While the grown-ups sat chatting on the porch, the four of us would gather on the lawn with the Corns' grandchildren. Dashing among the fireflies, we'd play the Argentine game of "Pottica" that Sheila had taught us. Later, sitting in the quiet of the evening, Lenny might tell us, in his slow and easy way, about the time that Harry Truman had stopped by his house for a visit while he was campaigning for president. Truman had sat right here, Lenny would tell us, on the very porch where we were now. Truman had been a good and honest man, Lenny said. A Missouri man.

There were other farmers my father knew and liked, too. Coy and Agnes Taylor had come from generations of farmers and knew all the local legends. It was Agnes who'd told us that Jesse James and his gang had once slept in the corner of our wheat field while fleeing the law. Then there was Mr. and Mrs. Weist, whose only son had gone crazy, claiming a radio in his head was transmitting messages from outer space. It was Mr. Weist who would come to my mother's rescue while Joe was away on trips, helping her round up cows or horses that had broken out of their pastures. Each time my mother crept out onto the roof to wash the upstairs windows, she'd scribble down the numbers of these local farmers. Just in case she fell, of course.

In those first years on the farm, Joe turned gladly to these taciturn Midwesterners for friendship and farming advice. Whether it was about calving in springtime, bringing in the hay, or selling the wheat crop, my father seemed to delight in the art of farming. But as the years passed, he became increasingly hostile and paranoid. He would always remain friends with Lenny and Sally Corn. Yet sooner or later, whether with the local farmers or the townspeople, a disagreement would arise, turn bitter, and spoil a friendship.

THE WORM IN THE APPLE OF PARADISE

"What I just don't get," says my mother now, "is why your father claimed to love Oak Grove so much, but then hated all the people." My mother is right. Joe did everything in his power to keep the world from intruding into his paradise, drawing the circle of his wife and children tightly about him. But even my father couldn't keep the local community from entering our lives. One year, the town let Joe know it didn't like him so much, either.

I must have been about eleven or twelve, on the delicate edge of adolescence. Joe had just bought the Henderson farm next door. This one-hundred-acre plot of land bordered our horse pasture. It came with a long, low-lying barn, a chicken coop, an outhouse, and a small white farmhouse with a blackberry tree in the front yard. To get to it you either walked or drove down the tarred road in front of our house, following it as it turned sharply downhill. Halfway down this hill on the right was a gravel driveway that led into the Henderson farm. Sometimes, after dinner, if my father was home, we'd wash up the dishes and then take a family walk along this road. As my parents ambled along, sometimes holding hands, the four of us would play around them like planets orbiting twin suns. At the top of the hill, my parents would stop and contemplate the high ledge with its commanding view of the valley of patchwork farms. One day on this spot, they said, they'd build their retirement dream house.

But the power that came with doubling his property did something to my father. The land that he owned both to the left and right of the county road now became his dominion. The steep hill leading down to the Henderson farm had long been a local lovers' lane. Boughs of thick branches met and arched over it, providing a mantle of cover for necking teenagers.

This kind of disrespectful behavior on "his" road enraged my father. Seething about these deviant kids messing around so close to his family, Joe resolved to do something about it. He also decided to bring me along for the ride. Over the course of several weekend nights, no doubt after he'd downed more than a few beers, Joe ordered me into the front seat of the truck and set off down the road. My father never said exactly why he took me with him on these raids. To teach me a lesson about the dangers of sex? Something like that, I guess.

Beside my father in the cab, I slumped down as low as I could get in my seat. These were the older siblings of my schoolmates, and I burned with humiliation to be seen. Gossip in a small town like Oak Grove spread fast; I'd likely not escape the taunts that would be sure to come my way. Joe turned the carlights off, so as not to alert the miscreants in advance, and inched slowly down the hill. After spying an offending parked car, he'd pull up to a stop beside it and flick on his brights. Then he'd roll down his window and poke his head out.

"You kids have no right to be out here this late at night," my father would bark, probing the dark interior of the car with his flashlight. It might be nine or ten o'clock, but to Joe that was late enough. "I don't know what you're up to in there. But I want you to get the hell off my road." Blinking in the glare aimed into their startled faces, young girls with messed up beehives sat up and began buttoning their blouses. Teenage boys zipped up their jeans and ran their hands over their slicked-back hair. Mortified, most would gun their motors and drive off, brakes squealing.

But some were not so intimidated. "With respect, Mr. Carroll, you've got no right to tell us to get off county property," they'd challenge my father, before turning back to the embrace of their girls and refusing to leave. Nothing made my father angrier than this kind of insolent behavior. If they weren't going to leave, then neither was he. So he'd sit in his truck beside them, his engine idling, waiting them out. Finally, shouting loud curses in our direction, they'd give up and drive away.

Over the next month, the tension escalated in my father's battle to assert control over the road. At school, I could see the looks and hear the whispers from my classmates. One morning, we awoke to find trash strewn along the road in front of our house. The fright made me sick. I hated that my father had made other people hate us. I felt attacked, as if we'd been smeared. The problem was, I didn't blame them. The community we lived in may not have been his, but it was mine.

Joe was angry when he saw the trash, but not in any way that admitted shame. Stubborn, even proud, he seemed to welcome this revenge on the part of the local boys. It allowed him to get his own back. Although I begged my father to let us pick up the garbage ourselves, he refused to let us touch it. For several days, the bits of candy wrappers, soda cans, and scraps of paper stayed right where they'd been tossed. Rummaging through the litter, Joe discovered sales receipts from the local gas station. He paid a visit to the owner, and the perpetrators, who worked there, admitted their guilt. The next day, several sullen, sheepish boys pulled up to the bottom of our hill. They jumped out of their Chevvies and Mustangs and cleaned up each piece of trash. After that, no swooning couples ever parked on "his" road again. Joe Carroll had won the war over lovers' lane.

Despite my father's efforts, however, the outside world continued to intrude into his private refuge of Shalom Acres. For one thing, Joe himself brought it to our doorstep. Each time he returned from a trip, with his stories and souvenirs, a little more of this forbidden outer realm would find its way into our farmhouse. He introduced the worm that would eventually eat its way through the apple of our

Eden. I suppose my father thought that he could control our intake of humanity through the twice-yearly family trips we took. What he didn't realize was the way these trips would undermine our loyalty to the farm. And to him.

Flight itself would loosen our ties to our Missouri homestead. It would broaden our perspectives, widening them to include more and more of the globe. It would raise our expectations about what life had to offer beyond Oak Grove. It would make us restless to snap the limits imposed by place and locality. This conflict between the farm and the big, wide world played itself out in the layout of my bedroom. Out one window was a view of the soft, rolling Missouri hills. Waking early in the morning, I'd watch as the mists hanging on these hilltops melted in the rising sun. Season after season, I'd witness the hills turn from green, to red and orange, to shades of brown. I recall deliberately taking this view in, as if to imprint it on my mind forever; it is an image that has not dimmed with time. Out the window on the other wall, however, was a vista that included a horizon of twinkling city lights. When life inside the house became too hard, I'd sit on this windowsill and dream of walking down bustling city streets, doing exciting things and meeting extraordinary people. "Just give me a dime, and I'll climb out this window and run away," I'd moan dramatically to my little sister.

The big city was where Joe drove off to once or twice each week for his trips for TWA. Twice a year, winter and summer, I, too, drove to the airport for family trips. Of all the stages of flight, takeoff was the part I liked the best. If I was lucky, I'd be seated away from the rest of the family and could savor the moment in the walled garden of my secret imagination. As the plane would slowly taxi down the runway, I didn't just hear the engines begin to rev up. I felt it. Preparing to rise from the earth in the body of a plane was to me like being in the belly of an enormous bird gathering its muscles for a skyward leap. Outside my cabin window, I watched as the slow-moving propellers burst into a white blur of motion. The Lockheed Constellation we'd just boarded would shudder, and a roar and rush of sound would fill the air. Gripped by delight, seized with ecstasy, I would laugh out loud into the thunderous noise.

As the plane left the ground, soaring into space, so did my spirit. As we broke through the first layer of clouds into blue sky, I broke through into a world where the sun always shone. Where life was free of such pressing things as strict teachers, teasing friends, and overbearing fathers. As we flew west to California, my girlish imagination took wing. I would look down from my plane window and convince myself I could see wild horses running across the Rocky Mountains. I imagined myself dancing along invisible currents of wind, a ballerina of the skies.

I was never scared. Lightning, thunder, sheets of rain—even stormy weather couldn't dampen my enthusiasm. The bumpier it got, and in those days passengers could be bounced high and tossed from side to side, the more thrilled I became. In those moments, I was truly my father's daughter: an unafraid, bring-it-on, flying cowgirl aboard a plane bucking nasty weather. Others may have turned pale or thrown up in their complimentary barf bags; I was impervious to all danger.

Many years later, as a mother on my first flight away from home, I would lose the girlhood brio I'd felt when flying. It would never return, and traveling would never feel the same again. For the first time, I would become afraid of crashing and dying. There was too much to lose below. Back then—with the exception of one stomach-flipping flight on a small plane—little impeded my in-flight happiness, courtesy of the "up, up, and away" TWA experience. After our plane had hit its flying altitude, pretty hostesses, whose lips were bright with million-dollar red lipstick to match the airline's logo, and who were dressed in stylishly short, bright suits, would pamper us with hot towels, Coca-Colas with double maraschino cherries, Chiclets chewing gum, and glossy TWA playing cards. After being served hot, cellophane-wrapped meals by these beaming goddesses with their perfect hairdos, Joe would get up from his seat and go up to the cabin. Sometimes, he might come back and, two by two, introduce us to the crew. We'd pass through first class on the way up to the front, and I'd gaze in awe at the filet mignons on the plates of the rich. Once inside the cockpit, my father would greet the pilot, copilot, and flight engineer, who'd show us the instrument panel where Dad sat when he flew. But I only had eyes for the vista directly before me, the intimacy of endless sky a mere metal sheet away.

For me, the trouble with flying began as soon as we walked down the steep portable stairs and across the airport tarmac. Inhaling the smells of a new city, another rush of adrenaline would pour through my body. But as much as my curiosity was stimulated by the hotels, oceans, museums, and zoos of wherever we'd landed, I was never the traveler my parents and siblings were. On the ground, I had a sensitive stomach; the strange food made me sick. Many a vacation was spent throwing up in bathroom stalls. Walking and sightseeing caused my feet to swell.

There was also the tension between my parents. Something about being far from home brought out the goofy, maudlin side of Joe. In restaurants or on tour buses, he'd become loud and embarrassing, a clown on the town. In slurred, drunken speech, he'd insult waiters and tour guides. At night, my parents' arguments, awkwardly audible through the thin walls of their adjoining hotel room, would keep the four of us awake, whispering in fear.

Once we were airborne again and winging our way home, I'd feel lifted above the family tension that ensnared my young, developing self. I'd hug my souvenirs to my chest—the little Buddha from Chinatown, the vial of beach sand, the cheap gardenia perfume—and try to freeze memories of my trip in place. All too soon, though, we'd begin our descent, coming in to land over the warehouses and business districts of Kansas City. If taking off is infused with the promise of adventure, landing is about the journey's end. Descending from the air, I could feel my body begin to adjust to the density of everyday existence.

Silent and tired, the six of us would pile into our car for the long drive home. If we were returning from a winter trip, the farmhouse as it appeared from the country road would seem small and lonely on its barren hilltop. The surrounding fields were sallow in the January cold. The cattle and horses stood against the bleak winds, heads down, tails tucked in. If it had snowed, the Falcon sedan would likely get stuck in the huge drifts at the bottom of our hill. That meant we'd have to get out and wait while Dad put chains on the tires. Then, with all of us gathered behind the rear fender, we'd shove. "Push! Push!" Joe would yell from behind the wheel. When the car wouldn't move out of its rut, we'd trudge up the hill with our bags, our feet in their fancy traveling shoes freezing wet from the snow.

Arriving home from a summer vacation trip created a different kind of return. With no school, there was more space to reenter the atmosphere of my personal life. It still took time to adjust to the minutiae and chores of the farm. But the verdant lawn that we loved to tumble and roll down, and the hours I spent reading beneath the shade of our giant oak tree, helped to ease my passage from sky to earth.

Joe, too, had his own troubles with reentry. The conflict between whether he was a man of the air or of the earth was repeated in every departure and return, and he contemplated this as he lay dying. Even on the farm he so loved, the sky would continue to speak to him. On many a summer's evening, Joe would call us outside for our special evening ritual. He'd unfold six green lawn chairs, one for each of us, and we'd line them up in a row between the pink dash of peony bushes and the lime green Taj Mahal. Then we'd all lie down—Joe, Sheila, me, Colleen, Steve, then John—bare toes pointed to the grass, our faces turned upward.

Stars shone brighter and thicker in those days. My father, beer can in hand, would point out the constellations, so familiar from his days as a navigator. I can still see his face, pondering that of the sky peering back at him. The burning tip of his cigarette traces patterns in the dark as he points out the wonders of the heavens. "There's the Big Dipper, and over there, the Little Dipper. And that's the Milky Way."

After the launch of Sputnik in 1957, we began spotting the tiny, blinking satellites bobbing and weaving across the horizon. As the six of us would lie dreaming beneath the sweep of starred heavens, its presence both infinite and yet intimate, like the ancient Egyptian goddess of the night bent over the earth, my father would muse aloud about what existed beyond the planets and galaxies, and about the future of flight.

"Think there's life on outer planets?" he'd ask. "*I* do," I'd always reply with conviction, because I absolutely did. I was, after all, the daughter of an airman. The world out there, I believed, contained important secrets that I would one day decode. For somewhere, I knew, out beyond Earth's boundaries, lay many more interesting dimensions to discover. After my father had fallen silent again, we'd lie there in stillness, lifted above our fractured hearts and failed attempts at connection, saying nothing at all—each of us lost in our own thoughts beneath the big Missouri sky.

As Seen from Above

When Icarus first soared upward, he only had eyes for the sun. But since the French launched the first manned hot air balloon in 1783, flying has transfigured how we see Earth. During that first flight, one of the two pilots on board became so distracted by the expansive view below him that he momentarily forgot his duties. The lone pilot on the second manned flight, as recounted in *A Brief History of Flight*, was similarly overtaken. As he stood up in the middle of the gondola, Jacques Charles wrote later, he found himself lost "in the spectacle offered by the immensity of the horizon. When I took off from the fields, the sun had set for the inhabitants of the valleys. Soon it rose for me alone. . . . I was the only illuminated body within the whole horizon, and I saw all the rest of nature plunged in shadow."

Benjamin Franklin, in Paris on behalf of the new American republic, was witness to this historic encounter between human and sky. In a letter home, he wrote that the invention of flight was a discovery of great importance that would "give a new turn to human affairs." Franklin was right. Besides ushering in an age of travel and communication, flight would reveal stunning new perspectives about the planet we live on. As aviation historian Tom Crouch recounts, the archaeological ruins of long-vanished civilizations could suddenly be seen from the air. Remote places such as Antarctica, the world's highest waterfall, and high peaks like Mount Everest were glimpsed for the first time from above. The most mind-altering image of Earth provided by flight, of course, would be the transcendent view of our planet from space.

But as much as flight would reveal Earth as a geographical wonder of stupendous mystery, it would also show something else: its slow destruction. From space could be seen deforestation, oil spills, smog, and urban sprawl. As even America's apostle of aviation Charles Lindbergh would observe, many of the changes taking place on Earth's surface in the twentieth century were not for the best. "Trees disappeared from mountains and valleys. Erosion turned clear rivers yellow," he wrote in *Autobiography of Values*. Areas that once lay black when he'd been a young pilot, he continued, "now glowed with electrification." Even worse for Lindbergh, Crouch writes, was his sobering recognition of the role flight had played in creating these changes. Space exploration would always remain a passion for Lindbergh, and he would never entirely abandon his interest in technology and aviation. Still, in the closing years of his life Lindbergh would oppose development of the American supersonic transport aircraft, devoting himself to environmental causes.

Lindbergh was an intellectually curious man of many talents who grasped the moral dilemma posed by flight and technology. In a revealing example of aviation's dark side, however, he was unable to bring the same perspective to his own life. Following the death of his wife, Anne Morrow Lindbergh, it was publicly revealed that Charles Lindbergh had lived a double life, fathering seven children with three German women. When I consider his profession, I wonder whether aviation fostered in Lindbergh the emotional disconnection necessary to carry off such a massive deception. His vocation, I theorize, helped to insulate him from the complications of his life on the ground and loosened his family ties.

Likewise, when I reflect on the question my father pondered in the last days of his life—whether he was a flier or a farmer—I wonder if he missed the larger point. In my mind, the real question that should have been asked was how flying shaped Joe's psychology, as well as his relationship to the land itself. Did flight inflate his dangerous tendency toward mania, urging him to take on more than his inborn limits would allow? Did it weaken his connection to the farm itself, causing the fields, barns, animals, and his wife and children to shrink in proportion to his life in the sky?

A photo of our farm taken when I was a girl speaks to this point. When I was around fifteen, an aerial photographer stopped by the house and proposed shooting and selling us a picture of the property from the sky. Joe loved this notion. At dinner that night, he spoke with animation about seeing the finished results. When we received the black-and-white photo, and after all of us had oohed and aahed over it, I proudly pasted it into a family album, with the handwritten caption "The Carroll Farm: Shalom Acres." As seen from above, our two-story dwelling sits like a dollhouse in the midst of neatly cultivated fields. There, in miniature, is the storm cellar, the pool, the barn with the pickup truck parked out front, the tops of our beautiful trees, and the green lawn with the pastel dash of peony bushes. In a corner of the house, one of us sits in the shade. My mother bends over her vegetable garden, my brother floats in the pool, and my father is on his tractor lawn mower. A peaceable kingdom by any measure, just as my parents had first envisioned.

But when I examine this photograph more closely, two important details leap out at me. Standing at odd angles in the horse pasture are four posts set loosely in their dug-out holes: this was the jump my father had started to construct, but never finished. Those posts stood just as they were in the picture for years; Joe would never remove them. Joe had bought English riding gear and enrolled my sister and me in English riding lessons. It had been his goal to teach us all how to jump, just as he'd done at the Altoona Hunt Club. The horses, however, are nowhere to be seen in this photo, reminding me of the big auction that must have just taken place. For, as it turned out, we never would achieve our goal of taking family rides together. In another detail, I note the empty, scooped-out hollow in the back of our house. Years earlier, my father had bulldozed this area for the family tennis court he'd hoped one day to build, but never did.

These two details appear emblematic to me of the difficulty my father had with permanently settling into his two hundred acres of Missouri land, and with being faithful over time to his dreams for his family and his farm. But the problems my father suffered were America's problems, too. Even before flight, according to James Hillman, America has from its beginnings had trouble being rooted in the land. "America is the dream," he tells me, "but geography is the place. You don't live in America; you live in Nebraska. But the dream is

American." Partly, Hillman says, "this is because in the beginning it was foreign soil," making it hard for us to truly feel part of land that was not our original birthplace. Our inability to remain in one place also has its psychological effects, exacerbating our tendency toward compulsive busyness. "Being established in a region and a place, with its wildlife, local traditions, and natural habitat," Hillman tells me, "is crucial to stop the rush of time. Without it we're driven."

My father certainly aimed to establish deep roots at Shalom Acres. I recall many times when, home from a trip, he'd go about his chores, whistling while he mended fences or tended to a pregnant cow or horse. As a young father, he'd perch us behind him on his tractor or take us for rides in the big flatbed truck along backcountry roads. He devotedly practiced soil conservation by recontouring and terracing fields so they wouldn't wash away. He loved planting sweet red clover and spreading lime over the fields, as he once told my mother, because it "nourished the earth." He planted a vegetable garden, canning green beans at summer's end. I think in doing these things he sought also to nourish the earth of his soul.

But as the years passed he also drove himself at a furious pace as he tried to keep up with the demands of both flying and farming. He attacked fertilizing, planting, plowing, and slaughtering like a gladiator in the Coliseum, or a soldier in battle. He ordered us all about, especially my brothers, like a general with his troops. Over time, the farm became the place where Joe fell to pieces. More drunk than sober on his days off, in the end he wasn't so much grounded as run into the ground by his drinking.

Neil Russack, a Jungian analyst, offers his own perspective on my troubled parent's earth/sky split. Something in the saga of Joe's childhood tragedy, Russack tells me, and his adoption by his foster father, reminds him of Orson Welles's *Citizen Kane*.

In the movie, Welles plays Charles Foster Kane, who had been born an only child to a poor Colorado family. When the young Kane inherits a fortune, his mother, whom he loved, sends him to New York, where he's put into the care of a guardian who is also a banker. Loosely based on the life of the newspaper magnate William Randolph Hearst,

Kane also grows up to become a publisher. Along the way, his ruthless pursuit of power and wealth tarnishes his earlier dreams of doing good, and ruins two marriages. At the moment of his death, Kane whispers "Rosebud," the name of the sled that he'd had as a little boy—and the last time he'd been really happy. In other words, says Russack, all Kane had ever wanted was to "grow up as a normal child in a loving family and have a normal life."

Without really knowing my father, Russack is careful to tell me, he can only theorize about Joe. But his initial psychological idea, he says, is that just like Kane, my father was searching for the home he'd lost, or perhaps had never really had. "His childhood was disrupted by this traumatic incident with his father, and the family broke up," says Russack. "The whole business of going to live with a wealthy family and having his mother serve him was bizarre. It wasn't normal. That caused a split in him right there. He comes out of the womb of his mother, who then becomes a servant to him in this new house. While one would think it was a godsend, he was wrenched away from his roots."

I interrupt Russack to say that, as I've been told so often, people were just doing what they had to do to survive. "Yes, they were," he replies. "But that doesn't prevent psychological consequences from occurring. There was too much of a disparity between these two worlds. There was a total break and disruption, and then suddenly your father finds himself in an artificial world of wealth and glamour. He was poor, so he was enamored by all the money and power. But it must not have made sense to him; he must have felt unreal. There was no integration between these two worlds, and he couldn't make the connection."

It's against this turbulent backdrop, continues Russack, that my father met the farmer Ollie Boop, while staying with his foster parents. Because Ollie represented to my father something he'd never had, even in his own birth family, it led him to idolize the farmer. "Your father might have seen these normal families living in a normal way, taking care of their children and living off the land," Russack elaborates. "Something must have felt very healing in that."

Yet another split occurred, adds Russack, when my father's foster parents sent him away to flight school. Pilots during World War II, he says, "were the cream of the crop. To be in the Air Force was to be next to god, and he would have been venerated. Something about the magic of flying may have been an extension of his wealthy foster family." Even while he was building his aviation career, however, says Russack, my father would have continued to long for the home he'd never had. In his mind, the Missouri farmers may have been associated with his earlier, positive memories of Ollie. "Your father," continues Russack, "may have felt that the rural way of life was real in a way flying— although it may have spoken to his spirit—wasn't. There was a longing he had to get back to some kind of simple, natural life that he'd never really had, even as a boy."

The split between Joe's childhood family and his adopted family, Russack elucidates, was mirrored in his split between flying and farming. These were both beautiful sides of my father. But the tragedy was that he couldn't bring them together in reality. The problem was, he notes, that my father wasn't grounded enough to sustain the pull of these powerful opposites. "When his childhood got disrupted, something in him got cut. Just like a spinal cord gets cut, preventing the flow of nerve signals. Your father simply didn't have enough substance in him from childhood to sustain a marriage and the dualities of farming and flying. Nor could he even make a life out of one side. Flying all over the map would have further prevented him from getting the grounding that he was seeking from nature."

The kind of childhood trauma my father suffered, observes Russack, need not always end on such a tragic note. "Even when people are damaged, some of them can be healed," he tells me. If my father had been in analysis, for example, says Russack, the therapist might have been able to help him find ways of bridging his painful divide through developing new models and images. "Your father might have come up with a symbol that would have created a bridge between these two different worlds. This new image would have provided him with a framework for new energy to flow into life. But without that healing image, he became a victim."

At the end of our interview, I ask Russack if he sees any new image arising in our culture that would heal the imbalances of our worldview around nature. By way of answering, he brings up a dream that I had shared with him at the start of our conversation. In this dream, a tall, golden camel is accompanying me on a long journey through an austere desert landscape. In this dream I am not alone; a long line of people stretches as far as I can see behind and ahead of me. More remarkable, each person is traveling with his or her own camel. In the dream, I lie down beside my camel on the ground. I curl up beside his strong body and we both fall soundly asleep. When it's time to get up and continue the journey, I wake up the camel too quickly. He is startled and I'm reminded that he's a wild animal. But he soon calms, and we get up and go on with our journey.

One way of thinking about nature, Russack comments, "is that, over time, we've become split off from the realization that our human lives themselves are not separate from the natural world." But in my dream, says Russack, "the camel is carrying me along in a right relationship to nature." I can't impose my will on this amazing creature or he will wake up too fast and, like a real wild animal, turn dangerous and injure me. "This is an animal that knows the way," states Russack. "And he's going to carry you. So the dream reveals that you yourself are connected to something instinctive inside that knows better than your conscious mind how to go about this journey of life. You have an animal guide who's going to take care of you and guide you. And that itself is an aspect of nature."

While my father slept soundly in his comfy chair that quiet afternoon, I studied the creased lines of his face and considered again the conflict he was taking with him into death. Of Joe's twin loves, I realized, it was flying that had come easiest to him; walking the ground of his own life had proved the more difficult art. Although he'd possessed the potential for a stabilizing connection to nature that could have helped keep him sane, he'd overridden those instincts, poking and prodding at the wild animal inside himself, driving it into exhaustion until it had turned on him in a fury. Ultimately, the farm would turn against him, as he, too, would turn against the farm. I can't really blame my father for how things turned out. Besides, by living out the American dream of progress as fast and as hard as he could, he'd thought he was doing the right thing.

VII

The Snake in the Barrel

Rise and fall. It is one of the archetypal patterns of life, and one of its most ancient, cosmic lessons. But how one falls, the style of coming down, remains the interesting part.—**James Hillman**, *The Soul's Code*

ELLMUHN!! COLLEEEEN!"

My sister had just arrived from Los Angeles. We were in Hilda's bedroom on what my father liked to call "the Mexican side of the house," mindlessly watching a rerun of *Dallas*, when my stepmother's screams split the air. Jumping up, we ran into Joe's bedroom. It was not, as they say, a pretty sight. My father, dressed only in his pajama bottoms, had fallen out of his king-size bed.

Joe's legs were stretched out before him. His back rested against the side of the bed facing us, as if he'd slipped down from the edge as he was trying to sit up. His head was slumped to the side. A thin trickle of saliva ran from his mouth and down his unshaven chin, disappearing somewhere in the huge mound of his bare stomach. His eyes were closed; he was out cold. Hilda's petite figure was bent over him. She was crying as she tugged at my father's fleshy shoulders. As we entered the room she turned and looked at us, her dark eyes dilated wide in panic.

I felt my body grow heavy, as if I'd been nailed to the ground through the soles of my feet. At the same time, my mind sailed off into the sky like a balloon. All the years of my therapeutically hard-earned adulthood fell away. Once again, I was a girl confronting a crazy madman. A man who claimed to be my father. With effort, I willed myself back into the moment. I was a grown woman of forty-four, I reminded myself: a mother, a writer, an adult who knew what to do, or, at least, *should* know what to do with a drunk father. The truth was, I had no idea, and I never had.

Swimming against powerful currents of resistance, I crossed the room to Joe's side. "Dad! Dad! Wake up," I beseeched him. "What's wrong? Say something!" Just looking at his body crumpled on the floor, the spittle on his face, filled me with revulsion, as did his urine-stained pajamas. The stench pushed me back; I could hardly touch him. I glanced up at his bedside table and saw the cigarette still burning in the overflowing ashtray. A bottle of Smirnoff and a half-empty glass leered at me. That potent cocktail of emotion known only to the child of an alcoholic—the icy rage, the burn of hurt feelings, the desire to punish, and the impulse to save, all mixed in with ridiculous love and concern—churned in my gut.

We kneeled together on the floor beside Joe and my sister and I exchanged a look. "He is very, very drunk," said Hilda, intercepting our silent communication. Though I'd often seen my father like this in the past, it had been a long time. "*Si, si*, yes, he is drunk," Hilda said again. "Let's go. You and Colleen, the three of us, we'll lift him back into bed."

Hauling my obese, ill, and drunk father back onto his high bed, I knew, was never going to happen. Still, I wanted to oblige my stepmother, and I began to tug. It then occurred to me that my father might not only be drunk. What if he'd had a heart attack? What if what we were trying to do was damaging him? In addition to cancer, Joe had high blood pressure and emphysema; his oxygen tank stood in the corner. "Shouldn't we call the paramedics?" I asked my stepmother. "Something else might be wrong with him," agreed Colleen.

Hilda sat back on her haunches, a horrified look on her face. "No!" she said emphatically, shaking her head back and forth. "No. Your father will be very angry if you do this." Joe was just drunk, she repeated, pointing to the vodka bottle on the bedside table. Hilda had long ago reconciled herself to her fate as an alcoholic's wife. She'd chosen peace over marital strife and concluded that it wasn't her job to sober Joe up. She'd even confided in me once what a catch my father had been. Back in Mexico, she'd told me, she'd mostly known men who were macho and controlling. My father, despite his alcoholism, had been a gentleman, and had treated her with respect.

But I also knew that she was frightened of my father, and how he might react if we called for emergency help. Even at seventy-two years old, weak and sick, nearly voiceless, Joe could be intimidating. Still, it didn't feel right to just leave him on the floor, wrapped in blankets. "He's passed out on the floor," I said. "Even if he is drunk, maybe something else has happened." Colleen felt as strongly as I did. My sister and I assured Hilda that we would take responsibility, and so I dialed 911. "He *is* your father," said my stepmother, giving in.

Within minutes, an ambulance pulled up to the door and three emergency technicians jumped out. Grateful for their presence, I led them to Joe's bedroom, breathing in their strength and sobriety as if inhaling smelling salts. The three men took out their medical instruments and knelt in a circle around my father, checking his vital signs. They determined that he hadn't had a heart attack and then linked arms beneath his legs and back to hoist him onto his bed. As one of the paramedics stepped back, I noticed that he saw the vodka bottle. "Oh, is that what this is about?" he asked, glancing in our direction. I nodded my head, even as I hung it in embarrassment. "But he has prostate cancer, too, and emphysema," I said. "We think he should go to the hospital just to be sure everything is alright." All three nodded their heads in agreement.

Just as the medics leaned over my father to load him onto the stretcher, Joe came to. His eyes surveyed the scene surrounding him and he turned red with fury, like a bull backed into a corner. "Who the hell are you!" he rasped. "Get the hell out of my house! Who the hell called you here?" He turned and fixed his glare at the three of us. "I did, Dad," I said as calmly as I could. "We thought you'd had a heart attack," said Colleen. Surely, I thought, he couldn't really be angry with my sister or me. Stunned, Joe's eyes blinked. Then he turned his attention back to the paramedics, raining down curse words on their helpful heads. "Goddamn you to hell, you sons of bitches, get out. GET OUT of my house!"

"Dad, you're sick, you need to go to the hospital," I pleaded. But Joe was having none of it. "We can't take him against his will," said the paramedic with the calm brown eyes and curly blond hair. "If he's conscious, he has the right to refuse treatment." They packed up their medical bags and left as quickly as they'd arrived, whisking their precious normalcy away with them. "Don't feel bad. You did the right thing calling us," said the last one down the path, as I watched my medical angels disappear into the waiting ambulance.

Walking back to the house, I felt tired to my bones. Not a trace of hope animated my heart. All the careful work my father had done so far seemed to have crumbled. I'd allowed myself to forget the central fact of my father's life: that he was irredeemably and unrepentantly an alcoholic. Nothing would ever take this family wound away.

As I returned to my father's bedroom, I knew that Joe was in a fighting mood, and that he had words for me. As sick as he was, I was astonished at how he could still make me cower in fear. "Don't. You. Ever. Do. That. Again," he snarled in his cancer-roughened voice. His eyes were the same cold, hard blue I so well remembered. The words were every bit as venomous as when I'd angrily confronted him as a girl for backhanding my brother. "Now get the hell out of here and leave me alone," he said, turning over on his side. And so I did. It was our last evening in Corpus Christi. My sister and I left first thing the next morning. We didn't even say good-bye. His bedroom door was closed.

In the aftermath, bitterness of spirit wrapped itself tightly around my heart, squeezing out any compassion I had for my father. Even as I wrote columns on spiritual and psychological topics, I found myself unable even to pray for my father. Joe wouldn't die of cancer, I told myself. No. He'd end up dying in a fiery car crash, mangled by shards of glass and twisted metal, guilty of the deaths of his innocent victims. Or he'd wander outside in an alcoholic stupor in the middle of the night, and die cold and abandoned in a ditch by the side of the road— just like he'd always wanted. There would be no loving farewells, no soulful reconciliation, no apologies for wrongs done. Just a predictably melodramatic end to a calamitous life of adventurous highs and alcoholic lows.

When I discussed the incident with my brothers, I was surprised to discover that they saw things differently. "I can see how Dad might have felt humiliated," said John, gently. "He probably felt ashamed in front of you." His words got under my skin. Had I slipped back into the familiar rut of trying to save my father, I wondered? Had I once again become the heavy-handed daughter-healer I'd been as a teenager, rushing to my father's rescue in an attempt to return him to sobriety? Had I handled it all wrong? And if I had, what was the right way to be with a dying alcoholic father?

America's Drinking Story

Addiction is such a threadbare word for the mad force that tears through the life of the alcoholic, or the tempest that levels the drinker's family. I dislike just as intensely the overused, unimaginative words *denial*, *codependency*, and *recovery*. Having outlived their usefulness, they've turned into distancing mechanisms that detach us from the underlying emotional despair and physical anguish of the addict. In his comprehensive study *The Natural History of Alcoholism Revisited*, the psychiatrist George E. Vaillant expresses something of the unremitting harshness that comes from both being an alcoholic and growing up with one: "Outside of residence in a concentration camp," he writes, "there are few sustained human experiences that make one the recipient of as much sadism as does being a close family member of an alcoholic." Alcoholism and its consequences, in other words, are a form of torture—both to the alcoholic and to the alcoholic's loved ones.

But alcoholism is more complicated still, a stubborn condition that can never be boiled down to simple terms. As I learn from Vaillant's research, no two alcoholics are the same. The disorder, he writes, "has an unstable, chameleon-like quality that makes it difficult to pin down at any time." Alcohol abuse, he maintains, isn't black and white, but gray. Some experts who have studied the phenomenon, he writes, "doubt that any such entity exists."

213

Thus, according to Vaillant, who is a professor of psychiatry at Harvard Medical School, there are as many "alcoholisms" as there are alcohol abusers. Some alcoholics die, some stop drinking altogether, and some are safely able to return to social drinking. Each alcoholic has his or her own collection of symptoms and behaviors that, over the course of a lifetime, make up their unique narrative, or drinking story. Culture, too, plays an important role. Social attitudes toward drinking, economics, ethnicity, and legislation are all important factors that influence the way a child learns to drink, writes Vaillant.

Joe Carroll's own drinking story began long before he was born, shaped by America's larger saga with alcohol. When my father was born in 1922, America was two years into Prohibition. Jeannine Treese, the executive director of the Blair County Historical Society, tells me that at that time illegal moonshine stills were hidden in the dark folds of the Altoona mountains. This made the back hills a treacherous place. One of her grandmother's best friends, says Treese, was shot in those woods as she was gathering greens for a school dance. It was thought she was killed because she'd wandered too close to an illegal still. Although the bars were shuttered, there were back alley speakeasies where people could gather to drink. Despite these illegal sources of alcohol, however, consumption would decline under Prohibition's stiff penalties. Never since, says A. Thomas McLellan, a professor of psychology and a leading researcher on addictions, "has this country had lower accident rates. Even liver disease went down."

But Prohibition would prove to be a mere interlude in what was a deeply ingrained national habit. "There has always been drinking in America," declare historians Lender and Martin in their book *Drinking in America*. Beginning with the *Mayflower*, the earliest settlers used alcohol to ward off illness and body aches, and to aid digestion. To live without this "good creature of God," as the colonists called it, was unimaginable. Instead of coffee or tea breaks, colonists picked up the jug and enjoyed "eleveners" and "four o'clock drams." Alcohol could be found in the fields and at communal barn raisings, prayer meetings, polling places, militia drills, and political gatherings.

A person might think that church would have been the hub of

community life in colonial America. Yet it was the tavern—a highly regarded institution attended just as faithfully as the churches—where families gathered to gossip and talk politics over a mug of beer or cider. In fact, the colonial tavern was held in such high esteem, says Howard Shaffer, director of the Division on Addiction at the Cambridge Health Clinic, that "the first person whose child was admitted to Harvard, after the dean, was that of the tavern master." Drinking may have been socially acceptable, but drunkenness was not. Rituals and sanctions were in place, says Shaffer, to discipline the person who stepped out of bounds. The presence of many generations and both sexes at the tavern, he says, enforced a kind of natural regulation in early American drinking patterns.

The move toward independence from England would begin to change these traditions of drinking moderately. As individual rights became elevated over communal values, the social bonds that once held drinking in check began to loosen. Around the time of the American Revolution, settlers began brewing their own hard liquor rather than rely on imports from the Old World. Americans, write Lender and Martin, began to feel that "as long as drinking harmed no one but the drinker," it was nobody's business what they did. Indeed, it is worth speculating, they note, "whether democratic ideology itself was not an important factor in American drinking habits. The rise of this individualist ideology and the dramatic increase in drinking were parallel phenomena."

Along with an increase in drinking came the sight of inebriated citizens stumbling along and throwing up in public, offending the sensibilities of those Protestant Americans who idealized polite and virtuous behavior. One of the first to frame extreme drinking as a health threat was Dr. Benjamin Rush of Philadelphia. In 1784, Rush, who was one of the original signers of the Declaration of Independence and a friend of both John Adams and Benjamin Franklin, published *An Inquiry into the Effects of Ardent Spirits upon the Human Body and Mind*. Drawing attention to alcohol's addictive powers, he wrote that where alcohol was concerned, "even a saint would have a hard time controlling himself."

Benjamin Franklin would share Rush's concerns. As A. Thomas McLellan tells me the story, Franklin, in accord with the custom at the time, paid the employees at his printing presses in pints of strong beer administered throughout the day. When the pragmatic Franklin noticed that his workers were intoxicated all the time, he offered to pay them money instead—with the added stipulation that they couldn't drink on the job. Not surprisingly, profit and output soared. Together with Rush, Franklin opened the first treatment facility for inebriation at Pennsylvania Hospital in Philadelphia. McLellan, whose office at the University of Pennsylvania overlooks this storied building, says that Franklin and Rush founded their treatment center because "they discovered that people couldn't stop drinking. And so they reasoned that it had to be an illness. But it was also very much in the Quaker tradition—to do good, to do well, and to produce more."

As Americans headed west into the frontier wilderness, their drinking habits would edge further beyond the bounds of social control. Stripped of the inhibitory influences of family and community, drinking for the transient, "Type-II" frontier population of miners, cowboys, fur trappers, and drifters became a rude business. Instead of families gathering around a table, the consumption of alcohol was now accompanied by "gambling, whoring, and fighting," write Lender and Martin. Binge drinking became a born-on-the-range phenomenon. The Civil War was yet another benchmark in America's drinking story, Howard Shaffer tells me. Away from home, men began downing brews alone or with prostitutes. Drinking during the Civil War, he says, was also "a macho thing" associated with violence.

In examining the American drinking story and its background influence on my father, the influence of the Irish cannot be overlooked. This ancestral land of my Carroll grandfathers—where alcoholism runs deep in the blood and is colloquially spoken of as the "Irish demon" or the "Irish curse"—is legendary even today for its hard-drinking ways. If the Irish in Ireland used alcohol to numb the pain of centuries of poverty and political oppression, they would turn to the bottle in America to resist assimilation. Discriminated against for their Catholic faith, Irish men drank to bond and to strengthen ties of ethnic identity. By the nineteenth century, the stereotype of the intoxicated Irishman had taken its place on the crowded stage of the American psyche.

With this in mind, I search for any family drinking stories that might have been passed down the line of my paternal Irish lineage. None of the relatives I speak with can recall any mention of my grandfather, George Carroll, as a drinker. Possibly Prohibition played a role in this. It seems likelier that my great-grandfather, William Carroll, that much closer to Ireland and being a new immigrant, might have been possessed by the Irish love of alcohol. I recall the PR laborers' habit of stopping after work to swill down "boilermakers," and wonder whether this habit passed down to Joe from both his Irish and German grandfathers, and even possibly his father, instilled in him a love of drink.

In the period surrounding my great-grandfather's arrival on these shores in 1862, Irish and German beer had taken its place alongside whiskey as the favorite national beverage among the industrial working classes. But it was also around this time that a collective outcry against the scourge of alcohol would rise up and intensify in volume. This was the voice of women, who would play a central role in this new movement. Wives who were dependent on their husbands for support worried about wages lost to the barrooms—not to mention the vice associated with the backstreet dives and other "dens of iniquity" that had replaced the community tavern. Violence and sexual abuse perpetrated by alcoholic fathers, sons, brothers, and uncles against women and each other also plagued families.

By 1869, a Prohibition movement had begun to build momentum, leading to the formation of the National Prohibition Party. A coalition of preachers, women's rights advocates, and other reform leaders began lobbying to make alcohol illegal. Spurred by the Woman's Christian Temperance Union, write Lender and Martin, women with Bibles in hand organized pray-ins and began "kneeling in front of hotels, taverns, and anywhere else liquor was sold." Newly arrived immigrants from "wet" cultures, such as the Italians and Jews, became targeted for their "free and easy" drinking habits—despite the fact that they came from homelands where, as had once been the case in America, there were strict social sanctions against drunkenness. Anti-immigration sentiments fused with anti-drinking ideals. Liquor became associated with a "low class of foreigners" and a decadent and corrupt Europe.

Into this swelling tide of Prohibition frenzy stepped the barons of industry. Steady hands, a sharp mind, and the discipline to meet schedules and operate trains and automobiles were needed to launch the massive industrialization process underway in late nineteenth- and early twentieth-century America. Alcohol, as any sixteen-year-old with a new license is taught to understand, doesn't mix well with heavy machinery. Railroad employers began firing anyone (like my grandfather?) caught drinking on the job. Henry Ford, an ardent prohibitionist, vowed to fire anyone who drank—even in the privacy of his or her own home. William Randolph Hearst and John D. Rockefeller warned against alcohol's power to cloud reason. Andrew Carnegie, write Lender and Martin, advised young men on their way up to "never enter a bar-room, nor let the contents of a bar-room enter you."

This mighty push to get America to climb "to the final heights of Mt. Sinai," as one dry journalist put it, culminated in the Volstead Act of 1920, which outlawed the sale of alcohol. Lender and Martin theorize that among the forces shaping Prohibition was the Civil War's shattering impact on the young republic's newly forming identity. The flood of immigrants arriving between the 1860s and early 1900s, they say, also threatened to erode the union's fragile foundation. It is a further step in interpretation, but I can't help but wonder whether Prohibition wasn't also an effort on the part of a rebellious, insecure, young America to differentiate itself from its "European parent" by banning alcohol.

By 1933, Prohibition was over, and the pendulum would swing back in the direction of more liberal drinking attitudes. It was the height of the Depression. Mad with joy, drinkers crowded into bars, jostled for barstools, and raised their glasses at the news. My father would have been eleven at the time. I picture his family gathered around the radio, listening to President Roosevelt as he welcomed the "return of individual freedom" at the same time as he urged "the education of every citizen toward a greater temperance."

Fourteen years after the passage of the Eighteenth Amendment, America had changed. The country, say Lender and Martin, had tired of the rigid legislation of personal morality. The criminalization of alcohol had created a dangerous criminal underworld. Sobriety was no longer as critical as it had been to maintain social stability. World War I had been fought, and the tasks of industrialization had been accomplished. Formerly dry industrialists now urged Americans to relax and enjoy the products of their factories and businesses. Besides, consumerism, not abstinence, was what was needed to help the country emerge from the Depression. Repeal of the Eighteenth Amendment, write Lender and Martin, meant "the employment of thousands in a rejuvenated liquor industry and a bonanza in liquor taxes for fiscally starved governments."

Women had changed as well. The power they'd gained during the campaign for temperance had helped spark the modern feminist movement and mobilized them to win the vote in 1920. Ironically, as more women began to step beyond their traditional roles in the home, their attitudes toward alcohol consumption began to soften. They, too, as Lender and Martin note, began to indulge in the social pleasures of drinking. As if to confirm this narrative twist, the only family drinking story I'm able to uncover about my grandparents involves my grandmother. After big parties thrown by the Glovers—Joe's adoptive parents for whom she worked—Grandmother Carroll would pour all the leftover liquor from the glasses and bottles into a large bowl. Then she'd return up the hill to her old house, where she'd dispense her potent brew to her sons and daughters still living there.

It's hard to mark the exact moment when my father began his descent from a social drinker to a serious alcoholic. Alcohol had been an indigenous tradition of his early flyboy days. My mother recalls how, in Argentina and Israel, Joe would return from a flight and then head out drinking with his fellow pilots. They would sit at the table in a bar and toss back drinks as they came down from the high of flying. Even as my dying father recounted his war memories to me, he remembered happily crazy drinking nights in sultry Rio de Janeiro with fellow pilots, and how they'd lean out the windows of his apartment and flirt with the girls on the streets below.

But there's no doubt that his downward slide began with beer, the elixir of his manhood. Joe popped a can of Bud the way Popeye downed spinach: head back, throat muscles gulping, then swiping the back of his hand across his mouth in satisfaction. He drank so much beer, my father used to joke to my sons, that he figured he owned a share of the Clydesdale horses pulling the brewery wagon in the Budweiser beer commercials. When the family first arrived on the farm in 1955, recalls Sheila, my father was already downing eighteen beers a day.

By any measure, this was a prodigious amount of alcohol. At the time, however, it barely registered with my mother. Naively, she says, she believed that beer couldn't get you drunk. Raised in Argentina, where alcohol was interwoven with daily life, Sheila had grown up being given small sips of wine at the dinner table. No such thing as a legal drinking age existed in Buenos Aires; alcohol was never the taboo there that it was in America. This cultural difference between my parents may have inoculated my mother against alcoholism. Yet it would also slow her reaction to the gravity of Joe's drinking problem.

As the forties melted into the fifties and early sixties, anyone would have had a tough time separating the alcoholics from the social drinkers. With Prohibition a distant memory, America had swung to the other extreme on the drinking scale. A new era of finger-snapping cool was in the ascendancy. Those cocktails-in-hand hipsters, Frank Sinatra, Dean Martin, Joey Bishop, and Peter Lawford, were performing at the Sands Hotel in Las Vegas, and on Joe's radio by his chair. Hugh Hefner had brought sex and an alcohol-smooth way of life out of the closet, and Joe was mooning over the singer Lena Horne and her hip-swaying performances on *The Dean Martin Show*. All across the country, cigarettes dangled from lips or between index and middle fingers; martini glasses clinked, served by wives to their husbands returning home from work. Sometimes, before dinner, Joe and Sheila would sit by themselves in the living room, where they would sip wine and enjoy their special hors d'oeuvre: a half avocado each, with my mother's special dressing of ketchup and mayonnaise.

TWA, my father's employer, was a part of the new gloss of sophistication that lacquered postwar America. In magazines and posters, the friendly airline was touted as "luxury living aloft," which included liquor and in-flight movies. Marie Trainer, a retired TWA hostess and former director of the Airline History Museum in Kansas City, tells me that it was a "different world" then. She recalls mixing Manhattans and whiskey sours from the mini bottles of vodka and scotch served on every flight. It wasn't until the surge of international flights in the late sixties, Trainer says, that wine would be available to passengers.

The company's eccentric owner, Howard Hughes, notorious for his ties to Las Vegas and Hollywood, added another note of glamour. Jane Russell was his lover, and Cary Grant was one of his few close friends. Because of this connection, TWA appeared in more movies than any airline of the era. The 1959 movie *North by Northwest* starring Grant pictured a TWA airliner behind the actor's shoulder—"with no apparent relevance" to the movie's plot, as the authors of *TWA* note. The classy David Niven and the pert Debbie Reynolds were photographed boarding TWA flights.

Like Charles Lindbergh, Howard Hughes was another one of Joe's heroes. Although Hughes was a mentally unstable drug addict who referred to himself as "God" and drove TWA to the edge of bankruptcy, he'd also been a brazen aviator and a brilliant inventor in the field. Joe idolized Hughes. One day, my father came home from a trip and held us spellbound with a story of how he'd been chosen to show the eccentric Hughes around the cockpit of one of TWA's fleet of planes. "Boy, did the man know planes," said my father, his face lit up with pride. "And he was very nice. Quiet. Had long fingernails. But very polite." Dad always claimed that the reason TWA began to go downhill was because they'd forced Hughes out. Commenting on my father's choice of heroes, Dr. Jerrold Post remarks on the way they reveal his psychology. "These were really quite lonely, highly driven individuals. But your father recognized in them an individual questing that was perhaps intrinsic to his sense of himself, as well."

It would be close to thirty years before TWA would eventually go bankrupt. But in the immediate aftermath of Hughes' departure, the airline entered a golden period of financial success. My father, too, was enjoying a period of professional accomplishment. He'd switched from the piston-powered Lockheed Constellation and was now flying the sleek, bullet-shaped Boeing B-707 jet. The farm was flourishing, as were his four children. For several easy, peaceful, Christmases in a row, Joe had given my mother a crisp one-hundred-dollar bill, tucked into a large card placed under the tree. Another Christmas, he'd given her a full-length mirror. When my little sister asked him what his Christmas present was, Joe replied, sentimentally, "I get my present every time I see your mother's reflection in the mirror."

The first hint I had that there might be trouble in our rural Eden arose when I was eleven years old. It was 1962, and *That Touch of Mink*, starring Doris Day and Cary Grant, was playing at the movies. Joe admired both these actors and so my parents planned a special date night in Kansas City. After Agnes, the neighboring farmer's wife, had arrived to babysit, Joe and Sheila drove off down the driveway in their brand new, boat-size, frost-blue Chrysler station wagon.

My mind was a froth of envy as I waited up for my parents. There were no theaters in Oak Grove, which made going out to the movies a very big deal. Television ads of the platinum blonde, blue-eyed, impossibly adorable Doris Day swathed in a plush white mink coat flirting with the debonair Grant had made me heady with romance. So when my parents walked back in the door much later that evening, I was ready with questions. "How was the movie?" I asked excitedly, studying their faces, impatient for details. "It was alright," said my mother coolly, turning her back. "What did you talk about?" asked my sister. "Not much," said my mother. "Hummph," grunted my father, disappearing into their bedroom. Sheila's aloofness and Joe's distance took me by surprise. How could a movie with a title and movie stars like that disappoint anyone?

I had yet to make the connection between my father's drinking and my mother's bad moods. But neither had my parents, and my father persisted in his quest to bring a taste of the TWA good life to his farm-bound family. One Christmas morning not long after my parents' failed date night, we awoke to find a large, oblong box under the tree. After the four of us had torn into our gifts, unwrapping our chocolate-covered cherries, Barbie and Ken dolls, books, toy guns, and paint-by-number sets, Joe handed the mysterious box to Sheila. Removing the lid and opening the tissue paper, Sheila drew in her breath. Gingerly, she pulled out a full-length white fur coat. "Joseph!" she said, turning to my father. She always called him by his full name at important moments.

Joe flushed and smiled. "It's not real. It's fake fur," he said, his masculine pride flashing. "It's artificial, but made to look like real mink." The four of us shrieked and danced around the room like banshees at such opulence. None of us had ever seen anything like it before. We must be rich! But carefully, prudently, rich; for it was, after all, fake.

My mother pulled the coat on over her nightgown and gazed at her reflection in the full length mirror, with her admiring audience in the background. Happiness warmed the air. There was a side of my father that aspired to be a big-time spender, a man like Howard Hughes or Frank Sinatra, who lavished gifts on beautiful women. Now he basked in that role. Later that afternoon, after we'd gone to Mass and had fed the cows and horses, the family sat around the table spread with roast turkey, stuffing, mashed potatoes, and mince pies. Raising his metal beer stein high, Joe led the four of us kids in a cheer. This was the Joe Carroll ritual he'd created on those days when life was good, and he wanted us to show our appreciation for my mother. "Hip hip hooray! Hip hip hooray! Hip hip hooray!" we shouted in unison three times. My mother bowed her head, shyly receiving this show of affection.

Sometime later, Joe took Sheila and her new coat on a weekend trip to Las Vegas. I had adjusted to my father's constant traveling, but only because my mother was always home. As excited as I was for her, I hated watching her white fur–clad back walk out the front door, and I sulked. But just two days later, Joe and Sheila were back. They'd cut their trip short.

"I hated Las Vegas," my mother announced, her lips drawn down in severe displeasure. "All those casinos and that gambling. I was so bored. It's a terrible place. Seedy. I couldn't wait to come home." My father said nothing. As he always did when he was in a bad mood, he went into his bedroom and closed the door. After that, my mother only wore her fake fur to Sunday morning Mass. Perhaps like the women of the old Temperance movement, she'd wanted to redeem herself from the drinking life and all that came with it: the dancing showgirls, the gambling tables, the tawdry nightclub life. And the drunkenness and abuse.

Good Love, Bad Love

For me, growing up with an alcoholic parent was like skating on the frozen farm ponds in winter. Skimming over ice that was judged thick enough to hold my weight, I'd gain confidence and skate farther out from shore. Then, suddenly, there would be a loud boom. A long crack would appear, running straight through to where I was standing, and I'd skate back on trembling legs, remembering the stories of local children who'd drowned this way. I always managed to make it back safely. With my father, however, I was never really sure when the ice might break and I might fall into the freezing, murky waters, and drown. Every time I felt secure, the ground shook, cracked, and opened up beneath me.

A memory: My father's younger brother, Uncle Gene, has just phoned. A pilot for Pan Am, he's in Kansas City on a layover and would like to come for an overnight visit. Could Joe come and pick him up? His flight would be arriving around seven P.M. A visit from one of my father's brothers was as rare an event as a total eclipse. When they happened, Joe vaulted out of himself and into highflying hyperdrive.

Joe hung up the phone and began charging around the house, shouting orders. "SheiLUH! Where are the goddamn keys to the Chrysler? And where's my damn wallet?!" He began disappearing into his bedroom, then reemerging, smacking his lips as he sometimes did after sneaking a drink. As the late afternoon wore on, he grew louder and more pugnacious.

While Joe dashed about getting ready to pick my uncle up from the airport, the skies outside grew dark. I remember the thunderclaps, the lightning, and the dread that sliced through my stomach like dancing knives. Then the skies opened, and a Midwestern monsoon poured forth. It had been dry that year, and the moisture was needed. But the life-giving rain gave my father a death-defying idea. "I'm taking you kids with me," he barked. "That's an order! Let's go. Get in the car."

Before I knew it, I was huddled in the backseat of the Chrysler station wagon. As we pulled out of the driveway, I shrunk myself into a ball. How old was I? Somewhere between ten or twelve, but the trauma-smudged memory makes it hard to say. Soon, we were driving down the paved two-lane highway that led into town. As we sped through the empty streets of Oak Grove, I gazed longingly out the window at the stores, and then, just before the freeway entrance, the new Oak Grove Truck Stop. I stared at the bulky truck drivers in their caps and jackets inside the warmly lit interior. I longed to be with them, sitting in safe normalcy at the yellow Formica tables, sipping from hot mugs of coffee and eating Mrs. Phillips's homemade cinnamon buns.

The truck stop receded into darkness as my father turned onto the overpass, entering I-70, the freeway that would get us to Kansas City in a little over forty minutes. Joe was running late, and in his zeal to pick my uncle up on time he began to drive faster. The rain fell in gray sheets outside the car. "Dad, slow down," I begged him. "You're going too fast. What if we crash?" But Joe just laughed and pushed harder on the gas pedal. "Oh, ye of little faith," he said, quoting the one and only Bible verse he knew, as he raced down the rain-slicked highway. When my sister tried to fasten her seat belt, and when I drew in my breath in fear, Joe flashed us an angry glare. I felt sick and crouched on the floor of the car. The shadowy shapes of my silent siblings surrounded me; each of us was in our own private hell. "Hail Mary, full of grace, the Lord is with thee," I began to whisper to myself. Paralyzed with fright, certain that I was going to die, I forgot the words to the rest of the prayer.

My father's voice broke into my blind terror. "Look! Pell! Kids! We're going a hundred miles an hour!" he shouted. I raised my head over the backseat. Joe pointed to the speedometer. The four of us kids began to scream. "Dad! Slow down, slow down—we're going a hundred miles an hour! EEEEEEHHHH!" But my father pressed on in the pouring rain, the thrill of the ride making him as heady as the alcohol he'd downed.

By some miracle, we reached the Kansas City Municipal Airport alive. Perhaps Mary, after all, had thrown her mantle of grace over the Chrysler speeding through the stormy night. I remember no more welcome sight in my childhood than the tall and comforting figure of Uncle Gene as he loomed out of the darkness, standing on the sidewalk. Gene had the same sharp, blue Carroll eyes, the bulbous Irish nose, and the heavy jowls. He drank too, but he was blessedly sober that night. Brushing the rain off his black trench coat and shaking the water off his Pan Am hat, he climbed into the front seat of the car. Almost immediately, my father's mad mood dissipated. Even the rain began to let up.

Gene was the quiet Carroll; the brother of few words. "Hi, Joe," he said, as if he'd seen my dad days ago, instead of years. "Hi, kids," he added, turning around to greet us. And then we sat in thankful silence all the rest of the long, slow drive home.

Many years later, as an adult in my fifties, I'd relive this traumatic drunken car ride in a dream. I was alone in the car with my father. As Joe sped faster and faster down the highway, the rage I had not been able to feel as a child began to course through my veins. "Stop the car!" I shrieked, trying to break through the thick nimbus that seemed to envelope my father and made him oblivious to me. Finally hearing me, he slammed on the brakes. I threw open the car door and leaped out. "You could have killed me!" I spat. "Don't you *ever* do that again." This time, the "dream Joe" had the grace to hang his head in shame. Immediately following this confrontation, I found myself sitting in a room. The door opened, and to my surprise my three siblings walked in, each bearing a tray of delicious cheeses and fruits. Last to enter was my father, looking chastened and bearing the largest tray of all.

I puzzled over this dream for a long time. How could my father have appeared in the same dream as both violent and nurturing? By reliving the feelings of sheer fright, and by releasing my anger, had I broken some kind of spell, freeing the sane dad from the grip of the alcohol-possessed demon father? A glimmer of insight comes from psychoanalyst Michael Eigen's aptly titled book *Toxic Nourishment*. In it, I read about two kinds of "contaminated" parental love. The first kind of love is poisoned with hate: unwanted, unloved, treated badly, these children may not feel good about themselves—but they know what they are up against. Then there are the parents, writes Eigen, who truly love their children but whose love is poisoned by a mix of "bad with good," including worry, self-hate, and anxiety. Children of this set of parents suffer debilitating doubt, as they cannot reconcile that they are *really* loved with the fact that love can kill. Sorting out this benevolent/hurting kind of love would become my psychological legacy: the mystery that parents, in their godlike power, can both nurture and crush life.

Aided by my mother, cushioned by the lush fantasy life I led inside my mind, I did my best to grow up as normally as I could, in spite of my father's mad drinking bouts. Like a flower that twines through the cracks in concrete walls, I grew around the broken places in my childhood, reaching up and out for life and warmth.

My childhood friends cheered me up. When Joe was gone, there were sleepovers and slumber parties. But in the enforced solitude of my farm, books would become my savior. Upstairs in my bedroom, or outside beneath a tree, I'd step through their pages into alternate universes. There were horse series, and mystery series, and a series about a girl who wanted to be an archaeologist. To keep myself going and growing, I dreamed big things for my future. Inspired by a young Sally Field in the television show *Gidget*, I imagined becoming a surfer girl running around on the beaches of California. On a trip to San Diego with my parents, I rented a surfboard and took my dream for a test dive. But when a big wave came up, pushing the heavy Styrofoam board against my mouth and knocking out my front tooth, I switched fantasies. I developed a fascination for the famed female aviator Amelia Earhart. I began to daydream about becoming the first woman on the moon. I joined an astronaut's fan club and decorated my bedroom walls with pinups of John Glenn and Alan Shepard. On my sister's side of the room, model airplanes hung from the ceiling over her bed. Even when he came upstairs to say goodnight, Joe never mentioned anything about his daughters' dreams of flying.

I was fourteen when a number of setbacks on the farm and at work pushed my father's alcoholism out of the background and into the open. The first twist of misfortune occurred in the grassy cow pasture behind the big barn. It was late spring. A dry spell had left the fields barren of the grasses that kept our herd of Herefords plump. To make up for the lack, it had become necessary to feed the cows grain. Climbing into the black pickup with Steve and John one day, Joe headed down the hill to the pasture. Once inside the gate, the cattle milled around, bellowing to be fed. Suddenly, a young calf turned frisky.

Twirling and lunging like a bovine kickboxer, it spun around and aimed a kick right at my father's leg. In a split second my father went down, his knee shattered. Somehow, Joe managed to drag himself across the pasture, climb behind the wheel of the truck, and drive himself and my young brothers back to the house.

The sound of the wheels crunching the gravel in the driveway and the loud honking of the horn brought my mother running. Sheila put my father in the Chrysler and drove him to the hospital in Kansas City. Once there, the doctors set his knee and encased it in a plaster cast. It would be six weeks, they told him, before the cast could be removed. Joe had worn a cast once before when he'd sprained his wrist. It had driven him so mad then that he'd taken a saw to it with his other good hand. But this was different; if he removed his cast now, he'd never walk properly again.

Grounded from both flying and farming, Joe was good and pissed off. Taking up residence in our newly built, brick-lined family room with the wood-beamed ceiling hand-varnished by the four of us, Joe brooded in his armchair. His cast-clad leg was stretched out on the hassock in front of him. On the side table next to him were his ship's wheel ashtray, a coffee mug, Johnson's baby oil, and an assortment of pain pills. A flyswatter and a knitting needle for scratching his leg when it itched beneath the cast were also on the table.

I'd just finished my first year of high school. Determined to overcome the reputation I'd gained in junior high as an awkward "cootie bug," I'd set out to become one of the popular girls. I would rise early before school and closet myself in the tiny upstairs bathroom beneath the eaves. Here, each morning, I'd set out my little pots and tubes of Max Factor makeup and apply bright blue shadow to my eyelids, thick black mascara to my lashes, and white frosted gloss to my lips in order to turn myself into a mod sixties girl. I would take out the curlers I'd slept in, and tease, plump, and then spray my dippity-doed brunette hair into a big, stiff bubble with a perfect little flip at the ends.

The next hurdle to clear was my father, for whom the application of makeup was the first step on the road to whoredom. Head down, I'd make my dash for the front door. "Wipe that face off!" I'd hear him yell, as he scuffled after me on his hated crutches. As I waited for the bus at the bottom of the hill, I'd roll up the band of my skirt until a good length of my thighs showed. All these efforts paid off. I knew nothing about football or basketball. I couldn't even do the splits. But I was perky and nice, with a really big smile that everyone seemed to love, and with those talents I made the A team of cheerleaders that year.

As determined as I was to live the life of a normal teenager, it was clear to me that something had begun to go seriously wrong in my father's head. One day, I sought him out to ask permission to go into town and found him in his easy chair, his leg up on his hassock. The television was off, and Joe was staring out the sliding glass doors that opened onto the vista of soft hills. His posture and the expression on his face caught me by surprise. His head was tipped to the side, cradled in his hand that was propped up on his elbow.

"Daddy, can I go into town to Virginia's house?" I asked. Joe's eyes flickered open, and he turned to stare at me. His bloodshot eyes were so fractured with craziness that it caused a shock to run through my body. His nose looked different, too. It was red and big with purple veins, as if a spider had spun its web beneath the skin. I recall wondering where my father had gone. This weird man in the chair did not seem to be related to me.

Joe turned away and continued to stare out the window. "What do you need a friend for?" he said. His words were thick and slurred. Nausea twisted in my stomach. "I just want to go and see Virginia," I said again, dancing on my feet. I wished only to be young, to believe that nothing was wrong with my father, to hold on to the beauty of a Saturday morning. "Mom will drive me, and I won't be gone for long." Silence. Joe finally roused himself, narrowed his eyes, and turned back to me. "Can't trust friends, can't trust anybody," he said. "It's dangerous to have a friend. They'll only hurt you. Take advantage of you. Why would you want to trust Virginia? The only thing a person can trust are those hills out there." Joe gestured out the window. "Only the hills. Only the hills."

"How can you say that?" I retorted. I was angry now. "Friends are the most important thing in life. We all need friends. You can't keep me from my friends!" I was frantic, as if defending my right to life itself. But really, it was my father I was trying to keep alive. Around and around the two of us went, until Joe began to pass out. As his eyes fluttered shut and his head fell back, he gave me the permission for which I'd fought so hard. "Run along, run along, go on and play with Virgginnie-ay," he muttered. "But remember: don't trust her."

That moment is sharply marked in my memory as a pivot I turned on, losing, in the completion of that circular motion, the innocence of my girlhood. An eclipse of madness, like the disc of the moon as it begins to cover the sun, had begun its slow passage across my father's mind. It didn't take us long to figure out that Joe had begun combining his pain pills with vodka. Not that any of us could do anything to stop him. Bored and drunk, Joe devised a new ritual called a "masaky." A mangled version of the Argentine word *masaje* for massage, this was his code word for a scalp rub, and it fell naturally to my sister and me to supply it.

"Hey, Pell! Neen!" my father would shout from his chair in the family room. "How 'bout a masaky? Just a quick one." Upstairs in my bedroom, my head in a Dinny Gordon novel about an archaeological dig in Greece, I pretended not to hear. "Pell. Neen. One of you girls get down here now," Joe would shout again, his words slurring together. After arguing back and forth with my sister—"You go," "No, you go"—I finally gave in. I closed my book and threw it on the bed, trudged down the stairs, through the living room, and into the family room.

I knew the drill. Standing behind Joe's chair, I picked up the plastic bottle of sweet-smelling Johnson's baby oil, squirted a few drops onto his shiny bald pate, and began gingerly rubbing circles with my fingers. "Ummmm, that's good," Joe murmured contentedly. "Makes your hair grow, ya know." Battling my feelings of revulsion, I massaged the top of my father's head, my mind light-years away in either ancient Greece or the football field at Oak Grove High. At moments like these, my fantasy life served me well, allowing me to detach from a repugnant reality. Finally, Joe would release me from the hated ritual. "Run along now, run along. No time for your old dad, but that's okay," he'd say plaintively, as he slipped back into a stupor.

At the time of his accident, Joe was forty-four years old. It was the first time since his own father had died thirty years ago that life had knocked him back. Up to this point he'd been on an upward, fast-moving trajectory away from his past and toward unfettered independence. Now Joe had fallen on hard times. It wasn't quite the same, but just as his father had once been bedridden, now he, too, was confined to the house. Psychologists speak of the way a harsh blow can sometimes reactivate an older, underlying trauma.

Even if Joe didn't know it, a part of him must have been swamped by long-buried feelings dating back to the Depression and his father's death. Old fears of poverty, abandonment, and helplessness must have risen up, coloring the present moment in shades of tragedy out of proportion to what was actually going on. Carl Jung once said that when something important is taken away from a person, they discover what it is that supports them. To this point, work had always supported my father, financially and emotionally. Now, faced with six weeks of forced inactivity, and what must have been terrifying inner turmoil, Joe had chosen Smirnoff.

About halfway through his six-week hiatus, something seemed to snap inside my father. One day, he got out of his chair, and, spurning his doctor's orders, hobbled outside. He climbed into the tractor seat, his cast sticking out to the side, and went about his farm chores like a man possessed. Whether it was because he was drunk, or because he just couldn't sit still anymore, he seemed bent on getting on with his life. Another reason Joe had found it hard to continue staying inside, I suspect, was the new hired hand he'd brought in to help out with the chores: Phil, a stocky black youth who lived outside Oak Grove.

The year was 1966, and that summer the burgeoning Civil Rights movement roiled the country. Race was on everyone's minds. Martin Luther King had taken his movement from the Deep South to the Midwest. As he led marches against racially biased housing practices in Chicago, King, as Michael Eric Dyson writes in his essay "No Small

Dreams," found himself confronted by racist crowds more hostile than anything he'd confronted in Selma or Birmingham. In the state I grew up in, relinquishing the long-held habit of slavery and racism had not come easy. Missouri had been mostly settled by white Southerners who'd imported slaves from Santo Domingo to work the ferries and to cultivate crops of hemp, tobacco, and grain. During the Civil War, over a thousand battles and skirmishes were fought across the state, some in towns close-by our farm, such as Lexington and Independence. So when it came to blacks and whites mingling on an equal footing, an old malignancy festered in the soul of my hometown.

At the time, when Jim Crow laws remained on the books in many municipalities, and separate-but-equal segregation stubbornly held sway, no blacks lived inside the city limits of Oak Grove. The only African-American man who, as far as I know, had ever lived inside the town—Nigger John, as the townsfolk called him—had died in a mysterious fire. Some said later that the fire had been deliberately set inside his trailer. Although kind to their own, many of the local people could be cruel to those they judged outsiders. Rumor had it that there were some townsmen who even belonged to the KKK. Even my sister and I were sometimes called, in an oddly affectionate way, "nigger lips" for our full mouths.

Anyone reading this book might think that my father would have been as prejudiced as the next white, narrow-minded person of the racially charged fifties and sixties. But they would be wrong. My father was hardly any kind of Civil Rights activist. Yet Joe, it turned out, wasn't exactly a racist, either. When we were little children and Joe had heard us call out "Hello, Nigger John," to the grizzled man sitting in front of the corner drugstore, my father had been furious. "He's Mr. John to you," Joe had lectured us with conviction.

Now my father took a real interest in Phil, his new farmhand. Phil was a smiling, good-natured guy. Besides Phil's easygoing personality, my father liked his work ethic and the fact that he knew a lot about farming. But Phil's agricultural talents had been gained at the expense of an education. At age sixteen, he'd never attended public school. Stunned to hear this, and perhaps influenced by the recent passage of the Civil Rights and Voting Rights acts, Joe set about righting this wrong. He drove out to visit Phil's father in his trailer and convinced him to meet with the school's principal. "Told him to go down to Oak Grove High and enroll Phil, and his other kids," said an animated Joe at dinner that night. "Told him to tell the principal to call me if he had a problem."

That my intrepid father had the guts to take up a young black man's cause at such a freighted cultural moment showed a stand-up side of him that aimed to do the right thing. It is a part of him I will always value. But Oak Grove, too, would show its better side to Phil. That fall, they'd welcome their first black student into the school corridors and put him on the football team. Though there were those parents who wouldn't allow their girls to get into a car with Phil, at least he wasn't beaten up or run out of town. Several years later, after I'd left home, the town would show an uglier side to a young black student who'd moved there with his adopted white parents. Outraged at the cocky young man who'd flagrantly dated the town's white girls, some boys had beaten the student repeatedly and had almost killed him. Eventually, scared for his life, he and his parents fled. Even today, Oak Grove remains a predominantly white town.

Finally that summer, the day came when my father's hated cast was removed. Just when life seemed as if it might settle down, Joe experienced another setback. On July 8, 1966, TWA, along with Eastern, United, Northwest, and National airlines, went on strike. As machinists demonstrated for higher pay and better benefits, the travel industry ground to a stop.

The massive shutdown hit a collective nerve. *Time* magazine described how air travel, now the fastest growing industry in the U.S. economy, had come to dominate twentieth-century life:

> As the biggest strike in airline history dragged through its first full week, disruptive effects large and small spread across the entire U.S. economy and throughout the everyday life of Americans. Thousands of vacationers canceled travel plans. Hotel bookings dropped. . . . Cut flowers wilted far

from florist shops; live lobsters piled up awaiting shipment from Maine. Manufacturers dependent on air shipment of electronic parts suffered production delays. Traveling salesmen and executives resorted to circuitous odysseys, chartered air taxis—or stayed home and used a phone.

As the article noted, the potential for growth in air travel at the time was still huge. An astonishing 60 percent of all Americans and 97 percent of the people of the world had yet to board a plane. Indeed, at the time of the strike, TWA had been on the cusp of ordering up fifteen Boeing B-747s, at a cost of $21 million each. These "whale jets," as they were dubbed, were scheduled to join TWA's fleet by 1970. Plans for the SST—the supersonic transport with the jet power to cross the country in a mere two hours and ten minutes—were also on the drawing board. "What all this tampering with time and distance will do to the passenger's psyche and physique," concluded *Time*, "remains to be seen."

Joe Carroll, of course, was living proof of how travel's "tampering" with body and mind could wreck the human biorhythms nature had so finely wrought over thousands of years. Our slavish devotion to progress and technology, Jungian analyst Ernest Rossi tells me, has become the most "tragic story" of our society for the way it has plundered our health. Deep in our collective psyche, he explains, we're possessed by an exploitative "empire-plantation-complex" that goes all the way back to slavery and the British Empire. To meet the pressures of living in such a driven society, he continues, we have to literally push ourselves like slaves.

Even my father's alcoholism, Rossi explains, could have been exacerbated by the irregular rhythms of his aviation career. The body, he says, has a built-in work–relax–work "ultradian" rhythm that runs in 90- to 120-minute cycles throughout the day: work for 90 minutes, then rest for 20 minutes. A kind of Icarus complex encoded in our very biochemistry, the body moves through its own landscape of peaks and valleys. Sever this God-given work–recover rhythm, however, Rossi warns, and we might slip over the edge into addiction. Either we're tired and need a lift, or we're overhyped and need something to help us relax, and so we look for help in a substance. Alcohol is unique, he concludes, because it offers a temporary lift, then a drop—so it gives both an up and a down, and that's why it's so popular.

Certainly, that summer some vital force in my father seemed to spin crazily out of bounds. As TWA struggled to find its way through the financial crisis brought about by the strike, so did he. He'd received no salary while waiting for his shattered knee to heal. Like other TWA employees, he couldn't draw a salary during the strike. Money became an obsession.

AUCTION

As the strike dragged on that summer, my father's mind grew feverish. Awash in alcohol and pain medications left over from his knee injury, Joe arrived at a stunning decision: he would hold an auction. He made the announcement at dinner. "Called the auctioneer. Man by the name of Haynes. Really great guy; like him a lot. Going to sell it all; get rid of it, horses, cows, tractors. You kids don't care about all that stuff anyway," he opined drunkenly. Pushing his captain's chair back from the picnic table, Joe left abruptly with an exaggerated "May I be excuuuused?" The rest of us sat in silence. "Well, that's that," said my mother, as she began to clear the dishes.

Over the following weeks, my father raced around the farm, readying things for the upcoming sale. Watching him, a hollowness began swelling my stomach. Inside that noxious space, knots twisted and tightened. Since I'd been a little girl, I'd always sucked my thumb. "It's because your father flies," my mother had once explained to me, which had seemed to make sense. Now, as my father schemed to sell my beloved Shetland pony out from under me with barely a word of explanation, I stole away to my room, hid under a blanket, and soothed my fourteen-year-old self with this infant-like habit. As always, I prayed to Mary and Jesus to stop my father, alternating Hail Marys and Our Fathers on my rosary. Sometimes, though I knew it was against Church rules, I'd bypass Mary and go directly to Jesus himself.

And, as always, nothing—not God, Jesus, or Mary—could halt Joe Carroll once he'd made up his mind. Even the resolution of the airline

235

strike eight days before the sale couldn't brake his momentum. He'd had posters printed, and Phil had tacked them up around town: "Due to a recent accident, I will hold a Dispersal Sale at the farm located three miles South of Oak Grove, Mo.," it announced. The poster was a black-and-white inventory of my father's dream to be a farmer. He'd decided to have the sale, my mother recalls, because he'd been angry at the calf that had dared to kick him. And so, by God, he was going to get rid of the cattle, and everything else that went along with the dream that had turned on him.

August 27, 1966, dawned as hot and humid as only a Missouri summer morning can be. The front lawn had been newly mowed, and the grass smelled sweet with dew. Not even a breeze stirred the cloudless sky. Trucks, tractors, and other machinery stood in straight rows outside the horse barn by the house. Saddles and bridles were neatly displayed. Down the hill and across the road, the Hereford cows and their calves had been herded into the barnyard. First to arrive was Jim Haynes, the auctioneer. Tall, lean, and stooped, his hawklike face with the beaky nose is still sharp in my mind. I stood on the front porch and watched as he and my father zigzagged among the equipment, gesturing and talking. Back inside, I helped my mother prepare the hot dogs and bake the Betty Crocker brownies that would be sold for lunch. Church groups typically provided lunches at farm auctions as a way to raise money. Joe had greatly annoyed the local church ladies by insisting we make and sell the lunch ourselves.

Around noon, I walked out to the porch and looked down the valley. A long line of Chevvies, Fords, Plymouths, and pickup trucks were slowly snaking their way up to our green house on the hill. The horses in their pasture had caught that something was in the air. Kicking their heels up and racing in circles, they whinnied in high-strung excitement.

Soon the farm was swarming with people. As if I'm gazing at an impressionistic painting from a great distance, I can still see the strangers and friends as they mill among the machinery and animals. There were farmers in overalls, women in cotton summer dresses, muscular boys dressed in tight jeans and shirts with their sleeves rolled up, suntanned girls in cute shorts and spanking white tennis shoes, and giggling children. It seemed to me that everyone in my known universe had come—not just from Oak Grove, but from surrounding towns like Odessa, Grain Valley, and Blue Springs. The auctioneer, who'd set up his lectern in the driveway in front of the alfalfa field, brought down his gavel at 12:30 sharp. His sonorous voice silenced the crowd. Like a priest, he sang out the litany of our farm's inventory, holy relics of my father's dream: thirty-six head of cattle, a one-thousand-gallon truck water tank, a New Holland Hayliner pickup baler, an Allis-Chalmers B Tractor with side mower, among other pieces of equipment. As the adults called out in response, haggling over the price of a cow, a saddle, or a plow, children ran and played in the background.

The beauty of this scene contrasted with the cries of the cattle and horses as they were led up long ramps into dark, strange trailers driven by their new owners. I can't remember this at all, but my sister tells me that we sat on the backs of our horses as Mr. Haynes auctioned them off. Her friends had told her that our horses would be sold to a glue factory and slaughtered, and she was petrified. My only recollection is of standing beside my father on the road in front of the house as he introduced me to the young couple who'd bought Sombra.

I looked down shyly at my feet. It seemed as if a moat surrounded me. My father is speaking, telling me that my horse will now be well cared for. I recall wondering in confusion what had happened to bring this about: Hadn't I spent hours riding and taking care of my horse? Hadn't we shared a close bond, this girl and her Shetland and my father and I, too, over the horses? But Joe turned on his heel and walked away, as oblivious to my hurt as to his own.

I stand in the middle of the road, numb as the truck and trailer drive away down the hill. Sombra's gold tail hangs out over the back gate. His whinnies float back to me. Fear and concern akin to how a mother feels as she watches her child disappear sluice through my heart. I don't cry then; but remembering the whole, sad scene of my horse being sold, I do now.

The dispersal sale was over by early evening. As the last of the cars departed down the tree-lined driveway, Joe sat inside the living room, counting his pile of cash. My mother walked in on this scene, saw my father's face, and recoiled. It was at that moment, she said later, that she realized that my father was going crazy. Mr. Weist, our neighboring farmer, had helped bring some things back inside the house. He, too, had seen my father's look. Taking my mother by the arm, he'd led her outside to the front porch. "Now, you call me if you need anything," he said. "Oh, I will, I will," my mother had responded breezily, masking her feelings. "No. I *mean it*. You call me anytime if you need me," he said again, slowly and with emphasis.

The day after the sale an empty quiet blanketed us all. The farm was bare. My parents were subdued. For the first time in years, there were no chores or animals to feed. I laid on my bed upstairs reading and, when I thought no one was looking, anxiously sucked my thumb. Before long, my father was back at work, flying America's skies. School started and life went on, like a wave washing over an accident on the beach, sucking all the evidence back into the ocean. Eventually, my father would buy sheep; he'd never have cows again. Nor did horses ever again gallop freely in the fields and woods of Shalom Acres.

THE BOTTOM OF THE BARREL

As 1966 became 1967, the world outside my small town continued to convulse with change. With some of Oak Grove's young men off fighting in Vietnam, Communism was on everyone's minds. Off in the distance, like a slow-rising cumulus cloud, the antiwar movement of pacifists, hippies, folk singers, and poets was amassing. I was no longer required to pin a black lace mantilla on my head before entering the church. Latin had given way to English in the service, and medieval chants had been replaced with folk songs. The moon, whose cycles had for centuries guided farmers, now beckoned as a new American outpost. Astronauts were the new cowboys. Nothing on terra firma seemed too firm, most especially with my parents. I watched their marriage disintegrate under the pressure of my father's alcoholism and became fascinated by the feminist notion that a woman could control her destiny by refusing marriage and children.

One day, during a debate in science class about the birth control pill, I impulsively raised my hand. Boldly, I announced my plans to hold off on marriage and family until I was thirty by taking the pill. In my town, where sex outside of marriage was a grave social sin and where it sometimes seemed that wedding plans began around the age of twelve, a statement like this was close to heresy. "You'll be pregnant and married by the time you're twenty-one," my teacher said, sarcastically. As it happened, so I was, albeit under different conditions than he'd imagined. But those patronizing words still sting.

By the time the summer of 1967 came around, our dinner table had turned into a verbal combat zone. When my father wasn't reaming me out on my new alliance with the "hippie dippy" peace movement, he and my mother were battling it out over, well, just about anything. The insults he hurled at her over our heads dripped with loathing. She was a pig, a mess, a fat slob, lazy, and disgusting. Adding to the tension in the house were the medical conditions afflicting both my brothers. Steven had developed Osgood-Schlatter disease, knee pain caused by sports and growth spurts, and had his leg in a cast. John had been diagnosed with septic arthritis and had been hospitalized. The burden of my brothers' care had fallen to my mother.

One humid day when Sheila was at the hospital, Joe went outside to clean the pool. I was sitting beneath the widespread branches of the giant oak tree in our front yard writing poetry. Colleen was reading "poolside," as Dad used to say. My father went inside the barn to get something. Abruptly, his voice rang out. "Neen! Get in here."

My sister jumped up in alarm and ran into the barn. Through the dim light she saw my father standing by the large barrel of diatomaceous earth, an organic compound he put in the pool filter to keep out bugs and reptiles. "Neen: I need you to reach in the barrel and get me a scoop for the pool." She started to step toward the barrel, but froze at his next words. "Damn snake's in there, so I can't do it." Trained to obey—or else—Colleen crept to the edge of the barrel, then leaned in to see for herself. A coiled snake hissed up at her. She leaped back in fright and refused to put her hand in, as any sane person would have done.

But my father was neither sane nor sober. "Goddammit, Neen!" he yelled. "Do what I said! What are you scared of, a little ol' snake?" But my sister refused, cowering by the door. "Goddammit!" he shouted again. "I guess I'll just have to do it myself." In disbelief, my sister watched as Joe stuck his hand in. Instantly, he jumped back, clutching his hand and yelling. "Neen! He got me, he got me, Neen!"

The snake had bitten my father, and now all pandemonium broke loose.

Their cries pierced my solitude and I jumped up and ran to the barn. Joe was holding his hand, while my sister was wringing hers. "He bit me, Pell. Neen, he bit me, the goddamn son of a bitch," he kept repeating. Then he tipped the barrel over, got out a hoe, and hacked the snake to death before it had a chance to slither away. Through my haze of shock, I could tell Joe had been drinking. Still, he had enough wits left to know that he needed to get to a doctor. My sister rushed inside the house, fetched some bandages, and then wrapped a tourniquet above the bite. My father dialed the local doctor's office with his free hand. "Better get in right away," said Dr. Bob.

"Get in the truck, girls," Joe ordered. "Pell, you're driving." My body went numb. I was fifteen, didn't have a license, and though my father had given me a few lessons, I'd never driven on the main road. Changing gears on the old Ford pickup had been hard to master; I still popped the clutch, and the vehicle lurched and sputtered. But disobedience was not a choice; besides, with his rapidly swelling hand, my father couldn't drive. My heart pounding, I climbed in the cab and slid behind the wheel. Joe sat in the middle, between my sister and me. It was only a three-mile drive into town. But as we turned down the long driveway, I felt as if I was driving off a cliff into empty space.

Stiff and upright, I kept my hand on the gear knob and my eyes fixed on the road ahead. Next to me, Joe kept up a running monologue. A brush with danger always had an immediate, sobering effect on my father. It was normalcy that he couldn't handle. Years of flying under all kinds of conditions had trained him to remain cool during an emergency. Now, as I ground the gears, his voice turned gentle.

"Just take it easy, there you go, just yoix the clutch, go slow, easy, there you go." Up to first gear, I chanted to myself, down to second, then up again, across and up to third, then down to fourth. Wiggle to the middle to take it out of gear. Despite my best efforts, the truck jumped like a jackrabbit down the driveway. Somehow, I made it out to the main road, and soon my driving began to even out. Just above town, I came to the hairpin turn nicknamed Dead Man's Curve.

I heard my sister suck in her breath in fear. "Now, Neen," said Joe. "Take it easy, Pell, just take it slow." I saw the town spread below me and felt my feet start to wobble on the pedals. What if we crashed and I killed us all in a fiery wreck? Gathering up my willpower, I steeled myself for the twisting descent. When I finally made it to the bottom of the hill, reaching the outskirts of town where the doctor's office was located, I felt a rush of relief. Once inside, Dr. Bob gave my father an injection of antivenom. I made the return trip smoothly, with only a few clutch jumps. Perhaps, as it is sometimes said, crises do turn out to be life's best teachers. By the time I pulled up in front of the house, I'd learned how to drive a four-gear pickup truck.

My mother was waiting for us inside. She'd just returned from the hospital. Her eyes were swollen and I knew she'd been crying. I'd driven with her to the hospital before to visit my brother, and I knew she sobbed all the way there and back. Each time she made the trip, she had to pass beneath a bridge that had been built the same year she was born, 1928. "That bridge looks better than I do," she'd say in her most dramatic, Elizabeth Taylor voice. I'd look at the bridge then back at her face, comparing her pretty visage to the crumbling stone structure. It had to be lonely for her, taking care of my brothers without a shred of support from my father—either for them or her. That day, as I watched my father disappear into his bedroom and head for his drink drawer, I dreaded giving her this latest news.

Almost immediately, my father began heaving and vomiting. A welter of red hives broke out on his stomach. The doctor had told my father that if he had a reaction it meant his body was rejecting the antivenom. After calling Dr. Bob for advice, Sheila turned around and once again made the hour-long drive back to the hospital in Kansas City, this time with my father in tow. In the emergency room, the physician on call examined my father. After administering another injection to halt his reaction, the doctor stood back, crossed his arms, and lit into Joe.

The reason he'd had such a bad reaction, the doctor dared to say, was because he was an alcoholic. He lectured my father sternly, and in detail, on how his drinking was ruining his health. My mother listened but didn't say anything. For the first time, someone was addressing Joe's drinking problem openly. To her great astonishment, my father took the doctor's broadside in passive silence. His usual blustering defensiveness was strangely absent.

Although my brother had been in another wing of the same hospital where my father was being treated, Joe didn't stop by to see his ten-year-old son. "I remember hearing something about Dad being in the hospital," recalls John. "But he never came in to see me." As my parents drove back home down the long, dark highway that night, neither of them spoke of what the doctor had said. Or of John. Glancing at the fuel gauge, my mother suddenly realized they were low on gas. "Joe, I need to turn off and get some gas," she said.

The old devils began to stir. "Naw, come on, let's see if we can make it home and fill up the car at the gas tank," said my father, referring to the fuel tank by the barn. My mother had reached her limit. She was in no mood for Joe's tricks. "If we run out of gas," she said in an oddly detached voice, more to herself than my father, "I don't know what I'll do." My father sat back in silence. He didn't say anything when my mother pulled off at the next exit to fuel up the car for the rest of the way back.

For several months after that, Joe didn't drink at all. It was a blessed hiatus. But all too soon his sobriety vanished, and the bottle was back in all our lives.

OUT OF A DARK AGE

Where alcoholism is concerned, it could be said, we've lived in a kind of dark ages. In retracing my own family drinking story, I look back in frightened amazement at just how dark those ages have been. Unlike many spouses of heavy drinkers at that time, my mother did not shrink from confronting my father's problems. At first, it was Joe's jerky mood swings that drove Sheila to consult our family doctor. Our kindly but dim local physician admonished my mother to be more supportive, and "to smile more and put a nice meal on the table." Sexy underwear, too, he said helpfully, might do the trick. My mother turned next to my uncle Paul, Joe's older brother. Paul, also a drinker at the time, told my mother to praise my father more, and to be sweeter to him. "Fed up," as my mother put it, with these patronizing words of advice, she paid a visit to our Catholic priest.

Father Red Socks, so-called because of the bright red socks he wore during Mass, inquired of my mother whether my father had been exhibiting a dramatic change in personality. "Yes," said my mother. "Does your husband have more than three drinks a day?" he asked next. "He has a hell of a lot more than that," Sheila responded tartly. "Sounds to me like he has a drinking problem," said Father Red Socks. He scribbled down a number on a piece of paper. It was for a local Al-Anon group, a new kind of support organization for the families of alcoholics.

Seated in a circle of women who shared her struggle, my mother felt that she'd found the mind she thought she'd lost. "I realized I wasn't going crazy," she said. She memorized the Serenity Prayer and gained a new perspective through hearing that a person can't control the behavior of an alcoholic. She surrendered to a higher power and tried to let go and let God take over.

For my willfully proud and tempestuous mother this kind of acceptance was almost next to impossible. Forgiveness and uncritical love, as well as the awareness that an alcoholic is not bad but rather weak and sick, are central tenets of Al-Anon and Alcoholics Anonymous. These gentler tactics fell on inhospitable ground in my family. As my mother admits today, she became stuck on that part of the Serenity Prayer that promises to have "the courage to change the things I can" while forgetting the next line, "and to accept the things I can't."

Indeed, if you backed her into a corner, my mother had always said, she'd come out fighting. Now, as Joe's drinking worsened, Sheila turned into a warrior-wife. His relentless drinking drove her to go after Joe "like an angry bulldog," she tells me. The morning after an all-day-

and-night binge, my father would sit in his chair, his head bowed, as my mother alternately argued, sobbed, scolded, demanded, or stonewalled. The toll this took was steep. When she chauffeured me into town for cheerleading practice or an after-game sock hop, she'd wear enormous dark sunglasses and a scarf, Jackie Kennedy–style, to conceal her tear-swollen face.

As I grew older, the realization that my father was a drunk increased in force until it became the overriding fact of my life. I took my cues from my mother and fought alongside her. I taunted Joe for being an alcoholic and a failure, and did everything I could to make his life more miserable than it already was. Unlike in other households, which kept happily mum on such taboo topics, nothing about my father's problem was ever whispered about. Far from it: we shouted it to the ceilings of our near-century-old farmhouse, which surely had never heard words spoken like these before.

"My father is an alcoholic," I learned to say blithely. I was proud of my openness; the Carrolls were different that way. We would not lie to ourselves about our father's affliction. We would put things on the table. Dirt would not be swept under *our* family rug. Now, as I write out the narrative of my father's drinking story, I see how my glib acceptance of my father's alcoholism was itself a form of escape. My family was a slowly sinking ship, and such easy proclamations allowed me to leap into a life raft and sail on with my life. Even though in later years I wrestled with the legacy of my father's alcoholism in therapy, something about Joe's drinking always eluded me. It became like a worn book that I carried with me everywhere, and yet whose pages I never bothered to read. "He's in denial. You can't change an alcoholic, you can only go on with your life," I'd say, flashing my little bits of knowledge.

I relate my father's tale of drinking to the Italian Jungian analyst Luigi Zoja, who has written about both addiction and fathers. Confessing my regret over the long periods of absence between my father and me after I left home, Zoja remarks, "Your father needed to deny his alcoholism. But you needed to deny affection, probably as a way to simplify things. So, by writing about him, you are trying to do something more complex, more complete."

By closing my heart to my father in order to blot out the hurt and disgust, I realize, I also shut out a more intimate knowing of the addiction he wrestled with. Without fully entering into the pathos he suffered as an alcoholic, I would never really solve the riddle of who the man was—or his influence on my psyche. Yet I can hardly blame myself for fleeing; outside Al-Anon, little exists to humanize the shame-afflicted relationship between an alcoholic and his family. How often, asks Thomas Moore in *Care of the Soul*, "do we talk about alcoholics or drug addicts as if they were not part of our community, as though their problem had nothing to do with us?"

As far back as Benjamin Rush in 1784, for instance, and as recently as the American Medical Association in 1956 and again in 1991, alcoholism has been recognized as a disease. Current research into the neuroscience of addiction views the addict as suffering from a chronic brain disorder, just as the pancreas malfunctions in someone with diabetes. Fifty percent of all alcoholic cases, psychologist and addictions specialist Thomas McLellan tells me, are accounted for by genetics. But as McLellan also points out, the statistical fact that half of the alcoholic population has no multi-generational family history proves that alcoholism cannot only be reduced to genetics. For while genetics may alert us to a person's potential vulnerability, as Harvard psychologist Dr. Howard Shaffer explains, "it doesn't solve the problem entirely. Because some people without the marker will develop alcoholism, and some people with the marker will never have it develop. It's a piece of the puzzle, but never sufficient to explain the puzzle." As a matter of fact, says Shaffer, he has come to believe "drugs or alcohol are not the sole repository of addiction—it's human experience. Ultimately, there's a final common pathway, which is the brain."

As researchers assemble more pieces of the intricate puzzle that make up alcoholism, they are discovering that in addition to genetics, other factors like temperament, cultural influences, PTSD, life experiences, and psychological disorders like depression, anxiety, narcissism, and bipolar disorder all fit together to create the larger pattern of addiction. In the portrait of my father that is beginning to emerge in this new light, his Irish heritage; his sensitivity as a child; the emotional shocks he endured growing up; the macho drinking culture of his brothers, World War II, and the early days of aviation and the fifties; and the torment caused by his inner conflicts were among the brushstrokes that painted the profile of his addiction.

Despite these gradual shifts in understanding, attitudes in popular American culture toward alcoholism remain mired in a judgmental moralism dating to the Temperance and Prohibition movements, and on back to the Puritans. McLellan has strong words on this topic: "Addiction has been considered variously a sin, a bad habit, a sign of moral decay, or weak will. The treatment then is to get thee to a nunnery, put you in jail, teach you a lesson, and dry you out," he bemoans, but "we probably wouldn't do that with someone who has diabetes; we wouldn't send them to a priest, or a thirty-day treatment program." It's very difficult, he continues, "to make what I still think is the right case: we can hate alcoholics; we can despise what they do, but we're just kidding ourselves if we think we're going to punish it out of them. I'd be happy to call alcoholism a sin if going to church made an alcoholic sober, or to call it a crime if putting someone in jail cured their drinking. But those things don't work." In the newly evolving model envisioned by McLellan and other experts, treatment would be multifaceted and lifelong, involving changes in lifestyle, diet, medications, psychotherapy, family involvement, support groups, and training in observant self-management.

Peering into the murky shot glass of my father's addiction, I find myself reflecting on another overlooked question on alcoholism: it may seem simple, it may even seem obvious, but do people, I wonder, turn to drugs or drink because they're searching for something right in the wrong place? Most therapies, including Alcoholics Anonymous, says Jungian analyst Michael Conforti, address the pathologies underlying an addiction: I'm an alcoholic. I'm sick, I have to give it up, I can't control myself, etc.

"For years," says Conforti, "I bought that approach as a therapist. But then I realized it didn't get me anywhere. It finally dawned on me that I had to ask a different kind of question of my patient: Where do you go when you drink? What do you access? What happened when you picked up the bottle and started drinking? What does it give you and how else can you get it?" If you can understand the symbolic drive, or the "angel behind the demon" of the addiction, says Conforti, you can begin to get at its roots.

To try to answer these questions on my father's behalf, to bring soul and imagination to his alcoholism, I follow the clues laid down by memory. One night when I was a teenager, I came downstairs to find Joe sitting in his chair in the dark. A coffee cup—a decoy for the vodka it contained—sat on the coaster. A Pall Mall glowed in the ashtray. The radio was on, and Joe was whistling along with the Henry Mancini tune (lyrics by Johnny Mercer) "Moon River": "Two drifters, off to see the world, / There's such a lot of world to see. / We're after the same rainbow's end— / waiting 'round the bend, / my huckleberry friend, / Moon River and me." Joe's softened, dreamy look and raised eyebrows signified that he was somewhere far away from his easy chair at the foot of the stairs, sailing down a winding river toward some mythical place.

Coming upon my father brooding in the dark like that always had an unsettling effect. Was he okay, I'd wonder, or was he losing his mind? Conforti wonders whether my father's drinking was a way to reconcile the man he'd become with the son of Altoona who could never go home again. Here's a man, he says, who "had a grand picture of a huge world, one that took him from Tel Aviv to Brazil to Buenos Aires. But how could he bring that vision into a personal life and a family, especially after he'd suffered a trauma? Suddenly, he found himself pretty high up, looking at the world from the vantage point of Icarus. He might have felt that he didn't belong anywhere. He could never really go home again and be the same guy; he couldn't put those pieces together. In many ways, the alcoholism might have been an addiction toward trying to integrate this much larger vision of the world that he had [with the boy he'd once been]."

Circling the image of my father drunk-dreaming in his chair, Jungian Sylvia Perera reflects from another angle. Joe may have been a solitary drinker, she comments, but that didn't mean he was alone in his head. "He may have gotten drunk to put himself back in a frame of mind, to return to more intense, exciting times from his youth, when he was drinking and flying with his buddies. So drinking might have allowed him to remember the past, and to get lost in his fantasies." Guzzling beer drinker that he was, my father may even, says Perera, have turned to alcohol out of a longing to reconnect with the roots of his Irish spirituality. These ancestral memories, she believes, carried down from one generation to the next, forming a layer of my father's psyche, and influencing his drinking unconsciously. Mead, the Celtic word for beer, I learn from Perera, was originally thought to be a gift of the Celtic goddess Maeve, and it was served in "great drinking halls" to strengthen kinship bonds. It was even used by shaman-priests who "quaffed the ale" to receive mystical visions and write poetry.

To think of something so profane as beer in a sacred context may seem like an odd notion to the modern mind, as does the idea of a goddess of alcohol, or that drink may be used in a legitimate way to access one's creative imagination or states of mystical ecstasy. But something in these old Irish traditions, as well as other ancient cultural rituals involving substances going all the way back to the ancient Greeks and Vedic priests, provides the key for understanding what ails modern-day addicts.

These libations were aids to altering consciousness, to changing the states of our minds. The need my father could not name could not be slaked because what he sought was absent in the very culture surrounding him: to get out of his head and into another way of being, whether that meant sleeping the sleep of a newborn, meditating on the face of God, or dancing beneath the stars in wild abandon.

Psychologist Ginette Paris elaborates on this theme. Anytime a person has an excessive need for something that is not essential to survival, she says, it points to something they're having trouble getting in the daily repertoire of feelings. And in the same way, when a culture is addicted to a certain kind of drug, it reveals something about the culture's repression. For example, Paris says that when she traveled to Morocco thirty-five years ago, smoking hashish was seen as something totally insignificant, almost like chewing gum! The whole mood of the country, even its architecture, she says, was stoned. What some Moroccans really wanted instead was to trade hash for a pack of American cigarettes, and to be "high on cigarettes." In contrast to their more communal culture, cigarettes provided the experience of feeling like a willful, heroic, separate individual—the archetype of the cigarette-smoking hero of the American movies of the sixties.

In America, the opposite is true. Our problem around alcohol, Paris points out, can be found in our overemphasis on those qualities of controlled self-sufficiency, work, order, logic, and ego consciousness that have come to dominate our culture. "Being proper 365 days a year will drive everyone crazy in very dangerous and unpredictable ways, because some element in society just cannot take it," she says. "A hyper-technological, hyper-rationalized society is as unbalanced as the anti-intellectual, Dionysian-intoxicated, intensely emotional states that are typical of alcohol intoxication."

For this reason, Western culture's problems with addiction, in Paris's view, stems from its failure to find equilibrium between the two poles. With an addiction, she says, we always think there's too much "Dionysos." But in fact, Paris continues, "addiction often means that there's not *enough* of the Dionysian element and by this I mean not enough ritual, not enough cultural development. This is true of every symptom of 'too muchness' that becomes destructive." Older and wiser cultures than ours, Paris tells me, recognized that the psychological health of a civilization rested on a balance between the disciplined "day world" and the more mysterious "night world."

All those storied Dionysian festivals of madness and revelry, in other words, were sanctioned rituals that allowed the wilder, more playful, uncensored, and unconventional sides of our human nature to come out and play, and to have their say. Those who live with alcoholics are often told, as I was, that when their loved ones are drunk they're not themselves. Yet, asks Paris, "Who is that person when they're drunk?" This "other person" who comes out under the influence of alcohol, she continues, "doesn't receive any attention. Not all alcoholics are the same when they are drunk. This other person may be a crying, vulnerable softy, an abandoned child; or he/she is an angry bully or a mean miser. . . . But to get out of addiction, one has to get acquainted with that Mr. Hyde." Even should a pill be discovered that would cause us to physically reject alcoholism, warns Paris, "the underlying problem would remain. The need of the expression of the *other* self, or should I say other *selves*, would still be there."

Likewise, she asks, "What is the need of the complaining, vulnerable, stupid side that so often peeps through the sappy behavior of alcoholics?" Especially in a culture that stresses ego and success so much, and where a person's only choice is to either go for it, or drop out and become a loser, says Paris, "where can we go where we don't have to be so on top of things without suffering terrible consequences?" Even should a pill be discovered that cures alcoholism, warns Paris, it would not remove a need for the alcoholic or drug-dependent person to express this hidden side of their personality, as eventually "this other self would come out in a double life as difficult to understand as the addiction itself."

So far, I've seen my father's alcoholism, along with his constant craving for excitement and adventure, as escapist—a flight from reality on the ground. But what if a flight from the everyday was sometimes the very medicine he needed, a necessary break from the twin pressures of his job and his farm and family? The Dionysian and Apollonian qualities Paris describes, for instance, played out in my father's chosen profession of aviation. From its early days throughout World War II, flying was characterized by high-stakes risk and daring. But in the era of commercial flight, with its carefully monitored schedules of takeoffs and landings, as I'll discuss in a later chapter, the qualities of control and mental sharpness were at the forefront. Could it be that as aviation became more regulated, Joe sought in drink the sensory pleasures that had been stripped from flying?

Up and down, manic and bored, ecstatic and sad: inevitably, my father's drinking story circles back to the Icarus riddle of how to handle the highs and lows of life. The only cure for alcoholism he'd seen, wrote Carl Jung in a fateful letter to Bill Wilson, had been brought about by spiritual experiences that caused a change of heart. "Alcohol in Latin is *spiritus*, and you use the same word for the highest religious experience as well as for the most depraving poison. The helpful formula, therefore, is *spiritus contra spiritum*." Reflecting on Jung's words, I wonder whether my own spiritual quest was in some way a search for the cure for my soul-sick dad.

As I remember again my father, lying on the floor by his bed, unconscious, I see him now through a different lens. Through writing this, and through my interviews with psychologists who have brought their research, depth of soulful imagination, and therapeutic sensibilities to alcoholism, my anger begins to soften. It isn't so much that I forgive as that I see Joe's individual suffering within a much wider context, and, in so seeing, I understand. I am humbled by this radical shift in perspective, and a Greek chorus of "if onlys" chants its refrain in my mind.

If only my father had been warned of his risk for alcoholism in a way that had been stripped of moral judgment. If only someone had said to him, "Joe, your digestive system doesn't break down alcohol in the best way." If only someone had taken him aside and said, "Joe, let's look at this in the same way as if you had diabetes." If only someone had said, "Hey, Joe, you're Irish. Why don't you read up on some of those legends about the great Celtic warriors? Or dance the Irish jig with those wild brothers of yours?" If only he'd allowed himself a day every now and then of sober daydreaming. If only he'd seen through the capitalist myths that had driven his body to exhaustion. Or had a therapist to whom he could talk about his childhood and the traumas of war. If only he'd found a spiritual path that had led him outside himself, into transcendent states of meaning and tranquility.

But maybe, in some mysterious way, the exercise of reliving the past is having an effect. Again and again in my dreams as I write this book, a different Joe keeps trying to emerge. I know that I must guard against my complex to heal and save, or to gloss over real horror. Nonetheless, in one dream, I'm lying on my couch, feeling depressed about my family past. Instantly, I become aware that a brown snake is in the house. Although at first I'm frightened that the snake will bite me, he insistently nudges my shoulder as if to tell me something. All at once the snake grows so large it moves to the front door and pushes it open. Flying out of the house, it rises into the air, an enormous, red serpent carrying a person on his back. Awed at this sight, I turn back inside, when suddenly my father enters the room. He is tanned, hale, strong, and dressed in a spring-colored pink shirt and green pants. He is grinning broadly, and says he has come to make me feel better.

VIII

Icarus's Daughter

But follow me: let me before you lay
Rules for the flight, and mark the pathless way.
—**Ovid**, The Story of Daedalus and Icarus

I'D NEVER MET A nurse like Andy Decker before. In my limited experience, nurses wore nondescript scrubs and were cool creatures of efficiency. So when a cocky, ponytailed young man dressed in Levis, a cowboy shirt with a pack of Marlboro Lights in the front pocket, and pointy-toed leather cowboy boots walked through my father's front door, I stared.

"Howdy!" he said, extending an arm covered in dense red hair and enclosing my hand in his unexpectedly soft grasp. "Name's Andy. I'm Joe's nurse. You must be Pellman. Heard all about you from your old man. Now what kind of a name is that?" Without waiting for my answer, Andy rambled on in his sweet-as-wildflower-honey Texan twang.

"That Joe," he said, a cheeky grin spreading over his face. "Gotta love him. What a character! He sure can make me laugh. He wanted to know if he could have a shot of vodka. I told him, 'Hell Joe, you're the one who's dying. It's your party! You can do whatever you damn well want to. Now don't tell that doctor of yours, but I might even have a shot and a smoke with you.'" Then Andy threw his head back and laughed like a rowdy guy at a rodeo.

I'd arrived back in my father's house the night before. The hellish bedroom scene of a month earlier had receded before Joe's accelerating decline. I decided I should get to know the brash new player on the stage of my father's dying drama and asked Andy if he'd like a cup of coffee. "Sure would," said my father's nurse. He sat down at the kitchen table awash in a pool of midmorning sun and began explaining his duties to me.

At this phase of my father's dying process, Andy said, his focus was on keeping Joe as comfortable as possible. As well as checking Dad's condition, it was up to Andy to monitor my father's pain levels and then prescribe the right dosage of morphine. Final approval always had to come from Joe's oncologist. But getting the higher doses of morphine necessary to treat my father's increasing levels of pain, said Andy testily, was always a challenge. "They're worried that your father is going to get addicted," he laughed sarcastically. "Now, how stupid is that? The man is dying!"

I had no problem with Andy on this point. To get all worked up over Joe getting hooked on morphine when he was on the cusp of dying seemed the most absurd thing I could imagine. My father's cancer had now spread to the bone; without drugs he would be in searing pain. I was less sure about my father's male bonding shots of vodka with his cowboy nurse; the other two members of Joe's hospice team had already testily informed me of their disapproval on this score. I studied Andy's open and welcoming face. I could see from his reddish hair and green eyes that he was probably of Irish or Scottish heritage. Put together with his Texas-size personality, the combination was at once laid-back and keenly intense. "So," I asked him, "You think it's alright for my father to drink while he's on morphine?"

Andy squared his shoulders defensively. "Sure," he said, his emerald eyes flashing. "He can smoke and eat anything he wants to. He's going to die soon, right? He's not going to be getting in any cars, either. What matters now is that he's able to enjoy his last days. A person has a right to go out the way they want. That's the beauty of hospice: it's Joe's death. He gets to tell us what he wants—not what we want for him. Like I said, it's his party."

Andy's face softened as he watched me mull over his words. "Your father doesn't have long," he said gently. "He can't drive anywhere, and he's losing his voice. Pretty soon he won't be able to get out of bed, or even be able to swallow a sip of water." He leaned in closer and peered into my face intently. The passion he felt for his work ebbed out of him and flowed around his words like seawater amid rocks. "I love this job, and I probably care more about the dying than I should," he said. "But the doctors are so screwed up when it comes to pain management. So afraid of addiction. Someone has to stand with the person who's dying. And I meet the most amazing people, at the most important point in their lives. What I do is a privilege. Now I have to get on with my job and see your father." He jumped up from his chair, grabbed his medical bag, and loped back to my father's room. His booming voice and laughter echoed through the house. If Joe's hospice nurse could bring him such joy in his last days, I thought, who was I to put a stop to that?

Half an hour later, Andy reemerged. "I'm late for my next appointment," he said, his fingers fishing for the pack of cigarettes in his shirt pocket. "Gotta take off. See you in a few days. But call me if your father gets worse, or if he needs more meds." I watched from the front door as my father's improbable Texas nurse with the ponytail leaped into his open yellow Jeep Wrangler and roared down the suburban street. Returning inside, I went to Joe's room. He was sitting up in bed, looking as pleased as if he'd just returned from a gambling trip with his new buddy.

"Hey, Pell!" Joe greeted me hoarsely, but happily. I sat down next to him on the edge of his bed. "How'd you like that Andy? He says I can die however I want. Boy is he neat! Gave me a new morphine patch, too." It hit me that maybe Joe liked his new nurse because Andy was like him, forever young, reckless, and defiant. Then a ray of sun glinted off the tumbler of vodka on his bedside table—and the one next to it, with a finger of clear liquid still remaining. Joe saw my eyes light on the two offending glasses. Immediately, a proud "I dare you to knock this chip off my shoulder" look came over his face. "Yup," he said defiantly. "Made Andy have a drink and a smoke with me. What a guy!" I could only sit back in submission. I just didn't have it in me anymore to challenge him. At this late stage, it was clear that my father was not going to change. And that was just how things were going to be.

Unconventional as his laid-back approach seemed to be, it was clear Andy had meant what he'd said: my father had the right to die on his own terms, even if that meant drinking and smoking his way to the grave. But it was also apparent that my father's cowboy nurse had been graced with an unusual talent for healing. That someone so well suited to my father's needs should appear at this critical time felt like yet one more blessing, as if arranged by some offstage director. My father patted the white square stuck to his chest contentedly. Because of its steady drip into his system, Andy had assured me, Joe's cancer-swollen body was numb. I watched my father's face relax as he began to drift off into restful sleep.

After Joe's tumble to the floor the previous month, we'd brought in a hospital bed for him with high railings. But, as we should have guessed, he'd refused to leave the comfortable nest of his old king-size bed. Now the rest of us took turns sleeping in it while we kept watch through the night. Putting down the bar, I laid down for a nap. I'd need some rest for the long night ahead.

As I closed my eyes, the thought hit me: Andy had long hair!

My father had changed, after all.

REVOLUTION

In 1968, the year that followed the kicking-cow accident, the TWA strike, the farm auction, and the snakebite incident, the world seemed to enter an eerie zone of free fall. Certainties that had held life in place for centuries tottered: the role of women and the place of African Americans in society, rules around sex and drugs, and long-held assumptions around war and peace. The nation's crazy liberation revolutions had burst these old containers with explosive force. To my father's enormous puzzlement and profound dismay, I continued to brim with excitement over these social changes.

In the fall of 1967, at the start of my junior year of high school, the peace candidate Eugene McCarthy had declared his run for the presidency. Jim Morrison and the Doors, my favorite rock group, had appeared on *The Ed Sullivan Show*. Defying the censors, who'd asked him not to use any drug-related words, Morrison had sung the word "higher" from his number one hit, "Light My Fire." In the nation's capital, Allen Ginsberg chanted to "levitate" the Pentagon, with thousands of protesters in the background. Thurgood Marshall was sworn in as the first black U.S. Supreme Court justice.

Except for the occasional eighteen-year-old who shipped out to Vietnam, these cultural and political upheavals were far removed from Oak Grove. Still, I was keenly aware of them through the images I saw on the nightly news. I was spellbound by the swarms of protesters. I began to live a split life. At home, I wrote fervidly religious Jesus poetry; took a correspondence course in Ancient Greek history; listened to the heady music of Bob Dylan, Joan Baez, and Judy Collins; speculated about converting to Judaism; and looked out my bedroom window, yearning to join the hippie revolution. At school, urged by my guidance counselor, I learned shorthand and typing to prepare for a career as a secretary, should the worst happen and I fail to marry. Continuing on my course to be "popular," I kept up with my cheerleading and social schedule of sock hops and slumber parties, where teenage boys made middle-of-the-night pajama raids in their daddies' cars. The sixties may have been rampaging throughout the country, but in my hometown the fifties still held sway.

That fall I'd been chosen as the junior class runner-up for homecoming queen. In my football-obsessed town, honors didn't come much higher for girls. One might have thought this would have pleased my father; it didn't. I was nearly sixteen, but Joe was determined to put a stop to my growing up. He'd refused to even give my mother the money to buy me a new dress for the homecoming dance. My good-looking date had a fine crew cut and was the upstanding son of the school principal. But that made no difference to my father, who held to his strict "no getting into cars with boys" rule, even for this special occasion.

For my mother, who'd grown up in the vibrantly social culture of Buenos Aires, my father's obsessive control around dating was an especially bitter fate. Number one on her list of expectations for both her daughters was romance, marriage, and a husband. Tucked beneath the nightgowns in her dresser were two sealed envelopes addressed

"To My Daughter on Her Wedding Night." Staring dreamily out the kitchen window over her cup of Lipton's tea, Sheila would reminisce to my sister and me about the balls she'd danced at as a young girl. "I hope one day you know the joy of putting on a beautiful ball gown and dancing a waltz with the man you love," she'd say, looking past the grain silo into her distant past. When or where she thought that might happen, I had no idea.

Now my mother became my ally—"going to bat" for me, as she used to put it, with my father. Somehow, she'd scraped the money together out of the food budget to buy me a plum-colored A-line dress for the dance. After much hectoring, she'd even persuaded my father to agree to let my date drive me home after the dance. On the morning of the homecoming game, Sheila took me to the local beauty parlor to get my hair set. Later that evening, after a day of much primping and preening, I was led by my mother to my father's chair. "Joe, doesn't Pelly look pretty tonight?" Sheila asked proudly. My father never even lifted his head from the *Newsweek* on his lap. When the handsome captain of the football team placed the sparkling tiara on my carefully teased and sprayed hair, then planted a kiss on my flushed cheeks, Joe wasn't present to watch me beam in happiness. He was at home, drinking.

Not that this bothered me. It had never been Joe's habit to show up for any of our sports or school performances. He'd long ago handed that parental task to my mother. The one time Sheila *had* forced my father to attend one of my sister's flute performances, he'd left in the middle of it to go to the local bar. After getting pie-faced smashed, he'd arrived to pick Colleen up on the sidewalk after everyone had left. Then he'd yelled at her all the way home, calling her a slut and a whore for wearing a short skirt on stage. So having my paranoid, zany, inebriated father at a public-school function wasn't anything I particularly wished for.

After I attained the pinnacle of what passed for high school success in those days, my interest in cheerleading and being popular went south. The cascade of events unfolding at the start of 1968 would profoundly alter my sense of direction. The year dawned expectantly enough. In Communist-ruled Czechoslovakia, the newly elected Alexander Dubček's proclamation of human rights and promises for new freedoms set in motion the exuberant Prague Spring. In America, *Rowan & Martin's Laugh-In*—the precursor to *Saturday Night Live*, and which we watched only while my father was away—had people chuckling irreverently over politics. Bobby Kennedy had begun campaigning for the Democratic presidential nomination, kindling the hearts of young dreamers like me with his vision of peace and justice.

Hanging over all our lives like a dark curtain was the Vietnam War. On January 30, North Vietnam launched the Tet Offensive against the United States and South Vietnam. The notion that this was a conflict America might lose was beginning to set in. For the World War II generation, failure to prevail was something they could not wrap their minds around. Families and neighbors squared off against each other, hawks versus doves. In my family, it was five doves to Joe Carroll's hawk. Joe felt strongly that winning the war in Vietnam was a simple matter of dropping more bombs. Hadn't the atomic bomb ended World War II, preventing him from going into battle?

On the last day of March, the Carroll family was sprawled out in the family room watching television. President Johnson was scheduled to give a speech on Vietnam. At eight P.M., regular programming was interrupted and the president appeared on the screen. Absentmindedly studying Johnson's face, with its jowled wings of gravity, I thought that he looked like my father. With his head cocked to one side and his brow furrowed over his large, square glasses, the strain Johnson was under was evident. Plodding through his speech in his Texas drawl, Johnson spoke of steps being taken to deescalate the conflict, while at the same time affirming American and Allied commitment of nearly 600,000 troops to help South Vietnam against the Communist-backed North Vietnamese—a staggering number of young men.

Toward the end of the speech, my ears pricked up. "Throughout my entire public career I have followed the personal philosophy that I am a free man," said Johnson gravely, "an American, a public servant, and a member of my party—in that order." As my interest continued to build, Johnson went on to talk about the "division in the American house," and the need for all Americans, "whatever their personal interests or concerns, to guard against divisiveness and all of its ugly consequences." Then, with immensely sad eyes, Johnson announced that, in order to keep the presidency from becoming involved in the partisan divisions developing that year, he had decided that he "would not seek, nor would I accept," the nomination for another term.

The announcement shocked both my parents. My mother jumped up from her seat on the plaid couch in disbelief. "What?" she cried out. At the same time, my father let out a low whistle and a "Jesus *Christ.*" Why that moment should have impressed itself upon my parents with such force and why it stood out in my memory is puzzling. But wherever we harbor a charged political memory, says Jungian analyst Andrew Samuels, we can be sure that it represents a critical juncture in the formation of our personal political identity. National and global collective events affect us intimately, he says, "at a personal and private level" through dreams, bodily reactions, and strong emotional responses. Rather than pretend they don't exist, believes Samuels, these instinctive responses to the body politic need to be honored and decoded.

Looking back at that moment as Samuels suggests, I believe that Johnson's stirring words about being a "free man" spoke to my desire to liberate myself from my father's control. At the time, I knew hardly anything about Johnson politically. But I, too, wanted passionately to be a free person. Likewise, the president's emotional words about healing the nation's divided house touched on the longing for peace I wished not only for my country, but for my own wartorn home. His choice to leave his position as the leader of his country, broken from a war gone bad, resonated with the pathos of the patriarchal father who'd failed in his responsibilities. Johnson's resigned air was not so different from my father's, and many other fathers, whose position at the top of the family hierarchy at that time was slowly eroding. I felt for Johnson, just as I felt for my father—even as I longed to be released from Joe's suffocating control and his ham-fisted, abusive temper.

Four days later, the world shook again. Martin Luther King, Jr. was shot dead, a bullet through the soul of the Civil Rights movement. Gathered around the television set once again, my family watched in fear as race riots erupted in cities across the country. This time, my father was away on a trip, and I felt his absence. My parents' personal stands against white prejudice—refusing to let us use the word "nigger," and advocating to let a black family attend the local school—had made me feel a part of this historic movement, if only in a small way.

In the months following, there was no letup to the gallop of political events. During the last week of April, student protesters at Columbia University in New York City occupied the administration building, shutting down the school. On Broadway, the counterculture musical *Hair* opened. On May 6, students and workers in Paris erupted in demonstrations that nearly toppled the government. Eight days later, the Beatles announced the creation of Apple Records; on May 17, the Catonsville Nine entered the Selective Service offices in Catonsville, Maryland, taking dozens of selective service records, and then burning them with napalm as a protest against the Vietnam War. Then on June 5, Robert F. Kennedy, heir to the "impossible dream" of Camelot and my young heart's hero, was assassinated. His slumped body lying on the floor of the Ambassador Hotel was a snapshot of a dream dying.

The emotional climate of that time, the alternating rhythms of wild elation and excruciating tragedy, was as if two jarringly dissonant pieces of music were being played side by side. An extreme, rise-and-fall, Icarus-like atmosphere was pervasive. A disbelieving depression over the assassinations of King and Kennedy flattened the mood of the public. The leeching away of young men to fight in forests half a world away preoccupied parents and girlfriends. At the same time the great loosening of ties that had bound society together for centuries released a wave of euphoria over dreams of a future free of war, sexual repression, discrimination against women and blacks, and where the colors of peace and compassion would bloom brightly. The young and impatient believed we'd have a new Eden within a few short years. Those more entrenched in the past clung to how they thought things had always been. Alongside the Vietnam conflict a culture war broke out: a conservative/liberal schism that has yet to heal began to cleave America in two.

Taking up my position on the liberal side, I began the summer before my senior year a different person. I had no heart anymore for cheerleading, sock hops, or slumber parties. The tension between my parents had escalated, along with the war and race riots, to unforeseen levels. Correspondingly, my ideals had risen to new heights. The world appeared to demand something of me.

Despite my town's traditional values—or perhaps *because* of them—it seemed to me that all it thought about was sex: who'd gotten to "first base," who'd "done it," who'd gotten pregnant and had to get married, who'd been spirited out of town for a secret abortion, what married man or woman had been caught cheating on backcountry roads. Throwing off this repressive yet prurient environment, I decided to enroll in a history course at summer school in Raytown, the suburb where my parents had first lived. There I made a new friend.

Sandy was the first real hippie I'd ever met, and I was entranced. She introduced me to the poetry of e.e. cummings, the delight of biting into a fresh pomegranate and letting the red juices run down my chin, the raspy folk music of Leonard Cohen, going braless, and smoking cigarettes in teahouses. She was also hooked into the hippie scene flourishing in Kansas City. While my father was away on trips, I talked my mother into allowing me to take the car and drive to the love-ins and antiwar demonstrations being held on the rolling green lawns of Volker Park on the Plaza downtown. There, amid large crowds of stoned youth costumed in fabulously flamboyant bellbottoms and tunics dripping with beads, Sandy and I delighted in placing daffodils I'd picked from the farm in the rifles pointed at us by smiling policemen. I also cautiously sampled a few puffs of marijuana and danced at a Jimi Hendrix concert dressed in a sunflower-yellow silk tent dress flowing over red tapestry bellbottoms that my mother had made for me.

The bright, psychedelic colors of peace, love, and freedom that were so enlivening to me only aggravated my father's darkening moods. He hated the changes that he saw in me, and he viewed Sandy as the cause. At the dinner table, he launched into drunken tirades against "*Califooornya*," that vortex of evil, debauchery, Communism, and radical antiwar dissent. His carefully constructed world was crumbling about him. Taken up in my whirlwind, I was blind to what must have been his panicked confusion over what was happening to me. Because I was the oldest, it was my fate to become the first child to go up against Joe, defying his rule. As I continued to demonstrate for peace on weekends, the air of violence thickened at home. Hardly a day passed without a screaming, crying fight between my parents. Huddled together with my sister and brothers, I'd try to reassure my siblings that things would turn out all right.

One gray, late summer Sunday afternoon, after a particularly nasty argument with my mother, Joe took his .22 rifle out of the bedroom closet and stalked out of the house. There had always been a rifle or two on the farm. Joe had received firearms instruction during the war, and he'd taught us to shoot. He'd stood the four of us in a row before a fence lined with Budweiser cans, then shown us how to hold the rifle steady, look through the sight, aim, and fire. But I was a born pacifist, and there wasn't anything about a gun that I liked. The powerful kick against my shoulder had knocked me back in fright. It repulsed me that the small metal bullet I shot out of the rifle had the power to take a life. It could also be that the combination of my hair-trigger angry, alcoholic father with a rifle in his hands was far more frightening than any gun could ever be by itself.

Yet as with so many other things in life, my father had a complicated relationship with firearms. As a farmer living in the country, he'd sometimes had to use his rifle to shoot a dog who was dying, or had turned feral after tasting the blood of an animal. He'd return from this unpleasant task silent and closed-mouthed, his rifle dangling at his side. And unlike a lot of the other farmers in the area who liked to hunt, my father had an aversion to it. Even when he'd let some of his TWA friends come out to the farm to shoot gophers, he'd stay inside, not even bothering to say "hello." Only one breed of animal failed to find protection under Joe's no-hunting rule: frogs.

There was nothing my father liked better in the summertime than fried frogs' legs, and our Missouri ponds were rich with the bug-eyed, croaking creatures. The best frog hunting, according to Joe, was to be had at night—and it had to be done with the four of us in tow. On a summer's evening after dinner, Joe would grab his rifle and order us out to the truck. We didn't have far to go—just a short, bumpy ride down the alfalfa field terraces until we reached the pond. Turning off the motor, he'd leave the headlights on, shining them on the still surface.

Attracted by the glow, frogs would begin popping up, their bright eyes big and blinking in the night. Making sure the four of us were well behind his back, Joe would aim his rifle, then pop them off, one by one. Sitting back with a contented sigh, he'd send us in to fish out the dead, floating amphibia. "Alrighty now, Pell, Neen, Steve, John. Time to fish for your supper," he'd shout. "There's a big one, over by the bank!"

Sitting on the fender of the pickup, Joe would relax with a cigarette and a Budweiser while we fumbled around among the tall bulrushes and brackish water now stained with blood. Dragging the pond for the limp bodies of these slimy green creatures, I'd squeal, recoiling from their clammy touch and the squish of stinky mud between my toes. I was frightened of the water snakes that lurked in these Missouri ponds, and the bony-sharp crabs that I'd once fallen on as a girl. Back at the house, my father would busy himself cutting up the carcasses, piling up their limbs. The next night, my mother would serve us frogs' legs dipped in flour and fried in salt and butter. "Ummm, ummm, tasty" my father would say, swilling back a beer.

So on that afternoon when Joe took his rifle from his bedroom closet and strode through the front door without a backward glance, I wasn't sure what to think. It was out of character for him to go outside alone with his rifle; I'd never seen him do this before. The ends of my nerves were frayed with worry. As the hours wore on, and we grew more concerned, I became convinced that my father had gone into the woods to shoot himself. A couple of suicides had recently rocked the town. A woman had been found facedown in a creek, and another had hanged herself from her living room ceiling. Horrible images flooded my mind.

Several hours later, just as it began to rain, the front door opened and my father walked in. Glancing at my tense face—I'd been waiting for him in the living room—he laid his rifle down on the hallway table, went into his bedroom, and slammed the door shut. We never did find out what he'd done with his firearm that strange afternoon. The .22 stayed on the table for some time, though. I guess he left it there as some kind of warning—an ominous symbol of the undercurrent of emotional violence rippling through our house.

CONVERSION

By August, Richard Nixon was the Republican nominee for president. On August 20, Warsaw Pact troops invaded Czechoslovakia, bringing an end to the Prague Spring. Two days later, antiwar demonstrators, enraged by the Democratic Party bosses' nomination of Hubert Humphrey over the peace candidate Eugene McCarthy, clashed in the streets with the Chicago police.

Not long after that, the conflict between my parents arrived at an impasse that put me in the middle. One Saturday night, rather than cruise Main Street with my friends, as I'd used to do, I chose to stay home. My parents had gone to bed and my little brother and I were munching on a bag of Lay's potato chips. Curled up on the couch, we were watching *Chiller*, one of the newly popular horror shows. In the middle of a heart-thumping episode about giant grasshoppers taking over the sewers of New York City—a scene forever melded in my mind with my parents' bad marriage—I heard my mother's shouts: "Kids! Kids! Help, help!" I raced to my parents' bedroom, my brother close behind. I opened the door a crack and saw my father with his arm raised over my mother. She was turned away from him toward the wall and was halfway out of bed.

"You stop that!" I yelled out. By now, I'd become my mother's avenger, though I still don't know where my voice came from that night. Sheila half fell out of the bed, sobbing. My father slowly rolled over, then sat up. "Oh, for God's sake, I wasn't doing anything," he groaned. "Sheila! Shut the hell up! Get back in here. Get back into bed." But my mother was on her way out, and she fled past me in tears. "He was trying to hit me, he was going to beat me," she cried. "Close the door," my father grunted, and I did.

That night my mother slept upstairs in my room. I made up a bed for myself on the living room couch. Scrunching down beneath the covers, I hardly closed my eyes for fear my father would get up and beat my mother or me, or my brothers and sister, in a drunken rage. The next night, and for months of nights after that, my mother continued to sleep upstairs in my bed. Sometimes, my father would get up in the middle of the night. Drunk and trailing burning cigarette ashes, he'd falter through the dark to the bottom of the stairs. "Sheila, goddamn it, get down here," he'd mutter. Then he'd start up the stairs.

Always on guard against just such an intrusion, I never slept very well. I'd awaken in an instant and fly from the couch to bar his way. "You leave her alone," I'd say, fierce protector of the family against my father, the alcoholic monster. How strange, I think now, that my father would actually obey me! He'd turn away dejectedly, his shoulders slumped forward, and shuffle back to his room. When morning came, these nocturnal confrontations vanished into the daylight as if they'd never happened.

As time passed and my parents' separate sleeping arrangements became routine, my temporary bed on the couch became a sanctuary. Long after everyone had gone to sleep, I'd stay up late. Encircled in the glow of the living room lamp, protected within the solitary enclave I'd created for myself. While browsing at one of the New Age bookstores that had opened in Kansas City, I'd picked up two books: *Contemplative Prayer*, by the Trappist monk Thomas Merton, and *The Tibetan Book of the Dead*, a Buddhist text on the afterlife. As I explored these spiritual classics in the dark night, something inside me opened up.

New worlds take many forms, whether it is Christopher Columbus stumbling upon America or the Wright brothers discovering flight. Now, as I paged through these two books, one Christian, one Buddhist, I entered what was for me an unexplored dimension: the world of the spirit. Although many of the concepts were difficult for my beginner's mind to comprehend, the words rang with an old familiarity. Prayer and nature had always been my refuge. But now I underwent a profound conversion experience.

Pondering Merton's meditations on the reclusive Desert Fathers, I sat with robed and hooded monks absorbed by prayer in the wilderness. Joining my solitary confinement to theirs, I felt part of a mysterious community far from my farmhouse. Studying *The Tibetan Book of the Dead*, I learned about the different *bardo*s: states of consciousness that Buddhist thought says the soul travels through after death. Something beyond myself, beyond the petty disputes that trapped my family in a bog of anger and paranoia, and beyond Oak Grove, began to open up. As simple as it sounds, the two books led me from darkness into light, from blindness to revelation. And so, as converted people often do, I felt, literally, saved.

The spiritual seeds planted then are still ripening. As it turned out, much work lay ahead for me. I would have to learn to disentangle my spirituality as a defense against the crippled parts of my psychological self from an authentic path that connected me to larger realities. In the meantime, the perennial wisdom of the teachings I'd come upon had given my peregrine soul refuge. Like centuries of seekers before me, I felt contained in something durable that could survive life's ups and downs.

I also began to think of myself as not belonging to my family. I would return from contemplative walks on the farm, where I'd chanted, meditated, and prayed, and approach the farmhouse on the hill as if I'd been "sent" from elsewhere. This splitting away from identification with my family was no doubt a way to survive the emotional chaos and upheaval. But it was also a time-honored, ancient way, and it helped me to get through difficult times until I had the grit and grace to turn around and face my past.

Amid all the cultural changes rocking my home and the country, a vocation of sorts began to take shape. By the time Nixon was elected president the day after my seventeenth birthday that November, I'd gone from peppy cheerleader and perky homecoming queen to Oak Grove's first hippie. My town, fortunately and to my surprise, embraced their new flower child with affection. Seized by the revolutionary spirit of the counterculture, I took up writing a newspaper column for the Oak Grove High School paper called "Wildflowers." In it, I wrote about things like love, peace, and reincarnation. In one column, radical for its time, I set the town on its ear, asking its Christian citizens to contemplate the notion that in a past lifetime they might have walked in the footsteps of Christ. When many took the idea more seriously than I'd ever imagined, I felt the first stirrings of the writer's power to open minds. I was coming home to something, and it felt right.

The world, too, was about to undergo a conversion experience that would change its self-image beyond anything humankind had ever imagined. On Christmas Eve, 1968, the Apollo 8 spacecraft entered the moon's orbit. The three astronauts on board became the first humans to see the dark side of the moon, and the first to gain a glimpse of Earth from the distance of outer space. The images they sent back were the first icons of a new age of revelation. The sight of the jeweled sphere rising over the moon's pearl horizon was like a vision of a heavenly world, one we lived on. Who knew that we occupied a planet of such rare splendor? Or that we whirled along magnetic loops, stars around stars and planets around planets, a gem of sapphire amid the galaxies, in a cosmic sea of infinite space? When the Apollo crew read out loud from the Book of Genesis, the world paused, silenced by the miracle collectively witnessed as one. To see the moon's unlit side for the first time was likewise rich in symbolic meaning. That which was light had its dark side, just as the human psyche had its conscious and unconscious.

That night, far below the drama unfolding above the planet, Joe brewed himself a cup of coffee. He'd been uncharacteristically sober as he'd watched the grainy shots on television. Beyond letting out a low whistle and a "How about that?" he hadn't said much. A week later, at midnight, he herded the five of us outside, shivering in the cold, for his annual New Year's Eve ritual. Silhouetted against the night sky, he aimed his .22 high and, as was his custom, fired several shots into the air. Then he made us all rattle and bang the empty Budweiser beer cans he'd strung together for our family celebration. One man asserting himself against the anxious uncertainties of life, where, as much as he tried, things refused to stay the same. It was a strange but fitting trajectory to a year marked by the scourge of violence and assassination, and yet also space travel and the flowering of a spiritual renaissance.

BLAST OFF

By the time my high school graduation came around, I'd begun to come apart from the tension at home. Even my newly awakened interest in mysticism couldn't protect me from the stress eating away at my family. At school, I brimmed and nearly burst with creative energy and fiery political rhetoric, wearing down teachers and classmates alike. I talked friends into making regular visits to a juvenile detention home, and prodded my English teacher Miss Miller into putting on *A Midsummer Night's Dream*, Oak Grove's first production of a Shakespeare play.

But at home I wore an expression of brooding anger—much like my mother. Looking back, I see that I followed in her emotional footsteps, mirroring her fury against my father. She, in turn, accused Joe of pushing me to the brink of a breakdown with his drinking. Due to my shaky state of mind, it was decided that I should be sent away to Tallahassee, Florida, for the summer. There I could be taken care of by Uncle Paul, Aunt Ann, and my younger cousin Sharon.

Entering the normalcy of my uncle Paul's house was the emotional equivalent of wandering into a safe haven after living on the streets. The warmth of the Florida sun, my aunt's soothing habit of watching soap operas during the day, and Sharon's sweet adoration was a salve to my raw feelings. The notion that a family could live such an ordinary life, uninterrupted by hot scenes and chill silences, was a new experience for me. Uncle Paul had stopped drinking years ago. He was worried about my father, he told me, but there was nothing he could do about it. He encouraged me not to think so much about the problems at home and to focus on the future. I got a job as a waitress at a fast-food restaurant, and on my off hours I read the latest counterculture book, *Stranger in a Strange Land* by Robert Heinlein.

On July 16, 1969, Apollo 11 blasted off from the Kennedy Space Center, headed for humankind's first moon landing. As my father's daughter and a child of the space age, I vibrated from head to foot with a champagne fizz of anticipation. Others, however, were less sure about the notion of humans leaving Earth to walk on the moon. Days before touchdown, some people's long-held belief systems had begun to quake. Aunt Ann was a devout Catholic of firm but simple religious beliefs. To this point, she'd believed that heaven was high over her head and that hell was below, beneath her feet. Now Apollo 11 was, literally, turning her world upside down.

"But in outer space, where the astronauts are going, there is no up and there is no down," Aunt Ann said, in great puzzlement. "So where are heaven and hell now? Where will I go when I die? Where will I go?" she asked anxiously, deeply perplexed. At the restaurant where I worked, a five-foot-tall, born-again spitfire of a waitress named Dollie held us all spellbound with her fierce denunciations of space travel. NASA was breaking biblical law, she loudly asserted, raising her fist in the air. The crew would never make it to the moon, said Dollie, preaching to her fellow waitresses with absolute conviction. For God would reach out his mighty arm and smite the evil spacecraft from the sky, turning it to cinders and ashes.

On the evening of the moon landing, I gathered before the television set with Sharon, my aunt, and my uncle. Untroubled by any of the fears shared by Aunt Ann and Dollie the waitress, I could hardly contain myself. When the first fuzzy black-and-white images began to emerge on the screen, the four of us went still. Staring intently, we strained to make out the dim shape of the bulky figure of Neil Armstrong as he descended the lunar module's ladder. When his foot touched the soft powder of the moon, my spirit took off. We all let out a cheer.

Instantly and unexpectedly, I felt a stab of homesickness. I knew my family would be watching, and I missed them. The sky and the space beyond it were, after all, my Icarus family's myth. Something in my face must have given me away. When regular programming resumed, Uncle Paul asked me if I'd like to call my parents. "Hey, Pell, wasn't that something?" said my father when he picked up on the other end. I felt tears sting my eyelids. It was time to go home.

I wasn't back for long. Uppermost on Joe's mind was keeping me away from anything to do with the counterculture movement, including my friend Maggie. While I'd been away, he'd insisted on enrolling me, against my wishes, in the Jesuit-run Saint Louis University. Parks School of Engineering, his alma mater, was now part of SLU, giving him a sentimental stake in sending me there. On August 9, when Charles Manson went on his brutal, murderous spree, my father's worst fears about hippies everywhere were confirmed. Barely a week later, the Woodstock Festival unfolded in all its naked decadence. Joe could not get me away from my new friend and into a Catholic college fast enough.

I arrived at Saint Louis University in the fall of 1969—a small-town innocent with a head full of radical political and spiritual ideas. I'd been led by my father to think I was being spirited away to a strict religious environment that would safeguard my virginity and return me to conservative politics. I in turn boiled with resentment and felt sure I was being imprisoned in some kind of nunnery.

But Joe had underestimated the reach of campus turmoil spreading across the country. Student unrest around the Vietnam War was at its height, and few universities were exempt. There was talk of a draft, and the trial of the Chicago Eight—the radicals who had spearheaded the demonstrations at the Democratic National Convention—had begun. Details of the slaughter of Vietnamese villagers by American soldiers at My Lai had emerged, stirring students to anger. No sooner had I eaten my first breakfast in Margarita Hall than I found myself swept up in a campus-wide protest movement against the ROTC. With banners to make, marches to plan, and rallies to attend, there was little time to study. I did, however, find time to fall in love with a tall, handsome Jewish boy named Mark from nearby Washington University.

Early on November 14, 1969, I boarded a bus with my newfound activist friends. A month before, hundreds of thousands of people had protested in antiwar demonstrations as part of the national moratorium to end the war in Vietnam. Now I was in a caravan of buses to yet another rally in Washington, D.C. Once we arrived, I huddled among the nearly half million demonstrators, shivering in the cold as we filed down Pennsylvania Avenue. One by one, each demonstrator stopped and paused before the White House. When my turn came, I held my candle high, made the peace sign with my other hand, and chanted, "All we are saying is give peace a chance." A lot of fun has been made of the antiwar demonstrations of those days. But for a few seconds, I felt the ennobling spirit that comes with being a free person in a free country with the right to go before the most powerful person in authority and speak my truth.

Our peaceful demonstration didn't last long. The next day, in the midst of a throng of students on the Ellipse, a stampede nearly knocked me over. "Run!" my friend Steve yelled at me. My eyes stung and I realized with a shock that we were being sprayed with tear gas. My roommate

Cindy grabbed my arm and together we took off, reaching the bus that would take us back to campus. At St. Margarita's dormitory the next day, exhilarated after my weekend of dissent, a message was waiting for me: "Your father called. He wants you to call him right away." I hadn't told my father anything about my protest, but I had a feeling he'd found out.

When Joe asked me over the phone where I'd been that weekend, I told him the truth. A long silence greeted my words. Too late, I realized I was up against the hard wall of his mean temper. "You are not to leave the campus ever again," said Joe in a steely voice. "I'm not sending my money to that school to pay for you to be one of those damn peaceniks." When I argued back, he hung up. It had been easier protesting to Nixon than my own father. Minutes later, a school administrator knocked on my door. My father, she said, had ordered me placed under "house arrest." For the next three months, I had to be in my room each night by nine P.M. or he'd cut off my tuition.

It wasn't hard to find a way around this edict. While my father may have thought he'd won that skirmish, in the end he lost the battle he'd waged to protect me from the counterculture. In December 1969, the first draft lotteries since World War II were conducted. Now the tentacles of war grew long, reaching into the homes and lives of families throughout the country. On May 4, 1970, four Kent State student protesters were shot dead by Ohio national guardsmen during a demonstration protesting Nixon's announcement to invade Cambodia, sending a chill through the antiwar movement, and closing universities around the country. On campus, death and the end of the world was on everyone's mind, as it had been for most of us since those elementary school drills preparing us for nuclear attack. Nothing made sense anymore. Anything that had once counted as normal, from college to getting married or getting a job, mattered little. Either we'd all die in a nuclear attack, or, come the revolution, we'd be living on communes growing our own food. If a future existed, we'd have to make it up. On a date with Mark, I sat transfixed by the movie *Zabriskie Point*, with its climactic scene of fiery annihilation. Not everyone was as caught up in the zeitgeist as I was. But everything in my background to this point had prepared me to fit right into it.

BREAKDOWN

By the end of my first year of college, I was dropping LSD and seeing the light of God shining through broken glass in trash heaps, a radiant experience still emblazoned on my soul. On one acid trip, I got in a car with my friends, and in a spooky scene reminiscent of the drunken ride my father had taken me on as a girl, my tripping friends and I sped down the highway, high as the stars overhead. Staring out at the horizon through the windshield, I became mesmerized by a band of light glowing in the night sky. In the grip of a mystical vision, dimensions of reality dangerously merged as one. I became convinced that our car was going to soar straight off the planet and into the next world, and I told everyone to prepare for rebirth. Afterward, coming down from my own Icarus flight, my euphoria persisted. Melding the spiritual realm with the earthly, I began to feel that death was something that would never touch me. "I'm never going to die!" I announced to my worried boyfriend.

"Did you ever think you were going to die?" Sylvia Perera asks me, after I tell her about my father's lifelong seduction of death. "No," I tell her. "When I was young I thought I was going to live forever." Perera pauses, taking in my words. "Same idea," she says. "Live forever, or die soon. Both ideas completely the end." Luckily for me, these experimentations with psychedelics were short-lived. My psyche was simply too open and sensitive for drugs, and in the end my tendency to get too high too fast scared both myself and my friends—who began to dislike being around me when I was stoned or tripping. Perhaps, in the end, what was scariest to me was just how like my father I really was.

Any interest I'd had in college evaporated. Academics didn't satisfy the new drive pushing me, and I was too emotionally charged to concentrate anyway. My psychedelic tasting of transcendent dimensions had only blown hotter the embers of the spiritual fire that had begun to burn in me as a young teen. What I really wanted now was to move to California, find a guru, and live in a commune. I broke up with my boyfriend, determined to be free. Then, a few weeks later, and just before the end of classes, I discovered I was pregnant.

My relationship with Mark had always been a bit of a Romeo and Juliet affair. His Jewish parents were not keen on their eldest son dating a Catholic girl; my romantically inclined mother, however, had been thrilled at this fateful piece of synchronicity. My having a Jewish boyfriend had seemed to carry forward a piece of her own life. She'd even sent me the beautifully embroidered Israeli blouse she'd worn while she was pregnant with me, so I could wear it to a dance at Washington University. But my father was another story. Joe—who'd lived at an historic moment in postwar Israel, who'd flown for El Al, who'd named his farm Shalom Acres, and who'd conferred upon me the Hebrew middle name of Sharon—was now dead set against his Catholic daughter dating outside her faith.

Pregnant and more scared than I'd ever been up to that moment in my young life, I had no idea what I was going to do. Telling Joe or even Sheila was not an option. All that I could envision was my mother's hysteria and my father's fury. When I broke the news to Mark, we sat trembling side by side. What had we been thinking, after all? Unlike me, Mark was very clear at the outset that becoming a father at nineteen was not something he wanted. But *Roe v. Wade* was still three years in the future. Although I knew abortions could be obtained, the idea of an illegal backroom procedure frightened me. Even if we decided to take this course, neither one of us had any idea how to begin arranging for it, much less pay for it.

Standing atop very shaky psychological ground, I made up my mind: I would move to a commune in San Francisco. I announced this news to my shocked and dismayed boyfriend. I told him that I'd raise the baby with help from my imagined communal sisters and brothers. When I telephoned my parents as classes came to an end, I hid the truth, saying I was dropping out of college. Because I would first have to find some way of earning money to get to California, I made the illogical, last-minute decision to move to Washington, D.C., with some college friends. I moved into a group house off Dupont Circle and got a job at a fast-food restaurant named Beefy's. Mark called me constantly from St. Louis, where he'd stayed for summer school. Out of his mind with fear for both of us, he told me that if I had the baby

274

I'd ruin his life. I resisted his entreaties, fueled by fantasies of growing organic vegetables with chubby toddlers playing underfoot.

Finally, one day, Mark called to tell me that he'd spoken with a campus counselor. She'd found a respected doctor in an area clinic where I could get a safe abortion. Lately, as the hot, sticky days had passed and no magical way had opened up to California, I'd begun to grow desperate. I was barely supporting myself, much less a child, on my salary from Beefy's. It began to dawn on me that both emotionally and physically I was simply not ready to have a baby.

When I went in for my initial examination, the doctor told me that I'd just passed the three-month point for a DNZ, the quickest and safest form of abortion. Now, he said, I would have to wait until the next stage, when I was closer to five months pregnant. I left the office in a daze. At the group home where I lived, and on my fast-food job, I began to feel as if I was living in a glass world. Encased in isolation, I couldn't seem to touch or feel anything. Once, in a moment of true despair—a destructive "What the hell does it matter anyway?" kind of Joe Carroll mood—I dropped acid. I began refusing phone calls from Mark, and barely spoke to my parents.

One day, as I was walking to work, I experienced a moment of grace. Out of the corner of my eye, I saw a vision of a lovely, wise woman. Warm and smiling, she emanated faith and love. Somehow, this apparition let me know, I'd make it through. Soon enough, the day came when a housemate drove me to the clinic in his flower-bedecked green Volkswagen bug and dropped me off at the entrance with a jaunty wave. Inside, a nurse led me to a room in a wing tucked out of sight; clean and white, it was empty of any other patients. After I'd changed and gotten into the hospital bed, a doctor came in and examined me.

When the doctor told me that the baby had already died inside me and that I would have had a miscarriage anyway, I wasn't surprised. I'd never felt any life inside me. As if from a very great distance, as if from a star in outer space, I told the doctor that I'd taken drugs before I'd known I was pregnant, and even once recently. He nodded his head but didn't say anything. His nonjudgmental reaction melted the wall of ice between me and my feelings. Tears began streaming down my cheeks.

After the doctor gave me the injection that would induce early labor, he left. I lay on my hospital bed, a helpless and lonely creature of all the forces that had brought me to this point.

When the fetus finally came out of me in a warm burst, I panicked and began screaming for a nurse. It was nearly half an hour before someone came to check on me. For almost thirty minutes I prayed with everything I had in my heart and wrestled with whether or not I should look at what had come out of my body. I didn't. When it was time for me to be discharged, I wobbled weakly toward the glass doors where I was shocked to be met by Sandy, my old friend. She'd flown in, she said, to take me home to Kansas City. It was an act of kindness I've never forgotten.

I returned home a walking, gravely wounded girl of just eighteen. Life on Shalom Acres had deteriorated badly in my absence. Family meals had ended; my father spent his days home passed out or shut up in his bedroom. Twice, my mother had visited a lawyer in secret. One terrible day, my father had gathered my sister and brothers together. Ordering Sheila out of the room, he drunkenly announced to my traumatized siblings that he and my mother were getting a divorce. My mother would be moving out, he said, and he'd have custody. By the time I walked up the front porch steps in late August, a truce of sorts had been called. As Joe and Sheila took in my pale, grim face and sudden weight gain, their faces furrowed in alarm.

For my first weeks at home I obstinately pretended that nothing was wrong. I'd dropped out of school, I loudly declared, because college degrees were just a means to get me into "the system." One day, my mother asked me to sit outside with her. Sheila had set up two chairs on the patch of lawn between the cistern and the storm cellar. The summer flowers she'd planted on the cellar hill had grown straggly with autumn's approach. I plopped down next to her. I felt butterflies; heart-to-heart talks between us did not come easily. But something about her manner toward me was different this time. She seemed strong, and maternal. "Now, tell me what really happened," she said, cradling her cup of Lipton's tea. Her evenness steadied me; my reserve crumbled. As the story rushed out, I braced for her usual gust of tears. But my mother sat quietly until I'd finished.

"I knew you were pregnant," my mother said thoughtfully. "In fact, I thought you were still pregnant. I went to see *2001: A Space Odyssey*, and in the middle, when they were floating in space, I had a feeling and I just knew." I shouldn't have been surprised at my mother's reaction. After all, Sheila had been raised by a mother who'd been a fierce advocate of birth control, and her "knowing" was another instance of her talent for psychic hunches. As my mother spoke empathically of how badly she felt that I'd had to endure such an ordeal, I felt a great relief at not having to bear my secret alone. When we came to the problem of whether or not to tell my father what had happened, Sheila decided that he couldn't handle the truth. Instead, we fell back on that tried-and-true strategy of powerless women through the ages. My mother decided I should tell him that I'd had a nervous breakdown.

Since my return to the farm, Joe had circled me cautiously from a distance. He'd also stopped drinking. Sometimes, I could feel him studying my face intently, and I realized that he didn't really believe my concocted story. One day that fall, when everyone else was out of the house, I sat eating a sandwich at the picnic table in my mother's usual chair at the head of the table. Joe, in his captain's chair, looked across at me.

"So," he said, clearing his throat. "Tell me more about this nervous breakdown of yours." I launched into my well-rehearsed litany of hurts: how he'd injured me with his drinking; how I couldn't study or concentrate because of his drinking; how he was ruining my life and everyone else's life by his drinking. I pumped up my delivery by contorting my face in what I hoped looked like terrible suffering. I leaped up from the table, punched the air with my fists, and paced nervously about the kitchen. As I spoke, I could see the pain on his face. He looked down at his plate as if he'd been hit by a slew of arrows.

But I couldn't keep up the pretense. Yes, at some deeply unconscious level of my psyche, his alcoholic parenting had prepared the way for what had happened. But I also knew that my shakiness at that moment had more to do with the lingering trauma of the abortion, losing my first love, dropping out of college, and feeling utterly lost, than directly with my father. "Do you want to know what really happened?" I asked, suddenly brave. Joe looked up at me; now *he* was the one who was afraid.

"Yes. Tell me," he said in a low voice.

"I got pregnant and had an abortion." My face and body flamed red with emotion.

There are moments in life a person doesn't forget, no matter how many years have passed. This was one. My father didn't move, his face a mask of shock and disbelief. For a man of his generation, of Irish-Catholic faith—no matter how irreverent he was—there was probably no worse sin a daughter of his could have committed. For a man of his narcissistic psychology, as well, my father could not handle the blow I'd just delivered to his fragile ego. That *his* daughter would do such a thing—to *him*, the all-powerful father! As the minutes passed, Joe's eyes grew bloodshot red, then black, with rage. When he stood up and pushed back his chair, I cringed. He turned away without a word, left the kitchen, and went into his bedroom. The door shut with a loud click.

For the next two weeks my father didn't speak, to me or to anyone. He didn't come to the dinner table and took his meals in his room. I began to feel as if my father's silence was killing me. I pleaded with him to talk to me. Although it was a relief not to pretend I was having a nervous breakdown, I was now scared of what terrible thing he might do, and the permanent damage my confession had caused to our relationship.

Then late one Indian summer afternoon, my father called up to me in my bedroom. Cautiously, I came downstairs. Without looking at me directly, he asked me to go outside with him, just as my mother had. My skin was clammy with fright as I followed his squared back outdoors. Joe led me past the clothesline with its billowing sheets and towels to the grassy area just beyond the pool, next to the barn where he'd been bitten by a snake. Gold-and-red-tinged leaves rustled softly in the autumn air. In an odd reenactment of my mother's ritual, he'd also set up two lawn chairs. He sat down and gestured to me to take the chair beside him.

Just as I'd been surprised by my mother, now I was taken aback by my father. In a steady, sober voice—he hadn't been drinking—Joe asked me to tell him, in detail, everything that had happened. Though he still didn't look directly at me, his manner was composed and deliberate. I spoke slowly at first, hesitantly choosing the right words so as not to trip his anger. But as he listened without interrupting, it became clear that Joe was genuinely interested in what I had to say. Now my words flowed out of me in my relief at being able to confide in him.

When I'd finished talking, Joe continued to look out over the hills. He silently crushed a cigarette beneath his heel, lit another, then inhaled deeply. The sun had started to sink in the sky, casting a rusty auburn glow. I could hear the bullfrogs begin their evensong down by the pond. My father, I thought in the lengthening silence, could make God pause, so skilled was he at the waiting game. I began to imagine the seasons turning, could see the two of us being covered in drifts of snow. Spring would come and find a father and his daughter still sitting, frozen to the plastic lawn chairs.

Finally, Joe sighed, turned to me, and began asking questions. He wanted to know more about the college counselor who'd referred me, and the clinic. He asked me about my job, the house I'd lived in, and my housemates. He was interested, even curious, about how all the details of an illegal abortion had been worked out. I recall now that Joe had ardently supported Barry Goldwater, who'd been an ATC pilot during World War II. The libertarian Republican Goldwater had also been a supporter of Planned Parenthood and, eventually, of abortion rights.

When his remaining questions had been satisfied, Joe fixed his gaze once again on the darkening horizon of hills. Then, in a tone of gentleness unusual for him, he said that I was too young to have had a child, that he was glad I'd come out of it safely, and that he was sorry that I'd had to suffer through such a difficult experience alone. I soaked in the rare experience of my father's paternal protection, as well as his friendship. It was a new sensation, but, as with my mother, one I liked. Talking this out with him had felt powerfully curing. I'd felt seen, I'd felt myself, and I'd felt grown up.

But it couldn't last. Joe looked me in the face. The angry old man was back. "And you tell that Jewish boyfriend of yours to stay away. I swear that if he ever steps foot on this farm," he spat out, his eyes narrowed into metal-blue slits, "by God, I will get out my shotgun and I will shoot him." Years later, in the midst of my retelling the story of my abortion to my therapist, Nona paused at this part. Nodding her head solemnly as if to drive home the point of my father's violent temper, she concurred: "And he would have."

LEAVING HOME, AGAIN

After this encounter with my father, the rest of the year passed without incident. I got a job and worked as a hostess at Stephenson's, the famous Kansas City restaurant where my parents had taken us during happier times. The following spring, I began attending a series of lectures by a succession of visiting meditation teachers at Unity Village, Missouri. There I met the spiritual teacher I'd long been searching for, and I signed up to attend a summer gathering. That July, I took a Greyhound bus to a meditation camp in the Arizona desert, outside a small town fittingly named Paradise.

On my journey, I read again from Thomas Merton's meditations on the Desert Fathers. As I stared out the bus window at the passing scenery, a memory stirred. During a family trip to San Francisco, we'd driven out to see the giant redwoods. As I ran and played with my siblings among the giants in the cathedral-like setting, I'd come upon my mother, startling her unexpectedly. She'd been standing in a ray of sun, staring into the light as if into a crystal ball. "What's the matter? What are you doing?" I'd asked, puzzled by the look on her face. "I was just about to hear God, see something," she said, sadly. "I was just about to hear the answer, and then . . . a shadow fell, and you came along." Her voice trailed off as tourists entered the clearing.

Now I was about to find the answer to my own questions that I'd put to God. When I arrived at the camp and took in the scene of long-haired, dusty, naked, spiritual seekers, I felt that I'd arrived at the place I'd long been looking for. Like St. Francis, who'd stripped off his clothes before a judge as a way to shed his family ties, I peeled off my blouse and turned my bare body to the sun.

Early the next morning, the gentle strum of a zither awakened me. I scrambled out of my sleeping bag, hugged my blanket around my shoulders, and followed the music and the stream of sleepy campers to an open area facing the eastern horizon. Seated in a cross-legged pose before my robed teacher, I was guided in a meditation on the orb of the sun as it slowly rose in the dawn-streaked sky. Over the next days, I bathed in the long hours of silent meditation and soaked my lacerated heart in the sweet balm of chanting. I forsook the name my father had given me—the name that had bound me to his strange fate—and accepted the new one my teacher had chosen for me as symbolic of my spiritual rebirth: Pythia, priestess of the Delphic oracle. I was not Greek, and I was certainly no priestess, but I'd always loved Greek history and mythology. And besides, I thought, Pythia was a lot easier to pronounce than Pellman. I'd found a new spiritual home, a new spiritual father, and a new identity. Or so I thought.

After the Paradise retreat, I returned home just long enough to pack a few clothes. At the camp I'd met my future husband, a kind, handsome, olive-skinned man of Armenian heritage. Terry had invited me back to California to be part of the commune where he lived, and I shimmered with happiness. I was going to live my dream. But first I had to say good-bye to my parents.

When I walked in the front door of the farmhouse, the familiar scent of cigarette smoke and fresh-baked Betty Crocker brownies wafted over me. The radio was tuned to Joe's easy listening station. As I crossed the threshold, my parents stared at me in disbelief. Instead of taking the bus back, I'd hitchhiked across Arizona and Oklahoma with a friend, whom I'd deposited in the city before hitching a ride out to Oak Grove. Although I'd been bathed spiritually, I hadn't washed in almost ten days. My skin was dusty and tanned almost black from the desert sun. My tangled, uncombed dark hair was twisted into two long braids, and I was braless beneath the T-shirt I wore loosely over my frayed and faded jeans. Dangling, turquoise-beaded earrings grazed my shoulders; copper bangles clanked noisily around my wrists; rings sparkled on my brown toes; and long loops of scented, wooden prayer beads hung around my neck. A beaming, wraparound smile graced my blithely innocent face.

Over dinner at the picnic table later that night, I announced to the family that I was moving to California to live in a commune. My father turned ashen. Mumbling beneath his breath—he'd been drinking—he warned me to look out for murderous Charles Manson lookalikes. My mother became hysterical. I sat beside her on the edge of her bed later that evening as she sobbed long and hard, her face in her hands. "But I don't understand. You're sleeping with too many men; no one will marry you. What will become of you?" she wailed, tears pouring down her cheeks. "Your father is drinking. I'm all alone. I don't know what to do. I just can't take it anymore. I just can't."

Guilt pierced my spiritual sunniness. I was all too aware that I was abandoning my mother, as well as my sister and brothers. Their strained, pinched, and sweet faces pressed in on me. My helplessness about leaving them, and their helplessness watching me go, nearly overwhelmed me. It nearly caused me to stay. Far down in some wordless, instinctive place, however, I knew I couldn't save them. I was not strong enough for the Herculean task of rescuing the Carrolls. I'd been thrown a lifeline, I'd found the life I wanted to live, and I had to go. Using my last free TWA pass, I flew out of Kansas City with my girlfriend the next day.

When Holly and I landed in San Francisco later that night, we hitched a ride out to Sausalito Beach in a purple-painted Volkswagen bus full of hippies. I had twenty-five dollars to my name and hadn't even told Terry when I'd be arriving. To save money, and for the sake of adventure, we decided to sleep on the beach that first night. As I shook out my sleeping bag beside the moonlit waves, I realized with a shock that I'd left my purse on the van's rooftop.

The next morning, I hitchhiked to the nearest phone booth and called home collect to ask my father for some money. "Just come home!" Joe shouted into the phone. "Just turn yourself right around, get on the plane, and get back here!" The phone clicked sadly as I placed it back on the receiver. It was too late now. I'd become my father's daughter and was declaring my independence for good this time. I was breaking his heart, but he didn't have the words to tell me.

Back on the farm, my father sat in his chair through the night, brooding, smoking, drinking, and shaking his head. "Where did I go wrong? Where did I go wrong?" he lamented. Then, "CaliFORNIA, CaliFORNIA," he'd say, smacking his forehead over the Sodom and Gomorrah of murderers and drug dealers into which his innocent daughter had disappeared. For her part, my mother tore up one of the mysterious envelopes addressed "To My Daughter on Her Wedding Night" that she'd kept hidden in her underwear drawer. Years later, I learned that it had contained a *Reader's Digest* article with advice to a woman on her first night of married life.

Soon, Colleen left home for college; not long after that, my brother Steve followed. Though he didn't like it, and though he stayed away from visiting me, Joe grudgingly began to adjust to my new life in California. Always sensitive to cultural changes blowing in the wind, even Joe himself had begun to feel the stirrings of his old restlessness. With just my youngest brother left at home, my father decided that it was time to sell the house and a hundred acres of the farm.

Joe wanted to move to Mexico. He'd heard Guadalajara was a pretty neat place to live.

THE LOST FATHERS

I keep on my writing desk two mementoes from my father: his TWA wings and his tie clip, embellished with an image of a rocket on liftoff. Emblems of his career, they call me, still, to the rim of the weightless horizon. Just as Daedalus fitted his son with wings of feathers and taught him the rules of flight, so my father imprinted on me the patterns of his life-myth. As my father had been smitten with sky-daring heroes like Charles Lindbergh and Howard Hughes, so, too, had I gravitated to the edge of my time. Joining up with the raucous revolution of the sixties had been my way of following in my father's footsteps—even as I fled from home and tried to sever myself from his values. Where change was, where risk and excitement was, there I'd be. Sure enough, just as my father eventually drunk-crashed, so I also flew too near the blazing sun and fell back to earth a merely mortal teenager in a lonely hospital bed far from home.

Although I was born the daughter of an aviator, no one ever told me about the myth of Icarus. No schoolteacher ever mentioned the reckless boy who, after failing to heed his father's warnings to navigate the middle course, plunged to his death in the sea on wings of wax melted by the heat of the sun. This was a loss, especially during the era when I came of age. The ancients may have known little about addiction or brain chemistry; they had no pills to prescribe for depression or anxiety. Instead, they applied the wisdom of stories as medicine for the endlessly recurring struggles that ail humankind.

The story of Icarus still speaks to us across the centuries because in it we recognize that familiar parable of flying high then falling low; rising to success and sinking to the nadir of failure; working hard and crashing; or getting drunk or high and being stone-cold sober. The Greeks recognized this dance of extremes as the endless up-and-down of life. The urge to touch the sun, to be greater than we are, is an especially exaggerated American trait. It is celebrated in every technological breakthrough, presidential inaugural speech, or *American Idol* contest. It is our spectacular, defining genius.

But it is also our tragic, fatal flaw. Through its lens our history comes into focus. It is the Founding Fathers enshrining the principles of individual liberty in the Declaration of Independence. It is the genocide of the Native Americans and the sin of African-American slavery. It is astronaut Neil Armstrong taking humankind's first step on the moon; it is the Challenger exploding into space. It is New York City's Twin Towers rising to touch the sky; it is terrorists in jets reducing them to rubble. It is the capitalist free market that turns a poor cabdriver into a wealthy entrepreneur—and then melts away his savings in an economic downturn, putting him back on the streets as a cabdriver once again.

And it is my father, sailing through the air in a jet only to return home to sit through the night drinking and grieving in darkness over the daughter who'd fled his house. For though the Icarus myth helped speed Joe's way from the railroad yards of Altoona to TWA's friendly skies, it left him unskilled in the art of fathering. Caught off guard, he could only watch and worry as I followed in his flying footsteps. But this, too, repeats the myth of Icarus, for as Daedalus prepares to escape with his son to a new country, his mantle of paternal responsibility begins to weigh heavily. Suddenly aware of the dangers of flight, the once carefree, inventive genius is now bent with worry over what might befall his inexperienced son.

Now, faced with my own headstrong behavior, Joe found himself in the unaccustomed role of Daedalus, warning me against life's dangers. Where before he'd tried to block the fact of my approaching adulthood, he began to plead with me to stay in college and get a degree. "How are you going to support yourself?" he'd ask, his face a creased map of parental anxiety. Having been born into a time when the very idea of the future itself was in peril, I had no idea what I was going to do when I grew up. I'd been born as the daughter of Icarus and raised in an Icarus culture at the dawn of the nuclear and space age: How *does* such a girl grow up?

Very slowly and over a long period of time, it turns out. Though I was propelled from home like a rocket, I wasn't even close for liftoff into an independent life. Emotionally, I felt less like I'd left my family and more like I'd been ripped out of it. Often in those first years away from home, I recall being unable to feel my physical body as "me." I would stand in front of another person and occasionally undergo the disorienting sensation of feeling their face transplanted onto mine. Something in my young, unformed self must have sensed that, as, daring as I aimed to be, I didn't have what it took to go too far from home.

During those heated discussions with my father about college, I'd begged him to enroll me in college in Kansas City. I might not have known what I wanted to do with my life, and home might have been a turbulent place, but I did have an instinctive desire to stay within close reach of my friends, family, and the farm I so loved. But guided by the myths of self-sufficiency, independence, and autonomy by which he'd autopiloted his life, Joe had done what he'd thought was best by sending me away. I, too, had pushed away my feelings of need and so had eventually done what he'd wanted me to do. I shut the door to my past, just as he used to shut his bedroom door in all our faces. After I left for California, aside from a couple of visits, I never went home again.

If as a teenager I was following in the mythic footsteps laid down by my father, I was also following in America's historical footsteps. Certainly at no time are our cultural ideals around independence and heroic individualism thrown into such bold relief as during that stormy coming-of-age period in a young person's life. The explosion of youth culture in the sixties only amplified those trends—one found in the DNA of America itself.

Reflecting on the psychological legacy of America's own coming-of-age-story, Canadian Jungian analyst Marion Woodman observes that our rebel ancestors "went through the anguish of breaking with the mother country, and even fighting and killing the soldiers of the mother. That gives you a fiery 'We did it!' spirit that marks the hero." She describes her reaction to a documentary she'd watched when she was visiting historic Williamsburg in Virginia. Woodman says that when she saw the reenactment of the young rebels suffering through an agony of spirit about whether they should fight England or return home to England, she "received a huge awakening about the ritual one goes through in order to grow up. One could say it was maturity for them to rebel, and that it would have been immature for them not to have rebelled."

Yet, she cautions, "American culture has gotten stuck in the rebel hero phase—a kind of traumatic separation that rejects the mother. It's one reason why the country finds dependency so threatening." Our idealization of the solitary individual courageously overcoming great odds to accomplish an outstanding feat, adds psychologist Judith Jordan, has led to "an ethic which elevates individualism and independence while scorning dependency as a sign of weakness."

Emerging Freudian theories around childhood development at the turn of the twentieth century would dovetail neatly with American ideals of autonomy. The developmental maturation of the child into an adult, for instance, was constructed on a classical Freudian model of separation—individuation: the progression of the child away from the ties of the family, especially the mother. By the 1950s and '60s, explains Jordan, the separate self was seen as the pinnacle of mental health. The standard then "was to leave home at eighteen and become your own person. The psychologies written at that time were characterized by a kind of 'Go West' frontier mentality. The notion of a healthy grown-up was that of someone who moved away from home to go to school in another city, and who then set up a home in yet a different city."

This "Go West," fly the nest, Joe Carroll style of American independence may have served to build an industrially successful country with outwardly self-sufficient individuals. But in its one-sided emphasis on external development, our myth of individuality ignores the glorious and dramatic interior world of ever-shifting feelings, intuitions, sorrows, and philosophical sensibilities and connections to larger, invisible realms of existence.

In fact, in today's technologically impersonal, globalized world, the stand-alone individual as a model of mental health may even have become a dangerous liability. Whereas those in therapy in Freud's time struggled primarily with issues around sexual repression and conformist cultural and family bonds that stifled individuality, those in the twenty-first century suffer more often from the malaise of modernity: isolation, depression, loneliness, and inner states of despair, deadness, and emptiness.

Because even psychological theories are influenced by the history of their time, the world we live in today, with its particular set of human dilemmas, has led many therapists to discard the paradigm of psychological development as a Revolutionary-like battle to separate from Mother England. New directions in psychoanalysis regarding the family, says post-Freudian psychoanalyst Stephen Mitchell, reinforce the idea that "people need to remain connected with each other throughout their lifetimes in complex, embedded environments." This orientation has recast the time-honored rite of leaving home. Instead, the goal of the young person, says Judith Jordan, is now seen to "have more to do with differentiating: staying connected, in other words, while engaging with their parents from their own unique standpoint, and creating other connections and relationships." The parent–child relationship in this sense is a kind of fertilizer to the child's inner world. What many therapists have learned from focusing on a person's private experience during analysis, Mitchell explains, is the "impact of the emotional presence and responsiveness of the parent in childhood: Were they there or not there? How were they there? What did they see in the child, what did they respond to, and what was threatening to them?"

Those who grow up lacking this kind of emotionally attuned upbringing can suffer what psychoanalyst Michael Eigen calls the "annihilated self," or a psyche filled with dread. Many of his clients, writes Eigen in *Feeling Matters*, discover that "something in the depths of their being feels 'off.' And whatever this 'offness' or 'wrongness' is . . . it poisons life, it spoils, it accuses, it nags."

Eigen's words stir memories of longings I entertained during adolescence, and even later, as a young mother and writer. In these fantasies, I would imagine a different kind of paternal figure than the one fate had dealt me, the kind of father some of my girlfriends had. This father was an easygoing man who played cards with me, or with whom I could affectionately kid around in light-hearted fun. A father who held his temper in check, who was protective without being abusive and domineering, and with whom I could safely share my secret worries and fears. I wanted the kind of parent who peeked out of my father in that rare moment in the garden, when I shared with him the trauma of my abortion.

But if I longed for a sweeter, safer relationship with my father, did he also yearn for the same with me? Joe's broken connection to his own parents, Italian analyst Luigi Zoja tells me, left him ill-prepared to cope with the feelings stirred in him by my going away. Joe, he explains, "had no grounding in the tasks of fatherhood. His own father had died in his adolescence, and his foster father had been an emotionally cool and unrelated man." My father's failure to shepherd me into adulthood, he believes, may even have contributed to his depression. Yet in this, says Zoja, my father was not alone, but "belongs to a lost generation of men who weren't able to transform themselves into fathers. And because of that, they were depressed."

Sadly, today the absent father, comments Zoja, is itself an image of a contemporary paternal archetype. This is the all-too-familiar weak father who, although unafraid to go to work or war, refuses to engage in his relationships. Even if he hasn't divorced or physically left the house, says Zoja, "he's no longer there." The silence of these fathers, writes Zoja, "deafens the analyst's studio. Every day, patients reprove their fathers for not having expressed themselves; for not having explained and defended their own points of view; for having been present but silent, for having offered no response to children or mothers."

As I've researched my father's past and how it came to shape him, I've often thought that women, who passed through the fire of feminism to emerge with broader definitions of womanhood, might have a lot to offer men. Indeed, it is worth considering that women as a whole have made greater strides toward integrating so-called masculine traits around worldly accomplishment and assertiveness than men have in the realm of feelings. Maybe, in fact, it will take another women's movement to lead our fathers, sons, brothers, lovers, uncles, and husbands to a more liberated understanding of masculinity.

A story I come across, retold by Jungian analyst Linda S. Leonard in her book *The Wounded Woman*, helps to light the way. In this fairy tale from Tajikistan, a courageous girl goes off in search of medicine that can help heal her blind father. There are no sons to do this task; her two older sisters try but fail in their attempts. Dressed in men's clothes, the youngest daughter travels to a faraway land where there lives a surgeon who possesses the medicine she seeks. Along the way, she overcomes terrible obstacles; aided by a wise old woman, she eventually locates the surgeon and obtains the medicine she needs to heal her father's eyes. Suspecting her true gender, the surgeon's son accompanies the intrepid girl home. Upon her arrival, her father greets her with tender relief. Weeping with gladness, the father says he will never again regret not having a son. Seeing that his companion is truly a woman, the surgeon's son falls in love with her, and they marry and live happily ever after.

Here is an image, comments Leonard, "of a wounded father, injured in his relation to the feminine, yet only the feminine can save him—the old woman has the knowledge and the daughters have the spunk and motivation." But in the process of healing her father, she writes, the girl, too, is healed, as she gains a "deep connection to her own strength and courage, to the power of her own feminine spirit, and to a loving relationship with the masculine." Leonard, whose book arose out of her own odyssey as the daughter of an alcoholic father, writes that "I have seen that finding a new relation to the father is an important issue for any woman with an impaired relation to the father. And culturally . . . it is an issue for every woman, since the relation to the cultural ruling fathers needs to be transformed."

"A loving relationship with the masculine"—my eyes linger on these words, imagining what that kind of world might be like. Perhaps, I think, it can only be achieved through a one-at-a-time, father–daughter, father–son process. Coming to the end of this chapter, I have a dream that is a modern-day version of my own Tajikistan quest. In it, I find myself in a large underground laundry room. I'm surrounded by enormous mounds of my family's dirty laundry, which it is my task to wash. Off to the side, sitting on a bench with his back to me, is my father. Surprised to see him again, I sit down beside him. "Dad," I say, putting my arm around his shoulder. "I've been learning new things about your life—especially the painful things I never knew before. I feel sorry for all that you had to go through." At these words, tears begin to fall from his eyes. Putting his face in his hands, my father begins to weep.

TOP LEFT: **The Carroll farm in winter.** Taken sometime in the fifties, this photo shows the Midwestern prairie landscape in its bleakest season.

TOP RIGHT: **The Carroll farm in winter**, under the prairie sky.

MIDDLE LEFT: **The old red barn.** Though it was never red, it once had been, and remained so in our imaginations. This is where hay and grain for the cattle was stored, and where we four kids loved to play.

MIDDLE RIGHT: **Slaughtered cow carcass.** Once or twice a year, one of our beef cattle was slaughtered, then cut up and stored at the local locker.

BOTTOM: **"Shalom Acres" from above.** Taken by an aerial photographer sometime in the late sixties, this photo shows the farm in all its beauty.

TOP LEFT: **Sheila picnicking in the pasture**. This photo of my mother was taken in the happier early years on the farm, in one of the lower pastures by our favorite pond, where we loved to have family picnics.

SECOND ROW LEFT: **Sheila on the riding mower**. While Joe worked the fields, my mother kept the green, sloping front lawn freshly cut, a job she loved.

LEFT: **Sheila and our new Chrysler** family station wagon. Taken sometime in the early sixties, Joe and Sheila were thrilled with their frost blue luxury car, a symbol of their rising economic status.

BELOW: **Joe training horses**. One by one over the years, Joe bred, then broke and trained a horse, until there were six: one for each of us.

TOP RIGHT: **Joe working on the farm**. This photo was taken in the fifties, during Joe's first years cultivating the fields on the farm.

TOP LEFT: **Joe and the four Carroll kids on the lawn**. Taken in the mid-fifties, from left to right: Steve, Pellman, John (in Joe's lap) and Colleen.

TOP RIGHT: **Joe and the four Carroll kids in the pasture**, taken in the mid-fifties. Pellman, Colleen, John (Donnie), and Steve (with his hat).

ABOVE: **Four Carroll kids in front of the farmhouse**: left to right: Pellman, Colleen, Steven, and John.

LEFT: **Four Carroll kids running toward the camera**: left to right: Steven, Pellman, Colleen and John.

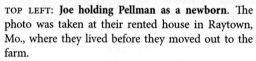

TOP LEFT: **Joe holding Pellman as a newborn.** The photo was taken at their rented house in Raytown, Mo., where they lived before they moved out to the farm.

TOP RIGHT: **Pellman on the farm in the alfalfa field.** Taken when we'd just moved to the farm, I'm about five years old, holding something I'd found in the cup of my hand.

ABOVE: **Joe and Pellman with her Shetland pony.** My mother christened our first newborn foal Sombra, Spanish for "shadow," as that's how he first appeared standing by his mother.

MIDDLE RIGHT: **Pellman as Oak Grove Homecoming Queen.** In the fall of 1967, I beamed with happiness to be chosen for this local honor by the high school's football team.

RIGHT: **Pellman as a hippie** in Paradise, Arizona. Taken in the summer of 1972, I'm on the brink of a new life, attending my first meditation camp in the high desert.

TOP LEFT: **Sheila and Joe** in front of the family room fireplace on the farm in later years.

MIDDLE LEFT:. **Final Carroll family gathering**. Taken by my husband Terry, this is the last photo of the Carroll family before my parents separated. Left to right: Joe, Sheila, John, Pythia, Colleen, and Steven, who is holding my son, Kabir.

BOTTOM LEFT. **My last family dinner on the farm**. On a visit home from California, Joe snapped this photo of the five of us seated around the familiar redwood picnic table.

top right: **Four Carroll children as young adults**. Home for Christmas, standing in front of the fireplace with the old railroad tie mantel.

MIDDLE RIGHT: **Fazl (Terry) and Pythia (Pellman)**. Taken in Marin County, California, where I'm married and living in a spiritual commune.

BOTTOM RIGHT: **Steven and Joe visiting Pythia** in Washington, D.C. Taken in 1986. Left to right: Steven, Pythia, and Joe.

TOP LEFT: **Don José and the Festival Queen**. When a local village asked my father to drive the newly crowned Festival Queen and her attendants around the square, my father—despite his expression—happily complied.

BOTTOM LEFT: **Joe in San Antonio, Texas**. This photo was taken at a restaurant on Joe's last family trip with his four children and his wife Hilda, just months before he died.

TOP RIGHT: **Joe's house in Chapala, Mexico**. John, youngest of the Carroll children, is standing on the balcony overlooking the pool.

MIDDLE RIGHT: **Lake Chapala, Mexico**.

BOTTOM RIGHT: **Joe's last house in Corpus Christi, Texas**.

TOP LEFT: **Joe's passport, 1975.**

TOP RIGHT: **Joe's passport, 1980.**

ABOVE: **Joe's last passport, 1985.**

TOP LEFT: **Joe's cremation: final blessing.** On the shore of the Gulf of Mexico, the family gathers with local priest Father Fred to pray over Joe's ashes. From left to right: Lily, Abe, Hilda, Amir, Pythia, Colleen, and Father Fred.

SECOND LEFT: **Joe's cremation: final journey.** Walking toward the ocean with the wind at our faces: From the back, left to right: Kabir, Hilda, Father Fred, Lily, Jules, Pythia, in front of Colleen, Amir, Steve, and Abe.

THIRD LEFT: **Joe's cremation: into the sea.** Amir throwing the urn with his grandfather's ashes into the Gulf of Mexico.

BOTTOM: **Joe's cremation: yellow roses, Icarus has fallen.**

IX

Don José and the Festival Queen

All men should strive to learn before they die what they are running from, and to, and why.—**James Thurber**, *"The Shore and the Sea"*

T HE PEBBLY SAND ON the beach spilled into my tennis shoes in soggy clumps. But I didn't care. I was running away from my father, racing along the shoreline of Padre Island in the midmorning quiet. Each flying footstep, each push of my chest into the gulf breezes, lengthened the distance between myself and the tomb-like house I'd burst out of. Slowing at a small promontory that jutted out into the glittering Gulf of Mexico, I clambered over granite rocks until I reached the water's edge. I settled into the lap of a large boulder and turned my face to the clear sky, breathing in drafts of fresh, salty air. After the chill of the air-conditioned rooms I'd just escaped, the sun's warmth was like a laying on of healing hands.

Joe was on his king-size bed and our family deathwatch had begun. Yet no one—not the hospice workers, not his doctor—knew exactly when Joe would draw his last breath. Unable to walk without difficulty, my father had become mostly confined to his bedroom. Going to the bathroom had turned into a major outing, like he was a little child being taken to the zoo. That morning, while Hilda had been sleeping and before the hospice aide had arrived, I'd had to help him pee. My sister had held the plastic container. Regressing to our twelve-year-old selves, we'd suddenly broken down in uncontrollable fits of giggles.

"Pee here, pee there, everybody keeps telling me where to pee," Joe had joked to relieve the tension. I'd run from the room, half laughing and half crying, appalled at this intrusion of my awkward adolescent self. But I couldn't help it; my father's dying was turning ever weirder. Now that it had become my responsibility to pay his bills, I'd started to go through the stacks of mail that had piled up. The night before, I'd come upon a notice informing my father that his fire insurance policy had been canceled. It was two months old. I'd walked into his bedroom, the paper in my shaking hand. Both my father and Hilda, who was sitting by his chair, were smoking, drinking coffee, and watching CNN. Out of the corner of my eye I'd seen the oxygen tank that stood upright in a corner, on the far side of the bed where my father lay sprawled out. An ashtray and matches had been on the desk next to it.

"Dad, did you know that your fire insurance policy has been canceled?" I asked gently. Joe looked at me with his faded blue eyes and smiled innocently. "No kidding," he chuckled. "Call that insurance guy and tell him the check is in the mail. You take care of it, all right? Attagirl." I nodded my head, and left the room. And all this time, I thought to myself, I'd been worried about my father's dying of cancer when one misplaced spark from his cigarette could have engulfed us all in flames.

Shaking away these thoughts, I stood up from the rock. I brushed the sand off my clothes and gazed out over the gorgeous turquoise waters under the impossibly blue canopy of sky. As I took in the great expanse of ocean and horizon, I felt the tight places inside myself breathe and expand. I shielded my eyes from the glare of the Texas sun and tracked the metallic dot of a plane as it flew across the horizon. In contemplating the plane's path through cloudless space, I could understand humankind's constant craving for mountain peaks and ocean cliffs, the heights of tall buildings or the sight of earth from an airplane window. Some instinct born of our birth in deep space calls out for great lengths, remote reaches, and drawn-out distances. Yet it's also in the natural order of things that our eyes can never linger long on these tall visions, but must narrow to the daily demands of small things, the work of everyday life.

I turned from the vista before me and began the short walk back to my father's house. My footsteps were slow, and I felt reluctant to reenter what my sister had taken to calling "the zone." I couldn't know then that soon Joe would come to rest at this very spot, or that my stepmother Hilda would return to Mexico, and that we would never speak again.

✳

Mexico. As places go, it's about as different from Missouri as any two points on the globe could be. How my father departed the farm and Oak Grove and came to live in the rose-scented village of Las Fuentes, Guadalajara, is yet another interlude in his roaming life story. "There are people who can be defined by what they escape from, and people who are defined by the fact that they are forever escaping," writes the English psychoanalyst Adam Phillips in *Houdini's Box*. It is not so much that we travel or move to another state or country, in other words, but why.

When he abandoned the two-hundred-acre Missouri farm he had so lovingly cultivated for over twenty years, my father was not fleeing poverty or disease, as his Irish forebear had when he'd come to America. Unlike his grandfather William, Joe had an income and a stable job. In part, it was that very regularity and security that would prompt this radical move to Mexico. "This is what money . . . pays for in ever more ambitious adventures," writes Phillips: "spectacular escape. People getting ahead of themselves. People getting away from it all." But the wind of the American dream was also at Joe's back, stirring his restless, rootless soul to be on the move again. We are largely, writes Wallace Stegner, "a civilization in motion, driven by dreams. The dreams are not dead even today, and the habit of mobility has only been reinforced by time," wanderers, orphans "running toward freedom."

In moving to Mexico, it was himself, and the confines of his madness and his maddening marriage, that my father was seeking to escape.

FATHER OF WILD RIDES

In the years that followed my own getaway to California, Joe continued his life of flying and farming. He replaced the troublesome Herefords with a herd of docile white sheep who'd never dare kick him. He purchased new farm machinery and experimented with planting crops of milo (grain sorghum) and soybeans. On the job, TWA was still the brightest star in the firmament of America's commercial airlines. Its red logo was the signature of first-class style and panache. In 1967, it had become the first airline to go all jet. Brochures described flying "smoothly above the weather," as you relaxed in "roomy, cloud-soft seats" en route to Paris or London. By 1969, the same year as the moon landing, the all-hell-breaking-loose political scene, and my ill-starred year in college, TWA had inaugurated around-the-world service.

Up in the cockpit, flight engineer Joe Carroll had a front-row, first-class seat on this global ride. He was approaching his twenty-year seniority, and he'd soon win coveted routes taking him to exotic destinations like New Delhi, Hong Kong, and Bangkok. Somewhere in the tumult around my leaving home, I recall how he'd fizzed with excitement over the news that his domestic routes would soon end and he'd be returning to his world-exploring days. Joe had waved his arms grandly and promised that we'd all be able to fly "non-rev" anywhere in the world for no more than a small surcharge.

But Joe was no longer the strutting, tire-kicking young man he'd been at the start of his career. Years of drinking, smoking, and sleeplessness had exacted a toll. It was around this time, my mother recalls, that he'd begun coming home "absolutely exhausted" after every trip. Past the fifty-year mark now, he became increasingly preoccupied with dying. "He was always instructing me on where his will was, and how much money I'd have to live on if he died," says Sheila. More of his days off were spent sleeping in his curtained bedroom. Preparing for a trip now seemed to require more pounds of flesh than he had to give. I learn with surprise from my mother that Joe had not welcomed the jet age. Initially, he'd thought that the advancement to jet engines wouldn't happen until after his retirement. In addition to everything else that had been upending my father's world at that time, so even had his one reliable constant, the airplane.

According to the data that my father had neatly tallied up in the worn logbook I find after his death, he'd put in 1,242 hours aboard the

PBY during the war, 1,698 hours on the Douglas DC-4 and DC-6 for FAMA, 700 hours on the DC-4 for El Al, and 7,315 hours aboard the Constellation for both El Al and TWA. It was while flying the four-engine, propeller-driven "Connie," as it was affectionately called, that my father had further honed his wartime skills as a navigator and flight engineer. In 1949, he'd graduated from an E.2, or "Aircraft Operational Engineer acting under supervision," to E.1, or "Aircraft Operational Engineer responsible for the operation of the aircraft power units and auxiliary systems."

Sometimes called the "third officer" or the "third pilot," the position of flight engineer first became needed when more hands were required in the cockpit to manage the increasing complexity of modern aircraft. With the development of multiengine transport and the rise of transoceanic flights, writes Denny Harmon in *The American Flight Engineer*, a third crew member was needed to manage the piston engines; monitor the fuel systems, cabin pressure, and temperature; adjust engine power during takeoffs and landings; and conduct pre- and postflight inspections. The need for aerial engineers on long-range military aircraft intensified during World War II; in May 1944, the Air Corps established a separate officer's code, 1028, Aircraft Observer, or flight engineer. One of the first airplanes to have an official flight engineer was the Boeing B-29 Superfortress—the aircraft used to drop the atomic bombs over Hiroshima and Nagasaki. Flight engineer–training peaked during the summer of 1945—the very time period my father, with his background in airline mechanics, was drafted into the Army Air Corps.

A common career path for commercial airline flight engineers was to advance to the position of pilot. El Al had wanted to train my father to become a pilot, as had TWA. My father's brother Gene, who'd started out as a flight engineer for Pan Am, had followed this trajectory. But even with the promise of a higher salary, Joe had refused to abandon his position as flight engineer. As much as he was an airman, engines were his first and lifelong passion, and he would remain loyal to them.

Alongside the images I have of my father in his crisp black-and-gold-trimmed TWA uniform are those of him at work on the farm:

the dark rims of grease beneath his fingernails; the pungent aroma of gasoline that clung to his work clothes; and the sight and sound of him happily tinkering and whistling beneath the hoods of cars, tractors, combines, lawn mowers, trucks, or any other machine. One reason my father hadn't liked jets, he'd told my mother, was because they weren't "hands-on" enough. Possibly, too, working on engines had kept him connected to the mechanical traditions of his father and grandfather.

In 1960, the year my father's logbook ends, TWA introduced jet service aboard the 707. Joe must have known that this shift signaled the death knell of his vocation. In fact, today the skills my father devoted his life to are performed by a computer. The jet age, as my father suspected, would replace mechanical craftsmanship with button-pushing. It would also blanch out of flying the bodily sensations of gut-belly fear and awe. Passengers of jets, writes T. A. Heppenheimer, "appreciated not only their speed but their freedom from harsh vibration and their ability to fly above the weather." Soaring at remote heights above clouds, snow, rain, ice, and turbulent winds, cushioned against the ear-splitting roar of engines, jets cruised the heavens in velvet calm. But where was the adventure in flying without the rush of adrenalin and a spiked heartbeat? Could flying still be a hero's quest if it lacked the felt thrill of danger, pitting humans against the elemental force of nature? As aviator Robert Wohl said, "no danger, no mystique."

In a striking chapter in his history of aviation, David Courtwright describes the mid-twentieth-century "formalization" and routinization of the frontier culture of flying. The gradual taming of what had once been a glamorous, high-risk sport began in the years after World War II. As aviation matured into a commercial passenger service, becoming increasingly safer, more efficient, and even banal, it lost its original, free-wheeling spirit. This "spiritual death, at the hands of . . . executives, bureaucrats, and engineers who rationalized, formalized, and reified its early frontier culture," writes Courtwright, "was a necessary prelude to flying's economic resurrection."

If flying was going to succeed as a capitalist venture, in other words, it would have to broaden its market beyond macho pioneer men and appeal to women, children, and even the elderly. Courtwright how marketing campaigns began to stress the safety of commercial flight. Pilots and stewardesses were given lessons in how to sound competent, reassuring, soothing, and comforting. But no single issue involving aircraft crew touched a deeper nerve with the public, he writes, than that of sobriety. The hard-drinking exploits of the original pilots, as well as the military aviators coming out of the war, had been legendary. Now ALPA, the Air Line Pilots Association, put its officers on notice that alcohol was the "number one destroyer of public confidence." Pilots developed tricks, Courtwright notes, "like alternate weeks of abstinence, to keep their drinking in bounds." This sentence clears up one of my family's biggest mysteries: Joe's religious adherence to his schedule of drinking on his days off, moderating his alcohol intake at work by drinking only at night on layovers between flights. Alcohol management, too, it turns out, was part of his training to become a flyer.

Aviators who'd felt flying in their bones—who'd tasted the tactile glory of the early days, when pilots dared the sun in planes that pitched and rolled, and who could veer off in any direction they wanted—suffered in the transition to commercial aviation. With pressurized cabins, radar to keep them on a predetermined grid of routes, and advanced technology, modern-day flying was more about concentrated monitoring than physical handling. "Piloting became less an experience of the senses and more an experience of the mind," writes Courtwright. He notes the intensely nostalgic tenor of frontier pilots' memoirs, who used words like "wonder" and "joy" to describe their experience of flying.

As I mull over this transition in aviation history, I remember an episode from my childhood. I was nine or ten when Joe began putting in the hours he'd need to get his state license to pilot small planes. He'd even drawn up plans for a landing strip on the farm (yet another project that failed to materialize). He did, however, carry through on his goal to obtain his pilot's license. As was his habit, he found a way to bring his family in on the final step—a solo flight. Why not, Joe enthused, take us all along for the ride? Because the maximum number of passengers allowed was four, it was decided that my youngest brother would stay behind with my mother. That left Colleen, Steve, and me to accompany my father on what would be for me an unforgettable, overnight trip to the Wild West tourist site of Dodge City, Kansas.

Initially, I was beside myself with excitement, as were my siblings. On the drive to the Grain Valley Airport, I squirmed in anticipation. I loved flying and saw this as yet another grand escapade. I clambered into the backseat of the plane and buckled up, while Joe did his final check. Almost as soon as the plane had lifted off the runway and into the sky, however, fear swept my body. For the first time in my life while I was flying, I became petrified of crashing and dying. I'd never felt this physically "up in the air" before. The din of wind howling outside the thin body of the plane, the shout and roar of the engines in my ears, and the vivid sight of the hard earth so far below, where I saw visions of myself lying like a crushed baby bird, made my stomach heave and my head whirl. Stuffing myself with SweeTarts and PayDay candy bars, I became sick and began vomiting in the backseat.

Joe wasn't angry with me. But he didn't give much heed to my jitters, either, and chuckled at my discomfort. He was, literally, in his element, and he was simply too elated to be brought down to my child's level of fear. A relaxed sky king at the helm, he was the father of wild rides. To my confusion, the more I puked, the more he laughed. After we finally landed at the airport in Dodge City, I tottered on wobbly legs to the hotel with my father and siblings. Just outside the entrance was a Disneyfied, oversize statue of the Western hero Wyatt Earp. As I passed this garish figure, with his cartoonishly large cowboy hat, lariat, gun, and holster, he seemed to leer at my yellow-bellied plucklessness. "Hey, kids, will you look at that!" yelled an enthralled Joe.

The tacky statue of Wyatt Earp and my father's attempt to reclaim flying as a physically felt adventure were emblematic of the problem heroes face as the frontier they've tamed becomes civilized. To what will they turn next for peril and adventure? Sure enough, as Courtwright points out, the sterilization of modern-day flying led to yet another unforeseen problem in commercial aviation: boredom. Flying at altitudes that practically obliterated the sight of the earth below, passengers drew down their curtains and concentrated on reading, catching up on paperwork, listening to music, or watching in-flight movies. Flight became as ordinary as driving. With the danger and mystique gone from aviation, advertisers began replacing images of planes with exotic tourist locales. Ads enticed passengers to fly to Paris, London, or the Caribbean. "The selling point," writes Courtwright, "became the destination." Traveling, not flying, had become the next new rush.

In the late sixties and early seventies, each of my parents would initiate a series of family trips abroad. When I was a junior in high school, my mother took my sister and me to Italy and Spain. About a year after I'd left home for California, Sheila invited me on a mother–daughter trip to Buenos Aires—a place I'd visited only once, as a three-year-old. At first, I hesitated. As I'd gotten older, I'd lacked the enthusiasm for travel the rest of my family felt so strongly. I was also reluctant to disengage from my new life. But a longing to see my mother's family and birthplace cut through my resistance, and I accepted her offer.

From the moment I stepped off the 747 Pan Am jumbo jet onto Argentine soil, I was swept up into my mother's loving and talkative clan. I'd never experienced even a single holiday dinner with multiple generations of family, much less a cousin or a grandmother. Empty places I'd never been aware of were filled up by a feast of relatives— my aunt, great-aunts, great-uncles, old family friends, and first and second cousins—all of whom thought nothing of indulging in hours of harmless gossip and talk of politics.

At family gatherings, young and old alike rolled back the carpets and kicked up a Scottish reel as they sang with abandon at the tops of their lungs. At tea in my Granny Attwell's charming apartment, I sat rapt as she clicked her knitting needles, cocked her head, and recited poetry. She confided in me her difficulties with her Catholic mother-in-law, now long dead, and voiced interest in my spiritual path. Everyone, she said with feeling, should be free to choose his or her own religion. The fragrant roses in my aunt's backyard and the glow of her polished copper, brought over from Scotland by my great-grandparents; the cobble-stoned, street-café-sophisticated atmosphere of Buenos Aires, with its overlap of European and Spanish culture, all touched chords. Here my American great-grandmother and Argentine great-grandfather had lived; here lay forgotten pieces of myself.

When I returned to Kansas City with my mother, I was blindsided by the abrupt change of atmosphere. Just twenty years old, I wasn't prepared for the visceral chill that hit me when I stepped off the plane. The sharp contrast between America's bigness and cool detachment and the warm Latin and maternal environment I'd left behind was palpable, even physical.

But things were only to get worse. Before we'd even left the airport, a full-blown Carroll melodrama commenced. After we waited at the baggage claim for a couple of hours, it was evident that my father, who was supposed to meet us, had forgotten. My mother's good mood instantly evaporated. The sullen look of resentment that had disappeared in Buenos Aires fell over her face like a widow's veil. We took a taxi back and walked through the front door into a house of unmade beds, strewn laundry, dirty dishes everywhere, an empty refrigerator—and an ominous silence. My mother collapsed in tears. She took to her bed and began a precipitous slide into despair.

Over the next several days, I sat by my mother's bedside as she tossed and turned. I hadn't known it then, but I was witnessing a breakdown—something close to the postpartum stress we realize now my mother had experienced after childbirth. At first, Joe had brushed aside my mother's anguish. "Goddammit, Sheila, what's the big deal? We were working, fixing fences, while you were gone. I just forgot to pick you up. Had to go to town for supplies."

But he'd been mean, and he knew it. He'd never liked Sheila traveling back to Argentina, or being free of his control, and now he was punishing her for slicing open his old wound of abandonment. On that first night back, Joe slept upstairs and I took up my old watch on the living room couch. During the day, my teenage brothers hung in the background, their faces furrowed with grown-up worry. As my mother alternately wailed and moaned, lashing the air with her arms, her body wet with sweat, I tried my best to calm her.

"Why did I come home? What kind of man is he?" she cried in my arms. "I was loved in Argentina, I had family. Now do you see what I left behind there? He hates me, he hates me . . . no one cares about me here. I don't want to live anymore."

Because I lacked any psychological understanding of what was happening to my mother, I breezily reassured everyone that she'd be all right. On the third morning, Sheila woke and sat up on the edge of her bed. Though she was exhausted, and sad beyond words, her sanity had returned. She showered and dressed, and we cleaned the house, bought food, and restored a measure of order. When I walked out the door a couple days later to return to California, I was hardly able, once again, to bear the sight of my family's faces. It would be years before I returned to the farm. By then, my parents and brothers were long gone.

As my twenty-first birthday approached, my father began to pressure me to take one last trip abroad. Because I wasn't in college, I'd soon lose my TWA passes. Joe was genuinely puzzled at my decision to spurn something he'd been working toward for years. How could I turn down the opportunity to travel anywhere in the world? Didn't I know that I was passing up what other TWA non-rev "brats" were clamoring for wildly? With every telephone conversation, he tried to persuade me to return to college. Each time, I refused. I felt happy in my communal spiritual life and had no desire to go back to school. I was getting an education, but of a different kind. And it was true. Northern California in the early seventies offered a crash course in multi-faith traditions, from Kundalini yoga to Sufi whirling, Vedanta, and Buddhism. And besides, I hadn't wanted to go on a trip that the man I lived with, Terry, couldn't go on too. I announced to my father that I'd be getting married soon.

Once he realized that nothing he said could change my mind, Joe invited me on one last expedition: a father–daughter journey on his current route that half-circled the globe. Something in the pleading tone of his voice gave me pause. Embarking on this trip, I speculated, would close the book on my childhood, both for my father and for me. But after what he'd done to my mother, how could I accept? Finally, after battling with my conscience, I laid down my sword and agreed to go.

Aboard the wide-bodied 747 once again, I found myself winging my way to Paris. This time, though, my own father was at the controls. After the dinner trays had been collected, I made my way down the aisle of dozing passengers to the cabin. The hostess in first class knocked politely on the door, then opened it to let me in. I poked my head into the cockpit and my father swiveled around proudly from his position behind the richly complicated panel of knobs, levers, and gauges. His TWA hat pushed back on his forehead, he greeted me with a jaunty smile and a "Hey, Pell!" Outside the window, the sky was a dark twilight, marked by fields of stars. I could see the sparkling patches of cities as they slid by beneath us. Momentarily turning their heads, the pilot and copilot greeted me. I'd be traveling with the same crew the whole way, and they were all in on Joe's father–daughter bonding adventure. "We hear you're hitching a ride with us," they joked. "Can't believe you'd want to come on board a flight with Joe Carroll at the controls! Sure you don't want us to turn the plane around so you can get off?"

From that light-hearted moment onward, our trip was charmed. On the bus rides that shuttled the airline crew between airport and hotel, and in the lounge waiting to board the next flight, I listened in to the banter Joe shared with his fellow pilots. As my father slept in his hotel room, resting up on layovers between flights, I explored, with what little time I had, the city we landed in.

In Paris, I visited old college roommates and walked along the Seine. In Rome, I sipped coffee in a street café and visited the Coliseum. In Hong Kong, I ran up and down the crowded, noisy streets, then took the famed cable car to the top of Telegraph Hill, from where mainland China could be seen hazily in the distance. There was more time for sightseeing in Bombay (Mumbai), India, where my father had a two-day layover. The first morning, Joe hired a driver, an exuberant man he'd befriended on previous trips, to drive us into the countryside dotted with temples. Back in the crowded bazaars with money Terry and my friends had given me for some of the Eastern exotica so in demand then, I loaded up on Indian instruments, beads, bangles, and colorful silks. When I returned to the hotel weighted down with goods, my father nicknamed me the "Bombay merchant." Not once did he mention Terry by name.

Israel, the country in which I'd been conceived, would be the last destination. Here, some part of myself had decided to undertake the greatest journey of all—the human experience. From the moment I stepped onto the streets of Jerusalem, the ancient city vaulted me beyond time. I walked along the stone streets of the old city, rubbed soft by the footsteps of centuries of pilgrims. I touched the Western Wall, and felt the prayers of the suffering; and while floating in the Dead Sea, I felt buoyed by Earth's great age. Standing atop the bare cliffs of Masada, the desert stared back at me, austere and inscrutable. As I explored the ruins of this old fortress, I felt yet another fragment of my historical identity fall into place. No wonder I'd never been entirely at home in Oak Grove. I was an all-American girl, but made from the soil of strangely disparate countries: Israel, England, Argentina, Scotland, Ireland, and points in between.

On our last night in Israel, my father took me out for dinner at a restaurant in Tel Aviv that overlooked the Mediterranean. One of the unexpected pleasures of this working trip had been Joe's sobriety. Because of his drinking-only-at-home ritual, there had been precious few moments of that in recent years. Now, at our journey's end, he grew reflective. I don't remember much of what he said; it was mostly a mood he conveyed of fatherly and familial love, and memories of a golden time, now vanished forever. After my father went to his room, I walked by myself along the seashore, puzzling over the happiness that warmed me from within. It was a feeling I hadn't associated with my father since girlhood.

Our return flight took off the next morning in the quiet before dawn. As we traversed the lightening sky, a crescent moon appeared briefly outside my window and then receded in the distance. The next day, when we drove up the gravel driveway in Joe's black pickup truck, my mother was there to greet us with a smile. Dad's favorite dinner, steak and baked potatoes, was waiting on the table. The distance we'd traveled, from the deserts of Israel to the prairie hills of Missouri, felt immense.

Escape, as the commercial aviation industry quickly figured out, is one of the time-honored purposes of traveling. At its best, travel can enlarge our vision of the world and reanimate lives that have become truncated from routine. Sightseeing in unexplored, foreign places can open new landscapes within. Freed from the mortal bearings of the past, psychoanalyst Adam Phillips notes, we lose our "sense of insufficiency and limitation." If we are lucky, we can bring this magic back home, using it to jog loose fresh ways of being and relating.

This was the gift of my trip with my father. Watching him at work had expanded the contracted image I'd formed of him. The man who'd so callously ruled over our family, and who could so coldly abandon my mother at the airport, was replaced by a sober, sane, self-contained, unruffled, capable professional who went about his work with focus and intent. Of all the many sights I encountered on that trip, nothing equaled this genuinely impressive side of Joe Carroll.

Looking back, I find it impossible not to conclude that my father was free to be his best self only when in the air. What preoccupied me after our trip was whether that side of my father had been real. When I returned to California, I found myself wrestling with my old problem of how to reconcile the decent side of my father with the parts of him that could be so fiendish and hurtful. Would my acceptance of TWA Joe, I wondered, be a betrayal of myself at the hands of Alcoholic Joe?

My mistake, I know now, lay in thinking I had to make a choice. One of the hallmarks of psychological maturity lies in being able to integrate the jarring oppositions of a parent into what's clinically referred to by psychologists as a "whole object." Much is gained, write Stephen Mitchell and Margaret Black in *Freud and Beyond*, "in the movement from the experience of others as split into good and bad to the experience of others as whole objects." Not only does accepting the contradictory nature of our parents this way diminish anxiety, it also helps because, as Jungian analyst Polly Young-Eisendrath explains to me, "internally, we're all constituted of our two parents."

For this reason, nothing is worse, says Young-Eisendrath, than "being left with the sense that one of our parents is all bad—so bad that nobody in the world would want to be with this person who is our parent. In a situation where the parent has been abusive, and there's not some effort to work that out, there will be a feeling of internal loss and psychic distress. All people feel that they are destined to become in some way like their parents—so it's terrible to fear that kind of destiny."

Given that I'd witnessed such extreme swings of behavior in my alcoholic father while at home, our father–daughter trip had given me something of great value. Observing my father in his work environment, I could appreciate Joe's skills as a flight engineer. I could respect the discipline, concentration, and attention to detail required of his craft. I could admire his ability to work within a team in a small cabin to keep a plane full of passengers safe and aloft through good and bad weather. I could take pride in his courage to follow his dream to become an airman, and his devotion to aviation. Most important of all, I could treasure the normalcy of the quiet, undramatic way he went about his job—so different a man from the father I saw at home.

I could even begin to claim these qualities as my own. As was pointed out earlier, fathers traditionally represent mastery in the outside world. "This is not about gender. It's not specific to men or women," explains Michael Conforti. "Many women have played the father role for their children. But when you find somebody who doesn't have a sense of how to enter the world in a meaningful way, or how to bring their gifts to bear fruit, you can usually pinpoint that to an afflicted father relationship."

Even so, biological sameness can make it easier for fathers to instill these qualities in their sons. By saying "yes, you are like me," writes feminist psychoanalyst Jessica Benjamin in *The Bonds of Love*, the father ignites his son's ambition, imbuing him with a sense of agency in the world. For daughters, however, this process is more complicated. Because men—particularly of my father's generation—had to achieve their masculinity by disidentifying with their mothers and women in general, it was harder for a father to see himself in his daughter. Deprived of this early affirmation of their power, girls grew up to become women who not only were unable to reach for the goals they dreamed of achieving, but they lacked even the desire to feel what it is they wanted in the first place. Clinicians today, writes Benjamin, recognize the need for girls to be able to identify with their father as a vehicle for being able to individuate. Girls, she says, should get what boys ideally get from their fathers. Likewise, boys should get the same affirmation from their mothers, too.

As things turned out, my sister—who was also taken abroad—and I would receive the better deal for these working jaunts with our father. Not long after I returned to California, Joe arranged to have my two brothers accompany him on a round-the-world tour, which included a layover in Thailand. Years later, I learned that after they'd checked into their hotel in Bangkok, Joe put my two barely teenage brothers in a taxi with instructions to the driver to take them to a "massage parlor." Once there, they received a lot more than a typical massage.

Afterward, my younger brother, in attempting to talk about what must have been a bewildering experience, made an awkwardly phrased, man-to-man remark to my father. Rather than respond, Joe's face snapped shut. He said nothing in response, nor, he made it clear, would he answer any questions. Discussion of the forbidden was forbidden. My father, however, had at some point taken care to let on to my brothers that he slept with hookers, as opposed to air hostesses—the whole thing, I suppose, something about his male prowess and keeping work separate from pleasure.

Whether my peripatetic father had remained a faithful husband was something the four of us had always whispered about. Perhaps it was the thought of all those brightly charming hostesses, combined with my parents' all-too-obviously unhappy marriage, but I'd always suspected that he'd cheated on his wife. The real surprise was finding out that, as seemed likely, he'd slept with prostitutes. Learning about this side of my father made me feel heavy with regret, as it still does. It was one more way he split his life into so many unrelated pieces.

This fracturing played out in other ways as well. Among all the various international journeys, there was not a single *en famille* Carroll trip abroad. This had torn at my mother and added to the mounting pressure on their relationship.

The day arrived when Sheila reached her breaking point. She told my father that she wanted to put their problems and his drinking aside and give the marriage another try. When Joe came up with the idea of selling the house and one hundred acres and moving to Guadalajara, Sheila readily went along with the idea. Relocating, they both believed, might be their ticket to a second chance. It might also help my father stop drinking, or so they both hoped. Now that Joe was flying internationally, he could live almost anywhere in the world. He could fly ten days, then rest up the remainder of the month. With only my youngest brother left at home, it seemed as good a time as any to leave the farm. And the country.

GUADALAJARA

From the moment my parents crossed into Mexico in early 1974, the decision proved a disaster. In his controlling way, Joe had told Sheila that even though they'd be living in a Spanish-speaking culture, she wouldn't be "allowed" to converse in the language of her childhood. This edict hadn't lasted long. As my parents passed through customs along the Texas border, the Mexican official examining their passports noticed that my mother had been born in Argentina. Smiling and gesturing excitedly, he engaged Sheila in rapid-fire Spanish. My father froze in fury at my mother's audacity. How dare she, he fumed afterward, go against his rules? They made the rest of the trip in tense, violent silence.

Once they arrived in Las Fuentes, a suburb of Guadalajara, my mother made up her mind once again to accept her fate as Joe's wife. As she and my father stepped across the threshold of the Spanish-style ranch house they'd rented before they'd left, she determined that she would accept my father's drinking and stop trying to change him. There would be no more crying and screaming, she vowed. She couldn't keep doing this to her children, or to herself. My father, for his part, had promised never to drink again.

Try as they might to keep their fragile truce, Mexico would be the stick of dynamite that exploded my parents' marriage. It had been twenty-three years since they'd lived abroad. Their new neighborhood was populated with intellectuals, professionals, artists, and retired Europeans and Americans. It might as well have been another planet, so different was it from Oak Grove. Even the weather was unusual. In contrast to the prairie landscape of Missouri, with its definitive seasons, Guadalajara's climate was a Camelot of perpetual springtime. Flowering hibiscus, wisteria, bougainvillea, roses, and jacaranda bushes cascaded in exuberant riots of color over pink adobe garden walls. At the end of their street, an old stone fountain splashed, and nearby a stout, serape-clad woman turned out steaming corn tortillas by hand. After the midday meal, or *comida*, the city of nearly three million inhabitants shut down for a nap. Dinner was around nine or ten; sometimes the neighbors didn't get to bed until two A.M. Everyone had gardeners and maids. Invitations to lunch, dinner parties, the theater, and the opera arrived. My youngest brother, possessed of a sharp intellect, thrived at his avant-garde private school.

Joe and Sheila went into shock.

Up in Marin County, California, I'd just given birth to my first son, Kabir. On a crackling, long-distance phone call, my father told me that he'd soon be coming "stateside" on a trip and that he'd like to swing by "Californeee-aayy" and see me. Mom couldn't get up to see me just yet, he added, saying that he'd explain more when we met. Several days later, sitting in the hotel restaurant, Joe eyed the tiny bundle in my arms. "Well, will you look at that," he said awkwardly, politely blowing his cigarette smoke off to the side. Disarmed by this new creature, considerately sober to mark the occasion, my father fumbled for words.

"What would you like to be called, now that you're a grandfather?" I asked, innocently. "Grandpa?"

Joe shot up out of his seat. He'd suddenly found his voice. "Grandpa! Grandfather! Good God. Are you kidding? Don't scare me like that. Don't mention that word around me again," he said, shaking his head. "Do I look like an old man to you? A *grandfather*. Hoo, boy. Don't scare me like that, Pell."

Next, Joe eyed Terry warily. They'd met just once before, a few months after our impromptu hippie wedding the previous year. At that first encounter, Joe had all but ignored him. He'd studiously look away whenever Terry had spoken directly to him, and turn in my direction to give his response. But the child in my arms meant that there would be no escaping the new man in the family. "Congratulations," Joe said stiffly, reaching out and giving Terry's hand a halfhearted shake. And then, just for a minute or two, my father melted. He hadn't said anything, but as he looked at the three of us sitting in the booth, his eyes softened.

"Well, well, will you look at that," he said again. Only this time, his heart could be felt in his words.

"By the way," said Joe, waving the waiter over for more coffee, "your mother's not doing so well." Sheila had not adjusted to Guadalajara's high altitude, my father explained. Since they'd moved, her blood pressure had shot up to dangerously high levels, and her doctor had advised her against traveling. But I knew there was more to Sheila's sudden spike in blood pressure. I'd heard from my siblings that my mother had again been teetering on the edge of sanity. The move had been hard on her; she missed the farm. When she visited, my sister had found her sobbing in the bathtub, heartbroken over the loss. "I've sold my home and I can't go back," she'd cried mournfully.

In an ironic twist to my parents' story, it was my immigrant mother— the cultured Argentine girl with the black curls who had jitterbugged to Louis Armstrong and danced with Moshe Dayan—who'd found her fate on the farm. Whether she was chasing a black snake out of the kitchen, tracking down lost horses and cattle, or shearing sheep with a local farmer, who'd admiringly called her "quite a dame," Sheila had put down deep roots in the Missouri soil.

To be sure, there'd been days growing up when I'd caught her crying because no one could discuss with her the subtle meanings of John Dos Passos's trilogy, *U. S. A.* Or that she couldn't write poetry like Keats or Wordsworth, or get the mystery novel she was plotting to come out right. Still she foraged through local junkyards and would creatively refinish cast-off country primitives, using them to warm up our old house, and starting a successful business on the side. She took up painting, turning out lovely still lifes on old barn wood. With the exception of my wild-card father and those times when he was home, hers had been a well-defined, reassuring cosmos of children, animals, nature, art, books, and small-town life. And now it was gone.

The farm and the family had been Joe's domain, too. But the rhythm of his life had been marked more by the pull of opposites. There was the century-old farmhouse, the weathered barns, taciturn farmers, plows, cisterns, grain silos, patchwork fields, livestock, and the dark quiet of woods. These earthbound elements were heavy with memory and belonged to a slower era of America's past. Though there was work and routine in flying, the planes my father flew in, and the immense hangars and airports he passed through, hermetically sealed him from everyday life.

As they had arisen in the twentieth century, modern-day airports, with their domed spaces and gleaming, geometrical interiors, had come to resemble docked spaceships about to launch. Outside floor-to-ceiling glass windows, dun-colored nature was discreetly cordoned off, lifting the traveler's attention to the heights. Animals and weather existed only as impediments to smooth takeoffs and landings. As passengers boarded and disembarked in a fluid stream of comings and goings, gliding along moving escalators in a kind of suspended anonymity, the weight of history fell away. Anyone who has rushed through an airport on their way to board a flight has felt, if only briefly, that mercurial sensation that comes with air travel, as if the edges of one's identity had melted away in the transitional space between check-in and takeoff.

As the years passed, and Joe had tilted further away from the muck and mud of family life on the farm, the two spheres of his life—sky and earth, work and family, sex and love—had begun to pull apart. Though moving to Mexico had been an attempt to bring it back together, my parents' fragile marriage had sundered beyond repair. As my mother sank deeper into depression and nervous anxiety, Joe inevitably started drinking again, breaking his vow and setting new records for alcohol consumption.

"So," Joe said offhandedly as Terry and I stood up to leave. "How about coming down to Mexico for a visit? Both of you," he added, turning to Terry with a rare gesture of magnanimity. "I'll get you discount tickets. A present for you and the baby. It would do your mother good, get her out of her doldrums." We were young, with little money, and the thought of a trip to Mexico sounded appealing. I'd also been worried about my mother.

Two weeks later, I found myself sitting, along with Terry and the baby, in the sunny living room of my parents' Mexican *casita*. My mother's spirits had lifted as soon as we'd walked through the front door. She was happy to hold her new grandson, and appeared glad to have us there. But I found her moody and inwardly preoccupied. In the morning, as we sat in my parents' turquoise-and-yellow tiled kitchen, Sheila sipped her Lipton's tea and talked obsessively about my father, his drinking, his temper, and then more about his drinking. Always, her anguish would turn on the same question: How could Joe sober up enough to fly but couldn't stay off the bottle at home? Since they'd arrived, she told me, he hadn't drawn a sober breath. Mexico had been supposed to change things. But to escape from the past, as Adam Phillips notes, is never so simple. "Wherever we go there is always the past," he writes in *Houdini's Box*. "We can change places in a way that we can't change histories."

Oddly, having tried to flee their past, my parents now found themselves living in a country permeated by history. Even the light in Guadalajara seemed old. Determined to distract my mother from her problems, Terry, Sheila, and I set out each day to see the city, my infant son strapped to my chest in my new front pack. These canvas carriers were meant to keep the baby close to the mother's heartbeat, but the very sight of one drove my father crazy. "You're going to smother that boy!" Joe would yell as we scurried out the door.

In the inhibiting presence of my husband and his new grandson, Joe for the most part kept his more loathsome side in check. Absent American television, we actually had some enjoyable conversations, intermixed with quiet reading. One night toward the end of our visit, I could see by the look in Joe's eyes that our good spell of family peace was about to be broken. Up all night downing vodka, Joe had awakened late midmorning the next day, drunk. As it happened, the house my parents had rented was next to an elementary school. If my father was in a foul mood, the sound of the children shouting outside at recess could make him furious. He'd call over to the principal's office and demand that the kids be ordered to be quiet in deference to his upcoming trip. This morning his rage was in full throttle.

"Goddamn noisy kids. I told that ass of a principal they should be kept inside," Joe railed, stumbling out of the bedroom in his dressing gown. Up to this moment, it had been a quiet morning. I'd been reading on the couch in the living room. Terry and the baby were sitting outside in the sunny back garden. My mother had a book open on her lap but had been staring blankly into space. "Oh come on, Dad," I said, trying to mollify him, as usual. "They're just children. You can't get mad at schoolkids."

"Goddamn right I can. Gonna sue that school. Gonna sue that stupid real estate agent who rented us this house," my father said, slurring his words. He walked over to his favorite chair, spilling hot coffee from his cup, and plopped into the deep cushions, his legs splayed. Beneath the robe, my father was entirely naked. Stunned, I glanced over at my mother, who raised her eyebrows and shrugged her shoulders as if to say, "See how bad it is?" Oblivious to the rest of us, Joe's head lolled forward onto his chest. In the background, a door clicked shut. It was Terry, walking down the *saltillo*-tiled hallway, cooing to our son. I jumped up and closed my father's robe, rearranging it over his legs.

I'd seen this sight before, only it had been years ago, on the farm. The memories are mixed with confusion and revulsion. Sometime after our swimming pool had been built, Joe had initiated a new family ritual: the naked family swim. "Pool time!" he'd shout. We gathered in the laundry mudroom with the beer keg refrigerator and stripped off all our clothes. Then, giggling wildly, all six of us—my mother and father included—we would dash across the lawn and dive into the water. God only knows what the dour Missouri farmer with the draft horses, whose fields bordered ours, thought at this unlikely sight.

At first, I'd delighted in these frolicking swims. Wrapped in the cocoon of pre-adolescent innocence, I relished the softness of the water against my body and the playful splashing among us. But our family idyll didn't last long. After I'd blithely invited a girlfriend to take a naked dip in our pool, word had gotten out in our gossipy town about the swimming habits of the odd-duck Carroll family. At school, I'd been teased and stared at by tittering students. The scales of innocence had fallen from my eyes; our family swim would never be the same. I looked down and felt a sharp sting of self-consciousness at the changes taking place in my pudgy, adolescent body. Suddenly shy, I began to hang back whenever the call to swim rang through the house. To my enormous relief, my mother finally intervened; for once, my father listened to her and our family ritual came to an end.

Joe himself, however, wouldn't give up the pleasures of nudity so easily. On a warm summer's evening, he'd strut around the pool, leather brown and as arrogant as some pagan warrior just off the battlefield. I can still see him as he skimmed for insects or checked the chemical levels, the drops of water glistening on his skin. In and out of the back laundry room he'd go. Though we lived in the country, our hilltop house was visibly lit up by the brilliant outdoor mere lights Joe had proudly installed himself. "Dad, put your clothes on," I'd beg him. "The neighbors can see you!" On the school bus, a boy from a neighboring farm had remarked to my sister that he'd seen our "old man walking around naked." But Joe hadn't cared. "You gotta live dangerously," he yelped, bringing out his stock response. At last, pressured by his physically maturing children, the day came when my father, too, had to put his clothes back on.

Now, years later, the move to Mexico had seemed to set off my father's old habit, only in a much more unseemly, drunken manner. Not long after my husband and I had returned to California, my aunt Fiona, Sheila's sister, arrived for a visit. She'd been sitting in the living room with my mother, Fiona recalled, when my father came in wearing a dressing gown. "He talked and talked and talked. He was a bit maudlin," she said. "And while he was talking, his dressing gown fell open, and all his privates were exposed. He wasn't even aware of it. In his good days," my aunt finished sadly, "Joe would never have done that."

Things got worse when my father dispensed with the dressing gown altogether. One afternoon, several of my mother's new friends stopped by unexpectedly. Just back from a long trip, Joe was asleep in the back bedroom. Over Mexican-blue glasses of iced tea and soda, the women were laughing and talking in a brew of Spanish and English. As their conversation grew louder, their voices rose. Suddenly, an awkward silence fell and all eyes turned to the arched entryway between the living room and kitchen.

There stood my father, framed by the mosaic tile, smoking a cigarette stark naked. "Hel-*lo*, ladies," he said, in an obsequious, saccharine voice. "Might I ask you to please, please, *seeel vooous plate* keep your voices down? I just came back from a trip, and I need my *beeyooty* sleep." Instead of turning and walking away, he remained rooted to the spot, swaying slightly, as he eyed the treats on the coffee table. For one awful moment, it looked as if he was entertaining the idea of joining my mother's guests on the couch. "Joe," Sheila said, jumping up, always the considerate hostess, even under the worst of conditions. "Why don't I help you back to the bedroom?" My father pretended not to hear. When he took a boozy step toward the coffee table, the women leaped to their feet and, in a daze, thanked my mother and fled through the front door.

When this latest bulletin from the family front arrived, I was resting with my toddler son. I sat bolt upright, the phone leaden in my hand, and stared hard at the many-hued rainbow painted on the light blue wall behind my bed, as if trying to superimpose its image over that of my father naked before my mother's friends. It was clear that things were falling apart in Mexico. More and more, I'd heard, Joe had sequestered himself in his bedroom, not even coming out for meals. I felt far away and helpless. Sure, my father had walked around naked before, but not like this. Had that moment arrived—the one we'd all been waiting for in crouched position, arms over our heads, as long as I could remember? Had he finally lost his mind? I began to worry that he might hurt my mother. The three of us who'd left home wanted her and my brother, who'd soon leave for college, to get out before something terrible happened. I recall telling my mother that I was afraid that my father, while he was drunk, might shoot her.

Possibly my mother's own fright and anxiety exaggerated the insanity we saw in my father. Like fun house mirrors, they reflected each other's craziness back and forth, distorting any traces of truth. And yet the volatility in my parents' marriage and my father's behavior had seemed to advance into more dangerous territory. It wasn't just that he'd turned into a sloppy drunk who couldn't keep his robe closed and who flagrantly exposed himself, or that he drank himself into oblivion, or that his temper was like a loose cannon aimed crazily at whatever came into view. It was all these things combined that turned my father into a threatening person more like some weird stranger in a bad part of town than a parent.

Even as I write down these memories of my exhibitionist father, I feel again the terror I experienced around him that used to well up and drag me down; the fear I'd struggle to cope with as a girl by singing sunny movie tunes like "Do-Re-Mi" and "I Have Confidence" from *The Sound of Music* to the trees and the sky.

On the night I work on this section, the bravado by which I've encapsulated these feelings finally drops away. I dream of being on a dangerous human rights rescue mission. Together with three men, I engage in a terrible battle. Afterward, I barely escape with my fellow freedom fighters, who've all been bloodied and wounded. One of the men has been severely burned and crippled in one leg. I help him onto the boat that has come to take us home. The rescuers in the boat stare intently at the injured man's leg, as if to impress upon him the severity of his injury. Upon waking up, I take the inner characters in this dream as a representation of those parts of myself struggling to be liberated from my bondage to a troubled family past, and to begin the rescue effort of caring for the severely crippled parts of myself.

As my father continued his hellish descent, my mother began her phoenix rise. As she mingled in Mexican culture, she recalls now, she was startled to hear herself speaking Spanish with an American accent. She looked in the mirror and wondered who she'd become. She began to remember the person she'd been before she married Joe Carroll. That woman, she said to herself, did not deserve to be treated this way. Her mother, she thought, had not given birth to her for her to live a life like this. And so, in late 1976, two years after their arrival in Las Fuentes, Sheila packed up the car. She took care to include the family photos, so that my father would know the full extent of what he would be losing with her departure. She planned carefully, waiting until my father had gone away on a trip. Together with my younger brother, who was headed off to college, the two made the long drive back to Kansas City, Missouri. After she'd dropped my brother off at the airport, she searched for a hotel room. Because of a large conference in town, there were no vacancies. She spent her first night in the backseat of her car.

Soon, she'd rented a tiny one-room studio to wait out her divorce. It was the hardest trip she'd ever had to make.

Like their marriage, my parents' divorce was an epic affair that lasted three years and was rife with sensationalism and backhanded maneuvers. My mother always suspected that one reason Joe had moved to Mexico was that, in the event of a divorce, he could hide his money from her. And hide it he did. When he was served divorce papers in New York, Joe tried to bribe the server. At a court hearing in Kansas City, he even attempted to "see" the judge beforehand to sway his opinion in his favor. More remarkably, he did all these things sober. As soon as my mother left, he stopped drinking. Cold. He'd show her, he told us, that he was no alcoholic.

Initially, I felt only enormous relief at the thought of my parents' separation. But now, as each of them competed for the allegiance of their four children, a new battlefront opened up. "Can't you stand up to your father?" my mother complained. "Tell him you won't speak to him until he gives me the money he owes me. I don't know why he thinks this divorce is my idea. He might as well have opened the door and hired a marching band to escort me out of the house!"

"Does your mother think I'm made of money?" Joe shouted over the phone from his hotel in New York to my sister at her home in San Francisco. "Where does she think I've got all this money stashed away? She's crazy. She's a parasite. Hell will freeze over before I give her one red cent."

When the little money Sheila had brought with her from Mexico began to run out, my mother took a job working in the antique toy department at Halls department store on the Plaza in Kansas City. A longtime collector of country primitives, Sheila's new job brought out her talents. But at age forty-nine, with no assets after four children and over twenty-five years of marriage, she seethed with bitterness over my father's refusal to give her support. In phone calls to me she voiced her despair. Often her depression was so dark and deep she didn't know if she even wanted to go on living. I recall pleading with her to call a hotline or to find a therapist. The day finally arrived when a judge in Kansas City awarded my mother half of the remaining acres of the farm. In the three years since they'd separated, she'd received not one penny of alimony. Laws at that time were so harshly skewed against divorcing women that it had taken her nearly a year just to get a credit card in her own name.

Hilda

The Carroll family emerged from the seventies splintered into six jagged pieces. During that decade we'd blasted apart, with no home to hold us together. My sister Colleen married and moved to Los Angeles to pursue her music career. My husband and I, now with three small sons, departed California for the high desert of Santa Fe, New Mexico, where we moved into our first home. I began to write. My brother Steven was traveling the world as an engineer, and John married and moved to Texas, where he worked as a journalist and editor.

My mother, the only one of us to remain in Missouri, quickly remarried a tall, white-haired, elderly gentleman who belonged to the local country club. Dignified and genteel, Sheila's second husband was everything Joe was not. But when her second husband began to slide into dementia, and grew paranoid and controlling, Sheila walked out the door and never looked back. It would be her last marriage. She moved into a townhouse in a Kansas City suburb and began to live life on her own terms. She became one of the city's most successful saleswomen and continued to travel.

Bravely for a woman of her generation, she went into therapy because, she told me, she didn't want to "die blind." Over the years, she evolved into an interesting and independent woman with a wide circle of friends and an eclectic array of interests in literature and the arts. She became, I believe, the person she'd always struggled to become. But like a river that goes underground, her Carroll past continued to stream beneath her new life, surfacing every now and then with renewed and surprising force.

And then there was Joe. In yet another one of fate's interesting sleights of hand, my father became the Carroll who stayed in Mexico. At first, I was taken aback at my father's decision. Though he never said why he stayed, I see now that returning to America might have posed a dilemma. Which of the four states his four children lived in, for instance, would he choose? He couldn't return to Missouri, for that was now my mother's territory. And anyway, as long as my father was within driving distance of an airport, it didn't matter where he set up his home. So, bidding farewell to the suburb of Las Fuentes, Joe rustled his Icarus wings and flew forty minutes south of Guadalajara, to land on the shores of Lake Chapala.

Others before Joe had sought refuge in the seclusion of Lake Chapala. Since the mid-fifties, it had been a popular enclave for expatriate Americans and other escapees. The largest freshwater lake in Mexico, Chapala is set like an oval turquoise into a high plateau, ringed by the Sierra Madre Mountains, mists and clouds shrouding its banks. In a villa in one of the lakeside towns arranged around the lake's fifty-mile-long circumference, the English author D. H. Lawrence penned *The Plumed Serpent.* Anaïs Nin, the feminist diarist, also found inspiration on the lake's quaint and quiet shores.

Though not as well read as my mother, Joe had literary interests. He always liked Ernest Hemingway for his muscular storylines in exotic locations. But he also enjoyed Taylor Caldwell, a popular Christian writer in the sixties and seventies who'd written historical Christian novels—a strange choice of reading matter for someone who hated the church. The Welsh poet Dylan Thomas was another favorite. With enough liquor in him, Joe would throw his head back and melodramatically recite part of the famous villanelle, "Do not go gentle into that good night. . . . Rage, rage against the dying of the light."

But Joe never really had the time to develop what I believe was an untapped philosophical side of his nature—a part of him that was like an inner Shangri-La he'd always tried, and failed, to reach. For this reason, Lake Chapala may have held out the promise of contemplation, an attempt, after all the theatrics of his marriage and career, to drop down to a deeper level. The reality, however, was that by this point Joe couldn't read much. His mind had stewed too long in alcoholic fumes to be able to concentrate much beyond work.

Ever on the move, Joe soon found something else to occupy his time. Sailboats, zippy motorboats, and water-skiers swirled around the lake's placid surface on ribbons of waves. Joe bought himself a little motorboat. Out on the docks and in the village bars, he mingled easily in Lake Chapala's more casual, free-spirited atmosphere. Freed from the trappings of his old identity as father, husband, and hard-working American, the more extroverted, unconventional, nuttier side of his nature that had always found refuge in Latin countries emerged in the more accepting Mexican culture. He even began to socialize.

One American expatriate Joe encountered would have a marked impact on his future. Jack was a pleasant, round-faced businessman from Chicago who'd invested in several lakefront properties. He lived with Rosita, a pretty young Mexican woman, and her two small sons. Jack was also a salesman. One of the first things he sold Joe was a tacky velvet painting of a voluptuous woman, naked from the waist up—a piece of art forever seared into our collective family memory. Such a fine piece of art deserved a suitable backdrop. For this, Jack had found my father a beautiful home in Ajijic, one of Chapala's lakeside hamlets. Constructed of white stucco in Mediterranean style, the spacious, two-story house had a red-tile roof and a wrought-iron balcony that ran the entire back length. Below the balcony, a series of graceful arches framed a wall of large windows that overlooked the lake.

The third thing Jack sold my father on was his girlfriend Rosita's sister, Hilda. At thirty-six years old, Hilda was nineteen years younger than Joe. Half Portuguese, half Mexican, she was slight, with wiry black hair, sienna-colored skin, and furious black eyes. Not long after they began seeing each other, Joe fell seriously ill. In those days, it took months to get a phone line in Chapala. With no way to call out of the country, no one told us until weeks later that my father had even been sick. When Jack heard about my father's illness, he sent Hilda over to take care of him. This she did with gusto, cooking and caring for my father until he recovered. It could not have been, in my father's eyes, a more successful courtship. Hilda was there for him in his "hour of need," he informed my sister later. Thoughtlessly, carelessly, he told us that Hilda reminded him of Sheila in her younger days. He invited her to move in.

Joe and Hilda's beginning, as all of my father's beginnings, appeared full of promise. Joe had found his new Utopia, as well as a beautiful

Eve willing to wait on his every need. Hilda, too, was blissfully content. A sweet, kind woman with a sad streak, Hilda had no work skills and suffered from her status as a single mother in a poor country. Life was not easy. The home and security Joe now provided her was a relief. So was the money she was able to pass along to her only child, a son who'd been mildly brain damaged by a drug overdose. Measured against this burden, what did it matter that Joe—in a switch of his language policies with my mother—forbade her to speak English so he could improve his Spanish? Or that he sometimes drank himself into oblivion? In her eyes, Joe was a prince who'd come to her rescue.

In phone calls and on visits to the states, Joe waxed lyrical about the delights of life with Hilda in Ajijic. Founded by the Nahuatl Indians in the early 1400s and colonized a century later by Spanish missionaries, Ajijic (pronounced *AH-ha-hic*) could have been a small fishing village anywhere in the world. Pigs ambled along the dusty roads, prodded by local farmers in leather *huaraches*. There was a charming main square along the pier, lakeside restaurants, and an outdoor market where Hilda and Joe bought fresh-caught fish and just-picked produce for the meals Hilda prepared. Devoutly Catholic, Hilda could attend Mass on Sundays in the five-hundred-year-old San Andres Church. With the help of a gardener named Carlos, Hilda planted a tapestry of orchids and scented roses in the garden.

Inside the cool, pastel-hued stucco walls of their newfound paradise, the two chain-smoked and watched endless hours of satellite television. In 1981, while on a trip to Florida to visit my aunt Eileen and uncle Gene, Joe and Hilda were married before a civil judge. Afterward, due to some trumped-up grievance on my father's part toward my aunt over an off-color joke she made, the couple took off in a sulk. Joe never saw his little brother again.

Though this falling-out marked yet another broken link in Joe's family line, it didn't seem to bother him much. Not only did he have a pretty young wife and a spacious new home, he had status. For that was the other thing about Ajijic: it gave my attention-starved father the chance to be a big fish in a little pond, in a way he'd never been able to achieve in Oak Grove. Taking advantage of TWA's policy that allowed employees to ship one car for free each year, he went shopping abroad for a Mercedes. In Belgium, a mechanic led a rapt Joe up to the second floor of his factory. There, in his inner sanctum, the mechanic threw back the canvas on a used white 230 SL Mercedes-Benz convertible he'd been tenderly customizing. Swayed by the mechanic's zeal, the polished wooden dashboard, and the plush leather seats, Joe couldn't resist.

My father and Hilda must have made an impressive sight tooling around the cobblestone streets of Ajijic in their flashy new coupe with the top down. Not long after the luxury car's arrival in Ajijic, the mayor from Ibarra, the next village over, personally called on my father. Would he, the mayor asked my father, be willing to participate in the annual Fiesta de San Nicolás, personally chauffeuring the festival beauty queen and her attendants around the town square in his Mercedes?

Joe couldn't have been more delighted. "Hey, Pell! You should have seen me; the girls were so *purrrdeee*. I drove them around and around the town square." I still have the Polaroid Joe proudly sent me. Framed in a white mat with gold trim, the photo depicts the great white gringo in his great white car. Across the top, Joe scrawled "Don Jose" in red ink, and "Fiesta San Nicolas" along the bottom. Joe sits behind the wheel, white straw cowboy hat pushed down low over his forehead. Large sunglasses cover the top half of his face. Joe stares into the camera like a scowling hangdog, wearing his vintage down-at-the-mouth look. One would never guess from the photo that he was as happy as he said he'd been that day. A red-and-white banner with the seal of Mexico is draped across the car's hood, strewn with gold petals and leis. Three girls, no older than sixteen or seventeen, are perched on top of the backseat; they, too, are serious and unsmiling.

The festival queen is dressed in a white, strapless gown, a red velvet cape with white fur piping, and a tall crown rising out of her dark mass of hair. The two attendants on either side wear strapless turquoise gowns and sparkling tiaras, though not as large as the queen's. Behind the car, a gaggle of children run to keep up with the chariot bearing its goddesses. As I stare at this photo, the memory of my own ride as a homecoming queen in the backseat of a Mustang convertible around the Oak Grove High School football field flashes across my mind. I think of the father I see before me now, who wasn't there then. But that was long ago, and the memory quickly fades to nothing.

Inevitably, as it always did, the crash came; also inevitably, it involved alcohol. One afternoon, during a visit from my younger brother, Joe took his boat out by himself on the lake. A storm came up. Clouds and rain swirled above and around him. Growing confused—he'd been drinking heavily—Joe put the boat in reverse, swamping it with water. It started to sink. With luck working its ways for my father, a passing boat noticed his distress and towed him back to shore. After helping Joe tie his boat up at the dock, the anonymous rescuers, who'd snatched my father from a cold death in the shallow waters of the lake, simply left him there.

So drunk he could barely stand up, my father stumbled to his car and passed out behind the wheel. Concerned local police found and dragged my unconscious father out of the Mercedes and into their squad car, then drove him home. My brother opened the door to a small posse of Mexican authorities, with a staggering Joe as their American bandit. After depositing my father in bed, John took the police into the kitchen and offered them sodas. He chatted with them in Spanish and found himself admiring the World War II Schmeisser machine gun one of the officers had slung around his waist. Once again, one of us had lived to tell another of my father's unlikely drinking tales.

Despite my father's frequent pleas and offers of discount tickets, I never did visit him in Ajijic. I'd heard enough horror stories from my siblings about their own visits to risk putting myself, or my family, at his drunken mercy. No matter that we were all now adults, with children of our own, Joe ruled over his home in Ajijic like a petty tyrant. The kitchen was "open" or "closed" depending on his whim, even to two- or three-year-olds hungry for a snack. John's Irish wife came in for grueling attacks at the dinner table, just as my mother had when I was growing up. The Irish were the "swine of Europe," Joe opined one night. "Lazy good-for-nothings who don't like to work." No, I had no wish to lay myself open to such scenes of verbal and emotional abuse again.

I hadn't, however, forbidden my father and Hilda from visiting me in Santa Fe. True to his dislike of the term *grandpa*, Joe never was a very involved, cuddle-up-on-his-lap kind of grandparent. As my sons grew older, Joe did, however, prove himself a charismatic character in their lives. He could charm them with Depression-era stories about smoking cigarettes rolled out of dry grass, make them laugh with his goofy jokes about the Budweiser draft horses, and blow smoke rings. He also, begrudgingly, came to admire his son-in-law, Terry, a successful businessman and committed father and husband. Besides, in my own home, I made the rules. I knew I couldn't stop my father from drinking altogether. But on one point I was always firm: Joe could not drink hard liquor in my house.

The empty bottle of Smirnoff I found on the kitchen sink most mornings of his visits showed me how completely useless my rules were against the ceaseless pull of my father's addiction. There were those who would have thrown Joe out, or forced an intervention. But at most, I saw my father only once a year, and sometimes not even that often. And I knew that if I made him leave I'd likely never see him again. It was also true that the only way my father would have gone to an alcohol rehabilitation center was if he'd been drugged and dragged there against his will. So as long as I was behind the wheel of the car whenever we were out, I accepted the situation for what it was. I simply didn't have the heart anymore for the dramatic confrontations of my youth.

In 1985, on one of Joe and Hilda's visits to Santa Fe, my father took us all out for dinner. Toward the end of the meal, Joe announced that he'd decided to retire from TWA. He was sixty-three years old and could have worked for two more years. Or so he said; at the time I had my doubts. These doubts persisted over the years until a conversation with an historian at the Airmen's Records Branch of the Federal Aviation Administration cleared my father on this score. Joe, said historian John Ryan, "had a perfectly clean record, with no accidents, incidents, or enforcements." Clearly impressed, Ryan said my father had been a skillful and experienced mechanic, ground instructor, and flight engineer. I still have the letter of congratulations

sent to him by C. A. Meyer Jr., TWA's president at the time of his
official retirement.

In the typed and hand-signed letter written on company stationary,
Meyer thanked my father for his thirty-four years of experience.
Because of his "dedication, loyalty and skill," Meyer wrote, "TWA was
a greater company." Saluting my father for his efforts on behalf of
TWA, he wished him a happy and rewarding retirement. In another
personal letter, E. J. Stroschein, General Manager of Flying, wrote that
my father had good reason to be proud of his contributions "during
this remarkable development and growth period. You have seen TWA
and world aviation move from the Douglas DC-3 to the wide-bodied
jets as participants, not just observers."

With none of these noble sentiments could I disagree, then or now.

YET EACH MAN KILLS THE THING HE LOVES

After my father died, I discovered two passports among his papers.
One was dated 1975, just after he'd moved to Mexico. In his photo,
he wears a plaid jacket. His face is stretched in a weird, clown-like,
ear-to-ear grin; a crazy, manic light shines out of his blue eyes. The
pages are a blur of purple stamps that track his travels through the
world. The other is dated 1985, the year of his retirement. Not even the
pretense of a smile graces this passport photo; the handsome young
airman has by now completely vanished. In his place is simply the
saddest-looking human being one could imagine, with a face as bleak
as those photos of starving orphans, tortured prisoners, patients with
pain-wracking disease, or beaten animals. The expiration date on this
passport is January 28, 1995: exactly ten years, less ten days, to the
date of his death. The pages in this passport are mostly blank, as are
the hollow, deadened eyes that stare out at me. I cannot look at this
photo for long. My father's haunted, hunted look seems to transcend
even himself, going beyond personal pain into the transpersonal realm
of human suffering. All light has been extinguished. Only flat darkness
remains.

It is this expression on my father's face, I realize, that has driven my
quest to understand the cause of such despair. Again and again, through

the telling of his story, and helped by the insights of psychologists, I've circled his wounded psyche. With each chapter, I've drawn nearer not only to an understanding of his pain, but something of the pain of the human condition. So much of it, it seems, has to do with love: love that begins with our parents and their parents before them and so on back in time, abandoned love, misunderstood love, thwarted love, withholding love, empty love, violent love, punishing love, love that ends with the lacerated hearts we hold in our own hands.

Consider, for instance, how Freud, the father of modern-day psychology, drew from Greek tragedy to illustrate his theories on family dynamics. Patricide, matricide, infanticide, thievery, jealousy, hubris, abuse, and incest all made their marks on the royal houses of ancient Greece, just as they have on the American family of modern times. Rage and guilt, madness and violence are the lodestars of these lineal tragedies, as they would be in my father's family chronicle.

As with all the difficult sides of my father, it is hard for me to look closely at the man who socked my brother in the nose, lifted a hand against my mother, terrorized us with verbal and emotional abuse, and whose drunken rages could make me feel as if the mechanism holding his psyche together might one day go haywire, and he might shoot and kill us all. It's tempting to condemn his behavior and shrink from investigating the deeper causes of his abusive personality. But that would not be in the spirit of this book.

"This side of your father that you describe as cruel, tyrannical, and abusive," says Jungian analyst Lionel Corbett, "there's a school of thought that says that kind of behavior is always revenge for abuse that was done to oneself in childhood. When people are abused in childhood they are understandably filled with hatred and anger. As a way to evacuate these uncomfortable feelings inside of themselves, they make other people suffer. Because it's so awful to be made to feel helpless and terrified as a child, they identify with the aggressor and make someone else feel helpless."

Corbett suspects that the primary source of my father's trauma may have occurred long before the trauma of my grandfather's death at the Christmas table. "Those who grow up to become paranoid, reclusive personalities like your father," he says, were usually "quite severely abused in childhood. They grew up in a household where people weren't trustworthy. At the very least, his social anxiety suggests a feeling of danger dating back to early childhood." Corbett's words remind me of relatives' brief references to the Carroll boys' "fear of being beaten" by their father; to my grandmother Carroll as a "mean German"; and also to my father's own memories of rejection by her.

Psychoanalyst Michael Eigen tells me that what strikes him about my father's story is the way "causality works in the human psyche." He describes the way my father's feelings of guilt over his father's death sickened over time into a kind of psychic infection of the soul. "The feeling that 'I did it, it's my fault' is one of the ways the human psyche organizes experiences," Eigen tells me. The danger in such an internalized narrative of self-guilt, Eigen explains, is that an innate sense of malignant destructiveness can take hold of the psyche, even creating a belief in a "horrifying confluence between inside and outside," or that one's badness can actually cause harm to others.

"It's my fault because I'm destructive. I've . . . killed my father, so I can kill anyone close to me. I can kill whatever I touch. Whatever I touch can die," Eigen imagines my father's unconscious monologue to have been. This metastasizing cancer of guilt may even have propelled my father's restless habit of constantly shifting environments, says Eigen. He may have had the feeling that "no one out there can handle me, or survive me, because I ruin everything I love or touch, everything I want." The feeling that we're too much for others to handle, Eigen points out, or that each person kills the thing they love, as Oscar Wilde writes, is not uncommon.

Through these dialogues I begin to see that my father's case wasn't that of someone who'd failed to achieve the American dream. On the contrary, it was that once he got all that he sought, he lacked the inner capacity to take joy in it, or to hold on to it and sustain it. Indeed, unless we "catch on to the destructive forces in our very beings," writes Michael Eigen in *Feeling Matters*, "our success is likely to be shaky." As he describes it, the human psyche is an underground battle between nihilistic, ruinous urges and more creative, fulfilling desires. Yet in our extroverted, capitalist way of life, where people treat even their relationships like business transactions, says Eigen, there's little place for exploring the underlying tensions and conflicts of our psychic lives.

Once again, Eigen picks up the recurring theme of America's disowned feeling life. "What counts in our society," he says, "is winning and getting on top. Feelings become second-class citizens. So we try to get on top of our pain and survive it. We toughen up and get resilient and find ways of pushing on through. Lacking even the language to name the sense that something feels wrong inside, we tell ourselves, 'It's just a dream. We're just making it up.' And so what's really wrong never gets addressed. Because the language, or the culture to address it, barely exists."

One of the biggest questions concerning the human condition, Eigen tells me, has to do with our sensitivity—something we typically harden ourselves against feeling. But, he warns, "if we keep trying to survive our sensitivity by playing it down and shutting it out, we're going to keep on causing catastrophes. In your father's case, for instance, he was trying to stay on top of his own guilt, rage, and pain. He had a couple of skills, and that enabled him to stay on top for some time—until he finally bottomed out."

Bottoming out and being at the whim of his moods is how I watched my aviator father come undone over the course of his life. My mother, too, could be overwhelmed by tidal waves of feeling that, afterward, left her exhausted and worn. I ask Eigen about these frightening, volatile swings in my household. In the exaggerated emotional life of the Carrolls, he sees something more universal at work.

"It's one of the confusing things about the human race," he replies thoughtfully. "We seem to have enough sane moments, but we're really quite mad as a group. Quite crazy, delusional, and maniacal. We have pockets of sanity, which delude us into thinking that we can control things. Or that we're better, more sane, or more rational than we really are. But I've always found the difficulty to be much deeper: we're mad creatures, and the madness will out no matter what we do. The job is to catch on to that, to become partners with our psychotic selves, and to learn to work with it [madness] on a deeper level. It's a mistake to think that if we just impose rules on these parts of ourselves they will listen to us."

Eigen brings clarity to something I had long wondered about. This was the idea that because my family was so emotionally expressive—to put it mildly—we were less repressed than other more controlled families. Eigen corrects this impression, pointing out that the idea is neither to shut down our feelings nor to let them run away with us. Rather, it's to be *related* to them, and to learn to engage our moods and feelings for the messages they're trying to deliver. My father, for example, says Eigen, needed "some kind of enlightenment experience where someone wiser than him could have said, in an authentic, convincing, and truthful way, that we have crazy minds. And that while it may have seemed to him that he was guilty of his father's death, it was megalomaniacal on his part to think that he was the cause."

I find myself wishing that my father could have been in therapy with a psychologically aware man strong enough to have stood shoulder to shoulder with him, braving the badlands of his psyche, educating him about the unhinged, explosive parts of his nature, and clearing their way to a place of understanding.

Terrence Real is a psychologist who writes compellingly about American masculine psychology. He is in the position, as Eigen uses the term, of enlightening men about the personal psychological origins of their rage, as well as the abusive climate within which they are raised, and which in turn shapes their intimate relationships: the mistreatment by their fathers, the terrorization of boys even by their own friends and peers, the danger of being seen as a wimp, and the need to learn how to beat someone up, simply to prevent being beaten. These injuries done to boys in their childhood, writes Real in *I Don't Want to Talk About It*, "operates like a fault line in troubled men, coloring their emotional lives, ready, given the right circumstance, to emerge anew. The wounded boy they have long left behind acts like a reservoir of hurt and shame."

To confront the abusive subculture that shapes American masculinity is to also reckon with the undertone of violence so frequently associated with the American character. I ask psychohistorian Robert Jay Lifton if he thinks, as so many judge us to be, that America is more violent than other countries. Lifton replies that although every country has its own version of violence, he tends to see us as more violent collectively in certain ways than other peoples. This has more to do, he explains, with historical and psychological reasons, than "for reasons of personal badness." In tones shaded with regret, Lifton tells me that our complicated legacy of violence can be traced to the "near deification" and "sacralization" in our society of a single, potent object: the gun.

"It's tied up with our American ideal of the heroic and with later commercialization. We saw ourselves as conquering the wilderness and the native peoples. And the gun was key to that. The gun is also called the great equalizer," he tells me. "So, ironically it was seen as a democratizing device. It was an expression of personal power that gave individuals some sense of control over life and death, perhaps compensating for the terror and fear that many people must have felt in this country in its early decades. So the gun became a symbol on many levels of a kind of organizing principle; as an expression of individualism and individual power; and as a way of dealing with anxieties about death and vulnerability. For all those reasons, the gun became more important to us than perhaps to any other culture." Lifton is grave, even mournful, about the country's self-defeating obsession with guns. He recounts a conversation he had with the distinguished historian Richard Hofstadter just before he died, who confessed to Lifton that of all his discoveries, "his most discouraging finding was the inability of Americans to come to terms with the gun."

What would it mean for America to come to terms with the gun, as both Lifton and Hofstadter suggest? I remember the animal fear I'd feel around the sight of my father's .22 rifle in his alcohol-shaky hands. I reflect again on Lionel Corbett's remark about how my father's cruelty could be tied back to the abuse done to him in childhood, as a form of revenge. I think, too, of photos of my father as a young man—see the promise of his youth and the tender idealism—and compare them to the lost, woebegone face staring out at me from his last passport photo. And I have come to believe that for America to come to terms with the gun, it would first have to come to terms with the extreme sensitivity of the human psyche; and how defects of love, trauma, and abuse can twist the sanest person's mind into madness and acts of violence.

The persecuted man who is my father stares out at me from his passport photo, as if to warn me of the truths behind these insights. Indeed, the time was drawing near when I would watch my father suffer the *cri de coeur* of his neglected psyche on his deathbed, and, at last, it would finally be heard.

X

Death in Texas

And even in our sleep, pain that cannot forget falls drop by drop upon the heart until, against our will, comes wisdom to us by the awful grace of God above.—**Aeschylus**

O N THE CHRISTMAS BEFORE my father died, I returned home to be with my family. Just so I'd know what I'd missed, Joe sent me a holiday card with an enclosed Polaroid of himself. In it, he posed in front of the Christmas tree that Hilda had decorated. Facing the camera in proud profile, his cancer-bloated belly sticking out, Joe tilted his chin high in arrogant defiance. "See me," the photo let me know, "I'm sick and dying. Why aren't you here?" Another photo pictured Hilda and Joe's long and lonely dining room table set for two, with poinsettias and heaping platters of mashed potatoes, cranberry sauce, and roast turkey. There was even a mince pie, Joe's favorite. But he'd been too sick to eat more than a few bites before returning to bed. The regret I felt over not being present for Joe's last holiday remains something I'll take to my own deathbed.

Dickensian themes of abandonment, deprivation, and loss had run through my father's childhood like a vein of dark coal. So I shouldn't have been surprised when a Dickens character of a different sort made his entrance during my father's last days: Ebenezer Scrooge.

Jungian analyst Lionel Corbett has described poignantly what he calls "the Scrooge defense." Mean, hard, sharp, cold, and bitter, Corbett writes in *The Religious Function of the Psyche*, Ebenezer Scrooge is

331

isolated and lacks empathy for others. Typical of those who suffer from narcissistic personality disorder, Scrooge's bitterness and cynicism are a defense erected to protect the vulnerable childhood self from further hurt. Yet when the spirit of Christmas Past appears to Scrooge, revealing his history in a series of flashbacks, Scrooge is able to grieve, finally, over the lost and lonely boy he once was. These powerful experiences break through his defenses, and "in the spirit of love, he sees himself as he really is," writes Corbett. "The memories of his childhood which emerge soften his heart, and allow him to cry again. As he does so he develops the capacity for empathy for the suffering of others."

A Joe Carroll version of the Dickens tale had played over the months of my father's steady decline. During this time I'd watched as the tried-and-true ways of approaching life that had sustained him for so long—the pale ghosts of old and dying warrior gods—gradually failed. In his refusal to go to the hospital was my father's unbending insistence on self-sufficiency and doing things his way. In his attempt to sell his house and move to a new city while barely able to walk or breathe, I saw the roamer after new horizons who would not die easily. In his initial, willful rejection of any medical, spiritual, psychological, or familial help was a man with an utter loathing of weakness. In the little newspaper clipping of a local basketball hero after his own name taped on his refrigerator door—CARROLL WINS!—was the indomitable American will striving to beat all odds and conquer at all costs, even when victory was impossible.

Yet by some wonderment as rare as the materialization of a ghostly presence, the spirit of Christmas Past—in the form of Maria, Gloria, and Andy (his hospice team)—had managed to slip past my father's prickly barriers, gentle as angels. As they'd guided him back over his life—reawakening memories of his mother, father, brothers, friends and adventures, war and work, and girlfriends, children, and love—the tight fist of his hardened heart had begun to unclench. Now, just as Scrooge had happily shared food and his fortune after his epiphany, Joe would be seized by a desire to celebrate what remaining moments he had with those he held most dear. If he really tried, he might be able to prevent a lonesome death on an unforgiving deathbed.

One of the first things to change was Joe's Scrooge-like grip on his wealth. Aside from occasional splurges, my father had been famously secretive and controlling with his money. But on all my visits to him in the months leading up to his death, he turned excessively and endearingly generous. He pressed money and credit cards into my palm and sent me out shopping with my stepmother. When my brother and his children came to see him before the holidays, my father gave them his credit card for a spree at the local toy store. Likewise, on my sister's visit to Corpus Christi just after the New Year, Joe pampered her with takeout dinners and yet more shopping trips. But this time, as her departure neared, Joe began to grow strangely agitated. In a statement wildly out of character with his former behavior, he began apologizing for not leaving her more money. Then he asked to see his will, and directed my sister to a built-in cupboard next to his bed. Colleen rifled through a disorganized stack of papers but found no will.

To this point, none of us had dared broach the charged topic of inheritance. There had been a brief mention of my father's outdated will when we were on the family trip to Austin. But we'd simply assumed since then that Joe had put his financial affairs in order. Though comfortably well off, my father was by no means a rich man. We knew that he owned a spacious suburban home by the Gulf of Mexico, a small boat, and a new Lincoln Town Car. We knew that he'd built Hilda a small house for that day, after he'd gone, when she'd return to her family. We figured that he probably had an IRA, a TWA pension, life insurance, and some stocks. We knew this last thing because over the final decade of his life Joe had become a devotee of the stock market. Forsaking traveling for investing, he'd spent his retirement years tracking the fluctuations of the Dow Jones Industrial Average.

The truth was, we'd always known better than to talk to my father about his money. As he'd made very clear, it was none of our damn business. But death has a way of blasting open even the most tightly lidded of family jars. When my sister's searches yielded no will on that January day in 1995, Joe's anxiety escalated. He pushed his tattered blue address book in her face and pointed to his banker's phone number.

Once he had Mr. Jenkins on the line, Joe requested that he come over "pronto." When the soothingly professional banker arrived early next morning, briefcase in hand, my sister led him to my father's bedroom and then left them alone. Hanging back in the hallway, however, she was tempted to listen in. A sharp tug on her arm interrupted her. It was Hilda.

"We must not eavesdrop," my stepmother admonished my sister. "Your father must die *con* dignity!" But Joe had heard the commotion. "Neen? Is that you?" he yelled out. "Come on in. I want you to hear this." Her pride wounded, Hilda retreated to the kitchen. After my sister entered the room, Joe asked Mr. Jenkins if he had a copy of his will. Puzzled, the banker shook his head no. My father grew more flustered. It was urgent, he said, that he make some changes. Mr. Jenkins arranged to come back in two days with an estate lawyer. If my father hadn't found his old will by then, they'd help him draw up a new one.

Later that night, as I listened to my sister's account of the missing will over the phone, I felt sick with apprehension. It was unlike my father to have been so agitated about his financial affairs, and to have included my sister in his conversation with the banker. Certain that he was entering his last days, I sent my sons to their father's and stepmother's house, called my editor, packed my laptop, and departed a snowy Washington, D.C.

When I stepped into Joe's dim, air-conditioned house that afternoon, the sight of him confirmed my fears. His skin was the cast of a gravestone; the whites of his eyes were a sickly yellow. His emphysema was worse, and his breathing labored. His legs were so swollen I thought the skin would burst. His feet were a bruised and bluish color. But his physical condition hardly seemed to matter. Boyishly happy, Joe greeted me with such relief it brought tears to my eyes. Hilda, however, turned a cool cheek to my kiss hello. Her mink-brown eyes were evasive and distant. The Texas-size drama that was my father's death was about to begin.

"I HAVE THE WILL!"

The doorbell rang at nine o'clock sharp the next morning. I opened the door and ushered in three tall men in suits and ties who looked to be in their mid-forties. Along with the bank vice-president, Howard Jenkins, there was Jack Hutchinson, an estate lawyer, and Randy Charles, a financial planner. I led the three men back to the kitchen and seated them at the round table. As I poured coffee for these latest additions to my father's dying entourage, Hilda went back to retrieve the star of the show. A bent but determined Joe entered the kitchen, clutching his walker, step by halting step. He carefully lowered himself into his chair and glanced around the table with a big smile. "Alrighty then, let's get down to business. Need to make changes to my will," he said, with a guileless grin.

Our guests were clearly shocked and the pity was plain to see on their faces. My father was so visibly ill, his condition so obviously terminal, that he looked as if his life clock had ticked to its final minute. His hands were shaking and his body trembled from head to foot. As I looked at him, I panicked that he might faint and fall out of his chair onto the floor, so I sat down next to him and pulled my chair close to his. Howard Jenkins spoke up first. "Sometimes you need someone outside the family to help you organize your affairs," he said, by way of introducing the estate lawyer and financial planner. Joe nodded his head vigorously. "I need to make changes to my will," he said again. "But I can't find it." The bank vice-president wondered if my father had put his will in his safety deposit box.

Joe's face brightened at this thought. "Bushky," he said, calling Hilda by her pet name. "Is the will at the bank?"

Hilda shook her head. "No, no. I don't know where it is," she mumbled, staring down at her lap.

Hutchinson and Jenkins exchanged a brief glance. "Have you looked through all your papers?" asked Hutchinson, the estate lawyer.

Yes, said Joe, he thought he had, but he couldn't be sure.

"When was the last time you remember working on your will?" asked Randy Charles, the financial planner, gently, as if he were talking to a child. "And who was your lawyer then?" My father's eyelids fluttered as he worked to remember.

Suddenly, they flew open. "I remember!" he cried triumphantly. "I had my lawyer in Houston draw up a new will when we first moved here. Let's see, it was a Mr. George. Pell, be a good girl and get my address book. It's in a drawer by my bed."

Exclamations of relief filled the room, as it seemed the mystery of the will was close to being solved. I raced to his bedroom then back to the kitchen and placed Joe's address book and the telephone in front of him. Fumbling through the pages with stiff fingers, he pulled out a card stuck in the back. "Read the numbers out loud, Pell," he said. As I began reciting the digits, my father picked up the receiver and began to dial.

In all the commotion, none of us had noticed Hilda's absence. So when she suddenly appeared in the archway that separated the kitchen from the living room, we paused, our words dropping off a cliff into dead silence. Slowly, my father put down the telephone receiver. For a small woman, Hilda packed a lot of intensity into her tiny frame. Now she stood before us like a Latin Annie Oakley, one hand clasped behind her back, as if clutching a six-shooter. Her head was thrown back and her face was contemptuous. Grandly, victoriously, she brought her hand out and thrust a sheaf of papers into the air. "*I* have the will!" she proclaimed.

Our eyes popped and our mouths gaped open in disbelief. I stared at my stepmother, my mind a whirl of thoughts. Now I understood. Whatever my father had, it was clear that Hilda saw herself in a fight for her fair share of it. Or, maybe, for all I knew, all of it. How long had she been hiding this will? And why hadn't she said anything up to this moment?

Howard Jenkins, the bank vice-president, was the first to break the spell. "Well, now, Mrs. Carroll," he drawled. "Isn't this a pleasant surprise? You've solved the mystery of the missing will. Congratulations! Why don't you sit down with us and we'll take a look at it?" Disarmed, but now clearly frightened, Hilda's mouth shook. For one crazy moment, I thought she was going to run out of the house and into the street, taking my father's will with her. Instead, letting out a gust of a sigh, she crossed the room, sat down, and placed the document in Hutchinson's hands. Then she put her head in her hands. Jack Hutchinson patted her back gently. "It's going to be all right," he said. "*Sí, sí*," said Hilda, fighting back tears. Then she got up and began making a fresh pot of coffee.

The three men turned their attention to the will, flipping the pages and running their fingers over the legal passages. They mumbled softly among themselves, an occasional phrase standing out: "Standard text . . . looks like it was drawn up . . . stocks are in a Schwab . . . IRA worth . . . let's see, the executor is listed . . ."

Finally, they looked up. "Joe," asked Jack Hutchinson in a measured tone of voice. "What are the changes you'd like to make to your will?" My father strained to focus. "I want to do what's fair," he said in his tremulous voice, turning to look at me. "I want things to be divided between Hilda and the four kids." Jack leaned forward and lightly touched my father's hand. "Joe, that sounds like a sound decision, and it shouldn't be a problem. Now, your older son is currently listed as the executor. Would you still like him to handle your estate?"

This was a problem. My brother had just taken a job abroad, which would prevent him from looking after my father's affairs. Joe furrowed his brow intently. In his genial twang, the estate lawyer explained to him that he could name the bank as his executor, or one of his other three children. He could name Hilda as executor, too, although, said Hutchinson, her limited English could present a problem. Joe thought for a moment, then turned to me with a big grin. "Whaddaya say, Pell? How about it?"

I couldn't have been more surprised. Of everyone in the family, I was the least financially proficient. Since I'd gotten divorced, I'd had a difficult time as I struggled to be both a writer and single parent. At forty-three, I still rented a home rather than owned one and had never so much as sold a stock, much less invested in an IRA. Joe himself had long despaired of me. He hated that my marriage had ended. He was fond of encouraging me to become a respiratory therapist because it was a job that earned a steady income.

"Dad," I said. "Do you really want *me* to do this?"

"You're the one who's here, aren't you?" he asked. Then the old fire sparked in his eyes—the same spark that shone as he drove off down the driveway when I was a girl, and waved to me in the window, as I did in return. The same spark that ignited my courage when he taught me how to drive a pickup truck; how to catch and saddle my horse; how to experience the adventure of flight and world travel; and, in certain rare, precious moments, had told me to "show 'em" I could write a book if I really tried. "You can do it, attagirl," he said now, slapping my knee. "I *know* you can. We'll do it together." His sudden faith in me undid years of needling inner mistrust and doubt.

Maybe, in the end, that is all we really need from our parents: the conviction that we are strong, smart, and creative enough to manage the challenges life throws our way. I reached over and gave my father a hug. "Okay, Dad," I said. "Let's do it!" As our three financial experts stood up to leave, I made an appointment with the estate lawyer for the following day. We'd all meet at the house the day after that to draw up the new will and determine how my father's assets should be divided.

After the door closed behind our financial team, I helped my father back to bed. The tension between Hilda and me was thick. Without a word, she immediately disappeared into her bedroom. From behind her door, I could hear her muffled voice rising and falling in an angry cadence. My stepmother was on the line to her family, I knew, talking about Joe's decision to revise his will—whether she would get her fair share or even be cut out—and making her post-Joe plans.

As much as she loved my father, Hilda had recently begun to make it abundantly clear that as soon as he died she'd be on the next flight out to Mexico. Just as my mother had been unable to adjust to Guadalajara, so Hilda had never taken well to living in America. She missed her extended circle of relatives and the familiar food and customs of her Latin culture. She also disliked our workaholic society and the way Americans put family last. She'd been happy only when she was shopping at the big-box stores that lined Corpus Christi's commercial strip, stocking up on goods for that day when she'd return south of the border.

The next morning, I was plunged into the world of finance. At the estate lawyer's gleaming high-rise office overlooking the Gulf of Mexico, I nervously signed the papers appointing me the executor of my father's estate. Along with that came a set of instructions, which,

Hutchinson told me, I had to follow to the letter. It would be my responsibility to sell my father's house and cars, liquidate his stocks, divide his belongings fairly among his heirs, and oversee the estate taxes. Every last penny, each item down to the last soap dish, had to be noted and accounted for. In preparation, I'd have to begin immediately sorting through Joe's papers and gathering together his stock portfolios, bank accounts, and insurance plans.

At the end of our conversation, Jack leaned back in his chair and looked at me thoughtfully. In all his experience, he said, he'd never seen someone as close to death as my father, and whose affairs had been in such disorder. If Joe died with the old will in effect, he told me, everything would go to Hilda. At this news, my heart began to pound. Was this why Hilda had hidden the will from all of us? And what would happen if he died before we finalized the new one?

I returned to the house and walked into the living room, sank down on the couch, and closed my eyes. Hearing soft footsteps, I looked up to see Hilda standing in front of me. Her face was set and her arms were crossed in front of her chest. "I have something to tell you," she announced, her voice hard. I nodded, waiting. "Your father had no money after his divorce. He told me that he gave it all to your mother," she said. "It was a tough time, and he told me that we had nothing. We struggled."

I wondered silently about the lakeside house they'd bought, the Mercedes-Benz coupe, the yellow Mercedes station wagon, the apartment on Spain's Costa del Sol they'd had for a while, the house he'd built for her, and the money he'd sent to her family. "And then when your father retired and started investing in the stock market, he asked me for my advice. He said I was good about picking stocks. I took care of him for fifteen years." I could feel my anger rising on behalf of my mother, who'd stayed home to raise four kids and feed the cows and horses and sheep on a hard patch of prairie farmland while my father was flying around the world and sleeping with hookers. I thought of the way he'd refused, when she'd asked, to let her work at the local library. But I said nothing, except to nod my head. Now was not the time to make Hilda my enemy.

As my stepmother continued to smolder with resentment, disappearing into her room or to the next-door neighbor's house for hours at a time, I began to feel as though I was trapped in a tawdry late-night movie. When I opened my father's so-called "files," which doubled as the space beneath the liquor cabinet in the living room, I was stunned to discover jumbled stacks of papers crammed in all the way to the top. I scooped out mounds of Schwab stock statements, medical bills, tax returns, yellowing Christmas and birthday cards, photos, and bank statements from Germany to Missouri, Mexico, and New York, and then dumped them onto the dining room table. I began to sort through the detritus of the past twenty years of Joe's life. Where had we ever gotten the idea that my father had been so financially organized?

This Herculean undertaking only further irritated my stepmother, who lurked in the background, casting suspicious glances laced with hostility my way. That night, I regressed to the fears of my childhood. As I lay awake, breathing in the ubiquitous cigarette smoke that belched from the air-conditioning vents, my mind began to misfire. For long and torturous hours, I became convinced there was a gun in the house. I imagined that Hilda might shoot my father or me before our appointment to redo his will the next day. Sometimes, our fantasies about others reveal more about ourselves. Maybe, in truth, I was the one so angry that I could have shot them both.

By the time our trio of tall Texans arrived at eleven A.M. the next morning, my heart was galloping with anxiety. They'd brought with them a Spanish-speaking woman to act as an interpreter for Hilda. We took our seats around the table, me next to Joe and Hilda beside the interpreter. The lawyer, banker, and financial planner each brought out their papers. Jack Hutchinson was the first to speak.

"Now, Joe," he said kindly, "we're here to help you rewrite your will." My father nodded his head, struggling to concentrate. "We need to accomplish two things today: list as many of your assets as we can, and arrive at a fair division between Hilda and your four children." Joe nodded again. He managed to light a cigarette with trembling hands, and to take a shaky sip of coffee from his mug. First came a rough estimate of how much Joe's estate was worth. Based on what I'd been able to pull together so far, he'd come in just beneath the limit where estate taxes would be levied. When Mr. Jenkins mentioned Joe's IRA retirement account at the bank, Hilda tapped the interpreter's arm. "What is an IRA?" she asked in Spanish.

I choked back my surprise. After all the intrigue over the will, it turned out that Hilda hadn't even known what was in it. It was obvious that with his second wife, my father hadn't needed to hide his money; he'd only needed to keep her from speaking English. The estate lawyer explained to my father that he could divide his estate evenly among Hilda and his four children. Or he could give half of it to Hilda and the remaining 50 percent to his four children to divide among themselves. It was up to him.

An awkward silence ensued. I looked out the window, struggling not to want more. After fifteen years of caring for my father and bearing with his drinking, Hilda merited more than her fair share. Besides, wasn't it "their" money, and not just "his" money? My more sane-minded self knew that beneath my stepmother's anger lay fear over her uncertain future. But the girl in me also wanted Joe to favor his children. Hadn't we suffered from his absentee fathering? Didn't we, too, deserve to be rewarded for enduring his alcoholic tempests? And weren't we his natural-born heirs?

Joe's gaze turned to me, then to Hilda. His face was crinkled with distress. Then he nodded his head graciously in my stepmother's direction. "I think it's fair to divide it in half," he whispered. I could see that his energy was failing. He turned to me. "I'm sorry, Pell," he said, his voice quavering. "I'm sorry I didn't leave you more money." Instantly, my heart melted at his words; now it felt unbearable to me that he would die feeling this way. Or that I could even have been so insensitive about Hilda. "Please, Dad." I said. "Don't say that. We didn't even expect to get this much. I'm very grateful, and we all think it's your decision." It was true. My siblings had been clear that it was Joe's money to do with as he wished. Funny that none of us saw it as Joe and Hilda's estate to decide together.

Fingers drummed on calculators and numbers were crunched as the final details of my father's new will were negotiated. The financial advisor brought out his actuarial tables. As the interpreter conveyed to her the details of her final settlement, Hilda's face began to widen into a smile. I could see that she felt relieved. "Toowa," as she called TWA in her Mexican accent, would take good care of her—if she was careful. After my father signed his new will in a spidery, illegible scrawl, there were relieved handshakes and congratulations all around. Then Hilda escorted our estate planners out the door. I helped Joe up from the table and led him on his walker back to his bedroom.

Later that day, Gloria and Maria arrived for their daily visit. I had started to usher them back to my father's room when Gloria asked if they could talk to me first. We sat down on the couch, facing each other. In my agitated state over the will, the two women seemed to me as soft and pure as Ivory soap or the Virgin of Guadalupe, untainted by money. Taking my hands in both of theirs, they asked me what was wrong. I'd never been much of a crier, but now tears streaked down my face as I broke down. I told them about the showdown that had ensued over my father's will, the tension between Hilda and me, and the guilt I felt discussing money with my father when he seemed so close to death. It seemed so tacky, I wept, to make my ill father talk about mundane things like his veterans insurance policy, or to make him divvy up his money between his children and their stepmother. It felt so, well, unspiritual, I said. In fact, it felt much worse than that. It felt like I was killing him.

Maria was the first to ease my stress. Putting an estate in order, she said, was as much a part of the dying process as was making peace with God and one's life. It was a difficult, thankless task, but necessary and worthwhile. It had to be done, and I shouldn't be ashamed of tending to such practical matters. And I was not killing my father: he was already dying. Though I felt a bit ridiculous, I also felt as if a dark spot that had been clouding my vision had been scrubbed away. Unburdened, relieved, I felt as if I could have kissed my two hospice social workers—and I did.

BORN AGAIN

Certainly Joe, in relinquishing his hard-earned savings, and in letting go of a lifetime of saving, spending, and constant, anxious fretting over money, was becoming unburdened of a weight he'd carried on his shoulders since that chill Depression day when he'd lost his father. Released into a kind of freedom he'd never known before, Joe now grew so light-hearted that if he'd possessed the energy he, too, like Scrooge, would have danced down the street, tossing coins in the air.

I'd never seen him so carefree before. Every time I left the house, he pressed a fifty- or hundred-dollar bill into my hands. All he wanted to do, it seemed, was call my siblings on the phone, eat, and relax. "Let's have takeout from Red Lobster!" he'd rasp, brandishing his Schwab credit card in the air, as eager as a ten-year-old. He seemed to want to draw life close to him, to have Hilda and me around him, and to be the last of the big-time spenders in the limited ways that he could. When he wasn't sleeping, the three of us spent lazy hours enjoyably munching on fried shrimp, sitting silently, or talking and watching television. Though much work remained for me to sort through the details of my father's estate, the tension between Hilda and me had dissipated. My stepmother seemed relieved to have a clear map for the next stage of her life.

But the changes in my father went even deeper than old habits around money. Far more surprising to me, things that once would have irritated my father now elicited wonder instead.

One afternoon, my sister, who had returned, took a break to practice her flute. Just as when she'd been young, she made sure to shut herself away to muffle her playing so as not to raise Joe's fury. I was sitting by my father's bedside when, despite her efforts, sharp, trilling notes pierced the afternoon quiet. I cringed, waiting for the caustic criticism I was sure would come, as it always had in the past. But the old Joe—the mean-spirited man who'd sarcastically ridiculed my sister's playing when she was growing up—was nowhere in evidence. Instead, something like reverence came over his face. His clouded eyes grew dreamy, and he looked into the distance. "Can you imagine how wonderful it would be to play an instrument like that?" he asked. "What a talent! I wish I could make music like that." He shook his head, marveling at my sister, as I shook mine in amazement at him.

343

I could, I know, have attributed the personality changes in my father to the operation he'd had and the hormones he was taking for his prostate cancer, or the mood-altering morphine. But to dismiss these finer feelings as nothing more than chemical reactions would have been cynical. His creative stirrings deserved a witness who would not do to him what he'd done to himself, and to others, over the course of his life.

As my sister played on, Joe's thoughts turned to my brothers. My father, who'd long withheld praise of his children, now practically bubbled with compliments. "John is such a good father," he said. "Really good with his kids. Better than I ever was. Good at his job. Good writer. And Steve, just think of it: All those big engineering projects he handles! Living all over the world. Don't know how he does it." Then he began to muse over his boyhood again, dreams from his past flickering across his face. "We didn't have much when we were growing up," he said. "No toys. No fancy things. When we were little, we played with sticks in the dust. But we had fun, running through the hills in the back of the house. We didn't even know we were poor, we were so happy playing with each other."

"He became a storyteller," remarks Sylvia Perera, also in some wonderment at Joe's transfiguration. "That's so Irish. In the mead hall in the old days the Irish bard would drink and then, his creativity loosened, he'd sing and recite poetry." This Irish gift for music and storytelling, she believes, lay dormant in my father until it was resurrected by his hospice nurses and my sister and me listening to him.

I turn over Perera's words and reconsider my father's strange habit of playing with his own. His odd way of elongating syllables into a language of his own made a new kind of sense, as did his bedtime stories, his elegant whistling, his sentimental love of certain songs, and even his drunken meanderings. Could it be that my father might have had within him the rough makings of a musician-storyteller, a talent that had been quashed somewhere along the way? When I share these thoughts with my sister, Colleen reminds me that, in fact, my father had once told her about a nun in his youth who'd accused him of having a "tin ear."

Depth psychologist Stephen Aizenstat observes that when a person comes to him caught in alcohol or drug addiction, he, the therapist, searches for that place in the family line where some creative capacity got stuck and wasn't able to find expression. Our family history, Aizenstat believes, has a mythological dimension. "Each of our parents, grandparents, and great-grandparents and on back," he says, "had a psyche filled with demons and muses." Disruptions to their creativity can be the result of large-scale calamities like wars and poverty, or family catastrophes like illness. Yet though these instincts may get submerged, he argues, they always come back, "either as creative potential, or like a genie trapped in a bottle, in the form of an addictive pathology." The very thing that was at the root of your father's alcoholism, in other words, is also where his genius was." Thus what often lies at the root of a drinking problem, says Aizenstat, "is the very muse that is a person's genius or talent. The seeds of our destiny, passion, desire, and uniqueness always lie in our pathologies and wounds."

Aizenstat further piques my interest when he tells me that what gets blocked in a family lineage can also be religious in nature. A spiritual figure in the family background, he tells me, might have become split off, driving a wedge in future generations between belief and unbelief. In my father's life story, it was he himself who'd bitterly denounced the Catholic Church for stealing his widowed mother's last dime to bury her dead husband. Sometimes, I wonder whether Joe's fury toward the priests was displaced rage he felt toward God for snatching his father away from him. Yet Joe had never entirely renounced the Church. Instead, he'd nursed his grievances at a low simmer, cursing and growling at the clergy, yet insisting that his four children be raised in his Irish father's faith. My mother's decision not to convert had further complicated the Carrolls' relationship with our professed family religion.

This storied ambivalence made for interesting Sunday mornings in my childhood. Whether my father was home or away on a trip, Sheila saw to it that, along with the rest of fifties America, her four children were up and dressed in their Sunday best. Sliding into the long pew in the modern suburban church we attended, my mother would enter first. One by one, my two brothers, sister, and I would enter after her, with my father coming in last to take his usual seat by the aisle.

When it came time for Communion, the four of us would stand up, file politely out of our pew, and take our place in line to receive the thin white wafer that was, as the nuns had taught us, the body of Christ. As they always did, Joe and Sheila would remain seated throughout this ritual. In all the many years of Sundays I attended Mass, I never once saw my father receive communion or take confession. I knew my mother wasn't a Catholic. But why, I'd wondered, hadn't my father ever stood up with us? Why were we being raised Catholic when our one Catholic parent hated the church?

I found out the answer to this question when I was around sixteen. It was a quiet Saturday afternoon, and I'd been eating lunch with my parents at the redwood picnic table in the kitchen. Suddenly, I'd been overcome with curiosity. "Dad," I asked, "why don't you ever go to communion?" Joe was sitting in his captain's chair, eating a sandwich. In lieu of an answer, he continued to chew, shooting me a dark look and warning me off this taboo topic. My mother began to squirm. She was angry, and I could see that she was spoiling for a fight. "Why don't you tell her the truth, Joe?" she finally burst out. My father kept his head down and continued to eat. Undeterred, Sheila persisted. "You can't keep this a secret from them anymore. The children need to know." My imagination spun into overdrive, as I began to suspect my father of some long-hidden secret sin.

"Sheila!" my father barked, his anger mounting. But my mother would not be stopped. "Your father had a vasectomy," she finally proclaimed, turning to me. "After John was born we decided that four children was enough. And birth control is a sin in the eyes of the church. You can't take communion if you've had a vasectomy." More embarrassed by this peek into their sex life than mortified at my father's apparently grave iniquity, I shrugged my shoulders in feigned boredom. At her words, my father left the table, his sandwich uneaten, and marched outside.

It's difficult to keep the flame of faith burning when your own parents have doubts about the tradition in which they're raising you. Although I credit the Catholic Church's mystical culture of candles, veils, robes, holy cards, incense, Latin, saints, and miracles with kindling in me a love for God, I never really felt as if I belonged. As our family fell apart, so, too, one by one, did all four of us fall away from the Church. When my parents moved to Mexico they also stopped going to Mass. I, of course, had shot straight from Catholicism into the heart of the spiritual renaissance in California.

One day, as the wheels of my parents' divorce were spinning, Joe called to say he'd be coming for a visit. As usual, I expected to meet him at his hotel. Instead, he surprised my husband and me by announcing that he'd like to stay with us in our communal household. Just for a couple of days, he said, clearing his throat. Uncertain what to expect, I made up a bed for him in my toddler son's room.

At first, Joe stayed true to his irreverent, jokey nature. In the gardens surrounding the three-story house that we shared with several families, a six-sided octagonal dome had been erected among the terraces of cascading flowers. Inside this spare space, seekers took meditation retreats. Soon after he settled into his room on the third floor, Joe peered out his window, which overlooked the garden. In the dusk, he saw a tall, clean-shaven man with long hair dressed in a flowing white robe chanting in the doorway of the retreat hut, his eyes closed. "Pell!" my father bellowed, his voice echoing throughout the house, "There's a ghost in the garden! And I can't tell whether it's a boy or a girl!"

Beneath Joe's bluff and bluster, it turned out, beat a heart that was hurt and in search of spiritual solace. Taking Terry aside, Joe asked for instructions on how to meditate. When his initial effort failed, he came to me next, disheartened and disquieted. "How can I get the thoughts in my mind to stop?" he asked plaintively. "They go around and around, like a damn dog chasing its tail. I just want some peace. They keep me up in the middle of the night. I just want to sleep."

I did my best, as had Terry, and gave my father some simple breathing techniques and visualizations. His attempts to meditate had touched me like nothing else thus far. For the first time, I glimpsed in Joe a real need for some sort of mental ceasefire, and a desire to connect with something meaningful and larger than himself. But it was not to be. "Just didn't work. Can't stop the thoughts from going around and around my head," my father said glumly. I patted his knee in sympathy, at a loss to ease the suffering of my own parent.

That would be our last conversation about spiritual matters. As far as I knew, my father had wholly surrendered to alcoholism. As I work on this book, however, my mother sends me the torn half cover of a faded TWA *Ambassador* magazine. Dating back to the mid-seventies, it's a memento that she's kept all these years. On it, my father had scribbled two quotations. One was from the historical Christian novel *Captains and the Kings* by Taylor Caldwell: "The individual who has experienced solitude," it read, "will not easily become a victim of mass suggestion." Opposite these words, my father had penned a quote from Albert Einstein: "Perhaps, some day, solitude will come to be properly recognized and appreciated as the teacher of personality. The Orientals have long known this." My heart wrenches as I read these quotations. I imagine my father pondering them, hungering to understand more about the deeper side of life, and glimpsing something purposeful and mysterious at work in his introverted nature.

Yet, as a familiar spiritual aphorism goes, when the soul is truly ready the guide will appear. For Joe, that teacher would show up just days before his death in the form of a local priest named Father Fred. He arrived on our doorstep like a Hail Mary pass in the last seconds of my father's life.

The story of how Father Fred came to tend my father's soul begins this way. The day after my sister left to return home, Gloria and Maria arrived for their visit. Together with Hilda, we all went back to Joe's bedroom. For a while, the four of us chatted idly. Then, as if out of nowhere, Hilda's face grew dark and she began to cry. She turned to the hospice workers and began speaking in a stream of Spanish, frantically gesturing with her hands. Gloria and Maria listened patiently and then translated.

"Joe," said Gloria. "Hilda says that her Catholic faith means everything to her. She would like you to have a Catholic funeral." Hilda nodded emphatically as they spoke. It occurred to me that it had been a while since my father had asked to be shot and thrown in a ditch. But Joe instantly recoiled at the idea. "No funeral," he said in his weak, husky voice. "No wasting money on a coffin. No money for the priests. Just cremate me."

These words were heresy to Hilda. "*Muy importante*," she implored my father. "*Muy importante*, my darling Joe."

At that moment, I realized that I, too, did not want my father to pass through the portal of death without a funeral. I wrestled with the principle that a dying person's wishes should be honored. At the same time, foregoing a funeral felt like we'd be allowing my father's life to go unmarked. It would only perpetuate his old habit of distance and disengagement from the customs of the living. Besides, in my view, letting Joe go into the afterlife without a proper funeral would be like sending him on a long journey naked and alone. "I think Hilda is right," I said. "Even if you don't want a funeral, it would help us after you're gone." Hilda looked at me gratefully; we'd found a purpose around which we could unite.

"Is this really important to you, Bushky?" Joe wheezed. Hilda nodded. Luckily, Joe's newfound euphoria predisposed him to want to please her, even if it meant making a deal with the hated Church. "Alrighty then, if that's what you'd like, then let's have a funeral!" he said, as if he were planning a party. Hilda's face lit up in relief. Crossing herself, she blew a little kiss to my father.

Immediately, an obstacle arose. Both Gloria and Maria were Catholic. They knew the rules. And in the Catholic Church, according to doctrine, Joe and Hilda's marriage was not valid: they were each divorced. In the eyes of the Church, they'd been living together in sin these past fifteen years. Technically, because of this, no priest, said Maria, could legally perform the funeral rites. It was clear this was territory they'd covered before with dying patients. But the news came as an insult to Hilda. No one in Mexico paid any attention to such silly rules, she claimed, drawing herself up straight. "And I am not living in sin with your father. We are married," she announced, her head high. Gloria and Maria huddled. There was a local priest, they said, who might be able to help.

In the early afternoon of the next day, a car pulled up outside the house. Through the drapes, I saw a van with handicapped license plates parked in the street. As the middle door slid open, I watched as a rotund priest of middle age and medium height struggled to climb out. Dressed in the black, high-collared shirt and pants of the clergy, he was wiping his perspiring forehead with a large handkerchief. I ran out to see if he needed assistance.

"Hello, hello, greetings," said the priest. "I'm Father Rodriguez. Just call me Father Fred, everybody does. Gloria and Maria sent me. You must be Pellman. I've come to see Joe." Reaching into the van, Father Fred pulled out a heavy cane. I took his arm and helped him inside. His wavy hair was thick and black, his eyes a dark and twinkling brown. It was tempting to think of him as a young, Spanish Santa Claus.

Once inside, Father Fred asked to sit down. "I had polio as a child, you know, and I'm lame in one leg, so it's hard for me to stand up for long," he explained, as I pulled out a chair for him at the kitchen table. "And this terrible heat doesn't help," he added. Out of the corner of my eye, I watched as Hilda appeared. Bowing, bobbing, and making the sign of the cross as she approached, she looked as if she was going to genuflect at Father Fred's feet. Later, I found out that she'd recognized him as the priest who performed singing Masses every Sunday afternoon on local television. Unable to attend Mass herself, she'd watched these televised services since her arrival in Corpus Christi.

Reaching up with his arms as Hilda leaned down, Father Fred embraced her in a large hug. "My child, my child," he said, sweat streaming from his face. "It will be all right." Straightening her spine and brushing away tears, Hilda stood back and poured Father Fred a cup of coffee. "Now," said our new family priest, the latest character to join my father's theatrical cast, "tell me about Joe."

Joined in our newfound alliance, Hilda and I set forth our case, pleading with Father Fred to find a way to give my father a Catholic funeral and burial. I sketched the narrative of Joe's life to this point, including his lifelong renunciation of communion and confession. I also told the priest how, after his initial diagnosis of cancer, my father had asked to be shot and thrown by the side of the road. That even though he was half joking, there was a current of something real beneath his words. As I spoke, I wondered if Father Fred would catch the undercurrent beneath *my* words: that my father had been a deeply troubled man. A host of broken and discarded relationships, I told him, was strewn along the road of life Joe had traveled to this point. But lately, with hospice, the hard shell of his indifference had begun to crack.

"Well, this is a difficult case," Father Fred sighed after I'd finished. "Better take me to Joe." I led the way to the bedroom, with Hilda helping Father Fred behind me. My father was sitting up in bed. Scattered pages from the *Wall Street Journal* covered the sheets. A bottle of Smirnoff was in plain sight on his bedside table, amid the usual clutter of coffee cups, pill bottles, and overflowing ashtrays. This was usually a sign that—visitor beware!—Joe was not about to pretty up who he was. CNN, as usual, was blaring on the television. Cigarette smoke hung in the room. "Hello," said my father, cautiously eyeing this priest who'd invaded his private sanctuary. His good mood had been eclipsed by a wary guardedness. I muted the television, pulled up a chair for Father Fred, and started to sit down. But the priest stopped me. "Joe and I need some time alone," he said.

Hilda and I returned to the living room. Sitting on opposite couches in silence, we listened to the voices and occasional laughter echoing from the back of the house. Half an hour later the door opened, and Father Fred called for us to rejoin them.

Given that my father hadn't talked to a priest at least since he'd married my mother, I couldn't have been more curious about what had transpired. I was happily surprised to see that Father Fred had moved from his chair and was sitting on the bed beside Joe. A rosary and an open Bible were on his lap. A little bud of hope opened up in my heart. There even seemed to be feelings of genuine warmth between the two.

"Joe and I have been talking," said Father Fred. "I told him it's not over until the Fat Lady sings!" The two men grinned widely, enjoying their joke at death's expense. Whoever this priest was, he had the same kind of magical talent as Andy the nurse to get my father to laugh in the midst of dying. "We've been having a good talk. But Joe told me that he wasn't so sure about the Church, right?" The priest's face grew more solemn, and my father nodded in agreement. "So, we're going to keep talking," continued Father Fred. "However, he's decided he'd like to have a funeral, for Hilda's sake. But in order to make things right in the eyes of the Church, I'm going to have to remarry the two of you,

Hilda and Joe. Then I can perform Joe's funeral service." With these words Father Fred's eyes twinkled, stirring images in my mind again of a jolly St. Nick. "Because Joe's illness is progressing fast, I'll come back tomorrow afternoon, and we'll have a wedding ceremony," he said. "But it has to be a secret, or I might lose my job. Pellman can be the witness."

Hilda jumped out of her chair and threw her arms around the priest. "*Gracias*, oh thank you, thank you," she kept repeating. I said nothing, silenced by the sheer unexpectedness of this new twist. After Hilda sat down, Father Fred spoke again. His face took on a deeper, humbler look. "But each of you has work to do," he said solemnly, looking first at Joe, then Hilda, and then me. "Joe needs to think about his death, what his beliefs are, and his relationship to God. He must work on healing his relationships with those he's hurt, and with himself, and finish up his business on this Earth by making amends. And the two of you," he said, leaning closer to Hilda and me, "need to stop thinking of Joe as only father and husband. As you care for him, think of his body as the body of Christ. You must do all these things for Joe as if you were sisters doing them for Jesus."

Father Fred's words rang through the room like a church bell quieting a city at the close of day. I turned and looked at Joe with altered perception. To care for my father as if he were Jesus. To see the Divine in him as it shone through the gauze of his flaws and failings. To assist in the healing of his suffering. In the holiness of the moment, whatever hostility remained between Hilda and me melted away. We gazed at each other, smiling shyly through our tears. Even my father seemed enveloped in the soft folds of grace.

After making the sign of the cross over the three of us, Father Fred stood up from my father's bedside with effort. Hilda stayed with my father as I accompanied Fred to the front door. But our newfound family priest had no interest in leaving. He wanted to talk. He limped into the living room and beckoned me to sit beside him. Was it true what he'd heard from Gloria and Maria, he asked, that I wrote about spirituality? I nodded. With this opening, the tables were turned. Clasping my hands in his, he began pouring out his life story.

His was a classic conversion tale, it would turn out, in a modern setting. Born to a Mexican family in a small town outside Corpus Christi, Father Fred had not always been religious. Before joining the priesthood, he'd lived on the fringes of society, traveling the country in theater troupes singing and acting. There had been lots of drugs, alcohol, sex, and other misadventures too outrageous to share.

He'd learned a lot about the human condition during those years, he told me. He'd also made lifelong friends and known love along the way. But then he'd begun to grow tired of the excess of his gypsy life. As he was preparing for the role of John the Baptist in the musical *Godspell*, he had a spiritual awakening. Seeking a closer connection to God, he'd decided to return to the faith of his childhood and become a priest. Even after entering the priesthood, however, he'd continued to follow his eccentric life star. He'd traveled to Latin America and joined with other priests in the liberation theology movement, helping the poor and the oppressed find social justice. After coming back to the States, he'd studied with alternative theologians and thinkers.

Finally, after all his journeys, Father Fred had returned to Corpus Christi. He'd made this decision, he said, in part to be with his family. But he'd also felt called to minister to the Mexican community of laborers and immigrants. His church parish, he told me proudly, was located in a poor barrio in a small town along the Gulf coast. Laughing, he described how his duties sometimes included going into bars on behalf of angry wives, breaking up fights, and returning drunken husbands home. As important as his ministry was to him, Father Fred confided, there were few people with whom he could really talk. He missed the exchange of ideas. His physical handicap, too, slowed him in carrying out his duties.

As I listened, Fred's faith and courage under such lonely conditions touched my heart. But I was also struck by the accident of fate that had led him to my family at such a critical point. What were the chances, I thought, that this quirky Catholic priest with such an offbeat background—a man familiar with many of the ideas I'd spent my life exploring—would show up on my father's doorstep at this very moment? And in Corpus Christi? With his crippled leg, his huge heart, his bohemian spirit, and his bright mind, Father Fred was what some call a wounded healer, someone who heals others out of their own suffering. As I had with Andy, Gloria, and Maria, I felt thankful for the support that had arrived in the form of Father Fred. Life with its mysterious powers could not have sent anyone more perfectly tailored to bring balm to my father, and to meet the odd needs of our family.

Joe and Hilda's wedding ceremony was scheduled for 5:00 P.M. the next day. At 3:30, my father awoke from a nap hungry for his favorite takeout meal. "Hey, Pell. Let's get some of that *deee-lishhh-us* Red Lobster! Whaddya say? We gotta have a wedding party. Now run along quickly," he croaked cheerfully, shoving the Schwab credit card into my hand. "I want lobster and fried shrimp. And get a lot of those soft rolls and extra tartar sauce and hot melted butter, ummm yumm, would you?"

Arriving five minutes past the appointed hour, I rushed into the house, two heavy, hot bags in hand. Hilda was waiting for me, a worried look on her face. "You are late," she said anxiously. "Father Fred is already here, waiting to begin." I placed the two bags on the kitchen counter and hurried back to the bedroom. Father Fred, dressed this time in traditional black robes, was seated by Joe's bed. On his lap were a small wooden box, his rosary, and a Bible. Hilda was perched on the bed beside my father. She'd put on makeup, curled her hair, and wore a flowery blouse. She'd even, I noticed, painted her nails a bright coral color. Joe was sitting up in bed, wearing a freshly laundered pair of blue pajamas that made his eyes pop. He was trembling and very tired. But he was trying as valiantly as he could to be a good groom for his new bride. His bedside table was mercifully bare; this was a good sign. I drew up the chair next to Father Fred and sat down.

The four of us now made an intimate circle. Within its space, an atmosphere of warmth and love welled up. Unbidden, the thought of Christ's words to his disciples, "Wherever two or more of you are gathered in my name, there shall I be," ran through my mind. Even *here*, I thought to myself: in this musty sickroom, with a dying alcoholic and his pills and cigarettes, in Texas, hard by Mexico. At that moment, my eyes met Father Fred's, and a small shiver went up my spine. "Are we ready to begin the ceremony?" he asked. "*Sí, sí*, we are," said Hilda. Joe nodded, as did I, swallowing the lump that had come to my throat.

Opening the box on his lap, Father Fred removed a small book. Then he took out a white mantle decorated with colorful images of the Virgin of Guadalupe and draped it around his neck. Fingering his rosary, he began to recite the Catholic wedding ceremony: "Father, you have made the bond of marriage a holy mystery, a symbol of Christ's love for his Church. Hear our prayers for Joe and Hilda. With faith in you and in each other they pledge their love today. May their lives always bear witness to the reality of that love. We ask you this through our Lord Jesus Christ, your Son, who lives and reigns with you and the Holy Spirit, one God, for ever and ever. Amen."

As Father Fred continued to recite the liturgy in his melodious voice, I closed my eyes. No matter the religious tradition, the doors to my soul were easily opened. I felt suffused by the redemptive spirit filling the room. The Catholic Mass, wrote Carl Jung, was an archetypal ritual that transcended the boundaries of history. It represents, he wrote, "the manifestation of an order outside time and involves the idea of a miracle." Certainly, it felt as if the room had been swept by a sanctifying force greater than any one of us.

Father Fred's voice interrupted my reverie. "Do you, Joe, take Hilda as your wife?" My father nodded and whispered yes, looking at his bride with love. "And do you, Hilda, take Joe as your husband?" Hilda murmured her assent. "And now," said Father Fred with a big grin, "we will have the exchange of rings." Spontaneous giggling erupted as Hilda looked down at the gold wedding band already on her finger. My father smiled, shook his head, and lifted up his left hand. In all his life, my father had never worn a wedding ring. And, he was letting us know, he never would. After our laughter had quieted, Father Fred concluded his ceremony with a blessing: "For all married people: for those who married yesterday; for the new couple, Hilda and Joe, married today; for those who will marry tomorrow. That they may savor the joy of being together, warm love, and children, a long life, wine, and friends. And a new day, every day. Let us pray to the Lord."

"Lord, hear our prayer," Joe, Hilda, and I responded as one. How, after all these years, had my father—and I—remembered this phrase? From what deep layer of memory had these words resurfaced? After Father Fred's final sign of the cross, we took turns hugging. "Peace be with you," we wished each other. Father Fred and I offered Joe and Hilda congratulations on their marriage.

One more order of business had to be taken care of that afternoon: my father's funeral. "Do you have any favorite psalms you'd like sung?" Father Fred asked Joe. My father shook his head; he had no idea. I wondered if some resistance to the idea of a funeral still lingered in my father, and that he hadn't had the heart to express. Father Fred made some suggestions; looking relieved, both Joe and Hilda nodded in agreement. After that, little more remained to be said. As Father Fred packed the instruments of his trade, the emotion contained in the room was almost more than I could bear. "Do you know how lucky you are to be there, witnessing all this?" asked my sister on the phone, after it was all over. Yes, I did, I told her.

Later, after Father Fred had departed, Joe, Hilda, and I shared our Red Lobster wedding feast, watching television together in companionable silence. It was, indeed, *deee-lishhhh-us*.

LOVE, AGAIN

Following my father's deathbed wedding, my relationship with Hilda continued to soften. Given how rarely I'd seen her over the years, as well as the language barrier, it had been difficult to really get to know my stepmother. Sometimes, I'd judged her as shallow, pigeonholing her as Joe's helpmate who waited on him, rather than his true partner. But a dream I had the night of their marriage ceremony changed that perception.

My nocturnal vision opened up as I descended steep, winding stairs to underground dwellings. There I discovered a hidden leper colony. As I walked among the low-ceilinged catacombs, I encountered a crowd of poor, crippled people—debtors, sinners, alcoholics, and addicts among them. Rounding a corner, I met my father and Hilda. Dressed in rags, they were sitting happily together, feeding each other from bowls of food on their laps.

Later, in analysis, my therapist Nona said the dream had been about love as it flourished in all the wrong places, like hardy dandelions in a manicured lawn. Love as it really was—freed of stereotypes and stripped of the straitjacket of perfection; love of the broken for the broken, of human for human. So much of my father's dying, it seemed, was turning out to be about the deepening of love, as if the mystery that is love can only be understood in our last days. For it is then, if we are lucky, that we behold the revelation that all that we've struggled with throughout our lives has really only been about one thing: that which really matters, which is love.

Spiritual psychologist Robert Sardello says that he tries to ask a basic question: What is the purpose of love in the world? Why do we go through all this pain and suffering? He answers the question by saying that love is the way the Divine element enters into us. In ancient Greece, he tells me, "whenever a deed of love was performed on the Earth the gods on Olympus experienced what they called nectar. In turn, when they received love, they poured forth love on the Earth." In Sardello's vision of love's possibilities, love becomes the most important initiation into soul work that we can experience. Helping my father die, in fact, would become one of the greatest labors of love of my lifetime. As I submitted to the tasks of tending my father on his slow march to death, love in all its different forms worked in me as a force. Old structures of how I'd felt toward my crotchety, misshapen father—angry, bitter, vengeful, critical—fell away.

But Joe, too, was being changed by love. We now had a hospice team of four—Hilda, Maria, Andy, and Father Fred—for whom the art of dying well was a high vocation. Their passion for their calling ensured that they entered my father's last days with profound engagement and patient attention to the most inconsequential detail. But Joe was lucky in other ways, remarked Gloria the day after the bedside wedding. Not every family, agreed Maria, was as fully engaged in a relative's dying process as ours was turning out to be. In their experience, many family members remained coolly detached as they waited for their loved ones to die. They shared stories of dying patients shut off in back rooms, carelessly abandoned to die alone.

I could hardly judge others for falling short. The physical tasks of cooking, cleaning, and caring for my father at the same time I was trying to meet writing deadlines, handle his estate, and field calls from my sons back home were taking a toll. I felt silly for fretting about my little dachshund, who was being taken care of by my close friend Lis. A good night's sleep was rare, and I was growing more exhausted. Often, Joe would be up for hours in a kind of quasi-wakeful state. Sitting up on the edge of his bed, he'd go through the motions of striking a match, lighting a cigarette, and sipping from an invisible cup of coffee. These were the habits of his lifetime, and they were dying hard. I worried constantly that my father would fall from the bed and hurt himself while I was asleep.

Then there was the never-ending wrangling over my father's medications. As Joe's pain levels increased, Andy would call in a prescription for a stronger dose of morphine. Inevitably, Joe's oncologist would balk, forcing Andy and myself to plead for relief. Waiting for her response, we'd all spiral in a tizzy of anxiety until, finally, she'd relent. Death is no easy matter, writes James Hillman in *Suicide and the Soul*: "dying is a rending business, ugly, cruel, and full of suffering."

And so my father's dying proceeded, ricocheting from heaven to hell, just as his own life had done. One morning, about ten days after I arrived, Joe woke up in a cheerful and sprightly mood. The fidgety unease of the night before had melted in the early morning sun, and he had a project for me: he was ready to entertain visitors. Handing me his familiar blue address book, he asked me to dial the number of one of his old TWA buddies.

I left the room to give him some privacy but could still hear him in his tremulous, sick, old man's voice trying to joke around about the good old days. "Hey, looks like I'm not going to be around much longer," I overheard him say. "Why don't you fly in for a visit? We'll drink some beer and sit out on the dock. Real pretty out there." This, of course, was a pleasant pipe dream. "Poor old Len," said my father when I checked in on him. "He's recovering from stomach cancer. Can't come out." When he dialed the number of another fellow flight engineer, Joe learned that he'd died the year before.

Next on Joe's list was his little brother Gene. Here his courage failed him. The two had not seen each other, and had rarely spoken, since the falling-out they'd had when Joe had married Hilda. Rather than make the call himself, he pressed me into service. My aunt was happy to hear my voice, although sad to hear my news. But she was cool to the idea of Uncle Gene traveling to see my father. It had, after all, been fifteen years since Joe had so high-handedly turned his back on them. My aunt considerately left that topic alone.

"Gene's not feeling well," she said. "I don't think he can make the trip. It would be too much for him right now." Then she put my uncle on the phone to speak to my father. "Howdy there, little brother!" said Joe bravely, if awkwardly. Neither of them were much good at talking on the phone—especially without the familiar prop of booze—much less saying a final farewell, after a lifetime, over the phone. After some faltering good-byes, Joe put the receiver down. For a moment he kept his gaze focused on the floor. When he looked up, I could see the tears trickling down his cheeks. Later, I heard that Gene, too, had cried after hanging up.

But soon Joe was on to the next call, this time to his older brother Paul. "Here, Pell, you do it," he said, pointing to Paul's number. "Tell him what's happening. See if he can hop on a plane and come on out for a few days." I went into the kitchen to make the call to Tallahassee, Florida. Aunt Ann picked up on the first ring. Again, I felt the awkwardness of the long years and great distances that had stretched out between the Carroll brothers and sisters, and me. After a strained silence, Ann put my uncle on the phone. When I told him that my father didn't have long to live, he began to sniffle. "I'm coming," he finally choked out. "I'll make reservations and call you back with my flight schedule." I ran back to my father's room with the news. As he did so often when he was happy now, Joe handed me the Schwab card so we could celebrate with takeout food from Olive Garden.

Then the phone began to ring and ring. It was as if the wind had picked up, filling the sails of the boat that would soon be carrying my father to the other side. My youngest brother John would be arriving for the weekend. Colleen, too, was making plans to return once again; this time she'd be bringing her daughter, Lily, with her. Calling from Cairo, Steven said he was making reservations to fly in over the next few days. Soon the house would be full with family, just like my father had wanted. Christmas, if a little late, was finally arriving for Joe.

But the excitement proved too much for my father. Taking a sudden turn for the worse, he lay on his back, his breathing harsh and labored. His eyes fluttered open and closed. Speaking became an arduous effort. He no longer paid attention to the television blaring in the background. "Joe might be starting to die," said Andy, sitting by his bedside. "There's nothing you can do now but wait."

That night, I kept vigil beside my father's bed. Joe shifted restlessly, his rattled breathing loud in the midnight silence. As the hours wore on, a cold fear, deep as a dark sea cave, grew in my heart and began to engulf my body. I started to panic. I felt too mortal, too small, to face death. All my spiritual resources drained away; I had no idea what I was doing. Irrationally, I felt angry with Andy, Father Fred, Gloria, and Maria for leaving me alone. I began to wonder if I should get up and say something to my father. If he really was dying, weren't there words or prayers I should be reciting? At the same time, I didn't want to intrude on his private process. Then a piece of advice a friend had once given me popped into my mind. As her father was dying, she told me, she'd overcome her shyness and told him not to be afraid. The soothing effect of her words had calmed his distress.

I got up and sat beside my father. His eyes blinked open. "What are you doing here?" he grunted, with a bewildered look. "Get back to bed. You need your beauty sleep." Taking advantage of this opening, I plunged in. "Dad, you're dying. And I know you must feel scared," I said, my voice thin as a reed. "But don't be afraid, there's nothing to fear. It will be all right." My father made the rough equivalent of a chortle. "That's easy for *you* to say," he croaked wryly. "You're not the one who's dying." I burst out laughing. Joe's talent for black humor was one of the sides of him that I loved the best. My father laughed, too, or tried to, in a grimacing way. But my instinct had been half right, for my question had breached his reserve. "So," he whispered, "what do you think happens when you die?"

This was not a question I'd expected. I thought carefully before answering. Sorting through the rich lexicon of images and beliefs that made up my own understanding of death and the afterlife, I settled on telling my father about near-death experiences. In writing an article on that subject, I'd been moved by the people I'd met whose lives had been changed. I saw their visions as the basis of a new theology taking shape around death.

"Well," I said, treading gingerly, "I've interviewed and read about people who say they've died and come back to life. And they describe going through something like a passageway or a vortex. Sometimes that can be dark and frightening. But they're helped by a wise being, like an angel or a teacher like Jesus or Buddha, who guides them to a bright light. Once they're on the other side of this tunnel, they find themselves in a beautiful place filled with even more light and love. Standing there waiting for them are people who have crossed over before them: parents, old friends, children, or wives or husbands." My father's eyes began to flutter, and I paused. He seemed tired, as if he'd already begun to float away. But he was listening.

"What happens next?" he muttered. I continued my narrative. "Then they're shown a review of the lives they lived on Earth. It's not a terrible judgment scene, like in the Bible. Instead, they're shown where they made mistakes. They might feel the pain they caused others, but not in a way that destroys them. They're being shown the lessons of that lifetime. They're also shown all the good things they did to help others. And they're given understanding for why things happened the way they did. And then, because it's not their time to die yet, and they have more work to do and people to take care of, they come back."

The quiet of the night deepened after I'd finished. Even if it hadn't benefited my father, my soliloquy had helped restore my own equilibrium. I began to trust again that forces more intelligent than myself would take care of the things I could not handle. For a minute I thought my father had fallen asleep. Then his eyes flashed open again. "You're lucky you've spent time thinking about God and these kinds of things," he said. "I wish I had. But it's too late." I put my hand on my father's hot and swollen arm. "No, it isn't," I said, with maybe too much passion. "It's not too late. I'll go out and buy some books on angels and near-death experiences. I'll get the Bible and some books on Buddhism and Sufi poetry, and read them out loud to you. We'll talk more about all this."

Joe was quiet. I wondered if the preacher in me had gone too far. Then he asked, "But what do *you* believe happens?" Again, I searched for the words that would convey best what I believed. I wanted to be truthful. But I didn't want to offer cheap hope, either. Death was much too important for that.

"I think that when you die your soul lives on in another place," I said to my father. "I believe that you go on growing and living. That you're surrounded by people you knew on Earth, and also by more advanced beings who are your teachers. I think you study the life you lived and learn from the mistakes you made. And I think you begin learning new things that you didn't get to do on Earth." Joe opened his eyes and looked into mine. "Sounds good to me," he murmured.

"Now go back to sleep," I said. I gave him a hug and crawled back into the hospital bed. As I lay awake, listening to his quiet breathing, I felt thankful for this small but beautiful blessing.

RESURRECTION, CRISIS, AND RESOLUTION

My sister arrived the next day, along with my five-year-old niece. Lily was a precocious little girl with wispy blonde curls and a head full of questions about the dying grandfather that she barely knew. Joe had seemed happy to see her and had insisted on sitting up to greet his granddaughter. She came dancing in to see him, the promise of the Carroll family future sparkling in her eyes. "Well, hello Miss Lily," said Joe. I could see that he was mustering all his strength simply to keep from falling over. Suddenly shy, Lily handed him a drawing she'd made. Joe swayed as he studied the colored picture. "Why now, that's very pretty. Thank you very much. And how old are you, Miss Lily?" As

Lily counted to five, I could see that my father was about to fall over. Taking Lily by the hand, my sister led her from the room. Before long, Joe had slipped back into a weakened state. He barely ate now, and could only take small sips of water.

I began to worry that Joe might not make it to see his two sons, or his older brother, Paul. He lay on his bed, his eyes closed, his chest rising and falling. The next morning, hours before my brothers' arrival, I perched on the bed beside him. "Dad," I whispered, unsure if he could even hear me, "Steve and John are coming in today."

Joe's eyes flew wide open. "Now what are they doing that for?" he sputtered weakly. "They should be working. They have more important things to be doing." For a fleeting moment, the thought occurred to me that my sister and I had work we could have been doing, as well. In fact, all throughout the course of my father's illness he'd leaned heavily on my sister and me, confiding in us the smallest details of his illness. Along with Hilda we knew about his blood pressure, his pulse rate, his bowel movements, his PSA levels, and the gooey phlegm plugging his throat. With my brothers, however, Joe maintained that traditionally staunch brand of manly courage, never mentioning to them his bodily aches and pains.

Leaving my sister to care for my father, I went out to buy groceries and run some errands before my brothers' arrival later that afternoon. After unpacking and putting away the food, I returned to check in on Joe. The sight that greeted me nearly knocked me back into the hallway. Joe was not only up and out of bed. He was standing upright all by himself in the bathroom, carefully shaving himself in the neon-bright mirror. He was even humming merrily. Hilda was running a bath for him, and Colleen was changing the sheets on his bed.

I had just enough time to run back into the kitchen and make a quick call to Andy. "My father's woken up again!" I shouted into the phone, standing outside the sliding glass doors in the kitchen. "He's not dying!" But Andy was coolly unsurprised. "This isn't uncommon," he said. "Sometimes when a person seems like they're on the brink of dying, they get a second wind. We don't know why that happens. Often it's because family is there, and they want to connect and say good-bye.

Could be the news that your brothers were coming was enough to wake him up."

When John and Steven walked into his bedroom later that evening, Joe was waiting for them expectantly. Neatly dressed in a clean shirt and slacks, he was sitting up in bed. He'd even found his voice, if still quavery, again. "You came all the way from Egypt," he said, clasping Steve's hand. "That's halfway around the world. Didn't have to do that. Shouldn't have left work. And John, you must have deadlines. You're busy, both of you. Go on now, get back to work, the both of you." In my father's world, men did not leave their jobs, even for the dying. He had not been by the bedsides of his declining mother, his foster parents, or his brothers or sisters who'd passed on before him. So when my brothers reassured him that they'd come because they wanted to be there, Joe was both bewildered and touched. Not that he could put those feelings into words. "So tell me," he said, "How's business? And how about that stock market? Almost four thousand!"

Joe's eleventh-hour resurrection lasted just long enough for my uncle's visit the next day. When my father's white-haired, burly, eighty-two-year-old big brother walked in the front door, Joe stood stock-still. Paul had always been the sensitive, even maternal, Carroll brother. Now he put his hands over his face and wept at the sight of the four of us. "I remember you when you were little," he said, tears pouring through his fingers. The four of us huddled around him, kissing and hugging him hello. After taking my uncle's bag to his room, I led him back to see my father. Awake and dressed for hours, Joe was sitting on the edge of his bed. As soon as his eyes fell on his older brother, he struggled to get up. Paul crossed the room before my father could rise, avoiding what surely would have been a fall.

"Hello, little brother Joe," my uncle said. He put his hands on my father's shoulders and gently pushed him back down. Paul was not crying now. In fact, I could see that he was being careful to act in a way that would be reassuring to my father. Or maybe he was just trying to act like a man. For he was, I could see, holding back his emotions to pay his respects to Joe's masculine pride. Paul sat down on the bed and took my father's hand in his own comforting large palm. For his part,

Joe was doing his best to act as graciously as he could, and to mark the occasion with the proper hospitality.

"Paul, big brother, good to see you," Joe croaked. He waved his arms in the air, grandly, but with effort, in Hilda's direction. "Bushky, coffee and sandwiches, *por favor*." Soon my father fell completely silent; though he struggled, he couldn't get out a single word. It was a painful sight. "I hear you're not feeling so well," said Paul, as gentle as a parent. Joe nodded like a little boy.

Unable to hold himself in check, Paul's blue Carroll eyes welled up with tears. "I remember you when you were just a baby," said my uncle, submerged in memory. "I used to hold you on my knee and bounce you up and down. You'd smile and laugh." His tears were falling now, running down the crevices in his Florida-brown cheeks. "You were such a cute kid. And then you grew up. And didn't we used to have fun?" My father moved his head up and down, a smile tugging at his lips.

The two old men stared into the space before them, hypnotized by images of the past that only they could see. One by one, everyone in the house filed into the room, sitting on the bed, chairs, the floor, or against the desk. As Joe listened on in silence, we joked, laughed, and reminisced. Over the next several hours we shared coffee, tea, sodas, and sandwiches in companionable warmth. Anyone who has ever sat in a room with a dying person, surrounded by friends and family, eating and drinking as you wait for the end, knows what this curious confluence feels like. It's as if the very presence of death draws to itself and then illuminates, in a shaft of light, the fleeting magnificence of life. As the afternoon faded into evening, my father fell back onto his pillows with a moan and a sigh. With Steve in the hospital bed keeping watch, Joe slept fitfully through the night.

The next morning, as we were all having breakfast in the kitchen, Andy arrived to check on my father. Before long, we'd all drifted down the hallway and into the back bedroom. From one day to the next, my father seemed to have slipped into a coma. He barely opened his eyes now, and didn't even try to speak. All his attention seemed drawn into the process unfolding within him. As we watched Andy check my father's vital signs, I could see my uncle begin to grow agitated. When he'd finished ministering to Joe, Andy stood up and gestured silently for us all to leave, giving my father some time to rest.

I walked into the living room chatting softly with Andy, my uncle and my stepmother following behind. They were talking together heatedly, and I wondered what could be upsetting them so much. Just as Andy stepped into the foyer to leave, Paul whipped around to face me. His arms were angrily crossed in front of his chest. His face was belligerent. "Joe's in pain!" he yelled. My uncle's words were like fire to Hilda's dry brush, and she ignited in fury. "I know, it is true. Joe suffers! It must stop!" she cried hysterically in her lisping English. I felt completely broadsided by this attack. What were they talking about? What could they mean? Now *I* crossed my arms, buttressing my courage and willing myself to remain calm in this latest crisis.

Paul waved his hands in the air before my face. "It isn't right. Joe shouldn't have to die like this. What is this hospice, anyway? All this makes me think of Jack Kevorkian. My little brother shouldn't be allowed to suffer like this. We're just keeping him alive for our own selfish reasons." As he spoke, Hilda wrung her hands in flustered agreement. "Listen to your uncle, Pellman," she said. "Paul is right. Your father must die *con* dignity. We can't keep him alive for us."

I realized with a shock that my uncle and stepmother were talking about euthanasia, about giving Joe a massive dose of pills or drugs to speed his death. I'd always known that this was not something I had it in me to do. The situation felt precarious; the emotions swelling the room could, I know, spin quickly out of control. Then it dawned on me that the truth was right in front of us. "But Joe hasn't asked to die," I said, drawing myself up. "He did, before he was in the hospice program. But then he stopped. The strange thing is that lately he's seemed to want to live, to be with us for a little while longer. He's the one who asked for you to come here. I know he looks terrible, like he's in pain. But Andy says he's not feeling anything because of the morphine. I think we should allow my father to die in his own time."

After I'd finished speaking, my uncle collapsed onto the couch. He put his head in his hands and rubbed his forehead tiredly. "You're right," he said. "Who am I kidding? It's not Joe's death I'm afraid of. It's my own." Hilda, too, quickly deflated, crumpling onto the couch beside Paul.

Throughout this exchange, Andy had stood, listening quietly. As Hilda led my uncle back to his bedroom to rest, I walked Andy out to his Jeep. "You handled that real well," he drawled, flipping open a lighter and touching it to the tip of his cigarette. "I've noticed a lot of older people in that generation are afraid of dying. Suffering, too," he said, taking a drag. "You'd think it wouldn't be like that, after all they've lived through. But I see it a lot." I waved good-bye to our hospice cowboy as he drove off into the bright Texas afternoon.

Over the next couple of days my father slipped in and out of consciousness. All around him, the house vibrated with life. Gloria, Maria, Father Fred, Andy, and the home health aide came and went. The next-door neighbor, Jenny, brought home-cooked casseroles and stayed and visited. The phone was in constant use. Lily danced and played underfoot. My uncle and brothers sat in the living room and talked sports, business, and politics.

By the third day of my uncle's visit, Joe was still in a state of semi-unconsciousness. But it was clear that something was bothering him. His forehead was creased with concentration, his body restless. Seated around the kitchen table, nursing cups of coffee, Father Fred, Andy, my uncle, brothers, sister, and I debated Joe's condition. According to Andy, his restlessness couldn't be caused by physical pain; the high dose of morphine he was on ruled that out. It seemed as if he was hanging on, but why? Furrowing his forehead, Father Fred thought perhaps there was something Joe had left undone. Could any of us, he wondered out loud, think of anything that could be making it difficult for Joe to let go and die?

"What about your mother?" asked Father Fred. I told him the story about Joe's "sorry, sorry, such a bastard" comment on his boorish behavior to my mother during their marriage. Andy brightened. "Has your mother said good-bye to Joe yet?" asked Fred. "Could someone act as a go-between?" The table went silent. Clearly, none of the four of us had any desire to get in the middle of our parents again. Then

Paul leaped up, delighted to have a task. "I'll call Sheila!" he exclaimed excitedly. He began to pace up and down. "I remember when we were young," he said, "and Joe and Sheila and my first wife and I drove from Pennsylvania to Missouri in a white convertible." He stopped, overcome by tears again.

After he'd composed himself, Paul asked to be left alone in the kitchen. From the living room, I could hear his voice as he spoke with my mother. It had been nearly twenty-five years since they'd last talked. Ten minutes later, my uncle hung up the phone and called me back into the kitchen. "I have a message from Sheila to give to Joe," said Paul, his words freighted with the importance of his mission.

Consumed as I was with curiosity, I restrained myself from prying. According to Father Fred, my uncle was bound to confidentiality. Striding down the hall, his head high like a knight on a quest, Paul entered my father's bedroom and closed the door behind him. A long, dense half hour followed. The conversation, I knew, would be one-sided, as my father could not speak. Then the door clicked open. Paul walked past me without a word, headed to his room. Many years later, my mother told me that she'd given my uncle a very simple message for my father: that she'd always loved him, and that she forgave him.

THE FINAL FLIGHT

The next day, Paul, a spent force, declared that he'd done as much as he could to help my father die. He'd made his peace and said his farewells, and it was time to leave. Now that my two brothers had arrived, he said, they could take up the manly duty of caring for my sister, Hilda, and me. His paternal protection was sweet. I felt sad as I hugged my gentle Carroll uncle good-bye. It would be the last time I would see him. He passed several years later.

It was clear now that Joe was actively dying. Save for a few ice chips to moisten his parched lips, he no longer ate or drank. This was a natural step in the process. His organs, said Andy, were shutting down. But this development came as a mortifying blow to my stepmother. To end years of feeding her husband felt like the amputation of her function as a wife. Sitting by Joe's bedside, undone with grief, oblivious now to the fact that Joe was dying, she ignored Andy's advice. "My darling, my darling," she implored, waving spoonfuls of fragrant scrambled eggs and bacon beneath my father's nose. "You must eat. You must get better." But Joe remained nonresponsive, his face a mask of cryptic self-absorption.

The time had come, said Gloria and Maria on their next visit, for us to choose my father's coffin, as well as an urn for his cremated ashes. The job fell to John and me. After being shut inside the house except for the occasional run to the grocery store, getting outside for a drive seemed like a welcome relief.

When I stepped inside the cool interior of the Seaside Funeral Home, I felt as if I'd entered the Model Showroom of Death. Piped-in music played discreetly in the background. Magnificent coffins of every size, shape, and kind of wood hung on the walls. There were burnished mahogany coffins lined with plush red velvet and gleaming brass handles; elegant walnut coffins with beige satin lining; dark cherry coffins with white silk, and so on, each one costing hundreds and even thousands of dollars. It was like looking at middle-class motor homes for the souls of the departed. The gaudy display overwhelmed my heightened senses, as well as my brother's. We exchanged silent, eye-rolling glances. "Maybe Dad was right about that ditch," John whispered in my ear. Against my will, I giggled, feeling rebellious and profane.

The funeral director, dressed in a neat suit, approached us. Cheerfully, yet with just the right tincture of sympathy, he shook our hands. I marveled at his smoothness, honed over years of selling coffins to the bewildered and bereaved. "We'd like something very simple for our father," said John. "Nothing fancy. And we'll need an urn, too." Excusing himself, the director left to get some catalogues and price charts. As we waited for his return, I glanced at the rack of literature next to me. It was stocked with pamphlets on loss and grief. Absentmindedly, I reached for one titled "Facing Death with Faith and Courage."

As I flipped through the pages, a highlighted quote caught my eye. "What people are coming to understand is that, while the process of dying may be scary as we contemplate the end of everything, what we enter into at the moment of death is so magnificent, so beautiful, so full of love, that it's a very powerful source of hope and comfort. There is a beautiful phrase from a tradition which says that if you look at death from afar, its specter is hideous; but when you approach it and see it closely, it has the face of the Beloved." What moving, inspirational words, I thought to myself.

Then I stood rock-still. The quote had come from an article I'd written: "Social psychologist Kenneth Ring, quoted by Pythia Peay in *Common Boundary.*" It was the very article on near-death experiences from which I'd drawn when I discussed the afterlife with my father. My brother's eyes widened in surprise when I showed him the passage, my hands shaking over the words. There we stood in a sanitized American temple of denial. And still, the living force of death had found and fingered us.

The funeral director hurried back into the room with his catalogue and pointed to the luxurious models of coffins and ornate urns. But my brother and I were quick to make our choices. A plain, pine coffin large enough to hold the body of a six-foot-tall man, and a simple urn for his ashes, we knew, was all Joe would want. We wrote a check and left, relieved to be outside again in the humid, salty air.

John was scheduled to return to work the next day. After some time alone with my father to say farewell—it would be unlikely that my younger brother would ever see Dad again—he drove away. With both my brother John and my uncle gone, the house fell still. Joe's party was officially over. There was little to do now but take up our stations, watch, and wait.

That night, Joe's breathing grew more labored, his body more agitated. Sparing Hilda, who was increasingly fragile with sadness and exhaustion, Colleen, Steven, and I took shifts at my father's bedside. By the next day, the tension of not knowing when my father was going to die, or how long his fitful quasi-coma would last, had begun to exact its emotional price. We were all frazzled, on edge with anxiety and sleeplessness.

Late that afternoon, we unexpectedly ran out of morphine. There would be no way Joe could make it through the night pain-free without it. After calling Andy, who phoned in a prescription, I drove to the hospital pharmacy and then stopped to pick up some Mexican takeout food for dinner. Walking into the kitchen, I put the keys down next to the containers of fajitas and tortillas.

Then I realized I'd left Joe's morphine back at the hospital. At half past five, I had only half an hour to make it through rush-hour traffic to get to the pharmacy before it closed for the night. When she saw what I'd done, Hilda snapped with anger. Picking up the car keys, she threw them across the room and then, screaming at me in a fit of panic, began shoving and pushing me out the door. I arrived at the hospital just as the pharmacist was turning the key in the lock. As I drove back, gripping the wheel with trembling fingers, I was overcome with emotion and tiredness. I began to doubt whether I had the strength to make it to my father's end.

Help arrived the next morning, when both Father Fred and Andy showed up within half an hour of each other. Both knew Joe's time was close, and they'd wanted to stop by and check in. After they each took turns sitting with my comatose father—one healer to care for his soul, the other his body—the two joined my siblings and me at the kitchen table. Propping his cane up against the wall, Father Fred sat down heavily, a worried look on his face. "Something's still bothering Joe," he said. "Something is making it hard for him to let go. Is there anything else, any unfinished business that you can think of that might be keeping him here?" he asked, glancing around at each of us.

Starved of rest, my capacity for reflection had reached its limit. But Father Fred was intent on examining Joe's conscience, and he needed us all to reach deep. Together, we ran down my father's checklist. He'd reviewed his past with the hospice social workers, Gloria and Maria. He'd helped settle his will; married Hilda in a Catholic ceremony; assisted in planning his funeral; made peace with his ex-wife; reached out to his four children, old friends, and his brother Gene; and had reunited with his older brother, Paul.

Whenever I'd been on watch, I told Father Fred, I'd continued my middle-of-the-night deathbed readings. My father had appeared to be listening as I read aloud to him from some of the world's religious texts. Sometimes, when I thought he'd fallen asleep and would slow to a stop, he'd mumble a word or two from what I'd just read, as if prompting me to go on. What more could a man of his lights—or any person, for that matter—be asked to do?

Father Fred had even heard Joe's last confession. This had been remarkable, given my father's lifelong distrust of priests and the Catholic Church. Though their exchange had been confidential, Father Fred had told me in a hushed tone that my father had reached some sort of truce with his childhood faith. But afterward, when I'd gone back to see him, Joe had given me a quizzical, skeptical look. "I like Father Fred. But you know I have my problems with the Church, right?" he asked me, as if trying to convey some message still left unsaid. I did, I replied. But then he sighed, and neither of us had said anything more on the topic.

As estranged as I felt from official Catholicism, I was comforted to know that my father would enter death with some spiritual protection. A ship needs its compass, after all. Still, it was clear that things between my father, the Church, and his soul had not been entirely resolved. Now I wondered whether this was what was holding him back. Could it be that he was suffering from the fact that he hadn't found a spiritual path that felt true to him, and that spoke to his own true and different soul? Or was it that he lacked the right relationship to God, whom he might soon find himself facing? But then, maybe that was something I was projecting onto him.

My father also had never apologized for his drinking. Not only that, he'd never even admitted to having a drinking problem. And though he'd expressed great pride in each of his children over these last weeks, he'd never once said that he loved us. In all my life, I could not recall hearing those words from my father's lips. But in these, Joe Carroll's last days, that didn't mean I hadn't felt his love. Accompanying my father as he completed his life's soaring arc, I'd felt abundant love pouring out of him—for me, for each one of my siblings, for his two wives, his brothers, and his parents. And for food, flying, farming, whistling, basketball, the news, coffee, cigarettes, politics, all things Irish, drinking, and all the crazy, wild things he'd ever done. When one reflects on the myth of Icarus, Thomas Moore reminds me, one should not make the mistake of being overly moralistic. For though my father, like the youthful flier, "had the disaster and the terrible crash," he says, Joe also had "the vision and the exhilarating experience."

Feeling the return of my father's love of life despite all the awful things that had befallen him, in fact, had been the single magnificent outcome of all his work. And who knew what he'd finally gotten the courage to put into words, yet had been prevented from saying out loud by his illness? As I sat by my father as his voice had vanished, he'd looked at me sometimes with hurt deep in his eyes, sputtering and straining to speak. In one incandescent moment, he'd sat up straight, stared wide-eyed into the air in front of him, shouted "Ma!"—then fallen back onto his pillow, silent again.

As I watched my father as he wrestled with invisible ghosts, I began to think that he might also be engaged in a practice basic to psychology: *working through*. The term originated with Freud, who endeavored to help his patients sweat out the dross of their neuroses, obsessions, and dark emotions. This was not about suffering simply for its own sake; it was about suffering through to some sort of unvarnished, hard-won self-knowledge: to examine, without defense, who we are and the life we have lived.

I will never know the exact nature of my father's angst in his last days. But I believe that as he faced death, he continued to be haunted by those cast-off, destructive, hungry parts of himself he'd long neglected: the unwanted infant, the traumatized boy, the homesick adolescent, the frightened pilot, the abusive husband, the hurtful drunk, the mad and crazy father, and the lost old man. And by the long trail of broken relationships.

Ironically for my father, the free fall he'd been in all his life had finally come to ground on his deathbed. And yet perhaps the timing was exactly right. "Religious literature is full of debilitating falls and disasters," writes Thomas Moore in *The Soul's Religion*, "all signifying entry into the mysterious and the infinite."

It could also be, too, I thought, that Joe was hanging on because he was afraid to die. In that, my father would have been only human. Even with "the highest personal development and liberation," writes

Ernest Becker, a person comes up against the real despair of the human condition: that after all the years of suffering and experience that goes into the creation of an individual, "we are good only for dying." Even the German poet Rainer Maria Rilke, one of the "greatest experts on death European art had produced," had suffered in his last days.

"If even Rilke—in his final moment," writes the Polish poet and essayist Adam Zagajewski, "does not find support in the fruits of his own spiritual work, does this mean that only a part of life—and a part of death—submits to a spiritual metamorphosis, while a hard, cruel layer hides beneath, indifferent to incantations, words, and images, the eternally frozen earth?" Indeed, does spiritual life, continues Zagajewski, yet leave in us "someone whom we have always been and will be, who does not submit to the transformations of the natural man . . . because he absolutely does not agree to imagining the end, the last sunset, the last supper, the last caress, the last dream, the last cherry"?

For all that I'd done to help turn my father's attention to the afterlife, to heal and raise his suffering up, even I could not imagine his end, could not let go as I knew I should the father with whom, after a lifetime of distances, I'd just begun to feel the delight of uncomplicated closeness. And to whom I wanted to cling as a daughter for just a few more moments. These thoughts were difficult to share that day with those in my father's dying entourage. But my feelings must have traced their design on my face. Sometimes, Andy said, his green eyes intent on my face, the dying hang on for the sake of the living. For that reason, it was important for all of us to begin our own letting go. Then, jumping up from the table, he left quickly. He had to get to another appointment.

Later that afternoon, Andy returned, pulling up in his Jeep. Bursting into the foyer, his cowboy boots tap-dancing on the tile in excitement, he practically shouted in my face. "I've found something to help your father!" he said, waving a cassette tape in the air. "It's called 'Last Flight.' A nurse gave it to me. It's a guided visualization of passengers boarding a plane for the other side." I swallowed hard. Truth be told, it struck me as an awful idea. "Well, it's worth a try," I said, trying to be politic. Going back to the bedroom, Andy checked my father once again. It couldn't be much longer, he said. Perhaps this tape would give Joe, the lone pilot, the boost he needed to come to the end of his life.

That night, after everyone had gone to sleep, I took up my perch on the hospital bed beside Joe. Maybe the tape would be helpful, I thought. It might speak to the aviator-adventurer in him, helping him to soar into unknown horizons. After applying a fresh morphine patch, I pushed the play button on the cassette player. Immediately, a loud, whooshing sound of plane engines readying for takeoff filled the room. Over the sounds of a noisy terminal bustling with the sound of travelers, the smooth voice of a hostess announced that a flight to the other side was ready for boarding. The tape continued, with the hostess showing the passengers—the dying—to their assigned seats. The flight's destination to the afterlife was announced.

As the voiceover continued against the backdrop of airport and airplane noises, my father began to toss and turn. As the plane lifted to takeoff, his agitation grew worse. Finally, his anxiety became so marked I turned off the tape. Who can tell what thoughts and images the tape had stirred in his silent, but obviously aware, mind. Perhaps it had triggered memories of hurrying to the airport, or working through long nights with no sleep as he monitored his aircraft's engines and fuel systems. Maybe it had made him feel late for something, as if he had to rush to get somewhere. Whatever the tape had provoked in him, it had not been peaceful. I knew from my studies of Buddhism that the soul's last thoughts can color its experience as it begins its journey through the landscapes of the next world. As I had done over the last nights, I began to meditate, surrounding my father's body with wide pools of tranquil light. Then, picking up a copy of a book on angelic encounters, I began to read aloud.

All through that night my father labored to breathe. At times, his body twitched and trembled; at times, he lay still, resting. It could not be long, I knew. But how long? Sitting beside Joe, my mind pitched between human and divine. I traversed Dante-esque landscapes of horror, fear, joy, and peace. I wanted my father to die so that his suffering would end; but I also didn't want him to die, and could hardly bear my mounting grief.

The next morning brought another visit from Andy and Father Fred. Hilda, my brother, sister, and I sat mutely over our coffee. The tape hadn't seemed to work, I told Andy. Gracious and philosophical, he said it was hard to know exactly what would speak to the dying person. But my father's fidgeting had made him think. Sometimes, he said, the person is ready to die before the body. The anxiety of a lifetime that has accumulated in the muscles can slow the dying process. If he administered a muscle relaxant to my father, it could help his body release tension, and allow him to let go. It wouldn't make him die, but it could allow death to take place.

Father Fred frowned at this idea. The soul, he said, had its own timing. My father's deathbed struggle meant that his soul was still working something out. We should have patience with this process. The Church did not sanction interfering in death's natural rhythm. Hilda, normally in agreement with Father Fred, now stood solidly with Andy. But I felt torn. I leaned toward Father Fred's side in the debate; I believed that Joe's death should be as natural as possible. But after another hour of discussion, I relented. I began to feel that perhaps my father did need the gentle boost that the tranquilizer could provide him. Eventually, everyone in the family came together on this idea. Even if Andy administered the muscle relaxant, it could still be hours, even longer, before my father died. It was possible that it might not even have an effect.

Father Fred gave his reluctant approval. But before Andy administered the shot, he recommended that we each go in, separately, to say our final good-bye. He advised that we call the rest of the family to let them know that my father was nearer death, as well. Almost immediately, I began to cry. Now that the moment might actually be here, no part of me wanted this to happen. I felt inconsolably sad.

As Andy had the day before, Father Fred now began talking about the importance of letting go of the dying. It was helpful to the person whose life was ending, he counseled, to feel permission from their loved ones to leave. They needed to be released from their obligations to the living. Andy nodded in agreement. Often, he explained, the dying wait to depart until they are completely alone, as they find it easier to slip away while no one is watching.

Andy left to retrieve the tranquilizer and my sister began to call the family. During a conversation with Sheila, she spontaneously handed the phone to my stepmother. By now, all Hilda's hard edges had softened. The two chatted briefly, even laughing together a bit. Somehow, it seemed fitting that, at this moment, Joe's two wives would speak without animus. It wasn't long before Andy returned. He administered the medication, and we went in, one by one, to bid our farewells.

When it came my turn, I perched on my father's bed and wept. Try as I might, I could not get the right words to come out. The approach of the end of Joe Carroll's life seemed to have stripped everything away but the girl who missed her father, who indeed had always missed him. It seemed to me that I had forever been saying farewell to a father who was always just beyond my grasp, always waving good-bye, always leaving for somewhere else. It had been the nature of our relationship, and it would never be otherwise.

Finally, I gathered myself together and said the words that had to be spoken. I loved him. I forgave him for the hurts. I hoped he forgave me for the ways I'd hurt him, too. I thanked him for everything he'd given me. I released him from the bonds of our tie and said his soul would find peace in the next world. And that I would see him again, on the other side. I left the room and, without speaking to anybody, walked out of the house and toward the Gulf shoreline, where I cried myself dry.

When I returned to the house, I bumped into Andy as he was preparing to leave. A primitive fear snaked through my body. "How will I know when my father's dead?" I asked. "When his breathing has stopped," he answered. "Then feel his pulse. When his pulse stops, he's dead. Then call me, and I'll come over, announce the time of death, and then call the coroner."

Then Andy hit his forehead in sudden exasperation. "Damn! I'm not on call tonight!" According to hospice rules, the nurse on duty was required to handle any deaths that came in. Still, Andy said he'd try to find a way around this bureaucratic obstacle. It would help, he said, if I put in a request to hospice headquarters. Andy had been like a midwife to my father's dying process. After everything we'd been through together, it seemed wrong not to have him there at the culmination of all our efforts.

THE LIGHT IN THE DARKNESS

There was little to do after Andy left. My brother went to his room and closed the door. My sister took Lily into the living room and began to read her a story. Hilda, however, began to clean the house. "When your father dies, people will be coming," she said, as she ran the vacuum cleaner over the living room rug. I wasn't sure who these people would be, other than the usual cast of characters who'd been coming in and out of the house for days. But lending a hand, I swept the kitchen floor, loaded the dishwasher, and cleaned the bathroom. The household tasks felt consoling, life's way of mingling the great with the small. As with sweeping and dusting, death seemed no more or less than the daily workings of everyday life.

After I finished my household chores, I turned on the television for Lily, who'd awakened from a nap and wanted to watch cartoons. With a start, I saw that the day before, January 17, a massive earthquake had rocked Japan. Over four thousand people had died. As I watched, I felt bound to the grief of the Japanese bereaved, a devastation magnified so many thousands of times over mine.

I thought of all the earthquake victims who'd been so violently snatched from life, with no chance of saying good-bye to those they loved. As arduous as it had sometimes been for all of us and for my father, it was impossible not to feel grateful for the great care that had gone into his dying. The long, slow ritual of farewell had proved satisfying. Not all of the past had been completely healed. Had that happened, it would have felt too perfect, too out of keeping with my father's character, and even life itself. But green shoots of grace now existed where only hard ground had been before.

Late afternoon wore on into early evening and our vigil continued. An eerie calm descended, as if death's proximity stretched this day forward into an endless future. We shared some stew that Jenny brought over. Hilda made a fresh pot of coffee. Steven returned to his room. Colleen lay down with Lily to read her to sleep. I went back to Joe's bedroom and settled into a chair. I picked up a book on near-death experiences and began to read aloud to my father.

After a while, I stopped. My father had grown more still, his breathing lighter and less labored. A palpable sense of solitude had begun to fill the room, like groundwater quietly seeping into a well. Then I remembered a phone call I'd received from my father after he'd received his diagnosis of incurable cancer. "Yello, Pell," he'd said. "You do that astrological stuff with the stars, don't you?" I did, I said, surprised. "Can you do my chart for me? I want to know what it says." Taken aback, I told Joe that I'd need to know what time he was born. "Eight A.M. sharp. Mum told me. Alrighty then, bring it with you when you come out. Bidey bo now."

At the time, I'd shrunk from the thought of giving my father a reading. I hoped that he might forget. But as soon as I arrived for my visit, Joe asked to see his chart. Reluctantly reaching into my briefcase, I took out the sheet of paper with its colorful, mandala-like circle filled with symbolic markings. When I handed it to Joe, his eyes widened in expectation. "This is a picture of the heavens at the moment of your birth," I cautiously explained. "Astrologers believe that the position of the stars is a map that gives clues to our individual destiny. They show us our strengths and weaknesses, what we're here to learn and accomplish." Joe was unexpectedly quiet, listening in a childlike, eager way to my words.

"So, tell me!" he said. Still hesitant, I launched into my reading, slowly making my way around the circle. I told my father about the planet Jupiter, king of the gods, that joined his Scorpio Sun, and how it had brought him luck and prefigured his larger-than-life experience of travel and exploration. I mentioned his moon in Sagittarius, placement of the journeyer and the "happy wanderer," as well as the nature lover. Lightly skipping over the Saturn that weighed heavily on his Mercury, the planet of communication, I mentioned his fifth house Mars, which gave him his love of risk-taking, romance, and had conferred upon him rebellious, spirited children. I pointed to Uranus, planet of foreign places and free-spirited unconventionality, in his seventh house of marriage. As I continued, I felt a rush of wonder at the way the patterns of my father's life had been laid out for him, even before birth, by the hand of fate. When I finished my journey around the circle of his chart, my father lay back on his pillow with a contented sigh. Often, after being told about their chart, people feel a kind of "rightness with the universe," as all the odd incongruities of their lives fall into a pattern of meaning.

I was glad I'd overcome my hesitation in reading my father his chart. There was symmetry in the idea that he, who'd flown by the stars and the sun all his life, and who'd pointed out the constellations to his children beneath a Missouri summer sky, would upon his death turn to the cosmos for a new kind of mythic direction. I thought, too, of the gifts we receive—even if indirectly—from our parents. Learning to navigate life by the symbolic wisdom encoded in the stars had been my birthright as my aviator-father's daughter.

Steeped in the solitude of the room and these thoughts, I was jarred out of my reverie by Hilda, who sat down in the chair beside me. Sipping from a cup of coffee, she began casually chatting about the early days of her relationship with my father. I felt annoyance rustle through me. I longed to be silent. Now I could feel my own Icarus spirit straining upward, resisting this drag on my attention by petty realities. I wanted to stay present to the movements of my father's soul as it began to leave his body. But even in death, life makes its claims, and I forced myself to listen as Hilda continued to talk. My father, I knew, would want me to be present for her, as well.

"Your father had a terrible temper when we were first together," she said. "But he told me I had a bad temper, too." My frustration level began to increase. I wanted tranquility to surround my father. Not this. "In the beginning, we fought and fought," Hilda continued, smoking a cigarette. "His drinking really bothered me." With effort, I listened, nodding my head, wanting in the worst way to swat away the smoke but resisting out of politeness. "He told me that we shouldn't have a gun in the house because I might shoot him! So then I made up my mind that there would be no more fighting between us. Whenever I got mad, I left the room. And we never fought again."

All through our conversation, I'd kept my eye on my father's chest. Suddenly, it failed to rise. His breathing stopped. His face didn't move. I turned to look at Hilda, who'd paused mid-sentence. We held our own breaths, suspended in an eternity of ticking seconds. When Joe's chest failed to rise again, we moved as one, kneeling on the floor. I picked up my father's wrist and felt a slight pulse. Then, nothing. "He's gone," I said. At these words Hilda threw herself on my father's body. An animal wail of lament rose from her throat. She began making the sign of the cross over my father's face. A jumble of prayers in Spanish and English began pouring from her, along with her tears: "*E nomine Padre*, son . . . our father who art in heaven . . . Hail Mary full of grace."

For myself, I couldn't help it. After the dark night, the sun had come out. I was overcome with joy, flooded with bliss. My father, at last, was free. The great moment had arrived and his suffering was over. The body that had so long shackled him in pain had released him from its grip. The wall beside his bed seemed to open like a window of light. A rush of wings and wind filled the room.

XI

Afterlife and Afterwords

This aristocrat, superb of all instinct,
With death close linked
Had paced the enormous cloud, almost had won
War on the sun;
Till now, like Icarus mid-ocean-drowned,
Hands, wings, are found.
—**Stephen Spender,** *"Icarus"*

HERE IS ONLY ONE force equal to death, and that is life, its wedded opposite. All too soon, the elongated minutes that unfurled with such infinite splendor after my father's last breath were interrupted.

For one thing, there were phone calls to be made. The first and most important call was to hospice. Andy could not record my father's death, said the operator. It would have to be the nurse on duty. Distressed that our father's favorite hospice nurse couldn't be with us, I pleaded. But the operator was unmoved. On the phone afterward, Andy fumed against the bureaucracy of his hospice organization. Then, recollecting himself, he offered his condolences. "You all did a great job with your father," he said. "I'm gonna miss old Joe. What a character!" A subdued Father Fred said he would be praying for Joe and would call the next day to discuss the funeral.

Then there were the calls to our far-flung family: my brother in Dallas; my mother in Kansas, who took the news solemnly and quietly; and my uncle Paul in Florida, who wept, promising to call Uncle Gene. There were calls to my children, and their father and stepmother in Washington, D.C., and to Colleen's husband and son in Los Angeles. Hilda, too, phoned her family in Mexico and notified Jenny next door.

Minutes after she hung up, the doorbell rang. It was Jenny, with a pot of chicken soup and neighborly support. Right behind her on the doorstep was the hospice nurse. Mildred was a kind and capable woman, but new and a stranger to us. Getting on with the business of death, I guided her back to my father's bedroom then returned to the kitchen to make coffee. We'd need the caffeine.

Together we'd decided, with Joe's consent, to allow his body to lie in rest for as long as the legal limit allowed—seven hours. We all agreed to this because we wanted to give his soul time to leave his body. And at my father's age, and in his physical condition, organ donation wasn't an option. My father had died at seven-thirty P.M.; this meant that we would keep our vigil until two-thirty A.M. By the time the hospice nurse had officially pronounced my father dead, filled out all the official forms, and called the morgue, it was well past nine o'clock.

After the nurse left, I went into the living room, where our ample-hearted neighbor was doing her best to entertain my sister and hold my stepmother together. Oddly, a wave of giddiness seemed to have come over the four of us. Neither Hilda, my sister, nor I had ever helped a person die before. At first, we felt light-headed with relief simply to have made it through the experience. Curling up on the couch in the living room, I listened to Jenny as she kept us laughing with her Joe Carroll stories. "When I first met your father I thought he was pretty strange," she confided. "Uptight and such a recluse. But then I came to like him. He was kind of a nut, but interesting, and he'd say the funniest things."

Taking advantage of Jenny's presence, I slipped back into Joe's room. In contrast to the mood in the living room and the ecstasy of the moments immediately following his death, a tender atmosphere, like a field at dusk, now prevailed. A soft lamp cast a glow on my father's newly motionless body. I sat down in the chair where all these nights and days I'd kept up my watch, resolved now to remain by my father's side until the last hour.

Soon, the high I'd been on shifted to a more formal, somber mood. Fear and awe set in as I observed the physical changes death was beginning to work on my father's body. The deep grooves and lines that had marked his jowly visage for decades were ever-so-gently smoothing out. His once-furrowed forehead was becoming high and rounded, as when he was young. The length of his once-restless body grew more peaceful with each passing minute. Joe was not entirely gone, it seemed, but in the process of leaving. This leave-taking was subtle, and proceeded in tiny increments of time, as the life in my father's body gently disentangled itself from its familiar physical abode. This slow separation of spirit from flesh was like watching two old friends parting ways. How paradoxical, I thought, that just as we become reconciled to the limitations of our bodies—to filling the outline of our physical fate—we must quit them.

As my father's body grew ever more pearl and waxen, a dense, dark volume filled the room. I floated in a sea of transitional space, impersonal as the cosmos. As I felt his spirit edging away, it grew on me that my father was never coming back. I'd never hear his voice on the other end of the line, shouting out, "Hey, Pell! So, whaddya have to say?" Never again would he make me laugh with his goofy projects, get a rise out of me with his provocative political remarks, or give me a lift by yelling "Attagirl!" Never again, too, would he hurt me with his drinking or his meanness and verbal abuse. But where had he gone? Where was the father who'd raised me now? What was happening to this person who'd been the ground from which I'd come, and who'd been swallowed up by death?

How sad it was, I began to think, that just as I'd come to love my father as I'd once loved him as a child, Joe Carroll had, again, gone away from me. There would be no return this time. Now he belonged to another region of the universe, a place just out of the line of our physical vision, seen only with the inner eye. Unsettled, I moved to a chair at the foot of his bed. The very fact of my living seemed an intrusion into the sure and steady workings of death.

In the deep quiet, I heard my sister enter the room and sit down beside me. The quality of our waiting was different now than it had been. The clock had struck midnight, and it was, in the poet Emily Dickinson's words, "the hour of lead." I saw us as girls, veiled and praying in the church pews after confession, fingering our rosaries in the incense-scented church interior. Only now it was not our girlish sins we prayed for, but our difficult father's soul. As if from far away, I heard Jenny say goodnight to Hilda and the door click shut behind her. A few minutes later Hilda came into the room, rippling into our pool of silence. I opened my eyes and saw her bend over my father's body.

"PellMUN!" she cried out, straightening. "CollEEN!" My sister and I jumped from our chairs, startled, our solitary watch shattered. "We must close your father's mouth, or they will come and take him with his mouth open!"

My stepmother was right: my father's mouth had fallen slightly ajar. Hilda flew into her closet and began rummaging through her clothes. Sweaters, blouses, shoes, and pants were tossed about in the storm of her search. Eventually, she emerged waving a lime-green, tangerine, and yellow flowered Oscar de la Renta silk scarf in the air. She hurtled across the room to my father's side and bound the designer scarf tightly around Joe's chin, then tied it up with a flourish, so that the ends stuck up in the air like floppy rabbit-ears on his shiny bald head. "There!" she said, patting his face in relief.

The sight of my father with a garishly bright scarf tied around his chin was too much. He looked like some sort of costumed Easter bunny. Horribly, improbably, I began to giggle. So did my sister. We fled the room. I could only hope that my father, with his wit and black humor, got the joke and was somewhere laughing, too.

Hilda was not amused. She followed us into the kitchen, took me by the arm, and shot my sister a dirty look. The two of them had always had a strained relationship; my father's death had only worsened things between them. Hilda marched me down the hallway and my sister followed. Dragging me into my father's bedroom, Hilda slammed the door in my sister's astonished face. "Your father is not ready to be taken away," she announced to me. "His body must be prepared. You and I must do this together."

I knew that my stepmother's fury was keeping her from falling apart, knew that she was disoriented with grief. Torn from the bulky anchor that had moored her for the past fifteen years, she bobbed like a cork on the currents of the new life into which she'd been suddenly plunged. With no wish to start a fight over my father's dead body, and out of respect for her as my stepmother, I surrendered to her wishes. But numbness spread through me. Could I really do this? Father Fred's advice to care for my father's body as if it were the body of Jesus came back to steady me. Uppermost in Hilda's mind, however, was what the undertakers would think of the condition of her husband's body, and how they might judge her, his wife, for any failure of personal hygiene.

Throwing back the sheet and seizing my father's feet, Hilda started back in horror. "*Dios mi!* My God!" she exclaimed. Apparently, although we'd been caring for my father during his illness, his jagged and overgrown toenails had escaped our attention. Hovering over Joe's swollen feet, Hilda began to clip intently. "They cannot see him like this!" she continued, as I gripped my father's ankles. Hilda then removed his diaper and we changed him into a clean pair of pajamas. Next, Hilda tucked a fresh sheet around him, and together we washed his face and hands with a warm washcloth. What I mostly remember, dressing my father's body, is how heavy he was—and the effort it took to heave him. Was this what women had done, I wondered, down through the ages?

By the time we'd finished it was growing close to the hour of departure. Soon, the funeral home would be arriving for my father's body. When the knock finally came, the house had been rendered as soundless as a sepulcher. Lily was asleep, and Steven, who'd remained grieving in his room through the evening, elected to be alone. I opened the door to a solemn-faced crew of four undertakers. They entered in their neat uniforms, speaking only in whispers as they wheeled the gurney into my father's room. So far, I had attended every stage of my father's dying. But this handling of my father's body I could not bear to watch, nor could Hilda or my sister. Soon they emerged, my father encased in a long, wide, emerald-green body bag. Carefully, the four eased the gurney out the front door and into the waiting ambulance. As I closed the door, not one thing more remained to be said or done. I collapsed into bed and fell into a timeless sleep.

I awoke late the next morning. Sunshine streamed into the house. In the kitchen, I made coffee and stared mindlessly out the window at

Joe's boat bobbing in the sparkling cove. Now that he was gone, I'd have to make arrangements for the boat's title to be transferred to his neighbor, Frank. This was as my father had wished. Once, while drunk, he'd stumbled and fallen overboard. He'd been saved from drowning just in time by Frank, who'd been looking out his window from his house next door. Frank had dived into the water, pulled my father ashore, administered CPR, and called the ambulance.

Yes, it would feel good, I began to think, to draw my father's life to a close and return to my own. I began to realize how removed I'd been these last months from the world, and all the things around which my life turned: my writing, my sons, my friends, my books, politics, gardening, my long walks, my dogs, the coziness of my little house. The mug felt warm in my hands; through it and the morning sun I could feel energy flowing back into me. Colleen, then Steven, came in, and each silently poured a cup of coffee. Together, the three of us sat in the balm of the beginning day. We said little, taking in like medicine the ordinary, uncomplicated delight of being alive. Trying on a day without Joe.

Then a loud sound split the air. The three of us ran into the living room. Hilda, still in her nightgown, had thrown herself on the floor. Out of habit, she'd awakened and gone into my father's room. Praying aloud in Spanish, she was crossing herself again and again. "He is gone!" she cried out, throwing her arms around my ankles and weeping. "He is gone!"

THE FUNERAL

There are three parts to a Catholic funeral: the vigil, or wake; the funeral Mass; and last, the burial, or the final commitment—in this case, cremation. Joe's vigil was held at the Seaside Memorial Park and Funeral Home on the evening of January 20, two days after he'd died. My three sons had flown in the night before, along with my younger brother and the rest of my sister's family. To see my children after these long weeks and months of caring for my father felt like heaven on earth. Maybe it was the proximity to age, death, and decay; but the normalcy they brought with them—their joking and horsing around, and their awkward, protective sweetness toward me—was stabilizing. They were the signs of life going forward, returned to me. Now, at the vigil, with all of the Carrolls seated before my father's coffin, Father Fred led our family in prayers and a recitation of the Rosary.

At eight o'clock the next morning, the family, up early and dressed in our dark, funeral best, split up into two cars: Joe's black Lincoln Continental and his beloved yellow Mercedes-Benz station wagon. We crossed the bridge that led from South Padre Island, where my father's house was located, and headed to Father Fred's parish in a small town on the Gulf.

In our funeral cortège of just two cars, we drove along the commercial strip that had by now become so familiar to me. There were Red Lobster and Olive Garden, Joe's favorite restaurants. There was Target, Walmart, and K-Mart, where I'd shopped with Hilda for my father's favorite stretch pants, which as he used to say gave him room to eat more, and where we'd picked out irons, towels, and children's clothes for her family in Mexico. Leaving this area behind, we began to wind our way among elegant neighborhoods of large and stately homes with landscaped lawns. This area gradually gave way to tree-lined developments with neatly squared suburban family homes. As these faded into our rearview mirrors, we entered an area of nondescript commercial warehouses and run-down apartment buildings. Out the tinted window of Joe's town car, I gazed at worn-looking tract houses with scruffy lawns. Dented pickup trucks and old cars lined the curb.

We crossed the railroad tracks leaving town, and I felt Hilda stiffen beside me. Those pedestrians who were out at that early hour stopped to gawk at the unlikely sight of the two fancy cars with their formally dressed occupants. It sunk in that Joe's service was taking place in a barrio, on the poor side of the tracks where the illegal and immigrant laborers lived.

After we parked, John took Hilda's arm and led the family inside. Entering the interior of Father Fred's church, I could see that it was a reflection of his own vibrant personality, a jewel of color and warmth. Murals of Christ's Stations of the Cross and images of the Virgin of Guadalupe painted in bright corals, greens, and blues decorated the walls, reminding me of the churches I'd visited in Guadalajara. The small domed ceiling over the altar enclosed and uplifted at the same time.

I lowered my gaze as we filed up to the front of the church and saw with a jolt that it was entirely empty. Rows and rows of wooden pews, their kneeling benches closed up, stood without worshipers. Nearing the front, I saw with relief two people sitting on the left side of the aisle: our neighbor Jenny, and the tall, white-haired widow down the street who'd also sent some meals over. We'd invited our hospice team, Gloria, Maria, and Andy. But they'd declined. It was impossible, they said, to attend the funerals of all those they cared for.

I understood. But the unpeopled church struck hard. I'd forgotten that my father's funeral would be different this way, that it would lack the usual attendees of coworkers, friends, church and club members, and extended family. The echoing hollowness reflected as nothing else ever had the life my father had led: a life lived on the run, never settling, never joining, always passing through, always on the fringe of things. I smiled bravely at our two neighbors as I walked by, glad at least for their presence. Hilda, my sister, my niece Lily, and I sat down in the first pew; the men in the family lined up in their dark suits behind us.

Then Father Fred swept out, his full white robes swaying behind him. The long ivory mantle draped around his neck was embellished with panels of traditional Mexican weavings and the roses and image of the Virgin of Guadalupe. His walnut-brown face with the large glasses and twinkling eyes that I'd grown so fond of was radiant. The empty church made no difference to him; indeed, he'd entered into his role with all the drama of a great actor before a packed theater. More than that, his sparkling spirit charged the air around us. And who was I, after all, to judge the scarce audience who sat before him? Was the measure of a man's life only in the number of people who mourned him? For all I knew, guests invisible to my eyes—Joe's departed grandparents, mother, father, sisters, brothers, and wartime and TWA flying buddies—crowded around us.

As Father Fred raised his hand, a bell tolled. I watched as two young attendants wheeled my father's casket to the front, stopping just short of the sanctuary. Stepping forward into the aisle, Father Fred "received" it, according to custom, with a special blessing. Returning to the sanctuary, he began to recite the liturgy, lifting us on his words.

Only my sister and I would speak for my father. After Communion, Colleen stood behind the microphone and recited two poems: "Do not go gentle into that good night," by Dylan Thomas, my father's favorite poem, and "It was not Death, for I stood up," by Emily Dickinson. Then, looking out at the rows of nearly vacant pews, I told the story of how, as a young girl growing up, I'd awaken early before my father's trips. How, leaning out my windowsill, I'd wave good-bye to him as he headed down the driveway. This, I concluded, whispering hoarsely through tears, would be my last wave to my father.

When I'd finished, Father Fred and the young man who was his assistant began to sing. Strumming their guitars, they turned toward each other joyfully, raised their faces heavenward, and sang out their hearts. I felt grateful for their faith and for their largeness of spirit. The church echoed to the dome with the sound of the psalm, "His Eye Is on the Sparrow," inspired by a passage from the Gospel of Matthew (6:26):

> Why should I feel discouraged, why should the shadows come,
> Why should my heart be lonely, and long for heaven and home,
> When Jesus is my portion? My constant friend is He:
> His eye is on the sparrow, and I know He watches me;
> His eye is on the sparrow, and I know He watches me.
> *I sing because I'm happy, I sing because I'm free,*
> *For his eye is on the sparrow, and I know he watches me.*

Father Fred sang to the cavernous church as though the pews were packed with rapt worshipers. I thought of the stories told of the Sufi dervishes. Gathering in graveyards as a reminder of the eternal reality behind life, dressed in tattered robes to signify their renunciation of the world, the dervish mystics would chant themselves into an ecstatic trance. In that state of consciousness, they'd greet one another as kings—because no matter their wealth or social standing, they recognized the Divine in one another.

He may have been Catholic, but Father Fred, handicapped priest to the outcast immigrants and day laborers, had to me the soul of a dervish. In the end, it could not have been a more fine and fitting funeral for my father. The shabby neighborhood, the barrio parish, the reproachful pews, and Joe's lonely and alcoholic soul made no difference to God, because, if I'd understood all the spiritual teachings I'd studied over the years, my father was loved all the more because of the cracked and broken places he'd been to over the course of his Icarus life. And because, in the end, he'd tried to understand, to mend what he could, and to be just a bit better. The heartbroken, vacant church on the wrong side of the tracks may have seemed a dismal place from a conventional viewpoint. But from the angle of my soul's eye, it was filled to the rafters with beauty.

Afterward, except for Hilda, who claimed to be tired, we all went out for a late lunch. Following the funeral, the shroud that had covered us began to lift. I understood now the purpose of all those ancient rites, where the bereaved bury their loved ones with provisions to accompany them into the afterworld. Such rituals are tools by which we can go on feeding and protecting the departed, suddenly so far removed from our human care.

And though I'd felt my father would never return from this final journey—well, I was wrong about that. Later that night, my father appeared in a dream. He was a young man, slender, with a full head of hair, and bursting with energy. We were standing together in a school hallway beside some stairs, outside a classroom. Overcome with emotion to see him again, I called out "Dad!" and then asked him how he was. He was fine, he said, but very busy. He had to get going and couldn't talk, as he was late for a class. He'd enrolled in music school, he told me excitedly, waving a sheet of music, and was learning to sing and play an instrument.

I could not have imagined a better transition to a new life.

Joe's "final commitment" took place two days later. When the call came from the crematorium that Joe's ashes were ready to be picked up, I phoned Father Fred. He'd be over later that afternoon, he told me. When his van pulled up, we all piled in. Our mood was even lighter now. As much as the poignant church service had meant, we knew this was the part that Joe would have loved the best.

Driving a little way down the road that wound along the Gulf Coast, we pulled up to a small promontory. At various times, we'd all made our escapes to this overlook. Here at the joint of sky and ocean we'd regained our sanity and perspective. As I stepped out of the van, the air blew wet and salty on my face. The sky scudded with clouds; wind shirred the gray water into silver scallops. After taking out the urn that held Joe's ashes, and the dozen yellow roses we'd brought with us, we made our way out to the water's edge. In the photo I have of that moment, we form a small phalanx, led by a limping Father Fred. Heads down, we face into the strong January winds whipping at our clothes.

Once we'd arrived at the edge of the embankment, Father Fred opened his large book, *The Order of Christian Funerals*. He arranged his mantle around his neck—the same one he'd worn during the funeral mass—and we took our places before him. As we bowed our heads beneath the bowl of sky, Fred read aloud the liturgy of final commendation. There is something about praying outdoors that gives wing to spoken words.

When Father Fred had concluded, I held up the plain, sealed metal urn containing my father's ashes. According to Catholic doctrine, which apparently does not look favorably on cremation, the body should remain intact at death. Joe had not liked this; true to his airman's nature, he'd wanted his ashes scattered. But in the end, to please Hilda, he'd worked out this compromise with Father Fred. Standing before me, Hilda held her hands over the urn, bent her head, and prayed her last words of farewell to Joe.

When she finished, I recited a prayer from my Sufi tradition: "May the blessings of God be upon you," I said, holding the image of my father before me. "May His peace abide with you, may His presence illuminate your soul, now and forever more." With that, I handed the box to my teenage son, Amir. Stepping out onto the edge of wet sand as far as he could go, he leaned back. Tall and lean, with Carroll blue eyes, my middle son, I realized with a shock, was the very image of the young Joe. Amir brought his arm forward and tossed my father's ashes far out into the deep waters of the Gulf of Mexico. As the urn sunk from sight, we all raced to the edge and threw our flowers in after my father, calling out our good-byes. I still have the photo of the scattered yellow roses, hastened by wind and current to the horizon's edge between sea and sky.

Icarus had fallen.

Visitation

After a brief trip back home, I returned to Corpus Christi one last time. As executor of Joe's estate, I had to appear in court, put his house on the market, sell his car, liquidate his stocks, and disperse any remaining possessions that my stepmother didn't want. My trip would overlap with Hilda's departure to Mexico by three days. I'd said farewell to my father; now it was time to repeat the rite with her.

As I walked in the front door, the house felt empty, swept clean of my father's presence. A wan and puffy-eyed Hilda greeted me with a tired hug. I put my bags in the back bedroom and the telephone rang. "Y'all going to be home?" asked a pleasant-sounding man. "I'd like to take a look at that Lincoln." I'd put an ad in the local paper the night before but hadn't expected such a quick response. About an hour later, I heard the sound of a car pull up in front of the house.

Two middle-aged couples climbed out of a Mercedes-Benz sedan. The men wore cowboy hats, and big silver buckles gleamed on their leather belts. Their wives were dressed in brightly colored athletic outfits. I'd already pulled the car out into the driveway. Immediately, one of the men crossed to the car and began looking it over, kicking the tires and squeezing the leather upholstery inside. The shorter of the two men, dressed in a blue polo shirt, walked over to where I was standing. Just as he approached, the door to the house opened and Hilda stepped outside. As she shook out a rug, staring intently in our direction, the man turned to me and put out his hand. "Howdy," he said, giving me a cheery shake. Then he jerked his head toward the house. "That your maid?"

I bristled, withdrawing my hand. "No," I said, offended. "That's my stepmother." The visitor had the grace to look ashamed, but only briefly. What he said next stopped the sun overhead. "Name's Joe Carroll. That's a real pretty car. It looks like it's in good condition. What's the mileage?" The man had to be kidding, I thought, in my confusion. I'd mentioned in the ad that the sale was due to a death in the family. Had he looked at the obituaries, then figured out that it was my father's car? But what kind of weird joke was it to introduce himself using my father's name? A cold chill settled over me.

"You're joking, right?" I said out loud, laughing just a little. The stranger squinted at me from beneath the rim of his hat. "What do you mean?" he asked. Then I looked at the signature neatly embroidered over the pocket on his polo shirt: Joe Carroll.

"I'm sorry," I said, as stunned as I've ever been in my life. "Joe Carroll was my father's name, too." The living Mr. Carroll stepped back, his face now colorless in the warm light. "You mean, your father, he's the one who just died?" I nodded my head. "His name is on the title of the car?" I nodded again. "He drove this car?" Yes, I said. But not for very long. "You know, this is a very nice town car, but I don't think it's right for me," said my ghostly visitor. Then he turned on his heel, gathered up his wife and friends, and jumped behind the wheel of his Mercedes. Except for Andy's Jeep, I'd never seen a car drive so fast down my father's quiet suburban street.

Back inside the house, I sat down. The eerie encounter had been like an electrical storm, flipping all my switches. When Hilda came in to ask if I'd sold the Lincoln, I told her what had happened. Her eyes grew wide, and she sat down, frightened. Ghosts were very real to my stepmother, as all of us knew. Sometimes, during the worst of our most wicked, barbaric moments, the four of us would joke that, after my father's death, we'd tease Hilda by calling her and pretending to be Joe speaking from the dead. But now our macabre joke was on me; it seemed that my father had found a way to speak from beyond his watery grave. My stepmother shook her head with great solemnity. "It is your father," she said, with conviction. I didn't doubt her for a second. What were the odds that another Joe Carroll in Corpus Christi would answer the ad for my father's car?

For the next several days, I continued methodically sorting through the piles of my father's papers, as Hilda packed. Because she'd always considered the house in Corpus Christi a kind of way station, my stepmother had never really settled in. Aside from some scattered family photos and Mexican pottery, there was little in the way of those personal touches that make a house a home. Nor was Hilda interested in taking much with her, having already decorated and furnished the house that was waiting for her in Mexico.

On the evening before she was due to fly out, Hilda and I decided to go out for a farewell dinner. We drove to a restaurant by the Gulf and sat outside on a deck overlooking the ocean. I'd held up pretty well so far, but the stress had started to get to me. I wasn't proud of myself, but I'd taken up smoking cigarettes—not many, just one or two at night. Now, on our last night together, Hilda and I ordered a bottle of wine. Soon we were smoking, drinking, and talking as if we were never going to see each other again. But then again, we weren't.

In the beginning, our conversation was light. We talked about her sisters, her son, whom she missed very much, and my own kids. She reminisced about visits she and my father had made to see my family over the years. As she began to speak fondly of my ex-husband, her tone changed. Leaning in across the table, she put her hand on mine. I braced myself, sure of what was to come next. "Why don't you remarry?" she asked. "Your father was so upset when you got divorced. He told me he wished you would find someone to take care of you. It made him sad to think of you alone, as he was dying."

I sighed and leaned back in my chair. It hurt to think that I'd made my father worry. I knew he'd been confused when Terry and I had separated, as he was the kind of man any father would have wished for his daughter. But we'd met young, at nineteen and twenty, both of us from families headed by an alcoholic father, swept up in the counter-culture and looking to each other for safe harbor. And although I was a very involved mother, it seemed, as I was just beginning to discover in the years after my divorce, that something in me could not fit into marriage. I had a solid relationship with Terry and his second wife, Anne, around our sons, and I felt satisfied with my family life. But

Hilda would have understood none of this. "I would like to remarry," I finally said. "It just hasn't worked out that way. But I'm happy with my life as it is."

Hilda pursed her lips and looked downcast. I knew that nothing I could say would dissuade her from thinking of me as living half a life because I was single. Then she leaned in close again. "I have something to tell you," she said, in a confessional tone. "I know that you loved your father very much. And I think"—here her eyes widened dramatically—"that you loved him more than the others."

Shocked at this statement, I protested; it certainly wasn't true. Perhaps she was trying to make up for having just made me feel badly. "I saw you cry, and I know you suffered like I did when your father died," Hilda insisted. "You are a good daughter. I know that you loved him the most." But Hilda wasn't finished yet, and she pushed on. "There is one more thing, very important, that I have to ask you," she continued, pausing to take a long drag from her Benson & Hedges Menthol Light. "I want you to promise me something. Promise me that you will change your name back to Pellman. You must do this last thing for your father."

This was something I had not seen coming. For a brief moment, I toyed with the idea of going along with this wish. How would my stepmother ever know the difference, after all? Maybe it would make up for having disappointed my father by divorcing and not remarrying. But in the end, I knew I couldn't even pretend to do what Hilda had asked of me. In the beginning, it was true, I'd forsaken my birth name and taken a new one to escape the heavy yoke that Joe had put on me. But the name that I'd gone by for nearly twenty-five years was now wedded to the life I'd created for myself. If my father's death had taught me anything, it was to be true to the life I wanted to live.

"I'm so sorry, I can't," I said, finally. I tried to explain the burden of the history that came with carrying the name Pellman. I tried to tell my stepmother that Pythia was my professional writing name, the name everyone knew me by, the name even my mother and siblings used. But it wasn't the answer Hilda wanted to hear. She leaned in again, insistent on accomplishing this last mission for Joe. "Your father told me that he never understood why you changed your name. He said he wished you would go back to the name he gave you. You must do this in his honor. It is the name that your father gave to you," she said, hard anger edging her voice. But something immovable in me would not concede to her, or my father's, demand. "No," I said. "I won't. I can't." Hilda sat back in her chair, and let out a long, disappointed sigh. "Well, okay," she said, turning up her hands. "You will be who you will be." Yes, I thought, so I would.

The next morning, I helped Hilda take her suitcases, bulging with stuff, outside. I'd offered to drive her to the airport. But she insisted on letting our neighbor Jenny take her instead. Standing in the driveway, I hugged my stepmother good-bye. For a brief moment, we stood looking at each other. Tears glinted, almost fell. Then Hilda climbed in the front seat of Jenny's car, and they drove off as I stood in the middle of the street waving. It was the last time I would ever see her. The several times I tried calling her in the months that followed she spoke only in Spanish and stumbled awkwardly upon hearing my name, as if she didn't know who I was or couldn't understand what I was saying. Then the receiver would click and the line fall silent.

After my stepmother left, I resumed clearing away the remnants of my father's life. Anyone who has ever emptied a closet, a room, or a house after the death of a loved one knows this ritual. They know the feeling that guts your heart as you sort through the material remains of a human life: the shapeless sweaters; the dry-cleaned suits standing in rows; the knife set short of two pieces; the freezer full of chicken, hamburger, and coffee; the kitschy wrought-iron clock on the wall; the challenge of what to store, give away, or sell in the estate sale. They know the catch in the throat that comes with stumbling upon the shabby little thing that is completely lacking in financial or historical value, and yet is somehow powerful in its capacity to dredge up grief and memory.

For me, this first occurred when I was cleaning out my father's bathroom cabinet. Tucked in among the Vaseline, Xanax, and Alka-

Seltzer were two sets of dentures. They looked so forlorn, sitting there. How had I forgotten that my father had lost all his teeth? According to my mother, when we kids were young, the dentist had told Joe that he had gingivitis and should have a few teeth removed. Going for the extreme, as my father did, he decided to check himself into the hospital and have all his teeth pulled, all at once. When my mother went to pick him up after the operation, she said, the nurses had told her that Joe had reacted strongly to the pain medication. "What a wild and crazy guy he is!" they'd said, laughing. Now it seemed wrong to throw out these fixtures of his life. But I couldn't keep them, either. In the end, I did the sensible thing. I threw the grinning teeth into a garbage bag and tied it shut.

Then there was the green satin Boston Celtics basketball cap, with the mischievous Irish leprechaun embroidered on it. I found this stuffed in a corner on the top shelf of his closet. Joe had loved the Irish in him, as I'd loved the Irish in him, too. It wasn't anything special, but I kept the cap, as I also saved his scratched reading glasses, his made-in-Ireland white wool cardigan, his broken Seiko watch, his TWA wings, his passports, and his pressed handkerchiefs.

I kept, too, the framed certificate marking his twenty-fifth anniversary with TWA, as well as the stacks of Christmas and birthday greetings the four of us had sent to him through the years. We'd meant more to him than I'd ever realized, I thought. There were things to box up and ship out: the engraved leather children's riding saddle my father had kept from the farm, and that he'd wanted my sister to have; the TWA cap and Tiffany key chain with the globe on it we'd given him for his birthday, for Steve. Joe had wanted John to have the yellow Mercedes station wagon that had so often crossed the border between Texas and Mexico, despite the fact that it was always breaking down.

Last of all was Joe's TWA uniform. That year, 1995, TWA declared bankruptcy. Though it would emerge with big plans to succeed, the iconic airline would be sold in 2001 to American Airlines. For me, TWA would forever be linked to my father and the airfaring tradition that shaped his life so fatefully. When I found his old uniform at the back of his closet, I buried my face in its pressed, dry-cleaned, dark folds, breathing in the scent of my father's travels and the memories of a long-ago childhood on a farm in Missouri. I brought it home with me, too. Sometimes, now, when I glance at it, I swear I can hear my father whistling, getting ready to leave on his next trip.

AFTERTHOUGHTS

As I come to the end of my journey into the heartland of my father's American life, I can say that I have come to know him—not completely, for there is something unknowable at the core of each human being. But reassembling Joe Carroll's life into a narrative has brought him down from the sky to human scale. A real man now stands in the place of the larger-than-life, Icarus-winged "Father" who shadowed me for so long.

The man I've come to know was a member of the Greatest Generation, and yet he stood a little apart. A creature of contrasts, he was rancorous, ornery, and rough; as well as inquisitive, affable, and intelligent. He talked in endless streams; he sat as silent as a sphinx. He was both far greater and more interesting—and far worse—than I ever imagined. He was victorious; he was a tragedy. He died and came to life again many times over, until I finally learned that our parents never really die, even after we bury them.

Where once I judged my father through an unforgiving moral lens, I view him now with more feeling. The hurt and crippling consequences I suffered as the daughter of an unapologetic, narcissistic alcoholic still remain. But living through the events of his life, from before birth to death, has educated my heart, allowing me to see through the defenses Joe had erected around his own. With the help of those therapists who assisted me, I've become more adept at taking in the good parts of my father and understanding the bad. The difficult aspect was learning how to do this without splitting the two in half, favoring one side and repressing the other.

I have learned that reflected in the glass of my father's addiction were longings for a mother's love; cravings to sleep in peace; a hunger for joy; a dreamy, musical imagination; and a yearning for spiritual transcendence. In his troubling exhibitionism was despair over not being cherished: a plea to be made visible in his parents' blinkered eyes, to be birthed from chaos into existence; a shout-out to the world to be special; and even a reveling in the physicality of his human body. In his desire to be a farmer was a humble attempt to fold his wings and come to ground in the permanence of a home he'd never had. In my father's flight patterns could be read both escape from a world he couldn't handle, as well as a daring reach for ecstasy and a dream that lay just over the horizon, but which he could never quite touch. For though the sky-seeking part of Joe aimed toward the sun, the earthbound part of him was inevitably pulled downward by the wound that would never heal. I learned from my father, who lived with one eye perpetually trained on the horizon, that a person should strive to live the kind of life that one should want to expand but never escape.

In coming to know my father better, I've also come to know myself more fully. Know thy parents, in other words, and know thyself. With a father like mine, this has not been easy. The fathers of the Greatest Generation and their fathers before them are, to a greater or lesser degree, the weakest link in modern family life. Because their inner stories were written in a different language than the language of their times, illegible even to them, it takes work to retrieve, translate, and reassemble the fragments of their experiences into some kind of intelligible pattern. But however little we have to go on, and however present or absent he was, each father story carries a piece of our own personal and cultural identity.

Through reliving my father's life, I also reexperienced my childhood. I discovered in myself the girl who was always trying to heal her father, always trying to fill the empty spaces inside of him, and always trying to resurrect his alcohol-numbed spirit. I found in me the girl who was scared of anger, both in herself and in others, and who, though she tried to connect, was so flooded by the wild, lush, and extreme emotions of her family that she had to close the doors of her heart in order to survive. This girl had a psyche that was too permeable to the moods of others. These parts of my childhood self carried over into adulthood, and made relationships difficult.

I didn't become an alcoholic like my father. But the same careening, up-and-down moods live on in my psyche. In my dreams, planes crash and take off again; I trek through frozen landscapes, hang from cliffs, and tremble on the edge of high peaks and yawning spaces. I scale mountains, only to fall back to the bottom. Veering between paralyzing uncertainty and unbounded optimism, I seek always the golden mean. Without the measured, creative life I've constructed for myself, it's possible I'd be on antidepressants.

Still, like my father, I can be a risk-taker. Where money is concerned, I've taken too many leaps into the unknown in favor of my creativity, ending up with little financial security and disappointing my family. Even as I've written about the dangers of the Icarus myth, this very book has been a risky flight to a creative height. Just like my father, I am a loner, and fit into the world differently than most. Anyone who knows me is familiar with my maddening stubbornness, a certain indifference to how the rest of the world lives, and a willful commitment to following my own path—all traits that belonged to my father.

Some of the ways I've been shaped by my father have been reactionary, though, and also show the ways we were truly different. Despite my early love of flying, I never became much of a traveler. I lack the physical constitution for it, and truthfully, it hasn't held much interest for me. I have a fear of heights, a distrust of tall buildings, and a need to stay close to the ground. Unlike my sensation-seeking, hard-drinking father—or because of him—I don't like change. I crave rhythm, order, continuity, and repetitive sameness in my daily life. Though like my father I tend toward introversion, unlike him I have a circle of friends who bear with my eccentricities, and I am close with my family.

Then there is the uncomfortably psychic part of me that sometimes dreams of things before they happen, even death. My father's childhood trauma was my childhood trauma. As a girl I felt keenly my grandfather's death and grandmother's grief, absorbed through my father's suffering. All this constellated in me an almost eerie attunement to the supernatural through dreams and precognitions, and sensitivity for spirit. These psychic senses were strongly activated during the events surrounding my father's own illness and death.

I've also learned through telling both my parents' stories that, as the novelist William Faulkner noted, "The past is never dead. It's not even past." Or, as Michael Conforti puts it, "You can never really leave home. Wherever you go, you always carry that piece with you." Yet though the past contains our origins, Conforti says, "it's not all of who we are." To consider the ways in which we are both our past and yet more than that is one of the more interesting explorations a person can undertake.

An image from my childhood speaks to the abiding satisfaction that can come from working with our personal history. Deep in the woods on the farm in Missouri where I grew up was an old, wooden foundation. Probably at one time a barn or a shed had stood there; all that remained was a square floor. Something about this platform of weathered and decaying wood drew me to it. Lying on the moss-covered planks, staring up at the treetops above, feeling the stratified earth beneath my back, I'd daydream about what had stood there before. But the stripped-down foundation also inspired dreams of the future—the house I'd build there for myself one day, the adult I'd be, the places I'd go and the things I'd accomplish.

Our past is like this old foundation, providing a specific structure and undergirding to our life. Perhaps the foundation we inherit is fine as it is; perhaps it needs repairing and fortifying. Or perhaps there are ongoing problems, like termites or creeping ivy, which require our continued attention. Maybe the house we've built on this faulty foundation needs to be torn down or remodeled. But once these tasks are completed, we can begin to design and build our own structure on its secured base.

This is also a description of depth-oriented psychotherapy, through which a partially built, shaky inner psychic structure is explored and gradually strengthened. The psychoanalyst Heinz Kohut, for instance, described a successful analysis as one in which the data which have been collected become ordered and fitted together into a deeper knowledge of the patient's mind and of the continuity that exists between the present and the past. At the end of a good analysis, he writes, "the analyst's knowledge and the patient's understanding of himself have taken on the quality of *wisdom*." Yet even at this final stage, Kohut goes on to say, this hard-earned self-knowledge is incomplete, as both the patient and analyst recognize that not everything has been solved, and that some of the old conflicts and symptoms remain. These frailties, however, he concludes, "are now familiar and they can be contemplated with tolerance and composure."

As I have also learned, our shortcomings and frailties carry within them a seed of purpose and destiny. "Pathology is the model that talks about what is wrong in us, and that deviates from the cultural norm," explains Michael Conforti. "Yet within the symptom is also a drive from the psyche toward a more creative or fulfilling direction." Out of our vulnerabilities, Freud said, will come our strengths. Lionel Corbett adds that for reasons unknown to us, "we end up with the family that best corresponds to our innate gifts," and that "the events that happen to us in childhood act to trigger those potentials."

Seeing my past this way helps me to better understand the double-sided legacy of my father's life. To put it simply, I can see how something meaningful came out of circumstances that at times felt nearly impossible to bear. For though growing up a Carroll bent me differently, it also fired in me endurance for the difficult. I have survived endless emotional crises and I am good at not falling apart under stress.

Without the sass and courage I inherited from my adventure-seeking father I would never have dared to put this self-disclosing family story onto paper. Without growing up on a farm, far from city life and steeped in nature, I wouldn't have been gifted with a love of solitude, a prerequisite for being a writer and a thinker. Without the atmosphere of ceaseless anxiety caused by my father's drinking, I'd never have turned inward and discovered the treasures within my imagination, and the stability of an ever-constant spiritual dimension. Without the crash course in madness I received in childhood, I'd never have delved into psychology and the intriguing world of the soul. Without my sensitivity to my father's pain, I wouldn't have compassion for the suffering of others.

Contending with my past has also hammered my youthful, zealous spirituality into something more serviceable and related to life. As the old hymn goes, it's brought me down to the place just right. I have as much appreciation now for the spirit of gravity as for the heights of spirit. Given my nature and background, I am cautious about meditation practices that take me away from the things of this world into a transcendent space. Because I naturally tend upward, I am careful to focus downward instead on the cycles of nature, the sacred in everyday life, the hard work of creativity and love, and the weight of being human. I haven't given up on my dreams and ideals. But having learned the lessons of Icarus from the sacrifices of my father—and from my own crashes—I take it slower now, and try not to get too far ahead of myself.

And what of America, that force of freedom and heroic individualism that shaped my father? In fleshing out Joe Carroll's life, I've also come to know better the character and psychological influences of my country, as if America, too, had undergone analysis in the process of writing this book.

I've learned that my cultural parent is noble, high-minded, daring, and forgiving. It is capable of tremendous sacrifice and astounding achievement. It is possessed of a generous soul. It is a beautiful dreamer and has as its motto the promise of a better life and freedom for everyone. It is independent to a fault. It aspires to live and let live. It bubbles with creativity: in writers, musicians, artists, entrepreneurs, and filmmakers. Should America fall down in failure, it always, always, gets back up to fight another day. It retains a certain innocence, while averting its gaze from its own dark shadow.

Indeed, as I've also learned, my cultural parent is restless, manic, hypercompetitive, and aggressive. It is unrepentantly boundless, recognizing no limit to its ambition. It is emotionally undeveloped and disconnected. For all its patriotism, it has a shallow, simplistic sense of its own complex history. It is addicted to the drug of the future. It can be a brutal taskmaster, cruelly rejecting those who fail to haul themselves up by the bootstraps through personal initiative and hard work. It can be pitiless toward failure and uncaring of those who fall by the wayside. It is psychologically ignorant of the ways it has been numbed and traumatized by war, terrorism, and the ceaseless up-and-down of economic swings. For all its religious devotion, it has a pernicious money complex that blinds it to the deeper side of life. Beneath its puffed-up patriotism, it has a weak sense of identity, it can't take criticism, and its pride is easily wounded. This can sometimes make it violent and dangerous.

This cultural parent of mine, I believe, is also lonely, adrift, and deeply depressed. It is at psychological risk. The fact is, as my father lived through the Depression, where people stood in breadlines, I am living through an American depression of a different sort. It is the kind where, instead of bread, children and adults line up for pills to ease the psychic pain of such intangibles as dark moods, nameless flat feelings, and a lingering sense of inner emptiness and chronic dissatisfaction. Few pockets of safety exist where we can safely explore these states or reflect on their deeper existential meaning, for, as James Hillman observes, "our fundamental value is to keep going, not slow down, reflect, or look back. These aren't highly regarded values in our culture."

I suspect, as do others, that our habit of devaluing inner reflection has something to do with our version of the hero—that basic image in which American individuality is cast, a myth imprinted on our national psyche since its inception. Somewhere along the way, as I learn from sociologists Robert Jewell and John Lawrence, the American hero became a caricature: an unknown cowboy/loner, gun in hand, riding to the rescue of an idyllic town threatened by evil. Think Clint Eastwood in *Pale Rider*, the Lone Ranger and Tonto, Superman and Spider-Man, or the steely Jack Bauer of Fox's TV show *24*, who rids America of terrorists, then disappears, his wife dead and his daughter vanished. Powerful though this myth may be, its downside, say Jewell and Lawrence, is the way it denies "the tragic complexities of human life."

The whole idea of the hero in our culture, adds psychotherapist Miriam Greenspan, "is a very masculine model of conquering emotions, including the conquest of fear," as if to suffer or be sad is somehow to fail. Venerating height as the metaphor for what is great or successful, she continues, makes us want to fly above things instead of bow low and go through them. "We don't value the usefulness of the journey through depression or melancholy, or see that it has its own kind of heroism," she says thoughtfully.

Our cowboy-hero also never looks back, but doggedly keeps going forward. Woe to the political candidate that fails to offer the optimistic vision of a bright future. Yet for a culture so intent on dismantling the old in favor of the next new thing, it's astonishing how little effort we've devoted to understanding the psychologically disorienting consequences of rapid change.

This is the predicament we find ourselves in today, as the country is not only suffering the consequences of a fast-paced way of life based on industrial-era survivalism and communally disconnected, me-first individualism, it's also witnessing the end of that era. It is simply no longer sustainable, both from an ecological *and* a psychological perspective. But the dying of an old way of life—whether it is small farms, the railroad, the auto industry, or even things like cameras or typewriters—brings its own kind of suffering. It can cause a destabilizing identity crisis, depression, drug addiction, and more. Like the patient in analysis who arrives with repressed stories or memories of the past, America would do well to begin the healing work of restoring its fragmented psyche to wholeness by drawing a connecting line of continuity between what was, what is, and what will be.

These American conflicts around the past and future, the old and the new, have played out in my own life. As I've written, it is through a twist of fate that Washington, D.C., is my ancestral home. Though it has taken me a long time to realize it, I have a history with the nation's capital. Here my eighteenth- and nineteenth-century relatives, steeped in the politics and issues of their day, were born, baptized, and buried. Here my Argentine great-grandfather met and married my great-grandmother. Here their son, my grandfather, attended school and lived with his cousins. It was to Washington, D.C., that my father traveled on the first trip of his life. It is here that my parents spent a romantic weekend as young newlyweds, and where they saw the cherry blossoms ringing the tidal basin. It is to this city that I traveled as an idealistic college student to voice my dissent against the Vietnam War; and where I lived through an endless summer while awaiting an abortion. Here I moved as a young mother, where I watched my children play on the steps of the Lincoln Memorial. And here, for almost three decades, I've made a life for myself.

And yet, so little did my own ancestry mean to me, so thick was the wall between me and my past, that I once wrote a feature story on the soul of Washington without even mentioning my own ancestral ties to the city's story. I saw only what those tourists who arrive here see every day: a place where the abstract principles of independence, liberty, and the rights of the individual that define America have been made visible in soaring monuments of stone. I adore those ideals; they define me in fundamental ways I'm still coming to understand. But in so many other ways they eclipse the personal dimension of the very individual ethos they proclaim.

What is it in America that remains so fixated on triumph and the gleaming horizon? Taking my question to James Hillman, he answers that, to the rest of the world, America has always held that image of "the city on the hill: the New Jerusalem, Zion, or the Promised Land that immigrants have to cross the water to get to. That is the image of the deep vision in the soul of America." This myth and the myth of the earthly paradise of finding gold in the streets that America still holds for people around the world, he tells me, are what compels people from Cuba to set out for America on a raft, or to smuggle themselves in the rat-infested hold of a Chinese steamer bound for New York. At the same time, says Hillman, "there is within the American soul this constant feeling of bitterness," because "once immigrants arrive here, they find that it isn't the Promised Land of their dreams."

For all that America struts the grandiose image it has of itself before the world, Thomas Moore has written, "there is a painful distance between the image we have of ourselves and the reality on the ground." If we were to put the nation on the couch, he continues, the corresponding psychological diagnosis to these symptoms of gran-diosity would be narcissism. A "huge vacuum that sweeps everything into the need for self," Moore explains, "narcissism can be seen every-where in American life—in the culture of celebrity, the fascination with constructing huge, tall buildings, and the need to do everything on a grand scale that dominates the culture. It suggests a vacancy, an emptiness with no life in it."

We can't fully know why this is America's pattern, reflects Moore. Yet by honoring Jung's principle to read the message in the symptom, he theorizes, America might see in its vacant narcissism a challenge to give more substance to its democratic principles. Even our fascination for doing things on a titanic scale—our "hugeness complex"—could be read as a symptom alerting us to a genuine need. "The soul needs bigness," says Moore. But, he continues, our obsession with "bigness and sprawl and making things huge and making ourselves bigger and bigger suggest to me that hugeness has value in America, it also means that our vision is not big enough. We've substituted physical size for grandness of vision. We could be much more of a light to the world if we worked to ground our power, rather than displaying it and protecting it defensively all the time."

What would it take for America, composed of such a tough bunch of plucky pioneers and hard-ass capitalist go-getters, to balance its perennially onward and upward-moving attitude with a more soulful philosophy? Without sacrificing our eagle vision, I believe, America might begin to redirect its attention to the fallen: those who have descended from health into sickness; from economic security to the edge of financial uncertainty; from professional success to joblessness; from happiness to melancholy, from sanity to mental illness, from sobriety to addiction, from war to mental trauma and crippled limbs; and from love to loneliness. Rather than judge the fallen as defective failures, we could have empathy for them as casualties of the competitive culture we all share. We might even learn from the fallen, finding wisdom in their stories.

As I learned from my father's life, we could, in fact, begin to balance our culture of striving and building with a culture of healing and deepening, reconciling our compulsive drive for change with cultivating what we already have—in honor, especially, of that vast land that we claim to love so. To do this, however, would mean overcoming our distrust of the inner life and embracing self-examination and even suffering, old-fashioned and anti-American as this may sound.

Thomas Moore calls this the "art of falling." James Hillman calls it "growing down." Michael Eigen likens it to the image of the Buddha sitting with the anguish of the human condition; to the suffering and resurrection of Jesus on the cross; or to the Old Testament Job, who had everything stripped from him. Eigen uses these religious images, he says, because in his experience as an analyst, inner work "is yet one more way to sit and be present to our suffering. In this way you might say that psychotherapy is a form of meditation or prayer. It is about trying to feel our way into who we are, and trying to become less destructive channels for the natures we've been given."

Psychoanalyst Jonathan Lear goes a step further, taking the unconventional approach that the psychological process can even be a kind of patriotic pursuit. Therapy, he explains, is where we cultivate a more philosophical dimension of what it means to be an individual: the foundation stone, after all, of Western democracy. As he points out in *Love and Its Place in Nature*, our entire American debate over individualism, while paying great attention to rights and liberties, remains "silent on what individuals are. Individuals are treated as atoms, with little notice given to subatomic structure." Individuation into an individual, Lear states, is "not granted at birth: It is a hard-earned psychological achievement that takes place over a lifetime of inner work."

Radical though it may sound to American sensibilities, this kind of inner work is also a form of heroism. Not as a replacement of traditional forms of outer heroic acts, but because digging around in our human nature takes courage and time, sometimes a lifetime. Individuals in therapy, Jungian analyst Ann Ulanov tells me, often feel humiliated to find themselves growing old and working on the same issues, year after year. "One feels shame that one can't just move on, as all one's well-meaning friends and family urge one to do. Talking over and over about the recurring problem that does not yield and will not go away makes one feel isolated and kind of crazy."

If only we could realize, says Ulanov, that at the core of even our most intimate personal problems, whether it's "betrayal, failure, or raging emotions," our personal suffering "circles around a problem that we all share," joining us to the human condition. Not just my father, for example, but many people suffer the problem of alcoholism and addiction. Not just my mother, but many immigrants must contend with the loss and disorientation that comes with adapting to a new culture. Not just myself, but many children grew up with an alcoholic, depressed, abusive, or emotionally absent parent. "If we can get to the deeper level of a personal problem," Ulanov tells me, "there is no difference between me and the 'other.'"

Ulanov likens dedication to this kind of patient, lifelong, inner work to the medieval workers who, stone by stone, helped to build the great cathedrals of medieval Europe. As many of these cathedrals took over a hundred years to construct, most of the builders spent the greater part of their lives laboring on a project they didn't expect to see completed in their lifetime. Yet they knew they were contributing to something that would survive long after they were gone. In the ongoing struggle with our recurring life problems, adds Ulanov, what matters most is that, through all the ups and downs, we make the effort to keep working on them. Even the suffering that is not resolved, and from which an individual is never completely free, she tells me, becomes "my brick, my job for the community, a kind of inner social action through which I contribute what I have learned."

The image of the great cathedral is useful in this discussion because it is that magisterial edifice of democratic principles that defines America that is in need of repair, reconstruction, and a new foundation in deeper values. Joining work on our personal problems to labor on our democratic society gives us a model for working in two directions at once: upward in the direction of the spire of our ideals, and downward in the direction of our limitations and our suffering.

Such an achievement could even be a fulfillment of that image in our collective soul: the Promised Land. In the imagination of the world, says Thomas Moore, America has always been seen as the "new world." "It participates in the myth of renewal and starting over again. All the old maps show America as *terra incognita*, or an unknown land." One way to work with our narcissism, he says, "would be to actually *become* that place of idealism and renewal the rest of the world sees in us. We could elaborate and stand behind our ideals much more than we do, rather than letting our democratic principles be merely empty words or 'floaty' things." Indeed, he says, we could "become a people worthy of recognition. All too often Americans publicly profess their democratic ideals, but when they get right down to it, they don't stand behind them."

✳

Joe Carroll belonged to the generation that sacrificed for the Depression and for World War II. They were the bulwark and the builders of the middle class. For this, they suffered a terrible loss of soul and psychological well-being. I began this book believing that an impassable chasm separated my Greatest Generation father's life from my own. I've since come to think differently. Now I believe that, through allowing history to be my guide and healer in the process of writing this memoir, I've accepted my legacy and inheritance as my father's daughter. My journey became itself the bridge that spanned the gap between us, a bridge that now connects the next generation with the wisdom I've taken from the lives that my parents, and ancestors, lived.

All throughout my work on this book, in fact, my father has seemed to accompany me, looking on in interest over my shoulder, appearing in my dreams. As I approached the end of his story, our story, America's story, he invited me in a dream to come and sit with him in a field on the farm and to "listen to the sound of the grasses in the wind."

Arriving at the last paragraph of this last chapter, Joe appeared in yet one more dream. I stand in a room enclosed within clear walls. Behind one wall, a couple is in distress because the man is pregnant and about to give birth. At that moment, an official emergency vehicle pulls up. Uniformed officers jump out and tell me that I've been accused of murdering my father. Shocked to hear this news, I tell them that I don't believe this is true. "However," I say, "if I did it unconsciously, then I'd like to know about it."

At that moment, I turn and see my father on the other side of the wall in front of me. He is ageless and vibrant with energy. His eyes are the same rare blue, but they shine with the uncanny light of the next world. His lips are exaggeratedly pursed, as if he is trying hard to whistle one of his Irish lullabies one last time. Like a little girl, I run to the door in the wall. "There he is! Dad!" I cry out, knowing that he will help resolve this crisis. I step through a doorway in the wall, but a force pushes me back, and I realize I can go no further.

My father and I live in different worlds now. Yet it is clear that he has come to my aid as I face my accusers—the personification of my own terrified guilt that by writing this book I've killed my own dad, smashed a taboo of secrecy, and overturned the natural order of things by trying to assist in the birth of a new masculine spirit. In a stark moment of reckoning, my father and I stare at each other across the boundary of life and death. Then, giving me a loving look, Joe lightly shrugs his shoulders and says, "Well, what are you going to do?" He whistles his song, turns away, and with a spring in his step joins with a large crowd of people moving toward something I can't see.

This Joe was still Joe: my "off to see the world" dreamer father. But in the shrug of his shoulders and his light-hearted whistle, he is shrugging off the weight of my guilt, reassuring me that he is all right. Still, in the intent expression on his face is a recognition of all that has happened in our family—and now of his fate in being the subject of this book, and mine in writing it. In working on the dream, I almost miss the most significant part: no more is my father the lone individual. He walks with others toward a new life.

For all their faults and failures, there is something magnificent about parents. Through the cracks in their broken places, they try to love us back. Through them history flows into us. Through them, we live and have life. And, through them, we learn how to be human.

Acknowledgments

THIS IS A BIG book with a big story to tell about a larger-than-life main character—and a grand cast of characters that helped to bring it into existence. To my mother, Maria Sheila Carroll League, I owe an enormous debt of gratitude. As I set out to write this deeply personal family story, her advice to me not to "whitewash" us revealed both her literary spirit and remarkable courage. Still, this was never an easy book for her to watch me write. Yet somehow she found it within herself to support me by providing me with old photos, telegrams, letters, scraps of paper she'd saved with my father's scribbled words, and her own notes of a time gone by. She graciously shared memories of herself as a young woman; of her and my father's romantic courtship that unfolded over several continents after World War II; and of their tragic, and yet also ultimately beautiful, American life and love story. Thank you, Mom: I could not have told Joe's story without you.

This book would also not have been possible without the rare combination of patience, forbearance, and miraculously generous financial support I received throughout the duration of this project from Terry and Anne Peay. I have always said that Terry was the best ex-husband a woman could ever wish for, and this journey has certainly proved the depth of his kindness and compassion, as well as that of Anne, his wife, and my children's loving stepmother. I am, as always, grateful for the remarkable family and friendship that we all share together, without which I could not have accomplished this project, and which has sustained and enriched my life in so many ways. I have also been blessed with good fortune in Taj Inayat, my cherished lifelong friend and Sufi teacher, for her generous financial support over the years for this book, for laughter and for the deep bond of friendship that we have shared for over four decades, and for her spiritual guidance that has nourished me as I traveled a sometimes rocky and wandering road. I would also like to thank Scott Brickman for his generous financial support of this book.

I also could not have written this book without the help of my three siblings Colleen, Steven, and John: thank you all three for helping me to recollect facts and dates; for hours of conversations probing the mystery of our troubled, alcoholic father; for reading early drafts of the manuscript; and for bearing with the painful process of stirring up buried memories and reliving old family dramas. No one knows the inside of this story better than the three of you; with no one else do I share that special brand of wicked Carroll black humor that somehow got us all through. I owe a very special thank you as well to my "soul" sisters-in-law, Tracy Staton and InYeong Lee, who have shared this journey with me over the years. This book is also for the next Carroll generation of nieces and nephews: Jules and Lily Leach, and Fergus, Aine, and Anjelica Carroll. What a lucky aunt am I to have all of you, and your love, in my life!

I am also grateful to my Carroll cousins, whose stories and experiences of growing up a Carroll helped to deepen my understanding of the family complex I'd been born into. They are: author, naturalist, and MacArthur Fellow David M. Carroll (son of Dick Carroll); Carol Corrado (daughter of Helen Carroll Mitterer); Sharon Carroll (daughter of Paul Carroll); Paula Carroll (daughter of George Carroll); Patrick Carroll and his sister Susan Blackston (son and daughter of Bob Carroll); Sophia Cooper Reyna (granddaughter of Jim Carroll); and my Aunt Renie (wife of Dick Carroll) for her memories of the band of Carroll brothers when they were young. I also want to thank especially Aunt Eileen (wife of Gene Carroll), for the love and affection she gave to me as a child, and for her generous sharing of Carroll family memories and photos.

A very special thank you goes also to my mother's sister and my aunt, Fiona Visser, also for her love, and for sharing her memories of Joe and my mother, Sheila, when they were young, as well as for her recollections of a long-ago childhood growing up in Buenos Aires. I also want to express my appreciation for her invaluable knowledge as our family historian, storyteller, and for the family tree that gave me the key to an incredible American genealogy. Warm gratitude goes also to my dear Argentine cousins Julie Lenton and Jean Hurst, for sharing their own childhood memories, and for deepening my understanding of that side of my family.

I am also indebted to my circle of friends: Sylvia Seret, Susan Roberts, Lis Akhtarzandi, Elise Wiarda, Janet Meyerson, Ann Cochran, Sally Craig, Harriett Crosby, Arlene Singer, Karen Parmett, Barbara Graham and Hugh Delehanty, Deborah Goldberg, Jim and Dodie Brady, Deborah Hughes, Ann Simpkinson, Nancy Kadian and Jack Mangold, Diane Perlman, Kristen Flance, and Ira and Ruth Rifkin for dream-sharing, coffee, dinners, walks, long talks, writing and journalism advice, and for providing such an incredible support system and sounding board over the years. Thank you also to my good neighbors Jack, Pauline, and Bernie; to friend and "computer healer" Susan Rodberg, for her service of almost twenty-five years; to Charles Sweeney, my tax preparer also of twenty-five years, who has followed this book's progress and eagerly awaited its publication; and to the very patient Barbara Offutt. Special thanks are owed to my Oak Grove childhood circle of friends, and for the long-ago memories we shared together: Virginia Dameron, Cheryl Clary, Jan Kimble, Debbie and Phil Ingolia, Janie Brown, Susie and Roger LaBeth, Jan Sause, Jim Arth, William Cornett, and Jerry Hoy, a very brave Vietnam veteran who shared with me what it was like for my father to go to war and then return home and suffer from PTSD. Thank you also to my Kansas City and New York friends Mark Edelman and his wife, Karin, for their interest and enthusiasm, and Malka Margolies, for her early support of this book.

I also owe a great debt of thanks to the many psychologists I interviewed over the years: for so courageously embarking on this unusual undertaking; for their patience with my questions; and for their insights into both my father's and America's psyche, and on specific topics such as alcoholism, narcissism, immigration and multiculturalism, depression, violence, and PTSD. Indeed, I amassed such a treasure chest of wisdom that it couldn't fit into the narrative of this book. It became necessary to create a companion volume of these interviews, *America on the Couch: Psychological Perspectives on American Politics and Culture* (Lantern Books). For their time and for their uniquely specialized knowledge of psychology and the human psyche for this memoir, I'd like to thank (in alphabetical order) Amir Afkhami, Stephen Aizenstat, Michael Conforti, Lionel Corbett, Mihaly Csikszentmihalyi, Larry Decker, Edward Edinger, Michael Eigen, Blaine Fowers, Miriam Greenspan, James Hillman, Judith V. Jordan, Harriet Lerner, Robert Jay Lifton, A. Thomas McLellan, Thomas Moore, Ginette Paris, Sylvia Perera, Jerrold Post, Ernest Rossi, Andrew Samuels, Robert Sardello, Benjamin Sells, Erel Shalit, Charles B. Strozier, Ann Belford Ulanov, Irvin Yalom, Polly Young-Eisendrath, and Luigi Zoja. I am also grateful to Jungian analysts Nona Boren and Tom Peterson, who guided me with such wisdom, who taught me the language of dreams, and who helped me to understand and come to terms with my psychological legacy as my father's daughter.

As much as psychology helped me to understand my father, so did learning the history of his times. For their time and knowledge, I would like to thank those historians I interviewed on the different periods that shaped Joe Carroll's life. Among them are documentary filmmaker Peter Vogt and railroad historian Dan Cupper for their knowledge of Altoona and the legendary and mighty Pennsylvania Railroad; Jeannine Treese, director of the Blair County Historical Society; Dan Hagadorn, Senior Curator at The Museum of Flight and Latin American Aviation historian; Frank D. McCann, of the University of New Hampshire, on the Brazil–U.S. relationship during World War II; Randy McGuire, archivist at Parks Air College in East St. Louis, Mo.; Marvin G. Goldman, El Al historian; Roy Hatanaka, Air Force historian at Fort

MacArthur in Los Angeles; Archie DiFanti, archivist at the Air Force Historical Research Agency (AFHRA) at Maxwell Air Force Base; Claire Saxon, president of the Air Transport Command Association and the wonderful ATC veterans she put me in touch with, including Richard Ravitts, and who shared their wartime stories; Charles Pinck, President of the OSS Society; Brent Stoley, Air Force historian at the National Museum of the Air Force; and those historians at the FBI, the Simon Wiesenthal Center in Los Angeles, the Air Force Historical Studies Office (AFHSO) at Joint Base Anacostia-Bolling, the Amervets Library, and the Air Force History Office at the Pentagon who so kindly took my calls and answered my questions. What a rich, untapped reservoir of knowledge these historians provide!

Every creative project has its unique "genesis" story, that moment when a spark is lit that fires a process that, if one is both lucky and persevering, leads in the end to a painting, a composition, or a book. For me, that moment occurred when, in 1995, my paths crossed with Lantern Books editor and publisher, Martin Rowe. At the time, I'd just completed a five-hundred-page manuscript in which I'd set out on a quest to analyze the American psyche through interviews with psychologists. When the manuscript proved too raw and unwieldy to publish, I took it to Martin in 1999, whose intuitive editorial eye instantly glimpsed the *real* story embedded in the text. "Here's your book," he said, pointing to several pages I'd written about my father. "Use his life as a way to talk about the myths of America, like our heroic individualism and independence." And so, I did.

As I learned things about my father's life I'd never known before, and as my research took me in unexpected directions, Martin graciously extended my deadline over a period of nearly fifteen years. In meetings in hotel lobbies as he passed through D.C. attending conferences on environmental issues and animal rights, or in his Brooklyn brownstone with his lovely wife Mia, Martin read pages and offered advice. "Don't think of this memoir as a textile with different themes you're 'weaving' together," he said once. "Think of it in spatial terms, of height and descent, of earth and sky, of flying and crashing, like the myth of Icarus." For his now-legendary gifts as an editor and also as an author, for his patience and faith, and for the remarkable gift of his friendship, I want to acknowledge Martin Rowe. Without him, this voyage of discovery would never have taken place. What I discovered along the way changed not only how I saw America, it also changed my relationship to my father, and uncovered an American story I never knew I'd been living. I am also very grateful to the creative and dynamic director/producer team of Snapdragon Films for the luminous and evocative book trailer they made for *American Icarus* and *America on the Couch*.

I would like to thank my three sons, Kabir, Amir, and Abe. Over the course of the twenty years that it has taken me to write this book, they have grown into unique, kind, and good men with interesting lives, work, and families of their own. They have looked on and listened with interest as I've struggled to bring this project to fruition. I thank them each for putting up with their preoccupied and absent-minded mother; for their sweet, playful, and unconditional love; and now also for the gift of their wives, my strong, loving, and amazing daughters-in-law Alison Forrestel, Carolina Montoni (to whom I owe a debt of gratitude for her invaluable tech support and help in moments of crisis over the years), and Vera Bright. Joe would have loved each one of them—and now Kabir and Alison's daughter, my granddaughter, Eslyn Jane Peay. I look forward to the adventure of family as it continues through all their lives.

Last of all, I must mention my father, Joe Carroll. Though this memoir was written after his death, I felt his presence throughout the entire journey in my dreams. Sometimes he was young, brave, and strong; sometimes old, sick, and sad. Sometimes he was angry, frightening, and drunk; sometimes quizzical, funny, and loving. Or he was a presence looking over my shoulder, his voice breaking into my writing with his inimitable, "*Yello*, Pell!" Somewhere, I know, Joe is shaking his head over the fact that he, the humbly born son of a Pennsylvania Railroad mechanic and housekeeper who grew up to fly the globe, is now the subject of, and on the cover of, a book that tells the story of his American life.

Bibliography and Notes

All URLS valid as of November 4, 2014

I: Plaything of Clouds and of Winds

Samuels, Andrew. *The Political Psyche*. London: Routledge, 1993.

Jung, C. G. *Two Essays on Analytical Psychology*. Princeton: Princeton University Press, 1966.

von Franz, Marie-Louise. *Archetypal Dimensions of the Psyche*. Boston: Shambhala Publications, 1994.

II: The Sons of Altoona

Strozier, Charles. *Heinz Kohut: The Making of a Psychoanalyst*. New York: Farrar, Straus and Giroux, 2001. From a case study of one of Kohut's patients, whose psychological confusion manifested in a dream of flying east, while looking out the window at the southern horizon. This image was a clue to Kohut of his client's "self-state dream of disorientation reflecting his panic and fear of fragmentation at the impending separation. . . ." My own insights about my bad sense of direction are an extrapolation from this case study.

Turner, Frederick Jackson. *The Frontier in American History*. New York: Dover Publications, 1966.

de Tocqueville, Alexis. *Democracy in America, Volume II*. New York: Vintage Books/ Alfred A. Knopf, 1945.

421

Miner, Craig. *A Most Magnificent Machine: America Adopts the Railroad, 1825–1862.* Lawrence: University Press of Kansas, 2010.

Altoona, the Keystone City of the Keystone State. Altoona, Penn.: Altoona Chamber of Commerce, 1924 <http://www.altoonalibrary.org/sites/default/files/books/keystonecity/keystonecity_toc.htm>.

Emerson, Sylvia. *A Brief History of Blair County, Pennsylvania.* Altoona, Penn.: Blair County Historical Society, 1996. Can be downloaded here: <http://www.blairhistory.org/about-us/county-history/>.

"Pennsylvania Railroad Shops and Works: Special History Study (Chapter One)." National Park Service, Special History Study. Last updated October 22, 2004.

"Altoona Mirror's Souvenir: Containing an Account of the Semi-Centennial Celebration of the War Governors' Conference." Altoona, Penn.: Mirror Printing Co., 1913 <http://www.usgwarchives.net/pa/blair/wargovspix.htm>.

Pulling, Sr. Anne Francis. *Images of America: Altoona.* Mount Pleasant, S.C.: Arcadia Publishing/Tempus Publishing, 2003.

Needleman, Jacob. *The American Soul: Rediscovering the Wisdom of the Founders.* New York: Jeremy P. Tarcher/Putnam, 2003.

Takaki, Ronald. *A Different Mirror: A History of Multicultural America.* New York: Little, Brown and Company, 1993.

Vogt, Peter. "Altoona at Work: An Era of Steam." Altoona Railroaders Memorial Museum Project. Bethesda, Md.: Peter Vogt Productions, 1998.

Cupper, Dan. *Crossroads of Commerce: The Pennsylvania Railroad Calendar Art of Grif Teller.* Richmond, Vt.: Great Eastern Publishing, 1992.

Courtwright, David T. *Sky as Frontier: Adventure, Aviation, and Empire* College Station: Texas A&M University Press, 2005.

Takaki, Ronald. *A Different Mirror: A History of Multicultural America.* New York: Back Bay Books, 2008.

Hellinger, Bert, and Gabriele ten Hovel. *Acknowledging What Is: Conversations with Bert Hellinger.* Translated by Colleen Beaumont. Phoenix, Ariz.: Zeig, Tucker & Co., 1999.

Freight Rail Works. Association of American Railroads <http://freightrailworks.org/>.

Cahill, Thomas. *Sailing the Wine-Dark Sea: Why the Greeks Matter.* New York: Doubleday, 2003.

Mitchell, Stephen A., and Margaret J. Black. "Psychologies of Identity and Self: Erik Erikson and Heinz Kohut." In *Freud and Beyond: A History of Modern Psychoanalytic Thought*, 139–169. New York: Basic Books, 1996.

Kast, Verena. *Joy, Inspiration, and Hope.* Translated by Douglas Whitcher. College Station: Texas A&M University Press, 1991.

Binswanger, Ludwig. In *Joy, Inspiration, and Hope*, by Verena Kast. "Über die manische Lebensform" in *Ausgewählte Vorträge und Aufsätze*, Vol. II. Berne: Franke, 1955.

III: The World in Solemn Stillness Lay

Bowlby, John. *Loss: Sadness and Depression.* New York: Basic Books, 1980.

McCullough, David. *John Adams.* New York: Simon & Schuster, 2001.

Carroll, David M. *Self-Portrait with Turtles: A Memoir.* New York: Mariner Books/ Houghton Mifflin, 2005.

Freud, Sigmund. "Mourning and Melancholia." In *The Freud Reader*, edited by Peter Gay, 584–588. New York: W. W. Norton & Company, 1995.

Eigen, Michael. *Coming Through the Whirlwind: Case Studies in Psychotherapy.* Wilmette, Ill.: Chiron Publications, 1992.

Strozier, Charles. *Heinz Kohut: The Making of a Psychoanalyst.* New York: Farrar, Straus and Giroux, 2001.

IV: Love and War in South America

"Call to Colleges Detailed by Army . . ." *New York Times*, January 29, 1943. "Most of the Enlisted Reserve Corps students in colleges of the United States will be called to active duty at the end of the current semester, the War Department stated today."

Sherbine, Lorraine. "War Years Revisited." *Davidson Journal Archives: Alumni of World War II Era.*

Griffin, Susan. *A Chorus of Stones: The Private Life of War.* New York: Anchor Books/Doubleday, 1992.

Courtwright, David. *Sky as Frontier: Adventure, Aviation, and Empire.* College Station: Texas A&M University Press, 2005.

Lindbergh, Charles. *The Spirit of St. Louis.* New York: Scribner, 1953.

Lindbergh, Reeve. *Under a Wing: A Memoir.* New York: Simon & Schuster, 1998. As cited in Courtwright: *Sky as Frontier: Adventure, Aviation, and Empire.*

Fitzgerald, Scott. *Echoes of the Jazz Age.* In *The Crack-Up*, edited by Edmund Wilson, 13–22. New York: New Directions, 1945. Cited in Courtwright: *Sky as Frontier: Adventure, Aviation, and Empire.*

Ravindra, K., and John Waide. "From Parks Air College to Parks College of Engineering & Aviation: 75 Years of Legacy in Aerospace Engineering." In *Aerospace Engineering Education During the First Century of Flight*, edited by Barnes

McCormick, Conrad Newberry, and Eric Jumper, 821–833. Reston, Va.: AIAA, American Institute of Aeronautics and Astronautics, 2004.

Gann, Ernest K. *Fate Is the Hunter.* New York: Simon & Schuster, 1961.

Craven, Wesley Frank, and James Lea Cate, eds. *The Army Air Forces in World War II.* Washington, D.C.: Office of Air Force History, 1983.

——. *Volume I: Plans and Early Operations: Jan 1939–Aug 1942.* Chapter 9: "The Early Development of Air Transport and Ferrying."

——. *Volume II: Men and Planes.*

——. *Volume VI: The Army Air Forces in World War II.* Chapter 14: "The Foundations of a War Training Program."

——. *Volume VII: Services Around the World.* Chapter 1: "The Air Transport Command."

——. Chapter 2: "Airway to the Middle East."

——. Chapter 8: "Traffic Homeward Bound."

"Civilian Pilot Training Program." Wikipedia <http://en.wikipedia.org/wiki/Civilian_Pilot_Training_Program>.

"United States Government Role in Civil Aviation." Wikipedia <http://en.wikipedia.org/wiki/United_States_government_role_in_civil_aviation>.

Conn, Stetson, and Byron Fairchild. *The Framework of Hemisphere Defense.* Chapter XII: "The Establishment of United States Army Forces in Brazil." Washington, D.C.: Center of Military History, 1989.

"Growth of Air Transport Command." *U.S. Air Force Fact Sheet.* National Museum of the USAF <http://www.nationalmuseum.af.mil/factsheets/factsheet.asp?id=1690>.

La Farge, Oliver. *The Eagle in the Egg: The Story of the Coming of Age of Military Transport.* Boston: Houghton Mifflin, 1949.

McCann, Frank D. "Brazil and World War II: The Forgotten Ally. What did you do in the war, Zé Carioca?" *Estudios Interdisciplinarios de América Latina y el Caribe* (6):2, July–December 1995.

Conn, Stetson, and Byron Fairchild. *The Framework of Hemispheric Defense.* Washington, D.C.: Center of Military History, United States Army, 1989.

Rohter, Larry. "Natal Journal: A Has-Been Wonders How to Honor What Was," *New York Times,* June 20, 2001.

Brooke, James. "Natal Journal; Brazil's Glory Days of B-25's and Boogie Woogie," *New York Times,* April 26, 1994.

Wittels, David G. "I Rode the Fireball," *Saturday Evening Post,* July 1, 1944.

McAvoy, Tom. "To India and Back in 10 Days: Life Photographer Flies 26,000 Miles with 'Fireball Express,'" *Life,* June 5, 1944.

Neale, Mary Lou. "There *Are* Old, Bold Pilots," *Flight Plan*. Fairfax, Va.: Air Transport Command Association, 2001.

Aslakson, Carl Ingman. *Earth Measurer: The Autobiography of Carl Ingman Aslakson*. NOAA Library, 1979 <http://www.history.noaa.gov/stories_tales/ak1. html>.

Valenti, Jack. *This Time, This Place: My Life in War, the White House, and Hollywood*. New York: Three Rivers Press/Crown, 2008.

Gordin, Michael D. *Five Days in August: How World War II Became a Nuclear War*. Princeton: Princeton University Press, 2007.

U.S. veterans PTSD rates: Face the Facts USA: A Project of the George Washington University <http://www.facethefactsusa.org/facts/the-true-price-of-war-in-human-terms>.

Hillman, James. *A Terrible Love of War*. New York: Penguin, 2004.

Kaplan, Mark S., Nathalie Huguet, Bentson H. McFarland, and Jason T. Newsom. "Suicide Among Male Veterans: A Prospective Population-based Study." *Journal of Epidemiology and Community Health* 61(6): 751, August 2007.

Lifton, Robert Jay, and Greg Mitchell. *Hiroshima in America: Fifty Years of Denial*. New York: Grosset/Putnam, 1995.

Lifton, Robert Jay. *The Broken Connection: On Death and the Continuity of Life*. New York: Simon & Schuster, 1979.

Heppenheimer, T. A. *A Brief History of Flight: From Balloons to Mach 3 and Beyond*. New York: John Wiley & Sons, 2001.

"Boeing B-29 Superfortress 'Enola Gay.'" Smithsonian National Air and Space Museum. Washington, D.C. <http://airandspace.si.edu/collections/artifact. cfm?object=nasm_A19500100000>.

Goldstein, Richard. "Paul W. Tibbets Jr., Pilot of Enola Gay, Dies at 92," *New York Times*, November 1, 2007.

V: The Girl from Argentina

de Tocqueville, Alexis. *Democracy in America, Volume II*. New York: Vintage Books/ Alfred A. Knopf, 1945.

Attwell, Juan Sinclair. *Recollections from My Tours of Duty in the United States*. Abstract translated by Julio Kouri, former Cuban diplomat. Overland Park, Ks.: 2007.

"The Huyck Family in Holland and America, 1616–1896." Privately printed, Albany, N.Y., 1896.

Records of the Columbia Historical Society, volume 22. Washington, D.C.: Columbia Historical Society, 1919.

Dictionary of American Naval Fighting Ships. "Tarbell." Department of the Navy, Naval Historical Center, Washington D.C. <http://www.history.navy.mil/danfs/t2/tarbell.htm>.

"Stephen Cassin, Commodore, United States Navy." Arlington National Cemetery Website. Last updated September 24, 2007. <http://arlingtoncemetery.net/scassin.htm>.

McGee, Christopher. *A Gentlemanly and Honorable Profession: The Creation of the U.S. Naval Officer Corps 1794–1815.* Annapolis, Md.: US Naval Institute Press, 1991.

Nelson, Craig. *Thomas Paine: Enlightenment, Revolution, and the Birth of Modern Nations.* New York: Penguin, 2006.

Sharp, John G. *Biography of Commodore John Cassin 1760–1822.* USGenWeb Archives Special Projects <http://www.usgwarchives.net/va/portsmouth/shipyard/nnysharp3.html#cassin>.

Dapray, Helen Cassin. Private family memoir, quoting from a booklet published by the War of 1812 Society.

Davis, William Watts Hart. *History of Buck's County, Pennsylvania: From the Discovery of the Delaware to the Present Time, Volume I.* New York & Chicago: The Lewis Publishing Company, 1905.

Howard, C. L. "Yemenites Long Journey to Israel: The Magic Carpet." *The Jewish Magazine* online, September 2006 <http://www.jewishmag.com/106mag/yemen/yemen.htm>.

Alaska Airlines. "Operation Magic Carpet" <http:www.alaskaair.com/content/about-us/history/magic-carpet.aspx>.

Joffe-Walt, Benjamin. "Israel's Operation Magic Carpet," *The Jewish Independent*, October 22, 2010.

Goldman, Marvin G. *El Al: Star in the Sky.* Miami: World Transport Press, 1990.

Jung, C. G. *Dream Analysis: Notes of the Seminar Given in 1928–1930 by C. G. Jung.* Edited by William McGuire. Bollingen Series XCIX, Princeton: Princeton University Press, 1984.

——. *Two Essays on Analytical Psychology.* Volume 7: The Collected Works of C. G. Jung. Translated by R. F. C. Hull. Bollingen Series XX, Princeton: Princeton University Press, 1966.

See p. 145: As I continue to discover, even beyond the scope of my writing of this book, my father may have been set apart for other reasons. Once again, this period in his life raises questions that he'd been involved in some kind of clandestine intelligence gathering. Just as the U.S. had been concerned about Nazi influence in

Brazil after the war, an FAA historian points out, so were they concerned about Nazi influence in Argentina. Her remark triggers memories of a time when, just after I'd left home, an older German friend who'd lived in Buenos Aires after the war had strongly asserted that my father's job with FAMA had to have concealed some kind of CIA or undercover involvement. "My father a secret agent? How ridiculous!" I'd said at the time, laughing. Now, however, I begin to wonder.

I turn again to South American aviation historian Dan Hagadorn, who spent twenty-seven years in military intelligence just after the war. At that time, he recounts, the OSS (Office of Strategic Services) was disbanded then reorganized as the CIA, with jurisdiction over Latin America. Although it was true that the Argentine airline FAMA at that time was hiring American personnel to help train their crews on their new fleet of Douglas DC-4s—providing in the eyes of some an ideal cover—Hagadorn doubts that Joe was a "card carrying agent" of the CIA. Still, he admits, the State Department during this postwar period "was very sensitive to any U.S. personnel working for foreign airlines." Joe, he said, would had to have gone through the State Department for approval and passport clearances. At some point in this process, he would have crossed paths with some agency of the U.S. State Department, such as the American Embassy in Buenos Aires. A more likely scenario, says Hagadorn, is that Embassy personnel would have introduced my father around, then taken him to the "right person" who would have said to Joe, in an informal way, "Hey, we really need you to be our ears and eyes on the ground. Help us out if you hear anything about Nazi influences, or anything suspicious."

At the suggestion of several historians, I file a Freedom of Information Act (FOIA) with the CIA. The response I receive is dense with obfuscating language. The CIA, it reads in part, "can neither confirm nor deny the existence or nonexistence of records responsive to your request . . . .Therefore, that portion of your request is denied. . . ." Hagadorn is not surprised. The CIA, he says, "is specifically excluded from the provisions of the Freedom of Information Act. They will accept your request, but they don't have to honor it." Thus, even if my father had been part of the CIA and had a file, he says, they "wouldn't have to give it to me. The reasons for that are pretty profound. They want to protect him, and anyone associated with him."

Again, as during my father's service in the war, I will probably never know the whole story; also again, I wish my father were still alive so that I could put these questions to him myself. What I do know is that a pattern of secrecy and silences is beginning to emerge—one that would persist even in later years, when the same

German friend and others implied that even Joe's job with TWA may also have been a disguise for some sort of CIA involvement. I was skeptical at the time, as I am now, and as my mother is as well. And yet in a conversation on this topic, she muses aloud that she sometimes wondered how we had managed to own a farm and travel and stay in hotels, on a flight engineer's salary that wouldn't have supported such a lifestyle.

VI: Israel on the Missouri

Lindbergh, Charles. *The Wartime Journals of Charles A. Lindbergh.* Orlando, Fla.: Harcourt Brace Jovanovich, 1970.

Creative Staff of Hallmark Editions, editors. *Kansas City: An Intimate Portrait of the Surprising City on the Missouri.* Text by James Morgan, editor of *Kansas City Magazine.* Kansas City: Hallmark Cards, Inc. 1973.

Historic Kansas City <http://www.historickansascity.org>.

Stegner, Wallace. *Where the Bluebird Sings to the Lemonade Springs: Living and Writing in the West.* New York: Random House, 1992.

Courtwright, David. *Sky as Frontier: Adventure, Aviation, and Empire.* College Station: Texas A&M University Press, 2005.

Karash, Julius A., and Rick Montgomery. *TWA: Kansas City's Hometown Airline.* Kansas City: Kansas City Star Books, 2001.

Hillman, James. "Beauty Without Nature: Refounding the City." *Uniform Edition of the Writings of James Hillman, Volume 2: City and Soul.* Edited by Robert Leaver. New York: Spring Publications, 2006.

St. John de Crèvecoeur, J. Hector. *Letters from an American Farmer and Sketches of Eighteenth-Century America.* Edited by Albert E. Stone. New York: Penguin Classics, 1986.

Bercovitch, Sacvan. *The Puritan Origins of the American Self.* New Haven: Yale University Press, 1975.

Slotkin, Richard. *Gunfighter Nation: The Myth of the Frontier in Twentieth-Century America.* New York: Athenaeum, 1992.

Wills, Gary. *Cincinnatus: George Washington and the Enlightenment.* Garden City, N.J.: Doubleday & Company, 1984.

McCullough, David. *John Adams.* New York: Simon & Schuster, 2001.

Hardy, Thomas. "The Darkling Thrush" <http://www.poetryfoundation.org/poem/173590>.

Heppenheimer, T. A. *A Brief History of Flight: From Balloons to Mach 3 and Beyond.* New York: John Wiley & Sons, 2001.

Lindbergh, Charles. *Autobiography of Values.* Orlando, Fla.: Harcourt Brace Jovanovich, 1976.

Crouch, Tom. "'The Surly Bonds of Earth': Images of the Landscape in the Work of Some Aviator/Authors, 1910–1969." In *The Airplane in American Culture*, edited by Dominick A. Pisano. Ann Arbor: University of Michigan Press, 2003.

VII: The Snake in the Barrel

Hillman, James. *The Soul's Code: In Search of Character and Calling.* New York: Warner Books, 1996.

Vaillant, George E. *The Natural History of Alcoholism Revisited.* Cambridge: Harvard University Press, 1995.

Lender, Mark Edward, and James Kirby Martin. *Drinking in America: A History, Revised and Expanded Edition.* New York: The Free Press, 1987. Unless otherwise noted, the section on the history of drinking in America is based on information from this book.

Rush, Benjamin, M.D. *An Inquiry into the Effects of Ardent Spirits upon the Human Body and Mind, with an Account of the Means of Preventing, and of the Remedies for Curing Them.* 1819. Full text available at <https://archive.org/details/2569031R.nlm. nih.gov>.

Karash, Julius A., and Rick Montgomery. *TWA: Kansas City's Hometown Airline.* Kansas City: Kansas City Star Books, 2001.

Eigen, Michael. *Toxic Nourishment.* London: Karnac Books, 1999.

Dyson, Michael Eric. "No Small Dreams: The Radical Revolution of Martin Luther King's Last Year." *LiP*, January 20, 2003 <http://www.hartford-hwp. com/archives/45a/288.html>.

"Airlines: Caught at the Crest," *Time* (88): 44, July 22, 1966 <http://content.time. com/time/magazine/article/0,9171,836118-1,00.html>.

National Institute on Alcohol Abuse and Addiction (NIAAA). According to the National Institute on Alcohol, "alcohol abuse is defined as a person who misuses alcohol periodically, but is not dependent. Alcohol dependency is defined as a person who cannot go without alcohol, and who exhibits symptoms of physical withdrawal" <http://www.niaaa.nih.gov>.

Interlandi, Jeneen. "What Addicts Need." *Newsweek*, February 23, 2008. Updated June 22, 2010 <http://www.newsweek.com/what-addicts-need-93767>.

Cheever, Susan. *My Name Is Bill: Bill Wilson—His Life and the Creation of Alcoholics Anonymous.* New York: Washington Square Press/Simon & Schuster, 2004.

Moore, Thomas. *Care of the Soul: A Guide for Cultivating Depth and Sacredness in Everyday Life.* New York: HarperPerennial, 1992.

Conforti, Michael. *Field, Form, and Fate: Patterns in Mind, Nature, and Psyche.* Woodstock, N.Y.: Spring Publications, 1999.

Paris, Ginette. *Pagan Grace: Dionysos, Hermes, and Goddess Memory in Daily Life.* Woodstock, N.Y.: Spring Publications, 1990.

Rossi, Ernest. *The 20-Minute Break: Reduce Stress, Maximize Performance, Improve Health and Emotional Well-Being Using the New Science of Ultradian Rhythms.* Los Angeles: Jeremy P. Tarcher, 1991.

Perera, Sylvia. *Queen Maeve and Her Lovers: A Celtic Archetype of Addiction, Ecstasy, and Healing.* New York: Carrowmore Books, 1999.

VIII: Icarus's Daughter

"President Lyndon B. Johnson's Address to the Nation Announcing Steps to Limit the War in Vietnam and Reporting His Decision Not to Seek Reelection, March 31, 1968." LBJ Presidential Library <http://www.lbjlib.utexas.edu/Johnson/archives.hom/speeches.hom/680331.asp>.

Moore, Thomas. *Care of the Soul: A Guide for Cultivating Depth and Sacredness in Everyday Life.* New York: HarperPerennial, 1992.

Cahill, Thomas. *Sailing the Wine-Dark Sea: Why the Greeks Matter.* New York: Doubleday, 2003.

Mitchell, Stephen A., and Margaret J. Black. *Freud and Beyond: A History of Modern Psychoanalytic Thought.* Chapter Six, "Psychologies of Identity and Self: Erik Erikson and Heinz Kohut." New York: Basic Books, 1995.

Slotkin, Richard. *Gunfighter Nation: The Myth of the Frontier in Twentieth-Century America.* New York: Athenaeum, 1992.

Mitchell, Stephen A. *Hope and Dread in Psychoanalysis.* New York: Basic Books, 1993.

Eigen, Michael. *Feeling Matters: From the Yosemite God to the Annihilated Self.* London: Karnac Books, 2007.

Zoja, Luigi. *The Father: Historical, Psychological, and Cultural Perspectives.* Translated by Henry Martin. Philadelphia: Taylor & Francis, 2001.

Leonard, Linda Shierse. *The Wounded Woman: Healing the Father–Daughter Relationship.* Boston: Shambhala Publications, 1982.

IX: Don José and the Festival Queen

Thurber, James. "The Shore and the Sea." In *Further Fables for Our Time.* London: Hamish Hamilton, 1956.

Heppenheimer, T. A. *A Brief History of Flight: From Balloons to Mach 3 and Beyond.* New York: John Wiley & Sons, 2001.

Courtwright, David. *Sky as Frontier: Adventure, Aviation, and Empire.* College Station: Texas A&M University Press, 2005. Robert Wohl, from *The Republic of Air*, as cited in this book.

Phillips, Adam. *Houdini's Box: The Art of Escape.* New York: Vintage Books/ Random House, 2001.

Harmon, Denny. "The American Flight Engineer." Flight Engineer History, Air Force Enlisted Forums. February 13, 2006 <http://www.afforums.com/ index.php?threads/flight-engineer-history.15324/>.

Stegner, Wallace. *Where the Bluebird Sings to the Lemonade Springs: Living and Writing in the West.* New York: Random House, 1992.

Mitchell, Stephen A., and Margaret J. Black. *Freud and Beyond: A History of Modern Psychoanalytic Thought.* New York: Basic Books, 1995.

Benjamin, Jessica. *The Bonds of Love: Psychoanalysis, Feminism, and the Problem of Domination.* New York: Pantheon Books, 1988.

Mitchell, Stephen A. *Hope and Dread in Psychoanalysis.* New York: Basic Books, 1993.

Eigen, Michael. *Feeling Matters: From the Yosemite God to the Annihilated Self.* London: Karnac Books, 2007.

McCullough, David. *John Adams.* New York: Simon & Schuster, 2001. "Like other young people [Jefferson wrote] he wished to be able, in the winter nights of old age, to recount to those around him what he has heard and learned of the heroic age preceding his birth, and which of the argonauts particularly he was in time to have seen."

Jewett, Robert, and John Shelton Lawrence. *The American Monomyth.* New York: Anchor Press/Doubleday, 1977.

Lear, Jonathan. *Love and Its Place in Nature: A Philosophical Interpretation of Freudian Psychoanalysis.* New York: The Noonday Press/Farrar, Straus and Giroux, 1991.

Real, Terrence. *I Don't Want to Talk About It: Overcoming the Secret Legacy of Male Depression.* New York: Scribner, 1998.

X: Death in Texas

Corbett, Lionel. *The Religious Function of the Psyche.* New York: Routledge, 1996.

McCullough, David. *John Adams.* New York: Simon & Schuster, 2001.

de Tocqueville, Alexis. *Democracy in America, Volume II.* New York: Vintage Books/ Alfred A. Knopf, 1945.

Perera, Sylvia. *Queen Maeve and Her Lovers: A Celtic Archetype of Addiction, Ecstasy, and Healing.* New York: Carrowmore Books, 1999.

Becker, Ernest. *The Denial of Death.* New York: The Free Press/Simon & Schuster, 1973.

Jung, C. G. *The Psychology of Religion: West and East.* Volume 11: The Collected Works of C. G. Jung, second edition. Princeton: Princeton University Press, 1975.

Hillman, James. *Suicide and the Soul,* second edition. Putnam, Ct.: Spring Publications, 2007.

Moore, Thomas. *The Soul's Religion: Cultivating a Profoundly Spiritual Way of Life.* New York: Perennial, 2002.

Zagajewski, Adam. *Solidarity, Solitude: Essays by Adam Zagajewski.* New York: Ecco Press, 1990.

XI: Afterlife and Afterwords

Spender, Stephen. *Collected Poems 1928–1985.* London: Faber & Faber, 1989.

Kohut, Heinz. *The Analysis of the Self: A Systematic Approach to the Psychoanalytic Treatment of Narcissistic Personality Disorders.* Madison, Wisc.: International Universities Press, 1971.

Lear, Jonathan. *Love and Its Place in Nature: A Philosophical Interpretation of Freudian Psychoanalysis.* New York: Farrar, Straus and Giroux, 1990.

Eigen, Michael. *Feeling Matters: From the Yosemite God to the Annihilated Self.* London: Karnac Books, 2007.

Index

24, 406
2001: A Space Odyssey, 277

AA. *See* Alcoholics Anonymous
abortion, 262, 274–80, 288, 408
absent parent, 411
abuse, 325
    alcohol, 213–14
    early, 45
    to Joe, 329
    sexual, 217
    trauma, 15
    verbal, 77, 323, 385
acceptance, 14, 19, 243, 304, 412
Acknowledging What Is (Hellinger), 42–43
Adams, Abigail, 66
Adams, President John, 66, 136, 215
    farming and, 178
Adams, President John Quincy, 134
addiction, 214–15, 400, 411. *See also*
    alcohol and alcoholism
    despair and, 213

pattern, 246
roots of, 247
Aeschylus, 331
Afghanistan War, 115, 119
Afkhami, Amir, 160
African Americans, 232, 256, 261, 284
Air Age, 95
Air Line Pilots Association (ALPA), 297
Air Transport Command (ATC), 95, 97,
    98, 99, 101–8, 114, 279
airlines
    Alitalia, 17
    American, 95, 146, 399
    Eastern, 95, 233
    El Al, 17, 148–51, 171, 274, 295
    FAMA, 17, 84, 85, 110, 146, 295
    National, 233
    Northwest, 233
    Pan Am, 17, 95, 189, 295
    strike, 233–36, 256
    Transcontinental Air Transport, 91
    TWA, 3, 4, 11, 17, 91, 95, 151,

About the Publisher

L ANTERN BOOKS was founded in 1999 on the principle of living with a greater depth and commitment to the preservation of the natural world. In addition to publishing books on animal advocacy, vegetarianism, religion, and environmentalism, Lantern is dedicated to printing books in the U.S. on recycled paper and saving resources in day-to-day operations. Lantern is honored to be a recipient of the highest standard in environmentally responsible publishing from the Green Press Initiative.

WWW.LANTERNBOOKS.COM